Claiming Citizenship

OXFORD STUDIES IN MIGRATION AND CITIZENSHIP SERIES

Migration and Citizenship Politics, edited by
Justin Gest, George Mason University
Sara Wallace Goodman, University of California, Irvine
Willem Maas, York University

Citizenship: The Third Revolution
David Jacobson and Manlio Cinalli

Claiming Citizenship

Race, Religion, and Political Mobilization among New Americans

Prema A. Kurien

OXFORD
UNIVERSITY PRESS

Oxford University Press is a department of the University of Oxford. It furthers
the University's objective of excellence in research, scholarship, and education
by publishing worldwide. Oxford is a registered trade mark of Oxford University
Press in the UK and certain other countries.

Published in the United States of America by Oxford University Press
198 Madison Avenue, New York, NY 10016, United States of America.

© Prema A. Kurien 2025

All rights reserved. No part of this publication may be reproduced, stored in
a retrieval system, or transmitted, in any form or by any means, without the
prior permission in writing of Oxford University Press, or as expressly permitted
by law, by license, or under terms agreed with the appropriate reproduction
rights organization. Inquiries concerning reproduction outside the scope of the
above should be sent to the Rights Department, Oxford University Press, at the
address above.

You must not circulate this work in any other form
and you must impose this same condition on any acquirer.

Library of Congress Cataloging-in-Publication Data
Names: Kurien, Prema A., 1963- author.
Title: Claiming citizenship : race, religion, and political mobilization
among new Americans / Prema A. Kurien.
Other titles: Race, religion, and political mobilization among new Americans
Description: New York, NY : Oxford University Press, [2025] |
Series: Oxford studies in migration and citizenship |
Includes bibliographical references and index.
Identifiers: LCCN 2024024075 | ISBN 9780197784099 (pb) | ISBN 9780197784082 (hb) |
ISBN 9780197784112 (epub) | ISBN 9780197784105 (updf) | ISBN 9780197784129 (digital online)
Subjects: LCSH: East Indian Americans—Political activity. | East Indian
Americans—Race identity—Political aspects. | East Indian
Americans—Government policy. | East Indian Americans—Religion. |
United States—Race relations—Political aspects. |
United States—Ethnic relations—Political aspects. |
Immigrants—Political activity—United States.
Classification: LCC E184.E2 K875 2024 |
DDC 305.8914/11073—dc23/eng/20240611
LC record available at https://lccn.loc.gov/2024024075

DOI: 10.1093/oso/9780197784082.001.0001

Paperback printed by Marquis Book Printing, Canada
Hardback printed by Bridgeport National Bindery, Inc., United States of America

For activists who work to create a more inclusive world

Contents

Preface ix
Map of India xiii

Introduction: Race, Religion, and the Political Formation of Indian Americans … 1

1. Race, Transnationalism, and Mobilization: Indian Americans 1900–1995 … 32

2. Religion and Transnationalism: The Rise of Intraethnic Divisions … 67

3. Ethnic versus Pan-Ethnic Mobilization: Indian American versus South Asian American Groups … 105

4. Enacting Cultural Citizenship: Majority versus Minority Religious Status and Contemporary Mobilization around Domestic Issues … 150

5. Enacting Transnational Citizenship: Majority versus Minority Religious Status and Contemporary Mobilization around India-Centered Issues … 193

6. Race, Religion, Generation, and Activism around U.S. Partisan Politics … 230

Conclusion: Claiming Citizenship: Race, Religion, and Political Mobilization … 274

Appendix: Indian American Advocacy Organizations Studied (At Least One Person Interviewed) … 295
References … 301
Index … 327

Preface

As an immigrant, I am interested in the ways in which immigrants and their children try to reshape their new environments as individuals and as groups rather than merely adapting to it. This book showcases immigrant agency by examining how and why contemporary immigrant groups become politically engaged in the United States. Specifically, it focuses on activists of South Asian and Indian descent and the advocacy organizations they have formed to make American society, policymakers, and politicians more receptive to the needs of their ethnic communities. It examines how race, caste, and religion interact with structures, cultures, and established political norms of the United States to shape varied political mobilization patterns. *Claiming Citizenship* presents a polyphonic account of the medley of concerns that galvanize a range of Indian American advocacy organizations. By political mobilization I mean involvement in partisan politics, as well as national-level attempts to educate and rally politicians and policymakers around domestic and foreign policy issues of concern to groups.

The individuals I focus on in this book either hailed from British India during the colonial period (my first chapter examines the migration of these groups to the United States at the turn of the twentieth century) or, like me, are immigrants or their descendants from the territory officially designated as constituting the postindependent "Republic of India." However, not all such individuals and groups identify as "Indian" Americans. As part of their activism some individuals and groups challenge the legitimacy of the accession of their lands by the Indian government or explicitly distance themselves from the Indian state and its policies for a variety of reasons. Thus, this book challenges the tendency to homogenize the nation-state (in this case, the nation of origin) by providing examples of the disjuncture between the state, or the government, and the "nation" as an entity to which its citizens and former citizens feel a sense of belonging and loyalty. Some of the questions this book explores include the types of identities and advocacy organizations that various groups mobilize around and the reasons for these choices.

My interest in political activism developed from earlier research examining how advocacy organizations representing people of Indian background were emerging in the U.S. public sphere around a variety of identities. I did not start this project with a focus on race, caste, and religion, however. Although I planned to include mobilization based on religion, I decided to avoid looking only at religious mobilization, since I wanted to move on from my past focus on religion. I was also aware that a common criticism of sociologists of religion was that we were "sampling on the dependent variable" and consequently were overestimating the role of religion. I tried several frameworks, including one that conceptualized Indian American political mobilization as based on a decentralized, pluralistic model of political mobilization, as opposed to the centralized, nation-state advocacy organizations of most other groups. However, none of the frameworks was satisfactory in explaining the diversity of Indian American mobilization patterns.

I finally realized that two important factors usually studied separately, race and religion, were interacting to influence the process of political incorporation and mobilization of Indian American groups. Quite late in the research, I also recognized that caste status, particularly privileged- versus oppressed-caste background, profoundly impacted the racial and religious identity of Indian Americans. Specifically, I found that differing understandings of race, as well as majority/minority religious status in India and the United States, both in turn influenced by caste background, served as prisms to shape variation in political mobilization patterns. Consequently, religion became the backbone of this project as well, something that I had resisted and did not expect.

Portions of the material presented in this book have been published elsewhere. The Introduction is based on the theoretical framework developed in "Race, Religion, and the Political Incorporation of Indian Americans," *Journal of Religious and Political Practice* 2, no. 3 (2016: 273–295. Chapter 1 draws on parts of three publications: "Who Are Asian Americans?," in *Choosing Asian America: A New York Reader*, edited by Russell Leong (New York: Asian American/Asian Studies Research Institute, 2017); "Shifting U.S. Racial and Ethnic Classification of a South Asian Group: Sikh American Activism," *Journal of the Social Sciences* (Russell Sage Foundation), Special Issue on Immigrants and Changing Identities (Fall 2018); and "South Asian Migration, Settlement, and Sociopolitical Incorporation on the North American West Coast," *Asian American and Pacific Islander Nexus Journal: Policy, Practice and Community*, Special Issue on Asians in Australia, Canada, United Kingdom, and United States (2017). Chapter 3 develops arguments first presented in "To Be or

Not to Be South Asian: Contemporary Indian American Politics," *Journal of Asian American Studies* 6, no. 3 (2003): 261–288 and "Who Speaks for Indian Americans? Religion, Ethnicity, and Political Formation," *American Quarterly* 59, no. 3 (2007): 759–783, later developed into the publication "Indian American versus South Asian American Diasporic Political Activism in the U.S.," *South Asian Diaspora* 14, no. 1 (2022): 1–20. Chapter 4 elaborates on parts of "Contemporary Ethno-Religious Groups and Political Activism in the United States," pp. 428–441 in The Wiley Blackwell Companion to Religion and Politics in the U.S., edited by Barbara McGraw (Wiley-Blackwell, Malden, MA, 2016). Chapter 5 is an expanded and significantly updated version of "Majority versus Minority Religious Status and Diasporic Nationalism: Indian American Advocacy Organizations," *Nations and Nationalism* 23, no. 1 (2017): 109–128.

This book, like my other publications, has been a long time in the making. While I first started working on Indian American political activism in 2001, a little after the September 11, 2001, attacks, which had a profound impact on South Asian Americans, I started research specifically on this project in 2007. A fellowship from the Woodrow Wilson International Center helped me to be in Washington, DC for the first half of 2007 (sadly I could not be there for the whole 2006–2007 academic year) and allowed me to begin the secondary research and the interviews. A grant from the Carnegie Corporation and a variety of small grants from Syracuse University (from the Alan Campbell Institute, Appleby Mosher, the Program for the Advancement of Research on Conflict and Collaboration, and the Summer Program Assistantship) permitted me to continue the research through subsequent short trips to Washington, DC; through phone interviews; and through secondary data analysis. I am very thankful for all these sources of funding. Several research assistants helped with this project. Vivek Srinivasan and Anirban Acharya conducted the bulk of the 20 interviews for this research which were not done by me. Sai Ma and Connie Etter did early work on literature reviews, and Jenna Sikka helped transcribe, code, and analyze some of the interviews. I gratefully acknowledge their contributions.

I presented portions of this research at a variety of venues beginning in 2007 including at the Woodrow Wilson International Center; Syracuse University; several American Sociological Association, Society for the Scientific Study of Religion, and Asian American Studies annual conferences; a World Congress of Sociology conference in Toronto; Case Western University; the University of Ottawa; the University of California, Los Angeles and Riverside;

Columbia University; Stanford University; the University of Pennsylvania; Rutgers University; Ecole des Hautes en Sciences Sociales (EHESS), Paris; the National Institute for Advanced Studies Bangalore and the Institute for Social and Economic Change in Bangalore, India; the National University of Singapore; Ewha Women's University, South Korea; and Waseda University, Japan. Comments and feedback that I received during these presentations were important in helping me think through many of my ideas.

I am very grateful to my department and to Janet Wilmoth for organizing a book workshop for me in October 2023. My reviewers, Nancy Foner and Irene Bloemraad, provided detailed and excellent feedback. My colleagues, in particular Selina Gallo-Cruz, Audie Klotz, and Janet Wilmoth, had good suggestions. I am ever so grateful to Audie Klotz and Leela Fernandes for other important types of help and support at crucial stages. I thank Marc Garcia for creating the data table for the Introduction, and Jaya Dalal for help with edits and the references. I appreciate the guidance Angela Chnapko (Oxford University Press editor) provided at every step through the long process.

My biggest debt of gratitude goes to the very many people, all high-profile, busy individuals, who took time to talk to me and patiently explain the history, goals, and activities of their organizations and the type of activism they had personally been involved in. Some have sadly passed on. It was heartwarming to listen to their remarkable accounts and see the passion they brought to their activist work. As they talked, I was often cognizant of how their work helped me, my family, and my friends in so many ways, including giving us access to many of the things we take for granted. I dedicate this book to activists who strive to create a more inclusive world.

Map of India

Alphabetical List of Acronyms of Frequently Discussed Organizations

See Appendix A for more details.

- AAHOA (Asian American Hotel Owners Association)
- AANA (Ambedkar Association of North America)
- AAPI (American Association of Physicians from India)
- AFMI (American Federation of Muslims from India)
- AIA (Association of Indians in America)
- AIM (Dr. Ambedkar International Mission)
- AIM (Association of Indian Muslims of America)
- AJA (Alliance for Justice and Accountability)
- AKSC (Ambedkar-King Study Circle)
- CAG (Coalition against Genocide)
- DFN (Dalit Freedom Network)
- FIA (Federation of Indian Associations)
- FIACONA (Federation of Indian American Christians of North America)
- GOPIO (Global Organization of Persons of Indian Origin)
- HAF (Hindu American Foundation)
- HfHR (Hindus for Human Rights)
- HSS (Hindu Swayamsevak Sangh)
- IAFPE (Indian American Forum for Political Education)
- IAKF (Indo-American Kashmir Forum)
- IALI (Indian American Leadership Initiative)
- IAMC (Indian American Muslim Council)
- KAC (Kashmiri American Council)
- MPAC (Muslim Public Affairs Council)
- RHC (Republican Hindu Coalition)
- SAALT (South Asian Americans Leading Together)
- SAFO (South Asians for Obama)
- SAHFA (South Asian Histories for All)
- SAKI (South Asians for Kerry)
- SALDEF (Sikh American Legal Defense and Education Fund)
- TSB (They See Blue)
- USINPAC (United States India Political Action Committee)
- VHPA (Vishwa Hindu Parishad of America)

Introduction

Race, Religion, and the Political Formation of Indian Americans

"It's amazing. Indian—of descent—Americans are taking over the country!" U.S. president Joe Biden exclaimed on March 5, 2021, referring to the large number high-level Indian American appointees in his administration, including Vice President Kamala Harris, whose mother had been an immigrant from India (Badrinathan, Kapur, Kay, and Vaishnav, 2021, 4). He was joking, of course, but by then Biden had appointed at least 55 Indian Americans in almost all wings of the government. By August 2022, Biden appointed over 130 Indian Americans to his administration.[1] In January 2021, four Indian Americans were sworn into Congress—Ro Khanna, Pramila Jayapal, Raja Krishnamoorthi for a second term, and Ami Bera for his third term. All were re-elected in the midterm elections, and in January 2023, a fifth, Shri Thanedar, was sworn into Congress. There were several high-profile Indian American appointees under the Trump administration as well, including Nikki Haley, former governor of South Carolina, as the ambassador to the United Nations; Seema Verma to run the Center for Medicare and Medicaid Services; Ajit Pai as head of the Federal Communications Commission; and Raj Shah as deputy assistant to President Trump and deputy communications director. In fact, political scientist Karthick Ramakrishnan argued that probably completely by accident, Indian Americans seemed to have been "disproportionately represented in Trump's nominations compared to other minority groups" (Kuruvilla 2017). Indian Americans were also a substantial presence in the Obama administration. President Obama hired so many Indian Americans, up to 75 to 80 at one point with 18 working in the White House, that some called him the "first Indian-American president" (Raj 2017). The first Republican debate of August 23, 2023, had just taken place as I was finalizing this manuscript, with media outlets claiming that Indian American candidates Vivek Ramaswamy and Nikki Haley both had standout performances (although in very different ways) and had raised their profiles.

Numbering 4.4 million in the U.S. census in 2020, Indian Americans are currently the second-largest group of immigrants in the United States, next only to Mexicans (Badrinathan, Kapur, Kay, and Vaishnav 2021, 1). They are also the largest "Asian-alone" (excluding multiracial people) group of Asian Americans. As early as 2002, James M. Lindsay, vice president of the Council on Foreign Relations, identified Indian Americans as most "likely to emerge as a political powerhouse in the U.S." (Lindsay 2002). "Forget the Israel Lobby: The Hill's Next Big Player Is Made in India" blared a September 30, 2007, *Washington Post* article. It discussed how Indian Americans drew inspiration from the American Israel Public Affairs Committee (AIPAC), the powerful pro-Israel lobbying group, and made the case that by following in the footsteps of AIPAC, the "India lobby is getting results in Washington—and having a profound impact on U.S. policy, with important consequences for the future of Asia and the world" (Kamdar 2007). Author Mira Kamdar was writing specifically about the U.S.-India civilian nuclear deal, a landmark agreement that required a change in U.S. and international regulations to permit the United States to sell nuclear fuel and technology for civilian purposes to India, a country that had not signed the Nuclear Non-Proliferation Treaty. After several rounds of negotiations and several holdups, the deal was eventually signed into law by President George W. Bush on October 8, 2008. In the article, Kamdar (2007) described an Indian American organization formed in 2002, the *U.S. Indian Political Action Committee* (USINPAC), referring to it as "the visible face of Indian American lobbying," and made the point, based on interviews with USINPAC leaders, that they had modeled themselves after the "Israel lobby."

When I began my research on Indian American political activism in early 2007, the first round of legislation around the U.S.-India nuclear deal had just been approved by Congress, and President Bush had signed the Henry Hyde Act in December 2006, which pledged that the United States would cooperate with India for peaceful nuclear energy development. Initiated in July 2005 by President George Bush and then–Indian prime minister Manmohan Singh, the agreement had faced considerable opposition in the U.S. Congress (it was also opposed by several parties and groups in India as undermining India's national sovereignty). However, several immigrant Indian American groups and individuals from around the country came together to mount an intensive fundraising and lobbying campaign. Wealthy Indian American men who until then had contributed to political campaigns without asking for anything in return responded enthusiastically since they saw the cause as one that would bring together and serve both their *janmabhoomi* (land of their birth) and their *karmabhoomi* (the land where they live and work). Supporters of the bill on the Hill acknowledged that Indian American mobilization had been crucial in getting the deal through Congress. In fact, then–U.S. undersecretary of state Nicholas Burns, the chief negotiator of the agreement, described the successful passing of the legislation as the "coming out party of the Indian-American community in the United States" (Haniffa 2007). The nuclear deal mobilization led several commentators besides Mira Kamdar to identify Indian Americans as a group that had emerged as a powerful influence in American politics and to compare it to the Israel lobby (Banerjee 2007; Kirk 2008; McIntire 2006). Consequently, the nuclear deal, and the concomitant Indian American mobilization, was the talk of the town (Washington, DC) in 2007 and I initially focused on this topic (see Chapter 3 for an extended discussion). I came to see that the best way to examine national-level Indian American political activism was to investigate the activities of key Indian American advocacy organizations (most with offices in Washington, DC) because they represented Indian American constituencies and brought their concerns to policymakers.

Over time, I realized that the nuclear deal mobilization represented an unusual example of apparently unified ethnic mobilization—actually, several Indian American subgroups and organizations did not get involved—and that it was just one way in which people of Indian background were becoming civically and politically engaged in the United States. While USINPAC was the only registered lobby group representing the Indian American community, it was not the only Indian American organization active around the nuclear deal. Several other types of Indian American organizations and Indian American leaders came together under the umbrella of the *U.S. India Friendship Council*; two prominent Indian American activists also came together to form the *Indian American Security Leadership Council*—both were temporary coalitions formed to push through the nuclear deal.

Although I began my research by investigating mobilization around the nuclear deal and the partisan politics behind it, I had a broader definition of political activism. Specifically, I was interested in the many ways that Indian Americans (whom I later came to define as immigrants and their children from the postindependent "Republic of India"—see the Preface) were mobilizing to demand recognition and resources for their cultural and religious identities, and to influence the domestic and foreign policies of the United States. In other words, I wanted to study how Indian Americans were *claiming citizenship* in the United States. I focused on civic and political activism in the U.S. public sphere, although some Indian Americans were active in other countries, particularly in India.

I soon came to recognize that Indian American patterns of activism *did not follow the model of other powerful American ethnic groups.* Ethnic groups are generally seen as homogenous units, and this "ethnicist and over-homogenizing" perspective overlooks internal differences in mobilization patterns within the same ethnic group (Però and Solomos 2010, 9). The literature generally focuses on cases where those who share national origins also share common political interests and mobilize around these interests. It argues that residential concentration, unity around a nation-state paradigm, and the development of one or more organizations representing the ethnic group, employing full-time, paid, professional staff, are prerequisites for successful influence (Haney and Vanderbush 1999, 344; T. Smith 2000).

However, Indian Americans manifested none of these characteristics. They are the most dispersed U.S. ethnic group (Portes and Rumbaut 2014, 94) and they have multiple types of advocacy organizations. There are a variety of organizations mobilizing around an Indian American identity, including trade organizations representing Indian American doctors, hoteliers, and information technology professionals that sometimes rally around broader Indian American issues. There are also a range of other organizations based on very different understandings of ethnicity and identity and consequently different goals. There are South Asian American organizations (Indian Americans make up more than 85 percent of the South Asian American population); organizations for Indian Americans of Hindu, Sikh, Muslim, Christian, and Buddhist backgrounds; organizations representing Indian American Democrats and Republicans; and even combinations of these such as the Republican Hindu Coalition that mobilized around Donald Trump's candidacy in 2016. Furthermore, there are generational differences, with adult, second-generation members getting involved in civic and political activism in very different ways and with different interests compared to their parents' generation. In other words, due to the diversity of the Indian American community, its civic and political demands have often been expressed through organizations catering to particular subgroups rather than through an organization representing the ethnic group as a whole. Unified ethnic mobilization is rare and does not take place through a single professional advocacy organization, or even through well-coordinated campaigns, but, as in the case of the nuclear deal, ensues through the mobilization of networks of activists around the country, the coming together of a variety of organizations of Indian Americans, and the formation of temporary, issue-based coalitions.

This, then, was the puzzle: *how were Indian Americans becoming a rising political force if they were not following the traditional, recommended model of political influence?* In *Desis Divided*, based on a study of South Asian Americans (or *desis*—individuals from the Indian subcontinent), political scientist Sangay Mishra (2016, 207) challenged the unified ethnic mobilization paradigm, documenting that internal cleavages, particularly based on religion, led to "multiple paths of political empowerment for different South Asian American subgroups." These cleavages and multiple paths of empowerment were clear from my earlier work (Kurien 2001, 2003, 2007b) and motivated this project. *Claiming Citizenship* goes much deeper than merely showcasing intracommunity cleavages and differential strategies for empowerment to explain how and why this happens and what the implications might be.

Large-scale international immigration has transformed the political contours of Western societies over the last few decades. The political mobilization of contemporary ethnic groups to claim public recognition and rights is raising questions about nationhood, citizenship, and secularism and has created dilemmas about how to institutionalize pluralism. The rise of the Internet and social media has also remade the mechanics of political mobilization and influence. Yet there is little understanding of how new immigrant groups become politically incorporated and influential in Western societies. What are the factors that motivate their political mobilization, and what strategies do they use to achieve political power? Is unified mobilization the only way to achieve political influence, and if so, what happens to groups that are internally diverse? This book addresses these questions through a study of Indian American political mobilization.

The Argument of the Book

I argue that two factors—race and religion—are crucial in shaping the social location of Indian American groups and the diversity of advocacy organizations. As a non-White group in a racially stratified society, many Indian Americans experience racialization. However, their racial status in the United States is "read" in a variety of ways (Morning 2001; Kibria 1996,

1998). Consequently, a variety of personal, group, and regional factors shape how race impacts their lives and how they perceive this impact. The rise of Hindu nationalism in India and the attacks of September 11, 2001, in the United States resulted in religious background becoming another important factor affecting Indian American experiences of belonging, both in India and in the United States. Indian Americans hail from a variety of religious backgrounds, and religion becomes the means through which they form communities and transnational links upon migration and settlement (Chakravorty, Kapur, and Singh 2017, 137, 271). Since religion also plays an important personal and public role in the United States, it becomes the political conduit to channel community concerns. This book shows that *differing understandings of the significance of racial identity in shaping the experience and incorporation of Indian Americans, as well as religious background (which in turn shapes perceptions of racial identity)*, produced much of the variation in the patterns of civic and political activism of various types of Indian American groups.

Both racial identity and religion in turn are shaped by another factor: the caste location of Indian American groups, something that is less evident to outsiders since it is not based on somatic difference. Caste is a very important source of social stratification in India, and as the numbers of Indian immigrants increased in the United States, caste groupings, outlooks, and stigmas were imported and implanted on U.S. soil. While most earlier immigrants were from caste-privileged backgrounds, particularly since the information technology (IT) boom beginning in the 1990s, some caste-oppressed groups have also been able to migrate to the United States. Ideas of social location, racial identity, ability, and entitlement are significantly impacted by caste status. A racial theory of caste first introduced during the colonial period that divides Indians into *Aryan* (part of the Indo-European people originating from the Caucasus) and non-Aryan groups continues to be deeply ingrained in the psyche of Indians and influential in shaping ideas regarding racial identity since privileged-caste groups in North India, as well as Brahmins and some privileged castes in South India, were classified as Aryans.

Religion and caste are interlinked. Twentieth-century British colonial censuses demonstrated for the first time that privileged-caste groups were a minority in India, which motivated early Hindu nationalists to designate untouchable castes as Hindus (until then they had been viewed as being outside Hindu society), despite great initial protests, to create a majoritarian religious nationalism (J. Lee 2021). The religious background, religious ideologies, and practices of subgroups are also affected by caste since conversion out of Hinduism has been a strategy followed by several oppressed-caste individuals and groups over the centuries as a means of trying to escape the worst caste abuses, in addition to obtaining self-respect and "mental liberation." Consequently, oppressed-caste groups, particularly *Dalits* (the self-chosen name of former untouchable castes), belong to a variety of religions. In short, caste background impacts religious background as well as understandings of racial identity and becomes a conduit to configure patterns of mobilization.

Generational status in the United States shapes the significance of caste identity. Even though many Indian immigrants try to transmit their "culture" (often a code for caste practices) and religion to their children, and caste societies have become established in the United States, the U.S. context constitutes an "interference" to ideologies and practices of caste, and consequently, many second-generation Indian Americans do not uncritically internalize ideologies of caste status in the same way as their parents. The American-raised generation is also keenly attuned to U.S. religious stereotypes and the nuances of U.S. racial ideologies and racialization, about which most immigrants are usually quite oblivious. Consequently, ideas of religious and racial location and identity of the second generation are often quite different from that of their immigrant parents, in turn impacting mobilization patterns (see Figure I.1).

There are also generational differences in how and why the two generations get involved in activism and advocacy. Immigrants generally get involved in American politics and activism through their participation in Indian American organizations, and politicians often recruit them to gain the financial support of the group. Usually, immigrant engagement in U.S. politics takes place after they have become successful in their business

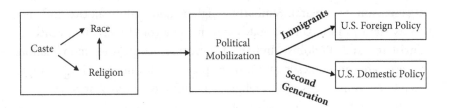

Figure I.1 Overall diagram.

or profession and part of the motivation is to gain status within Indian and Indian American circles. Many second-generation activists, on the other hand, develop an interest in advocacy, politics, and activism early on and often choose to go into law or public policy to facilitate a career in politics or policymaking. They are spurred by a desire to be part of the American political system and to be involved in policy formulation. While immigrant partisan involvement is often determined by the party of the politician who recruits them into politics, the second generation has a clearer and stronger sense of partisan ideology. Foreign policy or India-centric issues are of greater interest to the immigrant generation, while domestic issues are the primary focus of the second generation. Finally, generational patterns of activism are also gendered, with leaders and activists of the immigrant generation being male, while there are many women in the second generation who establish or lead organizations.

Claiming Citizenship shows that race and religion are not two different aspects of group life that can just be added together to comprehend the full group experience. Instead, race and religion, often working through caste background, *interact* to mold the mobilization patterns of Indian American groups that become active around a variety of religious and secular identities. Specifically, racial and religious identity (i.e., objective and subjective group characteristics) together with U.S. racial and religious regimes (i.e., the laws and practices of race and religion in the United States) influence the pathways of political mobilization for contemporary immigrants. Religion intersects with race. In the United States, religion has been racialized in post-9/11 America (Selod 2018). I show that race is significant not just in terms of somatic appearance and identity, and that religion is important not just as belief, culture, and social affiliation, but that both race and religion define *sociopolitical group locations* shaped by state policies. Specifically, racial identity determines whether a group mobilizes around a White model of political activism (with Jewish organizations being the exemplar) or a non-White model (Black, Latino, and early Asian civil rights organization exemplars). Similarly, religious and caste majority and minority status, in the United States and in India (of Hindu, Sikh, Muslim, Christian, and Buddhist Indian Americans), configures mobilization patterns around domestic and foreign policy issues in very similar ways, despite big differences in the religious beliefs, community organizations, practices, and economic profiles of groups. Institutional isomorphism, or the tendency to follow established organizational patterns of structurally similar groups, plays an important role (DiMaggio and Powell 1983). Dalit groups, many mobilizing around a revivalist Buddhism formulated by Dalit icon Dr. Bhimrao Ambedkar in the twentieth century, challenge the hegemony of privileged-caste Hindus but also have complicated relationships with other major Indian religious groups. This explains why they sometimes ally with Indian religious minorities and sometimes mobilize independently. Over the course of the research for this book and particularly more recently, Dalit groups have emerged as important U.S. leaders of multireligious, anti-Hindu-nationalist coalitions around attacks against minorities in India and around caste-based issues in the United States. *Claiming Citizenship* also makes clear why these identities (race, religion, caste) matter since they mold the goals and strategies of Indian American advocacy groups in very different ways.

Additionally, this book examines the dialectical process through which new ethnic groups conform to the structures and cultures of their host societies but also work to transform them to accommodate their unique needs. It shows the roles played by domestic and international influences on the political mobilization of immigrant groups in the United States. Consequently, it presents a template to understand how race, religion, national identity, and pan-ethnicity interact to influence the political formation and advocacy of new immigrant groups around both domestic and homeland issues, and the role that generational status plays in determining some of these patterns. While Indian Americans might represent a community that is unusually diverse, many other new ethnic groups have internal cleavages of different types. Social media amplifies the abilities of smaller groups to organize and mobilize and has been vital in contemporary Indian American mobilization. Perhaps with the advent of new forms of technology, Indian Americans might be the harbinger of a new type of group activism model, rather than being an exception.

Theoretical Frameworks

The Political Mobilization of Contemporary Ethnic Groups

Scholarship on immigrant political mobilization usually focuses on *either* activism around homeland issues, described as "diaspora politics" (Betts and Jones 2016; Moss 2022; Shain 1999), *or* activism around rights in their home countries, referred to as "immigrant politics" (Garbaye 2005; Nicholls 2019). This book focuses on *both* aspects and shows the connections between the two around the process of *claiming citizenship*. Ethnic organizations today operate in a context where multiculturalism, globalization, and transnationalism challenge definitions of assimilation and citizenship (Appadurai 1996; W. Brubaker 1989; T. Smith 2000). Citizenship includes legal status and rights to membership within a nation-state but also recognition of these rights by other members, which provides a subjective sense of belonging (Glenn 2011). Irene Bloemraad provides a bottom-up definition of citizenship that resonates with the approach of this book, describing it as a "relational process" by which immigrants and other groups make "membership claims on polities, people, and institutions, claims recognized or rejected within particular normative understandings of citizenship" (Bloemraad 2018, 4). This claims-making process and its outcomes are precisely what I examine here.

The term *multicultural citizenship* usually refers to top-down "government policies designed to positively recognize diversity and help minorities maintain cultural and religious practices while integrating them into public life" (M. Wright and Bloemraad 2012, 78). Although multiculturalism was never formally adopted as a national policy in the United States (unlike in Canada and Australia), multicultural policies to accommodate cultural, religious, dietary, and linguistic differences; reduce discrimination; foster cultural pluralism; and provide immigrants a sense of belonging and of membership were developed in the United States, as in Canada and Europe, in the last few decades of the twentieth century (Newfield and Gordon 1996, 76–77). *Cultural citizenship*, on the other hand, refers to "bottom-up" struggles for social inclusion by marginalized groups. First introduced by anthropologist Renato Rosaldo (1994, 57) to refer to the demand by racial and cultural minorities for full citizenship while maintaining cultural uniqueness from the "dominant national community," Rosaldo's definition was critiqued by Aihwa Ong (1996, 738) for implying that "cultural citizenship can be unilaterally constructed by minority groups" and refined to include negotiation with the state and its agents for the right to maintain cultural difference. In my research I saw how Indian American groups had to struggle and strategize to gain cultural citizenship—it was not simply achieved on demand. Despite the work of various individuals and groups over decades, this continues to be an ongoing process. Consequently, I use Ong's definition of cultural citizenship, which is similar to the claims-making, relational process that

Bloemraad (2018) describes. I examine the engagement and negotiations of various Indian American groups with the U.S. government and its representatives and their carefully planned schemes to gain rights and recognition and to claim belonging.

Whereas citizenship usually refers to membership in the country of primary residence, the concept of *transnational citizenship* recognizes that emigrants continue to feel a connection with their countries of origin and engage in cross-border political participation (Bauböck 2003). However, it is important to emphasize that they do this *as citizens of host countries that have global influence*. Similarly, migrant-sending countries have been developing schemes, called "diaspora strategies" (Ho, Hickey, and Yeoh 2015), to arouse the loyalty of diasporas to encourage them to send financial remittances, to make financial investments in their home countries, and to act as unofficial ambassadors to promote their homeland in their countries of settlement (Varadarajan 2010). Transnational citizenship activism can also involve the activism of diasporic groups who are minorities in their homelands *against* their home states, or "minority nationalism." The most-studied cases have been of ethnic groups that included a demand for secessionism, whether this demand was successful or not (R. Brubaker 1996; Varadarajan 2010, 37–38), but ethnic, religious, racial, and caste minorities might also mobilize in the diaspora around attacks against their groups in the homeland and around claims for rights. *Claiming Citizenship* uses and refines both concepts to study activism in the U.S. public sphere—cultural citizenship to discuss mobilization of Indian American and South Asian American groups around religious and cultural identities and practices, and transnational citizenship to discuss their activism around homeland issues. It also examines the role of the Indian state in creating policies to make Indian Americans feel vested in the progress and development of India.

The literature on U.S. immigrant political mobilization has tended to focus on how contemporary immigrants have been affecting American politics through voting behavior and participation in local administration (Bloemraad 2006; DeSipio 1996; Jones-Correa 1998a; T. Lee, Ramakrishnan, and Ramirez 2006; Stepick et al. 2003). However, their involvement in national advocacy organizations to claim rights and assert their cultural citizenship is likely to be more consequential and could result in the transformation of the American political system in important ways. Yet virtually no attention has been paid to national political advocacy organizations of contemporary immigrants who have entered the country since the passage of the 1965 Immigration Act. Perhaps this is because it generally takes a generation or two for new immigrant groups to enter the political mainstream of their new homelands (Mathias 1981). However, Indian Americans represent an unusual case of a group that has become a rising political force even in the first generation. Second-generation Indian Americans have been even more active at the national political level in both Democratic and Republican administrations and parties and as leaders of advocacy organizations.

Social media has transformed the landscape of both progressive and reactionary activism from the Arab spring and the Occupy movements to White nationalism and ISIS (Kidd and McIntosh 2016; Gerbaudo and Treré 2015; Berger 2016). For diasporas, social media has emerged as a vital platform to develop diasporic connections with each other, with coethnic diasporas in other countries, and with communities in the homeland (Alonso and Oiarzabal 2010; Retis and Tsagarousianou 2019). Finally, social media has also transformed the way advocacy organizations engage their supporters and the wider public, making it easier, quicker, and less expensive for them to get the word out, raise funding, and coordinate mobilization (Borge and Cardenal 2011). For all these reasons, then, the ethnic advocacy organizations of contemporary immigrants are likely to adopt different agendas and strategies of political incorporation when compared to those of the earlier waves of immigrants.

Political incorporation has been defined as both a process of learning the rules of the game and an outcome, the ability to influence policies and the political system (Hochschild and Mollenkopf 2009; Rogers 2006). Studies of contemporary immigrant political incorporation view the outcome of political incorporation as a variable shaped by differences in the *political opportunity structures* of the different countries (such as national ideologies, the type of polity and electoral system, laws dealing with the treatment of immigrants and refugees, and citizenship procedures, as well as the *characteristics and resources of immigrants* such as their ethnic identity, education levels, language ability, income and occupational background, social networks, organizational resources, and community unity (Bloemraad 2006; Hochschild and Mollenkopf 2009). How do these two characteristics interact to shape political incorporation? I address this question by examining patterns of Indian American political activism around both U.S.-based and India-based concerns. We see how immigrants create and capture new political opportunities in their host societies, leading to opportunities to expand citizenship.

Race, Ethnicity, and Political Incorporation

Race was a facilitating political opportunity structure in the incorporation of European immigrants in the United States. In fact, as Mathew Frye Jacobson points out (1999, 8), "[i]t was the racial appellation 'white persons' in the nation's naturalization law that allowed the migrations from Europe in the first place." He argues that "the civic story of assimilation (the process by which the Irish, Russian Jews, Poles and Greeks became Americans) is inseparable from the cultural story of racial alchemy (the process by which Celts, Hebrews, Slavs, and Mediterraneans became Caucasians)." Most contemporary immigrants in the United States are racial minorities, and this racial status is key to patterns of contemporary immigrant social and political incorporation (Jones-Correa and de Graauw 2013, 216–217). Consequently, many contemporary scholars use a racial lens to research the political integration of contemporary U.S. immigrants (J. Garcia 2012; Rogers 2006; Wong et al. 2011). Scholars have also noted that because of the "made in the USA" quality of racial formation, generational status is a significant predictor of racial identification, with second- and later-generation Americans more likely than immigrants to adopt and accept racial identities as Black, Latinx, and Asian American (Espino, Leal, and Meier 2008; Espiritu 1992; Lien, Conway, and Wong 2004; Waters 1999).

Despite the continuing importance of race as a political opportunity structure shaping contemporary immigrant politics, research on immigrant political mobilization shows the importance of ethnicity as a characteristic of immigrants since immigrants who belong to racial minority groups rarely identify in terms of broader racial categories and instead tend to mobilize based on national origin (Brettell and Reed-Danahay 2011; Jones-Correa and Leal 1996). Scholars argue that this is because immigrants do not feel any commonality of interests with other ethno-national groups that may be classified under the same racial umbrella (Bloemraad 2006), and because non-White groups want to avoid identifying based on race (Rajagopal 1995).

As mentioned, the U.S. literature on ethnic politics views ethnic communities as political groups and is generally based on a nation-of-origin paradigm. It generally looks at cases where the group, facing a crisis in the ancestral homeland, unifies around a nation-state organization and mobilizes to influence U.S. foreign policy (Ambrosio 2002; Goldberg 1990; Hamm 1996). There is some discussion of cases where there are competing lobbies within an ethnic group. But these are either situations where competing lobbies did not disagree on policy objectives (Gregg 2002) or cases where unity was eventually achieved (Goldberg 1990; Villarreal and Hernandez 1991). However, there is no discussion of ethnic groups where there are fundamental disagreements on policy objectives between various groups that do not diminish over time. The nation-of-origin model of mobilization overlooks how the political opportunity structures of *home* countries might mean that national identity may mean different things for groups from the same country.

There is a substantial literature that argues that majority and minority ethnic groups (defined in terms of numbers and political dominance) might have a different attitude toward their nation-state (Dowley and Silver 2000; Horowitz 2000; Staerklé et al. 2010). Majority and minority groups usually have very different histories, political interests, and social concerns in their homelands since the culture of the dominant group often tends to get institutionalized as the national culture, marginalizing minority groups (Gurr 2000; A. Smith 1986; Wimmer 1997). Consequently, it is likely that majority and minority ethnic groups will have different patterns of mobilization. There is some scholarship on this topic (Fair 2006; Kurien 2001; Wayland 2004). However, they usually examine individual instances of ethnic mobilization, or the ethnic mobilization of groups around separate sets of issues.

Religion and Political Incorporation

Ethnic majorities and minorities can be based on a variety of issues such as language, culture, or region. In the Indian American case, while each of these factors plays a role in creating subdivisions within the community, religion seems to be the biggest political cleavage. Globally as well, conflicts over religious issues have "intensified, driven by the resurgence of public religion" (R. Brubaker 2013, 14). Scholars who have compared immigrant integration policies in the United States and Europe show that religion plays an important role in shaping the political opportunity structure. They argue that because religion is viewed as normative and as a crucible of ethnic culture in the United States, it facilitates the integration of U.S. immigrants, in contrast to Europe, where religion hinders the integration of immigrants due to the more secular context (Casanova 2007; Foner and Alba 2008).[2] While there is some discussion of how religion shaped the political incorporation of earlier immigrant groups in the United States (Alba, Raboteau, and DeWind 2009), the issue of whether political opportunity structures might affect contemporary immigrant groups from different religious backgrounds in dissimilar ways has not been examined.

Religion and religious institutions can also mold the characteristics of immigrant groups. Religious institutions become social centers in the diaspora, shaping the characteristics of the group, since they provide immigrants with the resources to develop communities and identities (Hirschman 2004, 1228; Yang and Ebaugh 2001). Finally, race and religion often intersect to shape political activism. Racial separation among religious worship communities is the norm in the United States among long-established and more recent religious groups (Emerson 2006, 5; Foley and Hoge 2007, 68, 81, 84; Warner 2006, 239, 240). Consequently, if religious communities act as spurs for civic and political activism, the close relationship between race, religion, and political interests is to be expected (Espinosa 2013). Yet, there is not much understanding regarding how this relationship works for different religious groups. Through a study of Indian Americans, a politically active non-White group from a variety of religious backgrounds, this book provides a broader understanding of how both race and religion shape the political opportunity structures and characteristics of immigrants and the political goals and strategies of immigrant interest groups.

Global versus Domestic Factors Shaping Political Mobilization

Are ethnic groups motivated to get involved in the political process due to a desire to impact or shape the politics of their countries of origin? Or are domestic issues such as perceived discrimination a greater spur to political participation? As mentioned, the literature on established ethnic lobby groups in the United States generally focuses on how they mobilize to influence foreign policy (Ambrosio 2002; Haney and Vanderbush 1999; Wittkopf and McCormick 1998). There is an intense debate about the effect of multicultural citizenship and new forms of technology on ethnic lobbies. Some believe that globalization and multiculturalism legitimize the pursuit of parochial concerns by ethnic lobbies and will thus further the balkanization of the foreign policy process (Huntington 1997; T. Smith 2000). Others argue that ethnic lobbies representing the interests of new groups in the United States, aided by new forms of technology, will further democratic participation by a more diverse group of American citizens and will also result in the spread of American values around the world (Clough 1994; Shain 1999). Only careful studies of newer ethnic advocacy organizations can address the question of which of these two scenarios is more likely. Indian Americans can provide a good study to examine this question.

Domestic factors such as discrimination and attacks on civil rights can also serve as powerful motivators of political organization. For instance, groups like Jewish and Irish Americans mobilized to challenge racial and religious discrimination and to demonstrate racial, cultural, and political similarity with members of the wider society (Dollinger 2000; Goldstein 2006; Ignatiev 1995). Both groups successfully achieved "racial alchemy" to become recognized as "White" (Jacobson 1999, 8), and their religions were also integrated into Judeo-Christian America. However, the process has not been as easy for non-European groups. John Skrentny (2002, 8) argues that the African American mobilization for civil rights created a broader minority rights revolution in the United States as other racial minorities used their "tool kit of policy models." While the National Association for the Advancement of Colored People (NAACP) was formed in 1909, it developed a legal arm in 1940, the NAACP Legal Defense and Educational Fund. Particularly after the spectacular success of the organization during the civil rights movement of the 1950s and 1960s, it became a powerful model for minority groups. The Mexican American Legal Defense and Education Fund (MALDEF) was formed in 1968 and the Asian American Legal Defense and Education Fund (AALDEF) was founded in 1974 to mobilize around civil rights issues for their constituencies.

Most of these efforts were led by the second and later generations. There is some discussion regarding the difference between "immigrant" and "ethnic" politics, or the politics of the first- and later-generation Americans in the literature (Jones-Correa 2002, 2007; Garza 2004; Moore 1981; Reedy 1991). These discussions of generational differences in the case of Irish, Jewish, Mexican, and Japanese Americans focus primarily on how the orientation and pattern of political advocacy changed over time as the American-born generation took over control of politics, with the second generation likely to be more assimilationist (aiming to make good citizens out of their group members and have the group be accepted as fully American).

Multicultural citizenship has profound implications for the role of ethnic groups in domestic policy. It validates the demand for ethnic recognition and participation even without residential concentration, significant numbers, or assimilation. How does this change impact domestic policy? Indian Americans are a good paradigm of a group that has been able to achieve influence in the contemporary period despite being a small, dispersed minority. Indian American organizations focus on immigration-related issues; South Asian American groups focus particularly on post–September 11, 2001, policies that have adversely impacted their constituencies; religious groups like Muslims, Hindus, and Sikhs seek recognition and rights as American religions; and finally, trade groups representing Indian American doctors and hoteliers demand the removal of barriers to conducting their business and participation in national-level decision-making with respect to the health care and hospitality industries.

Strategies for Ethnic Mobilization

In the past, ethnic groups like the Irish, Cubans, and Jews were able to shape local politics and policies through residential concentration; control of political machines in big cities like Boston, New York, Philadelphia, Chicago, St. Louis, and San Francisco (M. García 1996, McNickle 1993; Reedy 1991); and, in the case of Latinos, through their numbers (Ochoa and Ochoa 2005; Marquez 2003). While in the past ethnic lobbies primarily exerted their influence through votes, many contemporary lobbies follow the model of the Israeli lobby and have shifted their strategies from votes to campaign contributions, high-level appointments, and media influence (Lind 2002). The AIPAC model, involving the creation of an organizational body to develop a "broad and unified Jewish American constituency" (DeWind and Segura 2014, 15), formulate strategy, and monitor the policymaking process in Washington, DC, has become a "gold standard" for ethnic lobbies (D. Paul and Paul 2009, 48; T. Smith 2000). Thus, many groups, including Cubans, Greeks, Armenians, and Arabs, try to imitate Jews and model their lobbying organizations after AIPAC. Organizations such as the Cuban American National Foundation (CANF), the American Hellenic Institute Public Affairs Committee (AHIPAC), and the Armenian Assembly of America are explicitly modeled on AIPAC (Haney and Vanderbush 1999, 344; T. Smith 2000; Uslaner 2002, 355–377). The comparison with Jewish groups also came up constantly in my own interviews with Indian American leaders and activists.

Although the literature on ethnic groups is based on a unified nation-of-origin model of mobilization, other research shows that a proliferation of ethnic organizations can contribute to ethnic political success. Scholars studying interest groups help us understand why there might be a diversity of advocacy organizations within one ethnic group. As organized interests have proliferated, they have become more specialized, occupying specific "issue niches." Consequently, interest groups aim to remain autonomous and to cultivate a recognizable and distinct identity so that they can become the spokesperson for a clearly demarcated segment of the public (Browne 1990). At the same time, they sometimes form alliances with other groups to further their agenda (Baumgartner and Jones 1993). Building on Robert Putnam's (2000) influential work on bonding and bridging social capital, Dutch political scientists Miendert Fennema and Jean Tillie (2001) argue that the denser the network of associations of a particular group, the stronger their civic community, which in turn enhances the likelihood that they will participate politically in the wider society. This is because voluntary associations are likely to have overlapping memberships (horizontal relations), as well as "distance-two" vertical networks where a member of group A can have access to a policymaker through a friend or common acquaintance in group B (Fennema 2004, 433). Using these ideas, anthropologists Deborah Reed-Danahay and Caroline Brettell (2008) show that having a variety of ethnic interest groups within a community can facilitate the political participation of immigrants since ethnic organizational networks are sites to construct dual ethnic-American identities, to learn about the political process, to engage in political activism, and to link with other ethnic organizations and mainstream organizations around the country engaged in the same goals. What is attractive about this literature is that it can provide a means to develop a model of ethnic lobbying that does not hinge on the unity of the group around an issue or an organization and that therefore might be applicable to groups like Indian Americans. They show that what is important is the networks that community members form through their organizations, not the specific concerns that individual organizations mobilize around. Consequently, under some circumstances, the diversity and multiplicity of organizations can be an asset to an ethnic group since the organizations focus on a variety of issues, both domestic and foreign; target different groups of policymakers; and are thus better able to represent the heterogeneity and needs of the community. It may also be a more realistic model for groups like Indian Americans that have multiple, cross-cutting cleavages.

Background to Indian Americans

India, now the most populous country in the world, has the largest global diaspora (18 million in 2020).[3] As we can see from Table I.1, the Indian American population in 2022 was 4.55 million. Most are foreign born (69 percent of adults in 2022), the highest percentage among the major Asian American groups, and most immigrants (69 percent) arrived in the country on or after the year 2000. They are among the most educated groups in the United States (78 percent of those who were 25 years or older had a bachelor's degree in 2022) and are also the highest-income group in the country. In 2022, the median annual household income of those above 25 ($206,848)

Table I.1 Indian Americans, sociodemographic characteristics.

	ALL	USB	FB
Total population, millions	4,549,067	1,396,829	3,152,238
Age (mean)	35	18	43
% Female	48.1	48.9	47.6
% Bachelor's degree or higher*	77.9	61.1	77.7
Median annual household income*	$206,848	$227,067	$204,222
Median annual income*	$95,009	$104,765	$93,742
% Poverty rate	7.57		
Nativity status			
% USB	30.7		
% FB	69.3		
Citizenship			
% U.S. Citizen	65.7	100	50.6
% Non-U.S. Citizen	34.3		49.4
% immigrated since 2000			69.0
% immigrated since 2010			44.9
Management, business, and financial occupations	19.1	23.0	18.6
Computer, engineering, and science occupations	27.5	15.7	29.0
Health care practitioners and technical occupations	8.6	19.6	7.1

* 25 and older.
Notes: FB, foreign born; USB, U.S. born.
Data: American Community Survey 2022.

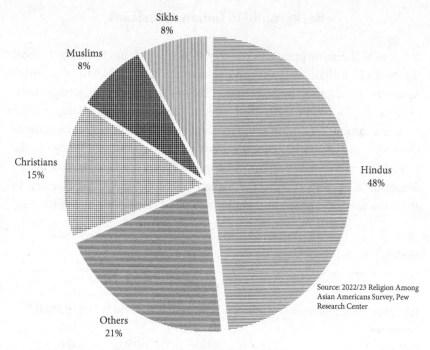

Figure I.2 Religious distribution of Indian Americans.

was much higher than those of U.S. households as a whole ($74,980) and of all Asian Americans ($120,000), but 7.57 percent lived in poverty.

Their migration began in the 1960s as students. The change in the immigration policy in the mid-1960s with the Immigration Act of 1965 allowed many of this group to stay and brought in a new group of immigrants as doctors, nurses, engineers, and other professionals. The 1990 Immigration Act created a temporary visa category, H-1B, for highly skilled foreign workers to address shortages in the U.S. labor market. Starting from the end of the 1990s, information technology (IT) jobs, particularly created to deal with the anticipated Year 2000 (Y2K) computer problem, led to a significant migration of Indian immigrants on H-1B visas. Over 70 percent of H1-B visas approved went to Indians from 2015 to 2020 (McCarthy 2021; Ruiz 2017; Zong and Batalova 2015). Consequently, a large number are concentrated in the fields of science and technology. Another significant mode of entry into the United States has been as students (many subsequently obtain jobs and stay on). From 2000 to 2022, India has consistently been either the first- or second-ranked source (after China) of international students in the United

States (Institute of International Education 2022). Due to the Indian history of British colonialism, Indian immigrants are much more likely to be fluent in English than the foreign-born population as a whole (Zong and Batalova, 2015), probably an important factor that has enabled even the immigrant generation to get involved in civic and political engagement. Indian Americans are scattered around the country, but more than half live in California, New York, New Jersey, Texas, and Illinois (Chakravorty, Kapur, and Singh 2017).

As Figure I.2 shows, about half (48 percent) identify as Hindu, although Hindus account for almost 80 percent of the population in India. Muslims are also somewhat underrepresented; in India they make up 14.2 percent of the population but only around 8 percent of those of Indian ancestry in the United States. Christians, on the other hand, constitute only around 2.3 percent of the population in India but account for around 15 percent of Indian Americans. Similarly, Sikhs in India are less than 2 percent of the population, but they make up 8 percent of Indian Americans (U.S. figures from Pew Research Center 2023; Indian figures from 2011 Indian census).

Most Indian Americans hail from privileged-caste ("upper caste") backgrounds. The ancient South Asian system of caste is not based on somatic difference[4] but rests on a hierarchical Hindu ideology designating the worth, ability, rights, and duties (*svadharma*) of hereditary groups, reproduced by marriage arranged along caste lines. Caste spread from Hinduism to other religious groups, which means that even though caste is not doctrinally part of many of these religions, caste practices are seen across South Asia. Caste ideas and practices are inscribed into the minds and bodies of people from childhood onward, with a structure of disciplinary power wielded by privileged castes that enforces these ideas and practices, including rules of caste deference. It is also embedded in most residential localities in India (even in metropolitan areas where certain localities are traditionally associated with particular caste groups), religious institutions, institutions of higher education and government jobs where caste-based "reservations" (affirmative action) are practiced, and the Indian political system where caste is an important political force (though in complicated ways).

There are four caste categories or *varnas*—*Brahmins* (priests), *Kshatriyas* (rulers and warriors), *Vaishyas* (merchants or agriculturalists), and *Shudras* (workers and service providers)—with the first three categories considered "upper caste." However, people in India identify based on their *jati* or local caste division and usually not their broader varna category. There are many ranked jatis within each varna and region and several thousand jatis. More than 30 percent of Indians are excluded from the *savarna* (caste) system: tribal communities and groups (8.6 percent of the Indian population according to the 2011 Indian census) and castes traditionally classified as *avarna* or "outcaste" (over 25 percent of the Indian population) including agrestic slaves and those forced to carry out jobs such as the disposal of human waste and dead animals. These groups were considered untouchable and could not walk on the main streets or enter Hindu temples, were not allowed to draw water from wells used by caste Hindus, were not allowed to obtain education, and had restrictions regarding clothing styles, jewelry, houses, and transportation they could use. *Dalit* is the self-chosen contemporary term to describe and unify a range of former outcastes. Dr. Bhimrao Ramji Ambedkar (1891–1956) was a venerated Dalit leader with a PhD from Columbia University, a DSc from the London School of Economics, and a law degree from Gray's Inn in London. He became the primary architect of the Indian constitution and made sure that untouchability was legally abolished and that civil rights for all and a variety of affirmative action provisions ("reservations") for oppressed castes and tribal groups were included in the 1950 constitution.

A small stream of Dalits who became educated through Indian affirmative action programs joined the H1-B migration. Since the IT sector is dominated by Indians, Dalit immigrants found that they were often subjected to caste stigma and discrimination by their fellow Indian Americans. Through Internet discussion groups, listservs and websites, and subsequently social media platforms, Dalits in America have been able to form transnational networks to challenge caste discrimination in India and the United States. Dalit Americans are from diverse social, economic, religious, and linguistic backgrounds but they unify around the figure of Ambedkar as *Ambedkarites*. In 1956, shortly before his death, Ambedkar renounced Hinduism, blaming it for caste oppression, and converted to a self-reformulated Neo-Buddhism (after a two-decade-long period when he explored other religions as a possible home for Dalits) along with hundreds of thousands of his followers. Consequently, a stance against "Brahmanical Hinduism" (privileged-caste Hindu ideas and practices of hierarchy) is generally considered integral to an Ambedkarite ideology. Some Ambedkarite activists, particularly from his home state of Maharashtra, grew up Buddhist or converted to Buddhism. Even though the caste system is prevalent among other Indian religious groups, it is not an intrinsic part of these religions and conversion out of Hinduism has been a common strategy to escape the worst caste abuses and to obtain self-respect and "mental liberation." As such, most Dalits, including in the United States, are not Buddhists but belong to a variety of religions or atheist traditions including *Ravidassia* (followers of the saint Ravidas) Sikhs, atheist *Periyar* (a term of respect given to anti-Brahmin activist E. V. Ramaswamy) supporters, Hindus from a range of sectarian traditions, and Christian and Muslim Dalits.

Race is not an indigenous Indian concept, but colonial scholarship superimposed racial categories onto caste. Nineteenth-century European scholarship based on a study of Indian languages and Vedic texts classified privileged-caste Indians as "Aryans," part of the Indo-European people originating from the Caucasus who had migrated to (or "invaded") India several thousand years earlier, displacing darker-skinned Indigenous groups in north India, with some Aryan groups moving south and integrating with the *Dravidian* people living there. Later colonial ethnologists linked caste and race based on nasal and cranial measurements (Trautman 1997). Various Indian groups appropriated colonial understandings of race to advance particular social and political goals. Caste reformers such as Jyotirao Phule (1827–1890) used racial theories to describe untouchable groups as Indigenous Indians, displaced and conquered by Aryan invaders. E. V. Ramaswamy or Periyar (1879–1973) developed an anti-Brahmin, atheistic Dravidian movement for lower castes in south India (particularly Tamil Nadu) in the early twentieth century, arguing that Dravidians (non-Brahmin south Indians) were racially different from north Indians and had been linguistically and religiously dominated by Indo-Aryans. However, Ambedkar ([1948] 2018) challenged the colonial theory of racial differences between privileged and oppressed castes and emphasized the racial unity of Indians as Indo-Aryans. Before 1923, Indian migrants in the United States drew on colonial scholarship to argue that as "upper-caste Hindus" they were Aryans or Caucasians, and consequently eligible for U.S. citizenship. Aryans and Dravidians are now understood as linguistic, not racial, groups; nonetheless, many Indians and Indian Americans continue to subscribe to the racial theory of caste (Thapar et al. 2019).

Indian Americans present an excellent example of how multiple interests function and interact with each other. There are a variety of religious groups among Indian Americans and deep cleavages between some of them. Indian Americans are also an important group to study the effect of ethnic groups on domestic policy because they have been able to achieve influence despite being a relatively small, dispersed minority. This study will also illustrate how intergenerational differences affect the understanding of ethnicity and participation in ethnic politics. While some Indian American leaders are interested in following the Jewish model and in developing one major professional organization that would represent Indian American interests, others feel that it is not possible or desirable for a single organization to speak for Indian Americans, given the size of India and the tremendous linguistic, cultural, and religious diversity of Indian Americans. They argue that Indian Americans need to develop their own model of ethnic politics, though there is no agreement on what this model should look like. Indian Americans are also a good group to focus on to examine the effect of multiculturalism and globalization on the strategies of ethnic lobbies since they engage in "long-distance nationalism," have been skillful at using multiculturalism to legitimize their demands, and are also particularly adept at using new technologies such as the Internet for community creation and mobilization (Kurien 2007a).

The Research

I decided to focus on the different ways in which people of Indian background in the United States were mobilizing around their "ethnic" (including pan-ethnic) and ethno-religious backgrounds and interests at the national level. The discussion here draws on a study of umbrella advocacy organizations, over 55 in all, that articulated the interests of a range of Indian regional and linguistic groups, and secondary research on many more (see Appendix A), representing different types of groups of Indian American ancestry (those mobilizing around Indian American and South Asian American identities; those articulating the interests of Hindus, Sikhs, Muslims, Christians, and Dalits of Indian ancestry; and those expressing the partisan interests of Indian Americans).[5] Some of this research was undertaken between the years 2000 and 2007 as part of other projects, but the bulk of the work was conducted between 2007 and 2018, with some updates in 2020–2021.[6] Between 2007 and 2021, I conducted interviews with 158 individuals, several more than once (a total of 168 interviews in all), with some help from eight research assistants (they conducted 20 of the 168 interviews). These individuals represented activists and leaders from the different types of organizations as well as some non–Indian American individuals in policymaking circles who were familiar with Indian American activism.[7] Following standard academic protocol, I change the names of my interviewees in this book except when the information provided can also be obtained through public sources or when the individuals were easily identifiable leaders of prominent organizations who had no objections to their names being used. When I use pseudonyms, I indicate this by using quotes for the name when I first use it in a section and by using only the first name, as opposed to the full name. As has been my practice, I did not use qualitative software to analyze my data for this project.[8] Instead, I listened to my interviews several times (usually during my regular long-distance drives) and later reread my material over and over, taking detailed and evolving notes until I knew my data intimately (also see Desmond 2012, 1302 for his description of a similar strategy). Before working on each subsection of a chapter, I would reread the relevant materials again and then cut and paste long excerpts from my primary materials, later culling from the excerpts as I began writing.

In addition to interviews conducted specifically for this project, I reviewed talks and interviews (conducted by others) of several nationally prominent Indian American activists that were available on YouTube. Finally, I attended several public meetings and events that had a bearing on Indian American politics and transcribed panel presentations available on YouTube of some meetings and events that I could not attend. In the summer of 2020, after the coronavirus pandemic shutdown, several advocacy organizations developed innovative virtual events and programs. I was able to attend several live events or view YouTube videos after the event. I also tracked Indian American and South Asian American activism around the 2020 national elections (in addition to the 2008 and 2016 elections) through Internet searches and keeping abreast with Indian American weekly newspapers such as *India Abroad*, *India West*, and *India Post* and conducted interviews with the activists.

Being an Indian American immigrant gave me easier access to the individuals and groups I studied, though my religious background (Christian, evident from my last name) made it harder to liaise with some Hindu advocacy groups who were suspicious of my motives. Similarly, my caste background (privileged caste, also evident from my last name) was an initial barrier to connecting with Dalit and Ambedkarite organizations and their leaders. Intergenerational differences within Indian American groups had surfaced in several of my earlier projects (Kurien 2007a, 2017a), so I was unsurprised to see it emerge as a cleavage in this one as well. As a university professor (and mother) who spends a lot of time with the younger generation, it was not difficult to relate to the positions and viewpoints of the American-born generation, despite being an immigrant. While both men and women received me warmly, as a woman, I was sometimes able to have more convivial discussions with my female interlocutors.

Plan of the Book

Claiming Citizenship demonstrates the complexity of identity development, the functioning and intersection of various types of mobilizations, and how racial identity, majority/minority religious location, and generational status impact the ways in which immigrants and their children mobilize to claim citizenship in their host countries. Chapter 1 presents a wide swath of Indian American history, between 1900, when Indians started arriving in the United States, and 1995. It focuses on the formation of Indian American advocacy organizations of various types around racial discrimination. The first half of the chapter centers the activism of early immigrants from the Indian subcontinent (1900–1946). Facing racism and exclusion in North America, which they attributed to the fact that India was a colony of the British, they mobilized for citizenship rights in North America *and* for Indian independence. In Northern California they orchestrated a global *Ghadar* (mutiny) movement for independence from British colonialism. When these attempts did not bring about desired results, a group of well-educated Indians took upon themselves the task of lobbying the U.S. Congress and President Franklin D. Roosevelt, particularly during World War II, for the citizenship rights of Indians in the United States and for U.S. support for Indian independence from Britain. By 1946 this group was successful in both these efforts.

The activism of post-1965 Indian immigrants is discussed in the second half of the chapter. A big discussion in the early days of settlement, as Indian immigrants lobbied for a separate category for themselves in the 1980 U.S. census (they were counted as "White" in the 1970 census), and as President Carter set up the infrastructure to monitor the progress of affirmative action, had to do with what type of "minority" Indian immigrants were in the United States (racial, cultural, geographical, advantaged, or disadvantaged) and how they could be categorized with respect to the U.S. census and affirmative action programs. Indian American organizations were able to create a new census category, "Asian Indian," for the census of 1980 and obtain racial minority status for Indian Americans as "Asians." They challenged some proposed immigration reforms that would have cut back on family reunification, obtained White House recognition for themselves as "Indian Americans" from President Ronald Reagan, formed a coalition with other Asian American groups, and mobilized around discrimination against FMGs (foreign medical graduates). They also challenged discrimination against Asian Americans in college admissions and in the workplace.

The rise of Hindu nationalism or Hindutva in India over the 1990s culminated in the coming to power of the Hindu nationalist Bharatiya Janata Party at the national level in 1998. Chapter 2 provides a background to these developments. It then draws on interviews with Indian American activists to discuss the significance of this event for the creation of separate U.S. advocacy organizations to promote the interests of Indian American Hindus, Muslims, Sikhs, Christians, and Dalits and describes the main bodies representing each of these groups. The chapter also shows how and why American groups that were religious minorities in India were motivated to organize to oppose political Hinduism and to form coalitions with each other to do so.

A prominent division among activists of Indian American background, particularly until around 2016, is that some individuals preferred to mobilize around national origin and others mobilized around a pan-ethnic paradigm as South Asians. Chapter 3 discusses the rise of Indian American and South Asian American organizations since the year 2000, the differences in their strategies and goals, and the impact of each type of organization on the Indian American community and on the American public sphere. It showcases the importance of generational status (immigrants versus the American-born generation) in shaping how racial identity and racialization as well as the history of religious tensions in the homeland were perceived. Indian American organizations were generally founded and supported by well-established Indian immigrants in the science and technology fields, and those who mobilize as "Indian Americans" generally identified with the nationalist ideology of India. India and Pakistan were formed through a bloody, religion-based partition; religious nationalisms are deeply embedded in South Asia, and the immigrant generation internalized these conflicts from their upbringing in the subcontinent. Consequently, their policies tended to be mostly foreign policy focused, against Pakistan and Islam, with Hindu underpinnings—almost all members of such organizations have been of Hindu background. Indian American organizations were mostly led by immigrant-generation, male entrepreneurs with strong ties with Indian businesses and consequently were also focused on trade and H1-B visa issues. Indian American organizations primarily allied with Jewish and Hindu groups.

Second-generation progressives who mobilized as South Asian Americans, on the other hand, used the pan-ethnic, racial solidarity model of Black, Latino, and Asian groups in the United States. In contrast to Indian American immigrant activists, they preferred to confront and challenge racialization (including the racialization of religion) as well as the religious divides of their parents' generation. Even though key leaders (particularly in the initial founding period) were from Hindu backgrounds, they emphasized a pluralist, multireligious model of advocacy; operated from a social justice framework; and articulated the interests of the full range of South Asian Americans, concentrating primarily on the more disadvantaged. Women were very prominent as leaders in South Asian American activism, unlike in Indian American activism. As American-born individuals, domestic issues and civil rights activism were of much greater interest to them than issues connected with India. They allied with immigrant rights coalitional organizations; with Asian Pacific American, Sikh, and Muslim organizations; and around caste discrimination.

Chapter 4 focuses on Indian American activism around U.S. domestic policy and examines and explains the reasons for the very similar patterns of activism of religious minority groups in the United States when compared with immigrant groups that become part of the religious majority (Indian American Christians). Organizations representing Indian American religious minorities in the United States—Hindu, Muslim, and Sikh—mobilized around several common issues such as anti-defamation, religious discrimination, and hate crimes after 9/11 to educate Americans about their religions, seek acknowledgment and recognition from the White House and the U.S. administration, and obtain accommodation of their religious practices. Since early 2000, these organizations have been led by second-generation activists. In contrast to many Indian American Muslims, Hindus, and Sikhs, second-generation Indian American Christians did not adopt a racialized discourse and did not participate in political activism as Indian American Christians. Consequently, Indian American Christian organizations have remained first-generation-male led and homeland oriented, focusing on attacks against Christians in India.

Chapter 5 examines how majority and minority religious status in the homeland affects the foreign policy activism of immigrant organizations.

With respect to activism around India-based issues, Hindu groups representing the majority religious group in India are the outlier: there is a big difference between the mobilization patterns of most Hindu American organizations and those representing religious minorities in India—Muslims, Sikhs, Buddhists, and Christian Americans of Indian ancestry. Both sides in the advocacy wars try to frame their grievances using racial and religious models that resonate with U.S. audiences. I use examples of the mobilization of Indian American religious groups around the status of religious minorities in India, the position of Dalits, the political situation in the former Jammu and Kashmir state (the only Muslim-majority state in India), and the Sikh Khalistani movement to show the fundamental divergence in the goals of the major Hindu American organizations (and even some secular Indian American organizations), representing the interests of the dominant religious group in India, and those representing Muslims, Sikhs, Buddhist, and Christian Americans of Indian ancestry who are Indian religious minorities. Hindu American organizations have generally explicitly or implicitly supported a Hindu-centric or Hindu nationalistic perspective, which considers the preservation of India's Hindu culture and heritage, and the assimilation of Indian religious minorities to a Hindu ethos, as vital for India's cohesion and progress. On the other hand, Muslim, Sikh, Buddhist, and Christian Indian American organizations have rallied to publicize attacks on their communities by Hindu-majority groups in India and to seek U.S. intervention and support.

The focus in Chapter 6 is on the activism of Indian Americans around U.S. partisan politics. It examines how all the factors discussed in previous chapters—race, religion, domestic and foreign policy concerns, and generational status—interact to shape the activism of Indian American advocacy groups around U.S. elections and the two major parties. It traces Indian American involvement in the Democratic and Republican Parties, from a nostalgia of the Reagan era when the Republican Party was alleged to have followed a big-tent approach and bipartisanship was common, to the bitter political divisions of the early 2020s. The chapter explains the differences in the approach of old-timer immigrant partisan activists and second-generation activists who came to the fore starting from 2004. Second-generation activists formed South Asian American organizations to mobilize around the Democratic Party, but there were some number who were Republican supporters as well. The chapter ends with a discussion of activism around the 2016 and 2020 elections. The election of Donald Trump in 2016 and the racism and xenophobia that his election unleashed around the country activated several Indian Americans (both immigrants and the second generation) to work to unite and mobilize South Asian Americans to flip swing states from red to blue. At the same time, Hindu nationalists started to pursue a bipartisan strategy to obtain U.S. support for India and Prime Minister Modi's policies.

The Conclusion provides an overview of what the Indian American case teaches us about the factors shaping immigrant and ethnic politics. How do race and religion impact social location, and why is this important to understand? How does this framing in turn reshape our understanding of how political opportunity structures and group characteristics interact, as well as mobilization around foreign and domestic policy issues? The Conclusion also discusses generational differences in political activism as well as the role of social media in immigrant politics. The chapter ends with an overview examining the Indian American model of mobilizing around a variety of identities and issues, rather than a mono-ethnic identity, and discusses whether diaspora activism portends an inclusionary or exclusionary future.

Indian Americans comprise a large and politically active population, a group that is non-White and largely non-Christian and non-Muslim, and one in which there are deep cleavages based on religious and caste identities. Although they might be unique in terms of their diversity and their varied patterns of mobilization, an examination of their patterns of advocacy and the reasons for the differences in the constituencies of each type of advocacy organization can help us understand the characteristics of groups and the political opportunity structures that shape different types of political activism. Consequently, Indian American political mobilization presents an excellent template to understand how religion, national identity, and panethnicity interact, and the role that generational status plays in determining some of these patterns.

Notes

1. See this report in an Indian newspaper https://www.thehindu.com/news/international/record-130-plus-indian-americans-at-key-positions-in-biden-administration/article65804233.ece.
2. Most contemporary U.S. immigrants are from Judeo-Christian backgrounds, but a substantial minority (around one-third) are not (Jasso et al. 2006).
3. https://www.un.org/en/desa/international-migration-2020-highlights
4. Caste was traditionally "made visible" through caste rules about clothing, footwear, jewelry, and bodily comportment.
5. Since I focused on advocacy organizations and their leadership, this research does not always represent the position of lay members of these groups who have diverse perspectives, as I realized from other research projects. This is a limitation of the study.
6. I focused on the history, mission, and activities of organizations; their leadership; and their strategies for advocacy. I also obtained information about their leadership, in particular their

backgrounds, the reasons for their involvement in the particular types of organizations, the civic and political activities they were involved in, and changes over time. I procured information about the organizations by analyzing primary data sources (their Internet websites and their e-newsletters), as well as secondary sources such as newspaper, magazine, and Internet articles.
7. In general, interviews were taped but in other cases I took detailed notes during the conversation and then typed up interview notes later that day. Many interviewees (including some who allowed me to audiotape the interviews) made clear that they were talking to me "for background" or context and that they did not want to be quoted, especially by name.
8. I tried using qualitative software many years ago and it did not work for me. I cannot make sense of context-free quotes since I feel that context is everything. Each person is located differently, which shapes their responses, and I need to know the interviewee and their background to understand their quotes. I also find that meaning making and analyses are dynamic processes. New literatures and deeper immersion in the data bring new understandings and insights. I found my experience of using qualitative software frustrating since it tended to ossify the coding and analyses in unhelpful ways.

1
Race, Transnationalism, and Mobilization

Indian Americans 1900–1995

"Our First Invasion by Hindus and Mohammedans" shrilled *the San Francisco Sunday Call* on November 18, 1906, with an eye-catching sketch of turbaned, bearded Sikh men, dressed in traditional Punjabi clothes, descending from a ship (Gilmour 1906). The piece, written by John Gilmour (who described himself as an Englishman who had lived in India when he was young), carried the subtitle, "Sikhs, Hong Kong's crack policemen from the Panjab have deserted and come to work on a railroad section at San Jose." Gilmour details how he was able to find a group of Sikh workers in town through the help of an Indian Muslim in the employ of an American farmer in San Jose. He learned that the Sikhs had not in fact deserted but had left Hong Kong to go to British Columbia, where they worked in quicksilver mines. Subsequently, they moved down to the San Francisco Bay Area to work on the railroad (Gilmour 1906, 6).

This chapter shows the many ways that race and shifting racist regulations were an overwhelming force shaping the lives of early Indian migrants. U.S. racial laws, including Jim Crow laws in the U.S. South, determined where they could live and work, and led to the revocation of their citizenship as well as the dispossession of their lands. The regulations hindered their ability to leave the United States and return, blocking further immigration from the subcontinent. Exclusion laws prevented men from being able to bring wives from the homeland, while anti-miscegenation laws prevented their marriage to White women (though these were sometimes circumvented). At the same time, Indian migrants used their racial ambiguousness in the United States to creatively navigate their way and to challenge racial customs and laws that discriminated against them and denied them citizenship rights. Racial lumping in the United States as "Hindoos" led to the development of solidarity among different ethno-religious groups from the Indian subcontinent. This chapter also demonstrates how U.S. racial identity and practices were fundamentally shaped by global factors, and how Indians resisted the American racial system using transnational resources, linkages, and arguments. In the second part of the chapter, we see how their status as a racial minority group shaped the mobilization patterns of post-1965 Indian immigrants in the United States in the first few decades of settlement, particularly around a census category and around racial discrimination in different spheres.

Between 1901 and 1910, 5,762 male immigrants from Punjab in British colonial India arrived in Northern California (Gould 2006, 90). About an equal number arrived in British Columbia in Canada over the same period. After the Continuous Journey Regulation of 1908 in Canada requiring migrants to arrive in Canada through a direct ship voyage (which, in practice, targeted Indians and prevented their migration), several thousand moved down to the Pacific West Coast of the United States (Johnston 2014, 18). Punjabi communities in the two countries were close-knit, and movement across the border between Canada and the United States was relatively easy at the time. The overwhelming majority of these Punjabi immigrants in the first decade of the twentieth century, around 85 to 90 percent, were Sikh, even though Sikhs made up only around 13 percent of the population of Punjab (McMahon 2001, 10; Sohi 2014, 8). Punjabi Muslims made up the second largest religious group among these early West Coast immigrants, followed by Punjabi Hindus. But they were all identified in the United States as "Hindoos, or Hindus" the (racial) term then used for inhabitants of India, which was also called "Hindustan," or the land of the Hindus. Several other articles from this period written by writers based in California and Washington, states where Indian immigrants were present in some numbers, referred to Sikhs as a "Hindu Invasion" (Takaki 1989, 296–297). Early immigrants worked in lumber mills, in railroad construction, and later in agriculture (McMahon 2001, 19).

Starting from the 1880s, a smaller group of Muslim men from a cluster of villages in the Bengal region of British India arrived at ports on the East Coast as peddlers of hand-embroidered *chikan* cotton, silk Indian fabric, and

Indian rugs. They peddled these wares on the boardwalks of beach resorts in New Jersey over the summer, and when the beach season was over, they moved down south to cities like New Orleans where they continued to ply their trade. Since "Oriental" products were fashionable at the time, peddlers adopted clothing and mannerisms to play up fantasies of India (including dispensing "magic" and ancient "wisdom") to give themselves and their goods an exotic value that attracted customers (Bald 2013, 50–51). Other Bengali Muslim men who worked as *lascars* or "native" seamen on British merchant vessels started arriving at East Coast ports and Gulf ports later, from around the time of World War I. These seamen used their networks to jump ship and find work in factories in interior towns, which were working overtime to produce goods and materials needed for the war. Some found employment in the service sector in New York City. As in the case of the West Coast Sikhs, newspaper articles of the day focused on the strange dietary and religious customs of the "Hindoo" sailors on the East coast (Bald 2013, 95–97). In the 1910 census, there were 492 "*Hindustanis*" in New York City, most of them likely to be Bengali Muslim seamen. One hundred and thirty-one Hindustanis were found in New Jersey and another 119 in Missouri (Das 1923, 17). This latter group was likely to be Bengali peddlers. Most of these Bengalis were sojourners; however, some married local Black women and settled in the United States (Bald 2013).

It is no coincidence that the two groups of labor migrants arriving in the United States from British India were from particular linguistic and religious backgrounds. British land revenue disrupted traditional farming practices, leading to migration out of many rural areas: both Punjab and Bengal were areas that were particularly badly affected by British agricultural policies resulting in famines and epidemics. Networks of kinship and ethnicity (where religion played an important role) in these "labor catchment areas" were routinely mobilized by British colonialists and labor recruiters to find workers for various types of specialized jobs (Ahuja 2008). Kinship links became a risk management strategy for recruiters, who had to provide loans for workers to make the journey from the hinterland and stay in boarding houses while awaiting work assignments. These modes of access to jobs were a jealously guarded resource maintained by ethnic groups. A consequence of these recruitment strategies was that different occupational niches within the colonial economic system were filled by different religio-ethnic groups, resulting in a highly segmented labor market (Ahuja 2008).

Sikhs were overrepresented among early migrants for another reason. As an older Sikh man from Northern California whom I interviewed pointed out:

> A lot of Sikhs were in the British Army, and so wherever the British went, Sikhs went with them. And a lot of them didn't return after the service was over, and they remained in those countries. And so that's the reason why the very early migrants to many parts of the world were Sikh ... you can call it a gift from the British to the Sikh community!

The British took over the Punjab region after a long and bitter struggle with Maharaja Ranjit Singh, the founder of the Sikh Empire (Gould 2006, 77–78). The British were so impressed with the military skills of the Sikh army that they designated Sikhs a "martial race" (Dirks 2001, 178–180), heavily recruited them into the British Army, and considered them to be an elite unit. The roots of the Sikh settlement in North America can be traced to the celebration of Queen Victoria's Diamond Jubilee in 1897, when a Sikh regiment based in India was sent to London to attend the rituals. In returning to India via Canada, they learned about work opportunities on the Pacific Coast of Canada and the United States and some returned, seeking work (McMahon 2001, 9).

A third, small group of migrants from India in the early decades of the twentieth century was composed of educated anti-colonial leaders—Sikh, Muslim, and Hindu. These migrant groups were also predominantly from Punjab and Bengal, regions that were experiencing political ferment and unrest. Bengal province was partitioned by the British in 1905, leading to large anti-colonial protests led by Bengali students (Jensen 1988, 5). Punjab experienced a series of famines and plagues at the turn of the twentieth century that radicalized many of the educated sections and led them to join the anti-colonial movement developing in many parts of the country (Puri 2011, 6; Sohi 2014, 18). Several anti-colonial leaders left India to escape British surveillance and to find safer bases from which to organize a nascent independence movement. Many came as students to enroll in American universities and learn about the U.S. political system (Sohi 2014, 21–22). The University of California, Berkeley was an important hub since the tuition was low and students could find work nearby in farms and canneries (McMahon 2001, 29). But Indian students were also to be found in many other universities around the country.

Race as a "Master Category" in the United States Impacted by Global Factors

U.S. scholarship on racial and ethnic categorization examines the meanings associated with what has been called "corporeal distinction" (Omi and Winant 2015, 107), or with national ancestry and cultural heritage. It focuses on the ways these factors are shaped by individual or group-level circumstances intersecting with state structures and civil society. Michael Omi and Howard Winant (2015, viii), two of the best-known scholars of U.S. racial formation, point out that race in the United States has "been a master category" organizing patterns of inequality and difference over the course of its history and that racial classification has been, from its inception, an inherently political project. Groups that today are viewed as "White," such as the Irish, Jews, and Italians, were initially considered racially ambiguous, or racially different from White Anglo-Saxons (Brodkin 1998; Goldstein 2006; Ignatiev 1995; Jacobson 1999). Race and ethnicity categories in the census have been part of the "nation-making process" where the state delineates the groups that belong to the national community (Jung 2015).

One major limitation of this literature is that it concentrates almost entirely on conditions *within* the United States: on the U.S. racial system or structure (Jung 2015), how immigrants undergo the process of "racial acculturation" to this structure (Roth 2012), and the micro-level racial fluidity that some individuals can achieve within this system (Saperstein and Penner 2012). However, the introduction of the "transnational turn" in U.S. immigration studies cautions us about the danger of methodological nationalism, or the assumption that key social and political forces are contained or confined by the nation-state (Wimmer and Schiller 2002). In the case of immigrant identities in the United States, homeland or other international factors can play an important role in how groups are categorized. Sociopolitical developments due to global events can bring about shifts in group identification. In other words, the process of immigrant identity change may not simply be a result of individual immigrants assimilating to, or struggling with, the domestic racial system. It is often an outcome of group-based political mobilization shaped by transnational factors. Global events can differentially impact groups within the United States, resulting in new patterns of activism around identity and categorization.

An important theoretical contribution of this chapter is to demonstrate the ways in which global, national, and local factors articulated to play a profound role in the changing racial identities of Indian immigrants. Specifically, we see how U.S. relationships with Canada and Britain shaped the form taken by racial exclusion policies targeting Indians and how early Indian immigrants drew a connection between their colonized status in India and their racial treatment in the United States to initiate a global *Ghadar* (mutiny) movement for Indian independence. The two world wars reshaped the global geopolitical landscape and U.S. strategies toward Indian immigrants. The entry of the United States into World War I against Germany resulted in the arrest and imprisonment of U.S.-based Ghadar activists since they were trying to get help from Berlin for their Indian independence movement. After the United States entered World War II, on the other hand, there was more support for Indian independence activists. Lobbying by Indian nationalists in Washington, DC making the case that support of Indians was crucial for victory over Japan led the U.S. Congress (through the Luce-Celler Act of 1946) to grant citizenship to Indians and to permit a small quota of immigrants from India every year.

Early Migrants, 1900–1920: Facing Racial Discrimination in North America

Sikhs are members of a religion founded in the Punjab in the fifteenth century. Many Sikh men, and some women, maintain their unshorn hair in a turban (men also maintain unshorn beards and moustaches) and carry a ceremonial dagger (*kirpan*) as these are articles of faith in the Sikh tradition. In postcolonial India, Sikhs make up only around 2 percent of the Indian population, largely concentrated in Punjab, while Hindus make up around 80 percent of the population. However, as we have seen, Sikh men dominated the early immigration to North America from British India (the colonial era lasted until 1947) in the late nineteenth and early twentieth centuries (see Kurien 2018). Sikhs mostly settled in the farming regions of Sacramento, San Joaquin, and Imperial Valleys in California, though some also lived and worked in lumber mills in Washington and Oregon. Many were married but had to leave their families behind when they migrated. Consequently, men generally lived together, in shacks provided by their employers in the farms and lumber mills where they worked, with "scarcely any intercourse with the Americans except in a business way" (Das 1923, 77). Some who were unmarried and lived in Imperial Valley in Southern California married Mexican women (Leonard 1994).

Sikh immigrant workers faced anti-Asian mobilization in both Canada and the United States. A Japanese and Korean Exclusion League formed in 1905 in both San Francisco and Vancouver by White labor union leaders was renamed the Asiatic Exclusion League by 1907 to include Indians among the groups that it opposed (Jensen 1988, 44). In 1907, a series of race riots directed against Indian immigrants by White workers took place along the North American West Coast. The first was in Bellingham, Washington, soon to be followed by others in Seattle, Everett, Vancouver, and parts of California (Jensen 1988). The 1908 Canadian law banning Indian migrants emboldened U.S. officials to take their own measures against the "Hindu invasion" of Northern California (Jensen 1988, 107). San Francisco immigration officials used a "likely to become a public charge" clause to exclude many Indians seeking entry into the United States beginning in 1909, leading to a decline in the number of Indian immigrants in the United States, from 1,710 in 1908 to 377 in 1909 (Jensen 1988, 111). Despite these small numbers, in 1910, a U.S. immigration commission issued a report on Indian immigrants, describing them as "the least desirable race of immigrants thus far admitted to the United States" and as "unassimilable" (Jensen 1988, 141). In 1912, American immigration officials were also able to pressure steamship companies to stop selling tickets to Indian laborers intending to travel to the American West Coast (Jensen 1988, 147). However, the Asiatic Exclusion League wanted legislative exclusion since they felt that would be a more reliable basis for keeping out Indian immigrants. This was discussed in Congress in 1913 and 1914 (see Linking Racial Discrimination below).

Bengali Muslim peddlers and seamen were also faced with racist laws restricting their entry into the United States. Bengali Muslim peddlers who started arriving from the mid-1880s were confronted with the Alien Contract Labor Law of 1885. While the act was to ostensibly restrict companies from bringing in immigrants for work, sometimes peddlers were also deported under the act. Over time, Bengali peddlers learned how to gain entry by exploiting loopholes in the law (Bald 2013, 14, 41–42). A "lascar line" (above 38 degrees north latitude) provision in the British Merchant Shipping Act of 1894 prohibited Bengali seamen from being hired on voyages to northeastern ports of the United States between October and March. In the United States, the 1915 Seaman's Act included a language requirement to prevent

Chinese and Indian seamen from working on American ships or entering on foreign vessels (Bald 2013, 112). Due to the acute need for labor, particularly during the period of World War I, however, shipping companies and U.S. factory owners in the Northeast were willing to circumvent laws to hire Bengali Muslim lascars. Consequently, around 20,000 to 25,000 Indian seamen moved through New York's port in the period between 1914 and 1924 alone. The networks that the lascars were able to build with other Bengali Muslims and with residents helped them navigate the many barriers they faced. Many Bengali seamen were able to jump ship and gain employment in U.S. factories in the Northeast (Bald 2013, 113–115).

Bengali Muslim peddlers moved to the American South at the turn of the nineteenth century when Jim Crow laws imposing a racial apartheid system were being implemented. By performing a "self-exoticizing" Indianness, they were able to obtain greater freedom of movement in the segregated South than African Americans (Bald 2013, 52). However, they were still confined to Black neighborhoods for their housing choices. Tremé in New Orleans became a center for Bengali peddlers. Around two dozen Bengali peddlers married Black or Creole women and settled in the area, while others remained itinerant (Bald 2013, 74). Bengali lascars who worked in factories in cities like Detroit; Baltimore; and Chester, Pennsylvania, also lived in Black neighborhoods. In New York City, there was a Bengali Muslim community in Harlem living alongside African Americans, West Indians, and Puerto Ricans. Around one-third of the New York group married women from one of these groups (Bald 2013). In their marriage certificates they were racially classified in a variety of ways: "white, colored, Negro, Indian, and East Indian" (Bald 2013, 170).

Linking Racial Discrimination in North America and Colonial Status—The Rise of the Diasporic Anti-Colonial Movement

As Indians became aware that the discriminatory laws against them in Canada and the United States had been passed with the approval and support of the British (Sohi 2014, 27), they realized that they could not turn to their (British-ruled) home country for support against discrimination in North America (unlike Japanese, for instance). Anti-colonialists started to link the discrimination that Indians were facing in North America with their colonial status in India. One older Sikh man in Northern California, "Dilraj," a descendant of an early Sikh anti-colonial leader, interviewed for this project, talked about how the White mobs attacking Indians in Bellingham had called them "slaves" and "coolies." According to Dilraj, Indian immigrants were "discriminated as slave Indians since they were not from an independent, free country. They were from a country which was under British rule." He continued, "And at that time they called them Indian dogs, or Indian slaves, or Indian coolies, [they said], you are not people, you are sheep, you are being governed by a handful of Britishers from ten thousand miles away and you are millions of people." Anti-colonial activists began to mobilize Indians in North America against British rule, calling for a revolution in India like the American Revolution (Sohi 2014, 66). They warned British colonialists that racial discrimination experienced by Indians within the territories of the British Empire (referring to Canada) could foment revolution in India (Sohi 2014, 34).

After the 1907 race riots in the Pacific Northwest, Indian immigrants on the Pacific West Coast began to form a variety of self-help community organizations. The *Khalsa Diwan Society*, a social organization that ran gurdwaras, was the first to form. The Vancouver Khalsa Diwan Society formed early in 1907 and opened branches in Washington, Oregon, and California a few years later (Sohi 2014, 50–51). Taraknath Das, an educated Hindu Bengali anti-colonialist, who had arrived in Seattle from Japan and then moved to Vancouver for a job with the U.S. immigration service, formed the *Hindustani Association* in Vancouver later in 1907, the first overtly political organization of Indian immigrants in North America (Buchignani, Indra, and Srivastava 1985, 21). Indian leaders like Taraknath Das and others moved back and forth between Vancouver and San Francisco, trying to mobilize the Indian communities in North America to work for Indian independence from the British. British agents closely monitored radical Indians in North America and reported on their activities to the British government, but also the governments of Canada and the United States. The first anti-colonial publication—*Circular-i-Azadi* (Circular of Freedom)—was published in San Francisco and Oakland in 1907 by Ram Nath Puri, a Punjabi Hindu (Sohi 2014, 51–52). Shortly after, in 1908, Taraknath Das also started an anti-British publication, *Free Hindusthan*, in Vancouver. Copies were sent to India and to Indian communities around the world. The

Canadian government protested the publication and notified the U.S. government and so Das moved to Seattle and restarted publication with the help of Seattle Socialists (Jensen 1988, 166–167). British agents followed Das's activities in Seattle. Das moved to New York in 1909 and started publication of *Free Hindusthan* again, this time with the help of Irish nationalists (Jensen 1988, 166–169). One of the important goals of the anti-colonial periodicals was to turn Sikhs in India against the British by telling them about the Canadian exclusion acts targeting Sikhs (Johnston 2014, 24; Sohi 2014, 53).

In 1906, Abdul Hafiz Mohamed Barkatullah, also known as Maulavi Barkatullah, a Muslim from Bhopal in Central India, formed the *Pan-Aryan Association* in New York City to fight against British colonialism (Afzal 1991, 1). One of Barkatullah's friends, Har Dayal, was a highly educated Indian revolutionary from a Hindu Punjabi background who had resigned from a British scholarship in Oxford to protest British colonial rule in India and had arrived in Berkeley in 1911. Dayal traveled around giving lectures to the wider American community and to Indians in North America about the evils of British colonialism in India. He was able to get more publicity for his ideas when John Barry, a well-known journalist, wrote several articles sympathetic to the Indian independence movement in the form of conversations with Har Dayal in 1912 in the *San Francisco Bulletin* (Jensen 1988, 176). These articles were reprinted by Dayal and sent to Indian communities in North America and India. Har Dayal asked his Indian audiences to prepare for a war of independence against the British, just like the Americans had done (Puri 2011, 56–65). By this time, the British had assigned a special secret agent, William C. Hopkinson, who had been raised in India, to monitor the activities of Indians in North America. Hopkinson hired Indian informants and especially focused his surveillance on Taraknath Das and Har Dayal (Jensen 1988, 164).

In June of 1913, Har Dayal, along with other Indian nationalists like Taraknath Das and Maulvi Barkatullah, held a meeting in Oregon to form an umbrella organization, uniting Indians in Canada and the United States—the *Hindustan Association of the Pacific Coast* (Buchignani, Indra, and Srivastava 1985, 51). Later that year, Har Dayal and others formed the *Hindustan Ghadar Party* for Indian independence in Oregon, with its headquarters in San Francisco (Sohi 2014, 57). The party aimed to get its message out through the weekly publication of the Ghadar newspaper, with its first publication on November 1, 1913, of 4,000 copies, mailed to every South Asian community in North America as well as many in India (Buchignani, Indra, and Srivastava 1985, 51–52). The newspaper periodically carried the following advertisement:

> Wanted—Brave soldiers to stir up Ghadar in India
> Pay—Death
> Prize—Martyrdom
> Pension—Liberty
> Field of battle—India
>
> (Jensen 1988, 183)

By 1914, nearly 5,000 copies of the weekly paper in Gurmukhi and Urdu were being circulated in North America. In six months, it reached East and Southeast Asia, Europe, Africa, and South America. In 1914, the movement also published 12,000 issues of a volume of poetry composed and written by Indian migrant workers, *Ghadar di gunj* (Echoes of Mutiny) (Sohi 2014, 59–60). The leadership of the Ghadar movement was strongly influenced by Industrial Workers of the World, as well as socialist and anarchist ideas (Buchignani, Indra, and Srivastava 1985, 52). Other leaders drew parallels between the struggles of African Americans in the United States and Indians in British India (Sohi 2014, 1, 69). The Ghadar movement emphasized the importance of religious, regional, and caste unity among Indian immigrants. Leaders like Har Dayal pointed out that the British had succeeded in controlling India through their divide-and-rule policies and that Indian nationalists had to rise above these divides (Puri 2011, 67).

In 1914, 376 Punjabi (mostly Sikh) passengers of a ship, the *Komagata Maru*, sailing directly from India to Canada (to challenge the 1908 Continuous Journey Regulation) were not even allowed to disembark in Vancouver and were sent back to India, many to face death or imprisonment. This incident angered Sikhs on the North American Pacific Coast. Ghadarites formed a committee for Indian independence in Berlin, known as the Berlin Indian Committee, in September 1914. They also received some financial help from the German government and arms and ammunition for Ghadarites in Bengal (Puri 2011, 134–135).

Several thousand Ghadar supporters left North America for India to launch an Indian independence movement. Others left from East and

Southeast Asia. However, the British government was prepared for this influx, having received intelligence about this plan. The Ghadarites planned an uprising in Punjab in February 1915 but were not able to mobilize regiments in India against the British since the British controlled the police and army and had many spies. By mid-1915, the British managed to crush the movement and put India under martial law by imposing the Defense of India Act (Buchignani, Indra, and Srivastava 1985, 64; Sohi 2014, 163–164). Those who were considered dangerous revolutionaries were sent to trial (291 Ghadarites by mid-1915), of whom 42 were sentenced to death. Most others were imprisoned (Buchignani, Indra, and Srivastava 1985, 64). Another large group was confined to their villages: between October 1914 and December 1917, 8,000 emigrants returned to India, of whom over 2,500 were restricted to staying in their home villages (Sohi 2014, 157).

The United States' relationships with Britain, an ally, shaped the exclusion policy toward British Indians. Between 1913 and 1914, U.S. Congress attempted to come up with a way to exclude Indians without specifically using race, ethnicity, or national origin, for fear that overt discrimination would cause unrest in British India. By this time, Australia, Canada, and other British colonies had already started excluding Indian immigrants using indirect criteria. In a letter to the Speaker of the House, Secretary of Labor William Wilson asked, "Can we, who are not connected by governmental ties or obligations with the Hindus, afford to do less for our people and country than those who are bound by a common citizenship under the Imperial [British] government?" (cited in Jensen 1988, 154). Consequently, Denver S. Church, a Republican from California, suggested an exclusion bill based on geography. President Woodrow Wilson decided to define a "barred zone" based on an imaginary line drawn across the map of Europe that had been used by geographers to demarcate Asia and Europe (Jensen 1988, 152–154). Since laws had already been passed regarding immigrants from Japan and China, and Korea was under Japanese colonial rule at this time, this law was effectively directed against immigrants from India (Jensen 1988, 152–154). In 1914, "Hindu Immigration Hearings" were held in the House. Anthony Caminetti, commissioner general of immigration (a Democrat from California who had been a strong proponent of anti-Asian exclusionism), used the Canadian 1908 exclusion law, which had, he assured committee members, "in fact been aimed at excluding Indians," to justify the need for a legislative solution to the "Hindu" problem in California (Jensen

1988, 156). A delegation of Indian immigrants sent by the Pacific Coast Khalsa Diwan Society and the Hindustan Association of America spoke at the hearings. They argued that Indian laborers were not undercutting the wages of White men since they undertook unskilled labor that White men did not want to perform, and that these men were only interested in working peacefully (Jensen 1988, 155; Hindu Immigration Hearings 1914, 4–5). The bill was not passed in 1914.

Once the United States entered World War I in April 1917 and declared war against Germany, it clamped down on the Ghadar movement and arrested Ghadarites, as well as American sympathizers and German officials and agents. A "Hindu Conspiracy" trial in San Francisco began in November 1917 to address planned revolutionary uprisings against the British in India in which people living in the United States had conspired. Indian immigrants defended themselves arguing that they were freedom fighters seeking to obtain an independent and democratic India, just like the United States had done in 1776. Most of the defendants were found guilty and imprisoned (Buchignani, Indra, and Srivastava 1985, 65; Sohi 2014, 184–194). The judge also ordered Indian defendants to stop distributing their "Hindoo publications" (Sohi 2014, 195). Another version of the 1914 bill including a literacy test and an "Asiatic Barred Zone" provision was passed in 1917 excluding laborers from a wide area from Turkey and the Arabian Peninsula in the east to some of the Pacific Islands in the west from entering the United States. Since there was little migration from other parts of the region except for India, the law mainly targeted British Indians. As a result, the legal immigration of most Indians, including Sikhs, into the United States was prohibited. This also meant that Indians who were in the country could not bring their wives and children from India. The Immigration Act of 1924 finally excluded all Asians from immigrating to the United States. However, students were still permitted into the country and others were able to enter illegally, usually through Mexico (McMahon 2001, 15).

This section shows that Indians migrating from British India played a key role in the development of a pan-Asian "Asiatic" category and identity in the United States, and that transnational factors such as the relationship of the United States with Canada and Britain, the outbreak of World War I, and tensions with Germany all played a role in shaping racist policies toward early Indian immigrants.

U.S. Racial Status: From Hindu Caucasians to Non-White Aliens

Since the racial status of Indians in the United States was ambiguous, the eligibility of the early Indian migrants for citizenship (then only conferred on immigrants who were "free White persons") was not settled until 1923 after the *United States v. Bhagat Singh Thind* case. Before 1923, Indian migrants in the United States drew on colonial scholarship that classified upper-caste North Indians as "Aryans" to argue that as privileged-caste "Hindus" they were Caucasians and consequently eligible for citizenship. They made a distinction between skin color and race, arguing, based on European race scholarship of the day, that skin color did not overlap with race (Haney López 2006, 58) and consequently that race should be established through ancient lineage and peoplehood. Between 1908 and 1922, around 69 Indians received citizenship in various states in the United States. In California alone, at least 17 Indian men were granted citizenship during this period (Jensen 1988, 255).

Bhagat Singh Thind, a turban-wearing Sikh, had come to the United States in 1913 for higher education and was active in the Ghadar movement (Coulson 2015, 15–22). In the middle of his studies at the University of California, Berkeley, he joined the U.S. Army to fight in World War I (he was the first turbaned Sikh in the U.S. Army) and was honorably discharged in 1918 when the war ended. He initially received U.S. citizenship, but it was revoked a few months later. In 1919, Thind filed a court case to challenge the revoking of his citizenship. Following on the Ozawa case in which a Japanese American plaintiff had been denied citizenship on the grounds that although he might be "White," he was not Caucasian, Thind's lawyers drew on European colonial scholarship that categorized South Asians as Caucasian. They argued that as a "high-caste Hindu" of the Aryan race from North India, Thind was of Caucasian descent and therefore eligible for U.S. citizenship. They made the case that the caste system prevented interracial marriages in India, like the racial system did in the United States, ensuring the Aryan racial purity of "upper-caste" Indians (Haney López 2006, 104–105; Coulson 2015, 26). In 1923, Justice George Sutherland (a British-born judge) delivered the unanimous Supreme Court decision that while Thind might be Caucasian, he was not White as commonly understood in the United States and in Western Europe and was therefore not eligible for citizenship.

Many Indians in the United States were stripped of their citizenship after this court case. Since the 1913 California Alien Land Law prohibited "aliens ineligible for citizenship" from owning or holding long-term leases on agricultural land, Asian exclusionists in California also took the opportunity to deprive Indians of the land they owned (Jensen 1988, 265). Transnational factors were responsible for the momentous *Thind* ruling. While Thind and his lawyers used European colonial arguments about the Aryan race to make their case, Doug Coulson (2015) argues that the U.S. Supreme Court denied Thind citizenship under pressure from the British government because of Thind's involvement in the Ghadar movement.

Mobilizing around U.S. Racial Status and Indian Independence

Dalip Singh Saund, who eventually became the first Asian American in Congress (1957–1963), was another early Sikh immigrant (he was clean shaven and did not wear a turban) to California who came to study at the University of California, Berkeley, in 1920. He was also involved in the Indian nationalist movement. While at Berkeley, Saund was a member of the Hindustani Association of America and became its president. In his autobiography he wrote of that time, "All of us were ardent nationalists and we never passed up an opportunity to expound on India's rights" (Saund 1960, 38). He received a PhD in Mathematics in 1923 but could not find work as a teacher since he was not a U.S. citizen. Consequently, he worked as a farmer in Imperial County in Southern California. He identified as "Hindu" Indian and campaigned for citizenship rights for Indians in the United States.

Indians on the East Coast were also active around the cause of Indian independence. Lala Lajpat Rai, who resided in the United States from 1914 to 1919, was a founding member of the *Arya Samaj*, a reformist and nationalistic Hindu religious organization established in the late nineteenth century in the Punjab. Rai also became a leader of the Indian National Congress. The *India Home Rule League* was founded by Lala Lajpat Rai in New York City in 1917, and the inaugural issue of League's monthly journal, *Young India*, was published in January 1918 (Gould 2006, 231). Rai's India Home Rule League was more moderate than the Ghadar movement and, as the name suggests, advocated for home rule rather than complete independence. This was because Rai as a follower of Gandhi did not endorse violence, and the

Ghadar group had allied with Germany to create an armed insurrection in India. Rai focused instead on trying to make "the Indian cause palatable to the American mainstream" (Gould 2006, 239). He set up the *Hindustan Information Service* to lobby Congress to support the civil rights of Indians in the United States and Indian freedom struggle. The service provided Congress with pamphlets on Hindu deportation cases in the United States and vivid descriptions of the misery that Indians endured in British India (Gould 2006, 246). Six delegations were sent to Washington. Gould (2006, 231) marks this as the beginning of the "India Lobby" in the United States, when Indians started working in a systematic way to influence policymakers.

Many former Indian maritime workers working in New York City were involved with the more radical organization, the *Friends of Freedom for India* (FFI), which operated out of a laundry and dry-cleaning shop of an ex-seaman and which was led by educated Bengali radicals such as Taraknath Das, who were also supporters of the Ghadar movement. Indian seamen and ex-seamen would gather in this shop to obtain information about the political situation in India and share their hopes for Indian independence, "which would shake off all the old fetters, the religious and caste prejudices" (Bald 2013, 144). After encountering an anti-colonial Sikh activist and learning about the Ghadar movement, one of these former steamship workers, Dada Amir Haider Khan, a Muslim born in Kashmir, started carrying copies of the volume of Sikh Ghadar poetry, *Ghadar di gunj*, on his ship voyages out of New York City. He distributed copies and gave passionate speeches on the need for Indian independence from the British to Indian seamen and expatriate Indian communities all along his route (Bald 2013, 149). Ibrahim Choudry was an anti-colonialist activist in Bengal who found a job as a steamship crew manager to flee British colonial authorities in India. He became the manager of a British seaman's club in New York City specifically for Indian seamen. During this time, he got involved with the *India Association for American Citizenship* (Bald 2013, 180–184). This organization and another one, the *India Welfare League*, founded by Mubarek Ali Khan, worked to advocate the citizenship rights for the roughly 3,000 Indian laborers who had settled in the United States before the *Thind* decision came into effect (Bald 2013; Gould 2006). In this effort, the India Welfare League came head to head with, and was soon eclipsed by, two organizations—the New York–based *India League of America* and the *National Committee for Indian Independence*—both active in Washington, DC in the 1930s and 1940s. A Sikh, J. J. Singh, based in New York, was elected president of the Indian

League in 1939 and played a leadership role in the mobilization of Indians for India's independence and citizenship rights for Indians in the United States. The National Committee for Indian Independence was supported financially by the *Indian National Congress Association of India*, the Sikh-based organization on the West Coast, established by Dalip Singh Saund (Jacoby 2007, 251).

The India League of America and the National Committee for Indian Independence had broader goals than just reversing the negative effects of the *Thind* decision. As Gandhi's nonviolent *satyagraha* movement in India developed, Indian activists in Washington, DC recognized that they had the opportunity to obtain American support for Indian independence by countering the "massive propaganda apparatus" of the British and their allies in the United States (Gould 2006, 341). They were also interested in getting racist immigration policies banning immigration from India reversed, permitting a small group of highly educated immigrants from India to enter the United States every year. "Lobbying on the Hill was his forte," declares anthropologist Harold Gould (2006, 318) about J. J. Singh in his book on the "India lobby." J. J. Singh and his supporters (who included Hindus, Muslims, and Sikhs) active in Washington successfully convinced important American allies that the support of the people of India for America was "key to victory over Japan" in World War II (Gould 2006, 334), leading the Roosevelt administration to establish an India section of the OSS (predecessor to the CIA) in 1943 to forge alliances with anti-colonial leaders in India (Gould 2006, 377). Through J. J. Singh's close connection with Representatives Clare Booth Luce of Connecticut and Emanuel Celler of New York (Gould 2006, 394), he was able to influence them to introduce the Luce-Celler Act in 1946 in Congress, which granted citizenship to Indians (including having them restored for those who had obtained it prior to the *Thind* case) and permitted a quota of 100 immigrants from India to the United States every year. Affronted that his years of work around the country on behalf of Indian laborers were obliterated by the two upstart organizations, Mubarek Ali Khan of the India League of America went on to create the Pakistan League of America in 1947 (Bald 2013, 184).

After the passage of the Luce-Cellar Act in 1946, Dalip Singh Saund applied for naturalization and received his American citizenship in 1949. Soon after, he became active in politics, first locally in Imperial Valley in California (he was elected as a justice of the peace) and then as a candidate from Riverside and Imperial Counties to the House of Representatives in 1955.

In 1956, Dalip Singh Saund became the first Indian American and Asian American in Congress. He was re-elected twice but suffered a stroke in 1962 that left him paralyzed and ended his political career.

This section shows how Indian immigrants in the United States, though disenfranchised, marginalized, and even physically assaulted due to their racial background, were able to unify and mobilize both around rights in the United States and around India's independence from British colonial rule. This included people from different class, religious, and caste backgrounds. Early Indian nationalists worked hard to make sure that religion (though already a dividing factor in India) did not splinter the unity of the community in the United States. We also see how the shifting status of Indians in the United States and policies toward them were shaped by global factors and, consequently, that racial formation is a global and not merely a domestic process.

Race, the 1965 Immigration Act, and the Racial Classification of Post-1965 Immigrants

The movement toward the 1965 Immigration Act that would lift the racist restrictions against the immigration of non-European groups and go on to fundamentally alter the racial composition of the country was triggered by both international and domestic developments. While World War II forced the United States to permit some Asian groups into the country (besides Indians, also Chinese and Filipinos) as part of its attempt to gain the support of Asian groups against Japan, the subsequent Cold War put pressure on the United States to contrast itself to Communist countries as a democracy. Then–secretary of state Dean Rusk argued that immigration reform was essential as part of American foreign policy (Takaki 1989, 418). Domestically, the civil rights movement led to Congress outlawing racial discrimination in 1964. The debate around immigration reform was initiated in 1965 with the goal of abandoning the national-origins quota system.

A nativist backlash developed immediately, and to address his critics, Senator Edward Kennedy argued that

> our cities will not be flooded with a million immigrants annually. Under the proposed bill, the present level of immigration remains substantially the same.... Secondly, the ethnic mix of this country will not be upset....

Contrary to the charges in some quarters, S. 500 will not inundate America with immigrants from any one country or area, or the most populated and economically deprived nations of Africa and Asia. (Immigration Hearing 1965, 2–3)

Initially, the emphasis was on bringing in immigrants based on their employable skills (the creators of the bill fully expected that only European immigrants would fit this criterion), but conservatives insisted that family reunification be given priority over employability to maintain the Anglo-Saxon European racial and ethnic mix of the population. Consequently, the bill gave first preference to family reunification and second preference to "specialized skills" (Heller and Heller 1966, 8). However, as we know, this plan backfired since not many Europeans took advantage of the opportunity. Instead, the act opened the doors to the entry and settlement of large numbers of immigrants from Asia, Latin America, and Africa in the United States through the special skills provision but mainly through subsequent chain migration. Many in this group, including Indians (as we see below, this section), would go on to claim recognition as racial and ethnic minorities eligible for civil rights protections. Writing in the early 1980s, sociologist Nathan Glazer rued (1983, 8), "Certainly those who voted for both the Civil Rights Act and the Immigration Act never dreamed that the two would intersect to place the new immigrants in a privileged class as compared with most native Americans."

Between 1965 and 1975, almost 100,000 Indian immigrants entered the United States, beginning with just 582 individuals in 1965 and increasing to more than 10,000 annually between 1970 and 1975 (Fisher 1980, 12). Since the Indian American population in the United States was small at the time, most early post-1965 Indian immigrants entered through the special skills provision. According to Maxine Fisher (1980, 11), the Immigration Service classified 93 percent of Indians admitted in 1975 as professional/technical workers or their dependents. Whether these individuals were always able to get a job commensurate with their educational and professional background, however, was a different matter. Scholars writing about the early group of post-1965 immigrants describe the frustrations faced by many as they discovered that their Indian educational qualifications and work experience were not valued in the United States (Dutta 1982; Fisher 1980, 19–20; Helweg and Helweg 1990, 64–65). A survey of Indian immigrants conducted in Chicago in the mid-1970s found that 44 percent of respondents reported incidents of discrimination. Most related to being denied jobs or being passed over for raises and promotions. Other experiences of discrimination had to do with refusals to rent houses and apartments (Elkhanialy and Nicholas 1976b, 47).

We have seen that early Indian Americans were discriminated against, were officially declared as non-Caucasians by the Supreme Court in 1923, and were also central to the creation of the "Asian" category in the United States (responsible for the creation of the "Asiatic Exclusion League" in 1907 and, 10 years later, of the "Asiatic Barred Zone Act"). In the 1920, 1930, and 1940 census, Indians were listed as being of "Hindu" race under the "Other Asian or Pacific Islander" category (which also included Filipino and Korean). In 1950 and 1960, they were designated as "Asiatic Indian" but moved out of the Asian category and into the "Other Race" category. In 1970, however, the U.S. census category "Color or Race" classified Indians as people of "Indo-European stock" and they were counted as White (anyone who checked "Other" race was also placed in the White category). Only Japanese, Chinese, Filipino, Hawaiian, and Korean subcategories were included under the Asian race category (Gibson and Jung 2005). What brought about this change?

The issue of how to racially classify Indian Americans resurfaced as the post-1965 immigration from India began, but under very different circumstances than in the 1923 Thind case. With the implementation of the Civil Rights Act came the need to measure and track discrimination against groups. Since census data was used to do this, the census committee (the Ad Hoc Committee on Racial and Ethnic Definitions of the Federal Interagency Committee on Education [FICE]) had to come up with a systematic schema to classify the major American groups. The committee, through its deliberations, came up with the ethno-racial pentagon (Directive No. 15 of 1977) that would go on to have profound impacts on American society. While the primary categories (White, Black, Hispanic, Asian or Pacific Islander, American Indian, or Alaskan Native) were defined by race (with the exception of Hispanic, which was defined as an ethnic group), the committee decided to use ancestral geographical origin instead of color as the criterion for belonging in these categories. However, the question was where to draw the line to demarcate Asia, and whether it should include India. A second issue that the committee had to decide was which groups should be classified as "discriminated minorities" in the United States (Trotter and Michael 1975).

A 1975 report by FICE describes how people from the Indian subcontinent presented a problem to the committee as it tried to wrestle with these two issues. It is worth reproducing the full summary of the discussion below:

> The question at issue was whether to include them in the minority category "Asian" because they came from Asia and some are victims of discrimination in this country, or to include them in this category [Caucasian/White] because they are Caucasians, though frequently of darker skin than other Caucasians. The final decision favored the latter. While evidence of discrimination against Asian Indians exists, it appears to be concentrated in specific geographical and occupational areas. Such persons can be identified in these areas through the use of a subcategory for their ethnic subgroup. (Trotter and Michael 1975, 11–12)

In other words, the boundary of Asia was drawn east of the Indian subcontinent and Indian Americans were classified as "White" by the committee since they felt that Asian Indians did not face systematic discrimination and should therefore not come under the purview of civil rights protections.

The U.S. Census Bureau was faced with a variety of lawsuits around undercounts of minority groups and problematic census categories in the 1970 census and created advisory groups composed of minority representatives to examine the issue (Mora 2014). An Indian American organization, the *Association of Indians in America* (AIA), formed in 1967, mobilized to make the argument that Indians in the United States should be included under the category of "Asian" as they had been in the 1917 Asiatic Exclusion Act, and that they experienced discrimination (Dutta 1976). The AIA was the first pan–Indian American organization transcending regional and religious divides to form in the United States. In December 2007, I met with Manoranjan Dutta, a professor of economics at Rutgers University, one of the founders of the organization. He told me that his goal was to encourage Indians in the United States to become civically engaged in the wider society. At the first AIA meeting in Princeton in 1967 with around 60 Indian Americans from the New York/New Jersey region in attendance, he said he urged his audience to get "involved here," arguing that this was important for their career advancement and for the sake of their children who were growing up in this society. He cautioned, "If you dramatize [your ties and loyalty to] India, it will be a block to our career." The organization developed its constitution in 1970, incorporated in 1971, and obtained IRS exempt status in 1973 (http://aianational.com/). The first thing Dutta wanted to do to make a case that Indian Americans were a group that deserved the attention of policymakers was to show that they were in substantial numbers in the United States. However, since the 1970 census categorized them as Caucasian or White without a specific subcategory on the form and only extrapolated their numbers from the country-of-origin question administered to 20 percent of the population, the Indian American population was reported as being 78,000 in 1970. Dutta, however, felt this was a gross underestimate. Using his econometrics background, he estimated that the Indian American population was around a quarter of a million, about the same number as Korean Americans, who had a separate category for themselves in the census. Consequently, he felt that the first task was to obtain a separate category for Indian Americans to ensure an accurate count of the group. But what should this category be and in what larger ethno-racial group should Indians be placed? Due to the rationale used by the Ad Hoc Committee to classify Indian Americans as White, this question became intertwined with the issue of whether Indian Americans should be classified as a discriminated minority group.

While Dutta, in his interactions with the Census Bureau officials, promoted a separate listing for Indians under the "Asian" category, there was little agreement within the Indian American community on this matter. Dutta told me that there was opposition from the community regarding being classified as "Asian" since many felt that they had nothing in common racially, or culturally, with East Asians. Surveys conducted at this time in the New York City area (Fisher 1980, 125-126) and in Chicago (Elkhanialy and Nicholas 1976b) found that Indians questioned the relationship between race and color and that there was little consensus regarding how they wanted to be designated in either respect. Elkhanialy and Nicholas (1976b, 45) indicate that in a pretest of their questionnaire, they tried to ask Indian respondents in Chicago to indicate whether they viewed themselves as White or Black. But most respondents "were indignant about these categories; there was so much resistance to answering a question about race with skin color" that they changed their question to one solely about color. They report that of their 159 respondents, only 11 percent chose White and only 3 percent Black. The largest proportion, 70 percent, wrote Brown. Elkhanialy and Nicholas (1976b, 46) also provided a list of categories including East Indian, Indo-Caucasian, Indic, South Asian, Indo-Dravidian, Caucasian, and Indo-European, asking for respondents' approval or disapproval. While the most favored term was "East Indian" (36.7 percent), it was also disapproved of by 27 percent. Indo-Caucasian received 34 percent approval and 27.7 percent disapproval. The term "Indic" received around 30 percent approval and 19 percent disapproval. The most unpopular category was Indo-European (the designation for Indian Americans used by the census in 1970), receiving only a 6.3 percent approval rating. Respondents also suggested a range of alternatives, with Asian Indian as one of them. A much smaller study with 24 respondents conducted by Fisher (1980, 125) in New York City also found that most people picked Brown for color and several emphasized that they were neither Black nor White. She provided an open-ended question regarding what race Indians belonged to and most respondents used the traditional Indian terms "Aryan" and "Dravidian."[1]

The strongest organized opposition to the Association of Indians in America (AIA) position came from the *Indian League of America* (ILA), another pan–Indian American organization based in Chicago, formed in 1973, that opposed the AIA's attempt to speak for all Indian Americans. The ILA did not want Indians to be classified racially as Asians but instead wanted a separate category for them. On the basis of the Chicago survey (sponsored by the ILA), Elkhanialy and Nicholas (1976a, 7) recommended the term "Indic" since it had received the most support from the community. They recognized that this was not a term familiar to many Indians and consequently suggested that the ILA and other Indian organizations work to make the term understood by Indian Americans.

Dutta told me that George E. Hall, then chief of the Social Statistics Branch of the Census Bureau, invited both the ILA and the AIA to make presentations at the upcoming hearing. However, the ILA was not able to prepare their case in time (they asked for additional time, but the Census Bureau was not able to accommodate this demand), and consequently, Manoranjan Dutta and the AIA represented Indian Americans at a hearing at the House of Representatives on June 1, 1976 (see also Das Gupta 2006, 43). At the hearing, Dutta argued that there was disagreement about the racial identity of Indians and that the present category of race/color was unscientific. "The fact is that some Indians are Caucasians, and others are not. In addition, we wish to emphasize that not all Caucasians are White" (Dutta 1976, 35). He went on to make the case that if a category of color was included in the census, it should be separate from race and should add brown, copper, and other colors to Black and White (Dutta, 1976, 36). Dutta also referred to the 1917 Asiatic Barred Zone Act to point to a precedent for counting Indians as Asians. Consequently, he argued that Indians should be counted as Asian Americans, with a separate category, "Asian Indians" (Dutta 1976).[2] The recommendation of the AIA for a separate listing for Asian Indians was accepted by the Census Bureau in September 1977 (Fisher 1980, 121).

There was also disagreement within the Indian community regarding whether they should be reclassified as a minority. Here again, Dutta, representing the Association of Indians in America (AIA) at a consultation sponsored by the U.S. Commission on Civil Rights, argued that "one of the great myths in this country is that the Asian Americans have had no history of disadvantage" (Dutta 1979, 394). Again with the help of his econometrics background Dutta was able show that while Asians had a higher median family income compared to the national median, they also had lower personal incomes (the high household income was due to having more income earners in the family). Many were underemployed, were underpaid relative to their years of education, and were also likely to advance more slowly in their careers when compared to Whites (Dutta 1979). Since Asians were counted as a minority group, the AIA through its categorization of Indian Americans as Asians would obtain minority status for the group.

While 76.5 percent of the respondents of the Chicago survey strongly agreed that for official purposes people from the Indian subcontinent should be classified as a minority in the United States (Elkhanialy and Nicholas 1976b, 49), the Indian League of America (ILA) was strongly opposed to this move. The president of the ILA, Chandra Jha, questioned whether the overwhelming support of respondents for minority status was because only those community members who suffered discrimination had returned the survey. "The very fact that so high a percentage of those who had responded had faced discrimination causes me to wonder about those returns. I am reminded of the saying, 'It is he whose ox is being gored who screams the loudest.'" He also raised the issue of whether the discrimination that was reported was "serious" or not (C. Jha 1976, vii). The ILA felt that being classified as a minority would hinder "the progress made heretofore in assimilation" by Indian Americans (Hardgrove 2013). Another early Indian American leader whom I interviewed said that the ILA "looked at the Jewish community and argued that they [Jewish Americans] were able to get ahead without being counted as a minority and were eventually able to be counted as White." The ILA hoped for the same outcome for Indian Americans. Chandra Jha went so far as to argue that if Indians were reclassified as minorities, they would lose job opportunities if they then had to compete with other U.S. minorities for a small proportion of minority set-asides (Fisher 1980, 131). The ILA and some other Indian Americans also feared a backlash from Whites and other minorities and worried about the possibility that this backlash could even manifest as violence against Indian Americans (Fisher 1980, 131–132; Hardgrove 2013).

Mobilization around Racial Discrimination

Being declared a minority by the U.S. census did not mean that issues of discrimination were automatically addressed. Not all departments in the United States accepted the minority designation, and consequently, other Indian American organizations had to mobilize to obtain minority status. In 1982, Jan Pillai, a professor at Temple University in Philadelphia and president of the *National Association of Americans of Asian Indian Descent* (NAAAID), petitioned the Small Business Administration requesting them to recognize Asian Indians as a socially disadvantaged group, making them eligible for minority set-asides. Pillai hoped that this in turn would lead other government agencies such as the Department of Health and Human Services and the Environmental Protection Agency to also recognize Indian Americans as a disadvantaged group (Glazer 1983, 10). K. V. Kumar, another early Indian American activist, was able to get the Department of Transportation to include Indian Americans as a group eligible for set-aside federal contracts (Haniffa 2017c, 13).

In the 1970s the Indian immigrant community in the United States was small (the 1970 census recorded 76,000 individuals of Asian Indian ancestry). This group had come under the "special skills" provision of the Immigration and Naturalization Act of 1965 and were mostly highly educated, fluent English speakers from urban backgrounds in India who entered professional and managerial careers. Education was another primary entry route for a significant proportion of Indian Americans who arrived in the United States as students (Nimbark 1980). The small size of the community, its largely professional status, and the racialization they faced led them to unify and mobilize in the public sphere. More Indian immigrants and students arrived in the 1970s and language groups started forming. A *Joint Committee* was formed with the help of the Indian consulate to unite all the regional groups from India under an Indian identity to celebrate Indian holidays like Independence Day, Republic Day, and Gandhi Jayanthi (Gandhi's birthday). Dr. Thomas Abraham, then a graduate student and president of the India Club at Columbia University (which was very active in organizing Indian movie screenings, as well as musical and cultural events in New York City), took over as chairman of the Joint Committee in the mid-1970s. He told me that he tried to bring the rival organizations AIA and ILA together, but this effort had failed, leading the Joint Committee to form the *Federation of Indian Associations* (FIA) in 1976, an umbrella association to bring the various Indian groups together in the tristate area (New York, New Jersey, and Connecticut). The organization held the first India Day Parade in 1981 in New York City on August 16 (Indian Independence Day is August 15), with many floats, and this became an annual tradition. Abraham served as the first president (1976–1981) of that chapter of the Federation of Indian Associations. The ILA was in decline by the late 1970s and Abraham encouraged the formation of an FIA chapter in Chicago. Other chapters began to form around the country. In 1980, Abraham formed the *National Federation of Indian American Associations* to bring regional FIA organizations together at the national level.

Rina Agarwala (2015, 102) quotes a later president of the NFIA, who explained, "Color brought these early Indians together. Color matters in the US." As head of the Federation of Indian Americans, Abraham testified in Albany before the Select Committee on Immigration and Refugee Policy in 1980 about the types of discrimination faced by Indian Americans (*News India* Staff Writer 1980). Another Indian American organization, the *Indian American Forum for Public Education* (IAFPE), was formed in 1982 in Washington, DC by Dr. Joy Cherian to bring the FIA and AIA together to mobilize against provisions in the Simpson-Mazzoli Immigration Bill that would have cut down family reunification categories by eliminating the second-preference category permitting the entry of the adult children of permanent residents and the fifth-preference category that permitted the entry of siblings of citizens. Cherian said that he urged Indian Americans to get involved in the mobilization against the immigration bill, pointing to the fate of Indians in East African countries like Kenya, Tanzania, and Uganda, where they became economically successful but faced anti-Indian sentiment and even expulsion since they had not integrated socially and politically (see also Cherian 1997, 27). George K. Zachariah, a professor at a local university, spoke eloquently in the Senate on behalf of the Indian American Forum for Public Education (IAFPE), stating:

> There could hardly be a hospital in this country without an Indian doctor, a university without an Indian professor, a major engineering firm without an Indian engineer, or a highway without a resting place, generally a small motel, run by an enterprising Indian. One can hardly open a professional journal without a major article authored by an Indian in it.

The IAFPE argued that if the provisions of the immigration bill were modified to cut down on family reunification, it would greatly hurt the Indian community, which would be denied the same rights that earlier immigrants had to bring their family members (Hudson 1983a, 20).[3] Indian Americans mobilized around this issue for two years, and in the end, the provision to cut family reunification categories was left out of the immigration bill. Indian Americans were commended for being instrumental in maintaining the family reunification preferences by Richard Day, chief council of the Senate Subcommittee on Immigration and Refugee Policy, and by Senator Simpson himself (Hudson 1983b).

This mobilization helped Indian Americans obtain political visibility on Capitol Hill. In June 1983, Cherian was able to arrange for around 100 Indian American leaders to meet with presidential advisors in preparation for the 1984 elections (when Reagan successfully ran for a second term). In February 1984, President Reagan met with a group of representatives of the Asian American community, including representatives from the NFIA, IAFPE, AIA, and NAAAID. President Reagan assured them that the Civil Rights Commission would investigate complaints of discrimination by the Indian American community (Chakrapani 1984). Cherian realized the importance of Indian Americans forming coalitions with other groups in similar situations and went on to get involved with, and take a leadership role in, the Asian American Voters Coalition. In November 1985, he was elected chairman-elect of the coalition, and in 1987, President Reagan nominated him to the Equal Employment Opportunity Commission as the representative of the Asian American Voters Coalition at a White House signing ceremony for Asian/Pacific American Heritage Week. Cherian became the first Asian American to be named to a subcabinet position (he continued in the position until 1993). When his nomination was announced, Cherian declared, "I strongly believe this is an opportunity for Asian Americans to enforce anti-discrimination laws" (*Ameri-Asia News* 1987). Later, reflecting on what he was able to do in his position, he wrote that his mission had been "to bring an increasing sensitivity to national origin issues in the employment area while upholding all other aspects of the Civil Rights Act of 1964" (Cherian 2004).

In 1980, there were only 361,531 Americans of Asian Indian ancestry, but by 1990, the number had gone up to 815, 447. This was due to a second wave of immigration from India in the 1980s. Many of the second-wave immigrants were relatives of the early post-1965 immigrants, sponsored under the family reunification provision of the 1965 Immigration Act. The Indian American newspaper *India West* carried an article on July 11, 1986, titled "Indian Immigrants: Educated, Affluent, and Apathetic," by Eric J. Adams, about a conference on India in America: The Immigrant Experience, held in New York City, where the political apathy of Indian Americans was a theme. Adams quoted political scientist Amrita Basu, saying that the experience of discrimination could "galvanize" political activism. "One of the major reasons for the politicization of Indian associations—comprised largely of middle-class professionals—is the anticipation or experience of discrimination" (Basu, cited in Adams, 1986). Indian Americans in the region were soon to experience extreme forms of discrimination and hate crimes and to mobilize around them.

Indians in Jersey City, New Jersey, found themselves under attack beginning in 1987 by a group that called itself "dotbusters" (many Hindu women wear a *bindi* dot on their forehead). A letter sent to *the Jersey Journal* in July of that year, signed by "The New Jersey Dot Busters," stated, "We will go to any extreme to get Indians to move out of Jersey City" (cited in Misir 1996, 59). One Indian man was killed, another was beaten into a coma, and many Indian men and women were physically attacked or harassed. Others had their homes and businesses broken into and burglarized. Rocks, beer bottles, and mini bombs were thrown at Indian homes, and apartment buildings containing Indian families were covered with graffiti with racial slurs directed against Indians (Misir 1996, 66–67). Despite all this evidence of racial bias, the crimes were not labeled as being racially motivated by the police. The individuals arrested for the crimes were acquitted or given very light sentences (Misir 1996). Indian American activists in New Jersey invited Dr. Joy Cherian to the region and he helped them mobilize the local chapter of the Indian American Forum for Political Education (IAFPE) around the dotbusters issue. The organization contacted the NAACP and Jewish groups and with their help proposed a hate crimes bill that included stiff penalties for bias-related crimes. They were successful in obtaining the support of several assembly members and getting the Anti-Racial Harassment Bill introduced into the New Jersey House of Representatives. The bill was held up for a long time but was finally passed in the early 1990s. Dr. Ved Chaudhary, who led this battle, told me that it "took a long time and a lot of persistence to get this through." Indians were also beginning to face racial problems in Fiji, Guyana, and Trinidad. Dr. Thomas Abraham and others felt that it was time to form a global alliance to deal with these issues, and Abraham took the lead in forming the *Global Organization of People of Indian Origin* (GOPIO) in 1989 with a big conference in New York City.

At the Seventh Annual Convention of the IAFPE held in Atlanta in July 1989, racial and national origin discrimination was identified as a major problem affecting the Indian American community and an equal opportunity task force was created to bring issues related to this problem to the attention of the officials at all levels and branches of the administration. The IAFPE conventions of 1990 and 1991 also focused on issues of racial bias. The two issues that came up the most and "evoked the most passionate debate and a consensus for increased activism to correct these problems facing Indian Americans" were the glass ceiling, or obstacles to career advancement faced by Indian American professionals, and discrimination against Indian American students in admissions to top universities (Haniffa 1991). Dr. Ved Chaudhary and Dr. Dinesh Patel initiated these campaigns. In his conversation with me, Dr. Ved Chaudhary told me that through his work as a scientist at Bell Labs and his interaction with other scientists, he realized the commonalities that Asian American groups faced in these two respects. He joined the group Asian Americans against Affirmative Action (also called "4A")[4] and later joined the 80-20 Initiative created in 1998 (a national, nonpartisan political action committee focused on Asian American issues aiming to mobilize 80 percent of the community's resources to support the presidential candidate who the organization feels will best represent the interests of Asian Americans). Dr. Ved Chaudhary was particularly involved in the initiative's Educational Foundation. Dr. Dinesh Patel, a knee surgeon who was also a clinical professor at Harvard University, was also involved in activism from his early days in the United States. He was a founding member of the Massachusetts chapter of the IAFPE and president of the national IAFPE for a term. He told me that he and two other Indian American leaders had a meeting with President Reagan about "invisible quotas" against Indian American students and glass ceilings, particularly those that prevented Indian American women from career advancement, and that he had been active around these issues at the national level.

Indian American Trade Groups Form and Mobilize around Discrimination

Due to a shortage of medical doctors in the United States in the 1960s, thousands of medical doctors from countries like India "were actively recruited" and given plane tickets to the United States (McMahon 2005, 16). The numbers fell in the late 1970s as a backlash against the influx of foreign doctors started setting in. From 1983, Indian Americans started expressing concern about discrimination against *international medical graduates* (IMGs) (doctors from other countries) in residency programs, hospitals, and medical research facilities (McMahon 2005, 29). The New Jersey chapter of the IAFPE first initiated these discussions in August 1983 and the issue was subsequently picked up at the national level by the IAFPE in Washington, DC. In May 1985, Senators Quayle and Hatch introduced a bill to establish a limit on the number of spots that a hospital could fill with IMGs (McMahon 2005, 46–47). By this time, the *American Association of Physicians of Indian Origin* (AAPI) had been formed (in 1984), partly to deal with issues of discrimination. Dr. Navin Shah, one of the pioneers among post-1965 Indian American doctors, was one of the cofounders of this organization. By the end of 1985, IMGs made up 18 percent of all medical residents in the United States. At the behest of Dr. Shah, several groups of IMGs held their annual convention in Washington, DC in July 1985 and came together to form an alliance, the *International Association of American Physicians* (IAAP), to mobilize against the second-class status of doctors who received their medical training overseas (McMahon 2005, 52). Dr. Shah, on behalf of the IAAP, went on to hire an experienced Washington lobbyist to help with their efforts (McMahon 2005, 63, 79).

At the 1985 convention, the IAFPE, with the support of the AAPI, formed a task force to examine bias against Indian medical graduates and discrimination against Indian American doctors, nurses, and other health professionals. The task force also launched a campaign against a newly introduced Senate bill that would have cut Medicare resident training reimbursements for foreign medical graduates. The IAFPE task force wrote letters to all senators and sent individual and mass petitions. Task force members also lobbied in Washington, DC several times (*Overseas Tribune* Staff Writer 1986). The lobbying of the task force finally yielded results when the bill was passed in April 1986. No cuts were made to Medicare funding for training foreign medical graduates, but IMGs were now required to pass the Foreign Medical

Graduate Examination in Medical Sciences within a year of beginning residency (McMahon 2005, 59). However, there were other issues that still needed to be addressed.

Indian American leaders from the AAPI led the fight to have a special section of the *American Medical Association* (AMA) for IMGs to address discrimination against them and to challenge their "de facto guest worker status" (McMahon 2005, 88). When the AMA proved unresponsive, Dr. Navin Shah turned his attention to Capitol Hill. Over the course of several years and several testimonies from Shah and others representing the IAAP and ensuing discussions, Indian American doctors were able to demonstrate the many ways in which international medical graduates (IMGs) were discriminated against and win the support and sympathy of more members of Congress. By July 1990, when the hearings began, the AAPI had become far larger than the other groups composing the IAAP and came to dominate, something the other IAAP physician groups looked upon with unease. The American Medical Association (AMA), realizing that IMGs made up a significant number of the doctors in the United States whose membership dollars they needed, finally showed a willingness to support the anti-discrimination bill. Then–vice president of the AAPI George Thomas argued that it was the AAPI's work that brought about this change (McMahon 2005, 128). In October 1991, the anti-discrimination bill calling for the prohibition of discrimination based on the international medical degree of the graduate came up for vote in the House. President George Bush signed the act into law in 1992 and the AMA finally created a section for IMGs in 1997. The IAAP alliance declined after 1992 and disappeared by 1995 (McMahon 2005).

Many post-1965 Indian immigrants who arrived in the United States (not infrequently by way of East Africa or the United Kingdom) hailed from a small region of around a 100-mile radius in central Gujarat. Most of this group was from the Patel subcaste of Hindus and consequently had the last name Patel. Sociologist Pawan Dhingra, who conducted a study of Indian American hotel and motel owners, explains how the industry developed into an ethnic niche for Gujarati Patel immigrants. Early Patel immigrants arrived as professionals but, finding that they were unable to find work commensurate with their qualifications, turned to self-employment (Dhingra 2012, 47). At this time, there were several older hotels available to lease in San Francisco and other places and some Patels turned to leasing hotels. Later, they were able to purchase smaller motels. Other Gujaratis who were less qualified arrived in the United States through family reunification and had few good options except insecure minimum-wage jobs. Consequently, they joined relatives who owned motels or purchased motels themselves. Yet other Gujarati Patels turned to the motel industry since they felt that it had better financial prospects for them compared to the jobs they currently had. Hotel franchising exploded in the 1970s and 1980s. Gujaratis bought rundown hotels, upgraded them, and obtained franchises from established brands. According to Dhingra (2012, 68), the "racist targeting" that Patel motel owners faced led them to form their own organizations. In Nashville, Tennessee, a group started the *Midsouth Indemnity Association* in 1985 that later became the *Indo American Hospitality Association*. The *Asian American Hotel Owners Association* (AAHOA) began in 1989 in Atlanta. In 1994, the Indo American Hospitality Association merged with the Asian American Hotel Owners Association (AAHOA) (Dhingra 2012, 68). Dhingra quotes a journalist writing for an Indian American weekly newspaper reporting on the 1994 event. A representative of the AAHOA described the need for the association: "We were fighting discrimination on a whole smorgasbord of issues. . . . Bankers were not giving us loans, mainstream America did not recognize us as the right kind of hotel owners, the franchise owners did not want to give us franchises, and the real estate brokers did not want to deal with us" (Potts 1994, cited in Dhingra 2011).

In this section, we see that global geopolitical shifts were responsible for changes in U.S. racial policies toward immigration and for the 1965 Immigration Act, which has redefined the U.S. racial system, but also that the act was originally intended to bring in more European immigrants despite its broader race-neutral framing. In the debate about whether Indians should claim minority status in the United States, the split between those who saw Indian Americans as a White-adjacent group and those who saw the community as a non-White group impacted by racial discrimination became apparent. Perhaps for this reason, the IAFPE strategically recruited the help of both Jewish groups and the NAACP to help Indian Americans deal with the dotbuster attacks on Indians in New Jersey in the 1980s. As political scientist Amrita Basu predicted, experiences of racial discrimination did indeed "galvanize" the political activism of post-1965 Indian immigrants. Early community leaders like Dr. Dutta and Dr. Cherian addressed the importance of immigrant civic engagement around domestic issues such as racial discrimination in the United States rather than just around India-based concerns and loyalties.

The issue of whether transnational loyalties negatively impact immigrant integration is much discussed in the literature, with most scholars showing that politically active immigrants usually get involved in both domestic and transnational activism (e.g., see Ley 2013; Levitt 2003; Nagel and Staeheli 2008). We saw this with early Indian immigrants mobilizing around rights in the United States and around Indian independence, and this is a pattern we will see with more recent immigrants as well, although the issue is complicated with generational differences playing a role, as will be discussed in subsequent chapters.

Conclusion

An examination of Indian American activism over almost 100 years demonstrates the fluidity of racial formation. We see how and why racial and ethnic classifications, as well as identifications, can change due to the interaction between international factors (including developments in the home countries and other global changes) and domestic events. The three-way relationship between the United States, Canada, and Britain played an important role in the development of discriminatory policies against people from the Indian subcontinent in North America and helped shape how Indians in the United States identified themselves and mobilized to further their interests. The 1908 Canadian act banning further Indian immigration was passed with the approval of American and British authorities (Jacoby 2007, 91; Sohi 2014, 27). Anti-immigrant groups in the United States used the 1908 Canadian law to develop similar policies in Northern California and to include Indians among the Asiatic groups to be excluded from the United States. For their part, Indian nationalist leaders moving across the Canadian and U.S. borders worked to link the degrading treatment of Sikhs in North America to their status as the colonial subjects of the British Empire. They also emphasized the need for unity between religious, class, and caste groups. Leaders of the movement for citizenship rights in the United States such as Bhagat Singh Thind, Dalip Singh Saund, and J. J. Singh were strong Indian patriots, also working for Indian independence from the British. Transnational solidarities between Indians in different parts of the globe (including India, the United States, and Canada) were forged against British colonial rule, motivating Indian immigrants in the United States to rally around the cause of Indian independence along with their efforts to gain U.S. citizenship.

Early Sikh immigrants used Western ideas about an Aryan homeland in the Caucasus from where there had been a migration to Europe and India to argue that they were racially related to White Europeans and therefore deserving of citizenship. However, British worries about the development of the Ghadar movement in the United States shaped the U.S. Supreme Court's *Thind* decision, leading Indians to be reclassified from "White" to "non-White alien," which meant that they lost their citizenship rights and their land holdings. Although competing Hindu, Sikh, and Muslim nationalisms had arisen by this time in the subcontinent, Indian immigrants in the United States remained unified around their support for Indian independence from the British. The Japanese attack on Pearl Harbor and the entry of the United States into World War II helped to change the situation of Indian immigrants in this country. Needing Indian support for the war against Japan, the American administration and U.S. Congress became more sympathetic to the cause of Indian independence and the demand for citizenship for Indians in the United States.

Racial discrimination continued to impact post-1965 immigrants, but ironically, the boundary demarcating "Asia" was now drawn to the east of India to exclude Indians from civil rights protections and the argument that Indians were "Caucasians" was resuscitated by a census agency after the passage of civil rights legislation in the 1960s to argue that Indian Americans should not be brought under the protection of this legislation and should be classified as White. But Indian American organizations mobilized and were able to get Indians classified as Asians and consequently as racial minorities. However, we see that the community was divided on whether Indians should be classified as Asians or as racial minorities, and on how their race should be described. Indian American groups also organized to challenge discriminatory immigration bills and glass ceilings in education and the workplace. Trade organizations protested bias against Indian American physicians and hoteliers.

In short, this chapter shows the variety of ways in which early Indian Americans were active around racial discrimination (to assert a White status, and later, to repudiate this designation) and how they mobilized to claim rights as U.S. citizens. Racial discrimination and smaller numbers kept Indian Americans relatively unified, and different groups came together under an Indian identity (even though the basis of this identity was in dispute and there were some internal divisions) into the 1980s and early 1990s. All this would change as religion reared up as a factor dividing Indian Americans. The rise of Hindu nationalism in India in the 1980s set these processes in motion, leading to the splintering of the community, as we will see in the next chapter.

Notes

1. Fisher (1980, 32–33) writes that "Aryan" and "Dravidian" were terms that were often discussed by her respondents to describe the physiognomy of North and South Indians respectively during her fieldwork among Indians in New York City.
2. Dutta said that Native Americans wanted him to add the word "Asian" to "Indian," "otherwise Columbus' mistake would continue."
3. Cherian told me that he used the statements that the United States had made in the Helsinki Accord to advocate for the family reunification of the relatives of Jewish families from Russia.
4. Asian Americans are divided on the issue of affirmative action. The 2016 Asian American Voter Survey found that 64 percent of respondents said that they favored affirmative action programs.

2
Religion and Transnationalism

The Rise of Intraethnic Divisions

In the mid-1990s I attended a South Asian American conference in Los Angeles where some second-generation activists who had worked on Capitol Hill talked about how members of Congress were confused by the many Indian American groups that approached them with very different perspectives and demands. A member of Congress would be visited by someone who would try to recruit him to the India caucus (see Chapter 3 for details) by talking up Indian democracy and pluralism. A few days later, the same congressman would be visited by Sikhs criticizing India's human rights record, and some days later by Muslim groups criticizing India's policies on Kashmir. The activists said that this led to confusion about which group *really* represented Indian Americans and that members of Congress wanted the community to have one representative organization and to speak with a unified voice.

This chapter discusses some of the key events that led to religion becoming a major source of division among Indian Americans. Most of these events first emerged during the colonial period, primarily tensions between Hindus and Muslims, leading to the extremely violent partition of India and Pakistan, with a death toll of between several hundred thousand and a million, and over 10 million refugees in the northwestern region alone (Metcalf and Metcalf 2002, 218–219). Religious cleavages were tamped down during the immediate postcolonial period by secularist Indian leaders like Jawaharlal Nehru (India's first prime minister) who wanted to bring healing and prevent further violence. However, Hindu nationalism resurged in the 1980s. This in turn led to the splintering of Indian Americans in the public sphere with the establishment of organizations dedicated to developing a transnational Hindu political identity, on the one hand, and on the other, the formation of advocacy organizations by Indian religious minorities to bring attacks against their religions to the attention of the American public. The first part of the chapter provides a brief background to some historical events that led to religious cleavages. The bulk of the chapter focuses on the various religious advocacy organizations formed in the United States, the reasons for their formation, and the early issues that they mobilized around.

Writing in 2009, political scientist Daniel Philpott sounded a clarion call for scholars to recognize the importance of religion in public life and in politics since, "on virtually every continent, among populations of every world religion . . . the place of religion in public life has become more prominent and more controversial in the past generation" (Philpott 2009, 184). As religion resurged in immigrant homelands it impacted diasporas and the countries in which diasporas were living. As Hindu nationalism started growing in India, intracommunity tensions developed, leading Indian Americans to begin to mobilize around religious organizations rather than around pan-Indian American organizations. By the early decades of the twenty-first century there were far more religious than secular Indian American organizations, even counting the very many regional language-based groups that formed among Indian Americans (Agarwala 2016, 920; Chakravorty, Kapur, and Singh 2017, 137). This development was not just due to the resurgence of religion in India. It was also due to the role that religious organizations play in the United States.

Religion has been a significant factor shaping American history and society, as well as immigrant integration patterns, from the beginning of colonial America. Early European migrants arrived in the United States to escape religious persecution, and the New England colonies have often been called "Bible Commonwealths" because they sought the guidance of scriptures to regulate all aspects of the lives of their citizens (Hutson 1998). Religion was also important in impacting the settlement experiences of Jewish and Catholic European immigrants who faced xenophobia due to their religious differences and became targets of Ku Klux Klan attacks and, in the case of Catholics, attacks from the Know-Nothing Party (Alba, Raboteau, and DeWind 2009, 1). Jewish Americans established organizations such as the Anti-Defamation League, the American Jewish Committee, and the American Jewish Congress to deal with the rise of anti-Semitism in the early twentieth century (Dollinger 2000). Catholic Church leaders created Catholic parochial schools in response to anti-Catholic sentiment and, later, due to the secularization of public schools (Dolan 1992).

U.S. religious institutions have often played a central role in the process of ethnic formation. While religious institutions in the homeland often serve "solely as sites for religious practice" (Ebaugh and Chafetz 1999, 599), in the diaspora, they also become community centers. Many immigrants turn to ethnic religious institutions to obtain the emotional, social, and economic resources to deal with the displacement and alienation produced by migration, as well as the moral and cultural socialization of their children (Hirschman 2004, 1228; Yang and Ebaugh 2001). Consequently, many immigrants who may not have been religious in the homeland turn to religion and ethnic religious institutions in the diaspora (Kurien 2007a; Williams 1988).

Religion has been important to Indian immigrants from the early days of their settlement in the United States, and home-based religious practices, rituals, and community gatherings in rented facilities were institutionalized quite early on (Kurien 2007a). In the diaspora, immigrant parents turned to ethnic organizations to provide moral and cultural grounding for their children—these were most likely to be religious organizations. These organizations focused on the spiritual, cultural, and social needs of members, and until the 1980s Indian Americans remained relatively united in the public sphere, mobilizing around issues of common interest.

A Brief Background to Contemporary Religious Conflicts in India

Caste, Conversion, and Hindu Nationalism

In India, religious conversion has been a traditional strategy to try to escape some of the worst caste abuses. Several medieval saints like Nanak and Ravidas came up with new religions (Nanak founded Sikhism and Ravidas founded the Ravidassia religion) or new religious movements such as the Kabir Panth, founded by medieval saint Kabir, that rejected many forms of institutionalized religion (both Hindu and Muslim) and also emphasized freedom from caste strictures. Islam in the Mughal period and Christianity during the period of European colonization became additional options for those seeking to obtain some freedom from extreme caste discrimination.

Hindu nationalism or *Hindutva* was explicitly codified in the 1920s. Caste was central to this process. As Joel Lee (2021, 10) argues, "techniques of colonial governance [particularly the British census showing that privileged-caste Hindus were a minority] stimulated a politics of numbers," specifically Hindu fears that they would be supplanted by growing Muslim and Christian demographics. He points out that in 1900, "neither untouchables nor Hindus perceived each other as co-religionists" (p. 78), and in fact, untouchables were viewed as "the despised antipode of the Hindu" (p. 79). In response to the perceived demographic threat, and in the service of creating a majoritarian nationalism, Hindu organizations like the Arya Samaj developed *shuddi* (purification) rituals to "cleanse" oppressed castes and bring them into the Hindu fold (Lee 2021). This is what led Vinayak Damodar Savarkar, who first codified Hindu nationalism in his book *Hindutva* ([1923] 1969), to define the Hindu "race" as including Hindus of all castes who were attached to the soil of India. However, initially, the classification of untouchables as Hindus was strongly resisted by caste Hindus.

In the late colonial period, Dr. Ambedkar became embittered by the opposition of caste Hindus, including Gandhi, to abolishing untouchability and the caste system and to giving political power to untouchables. Consequently, in the 1930s he vowed to convert out of Hinduism, which he blamed for the situation of the untouchables. However, he rejected the conventional religious options that oppressed castes had turned to and instead converted to a self-reformed, *Navayana* (new) Buddhism (which he founded by reading a variety of Buddhist texts) in 1956, along with half a million of his Dalit followers.

Since Ambedkar's conversion, many of his Dalit followers, particularly in his home state of Maharashtra, turned to Navayana Buddhism. Some Dalits officially classified as Hindus do not self-identify as such since they worship personal or local deities that are not included in the pan-Indian Hindu pantheon of gods and goddesses and follow practices that are not part of Sanskritic or "upper caste" Hinduism. Others, such as followers of the South Indian leader Periyar (E. V. Ramaswamy), are atheists, though also officially counted as Hindu. Since the idea of India being a Hindu-majority country is based on counting lower castes and tribals as being part of the Hindu category, the caste system and the position of the lower castes is a sensitive political issue. Lower castes on their part have been becoming increasingly mobilized and assertive, challenging caste discrimination. There have been mass conversions of Dalits and other oppressed caste groups to Islam, Christianity, or Buddhism to protest caste atrocities.

The Hindutva ideology, first formulated during the colonial period, proclaims that the Vedic age, conventionally believed to be 1500–1000 BCE but dated at least as early as 3000 BCE by Hindutva supporters, represents the essence of Indian culture. Hindu nationalists view Indian culture and civilization as Hindu. They deem Mughals and British colonialists and the "pseudo-secular" Indian leaders (who are perceived to have discriminated against caste Hindus by instituting affirmative action programs for lower castes and special protections for the personal laws and the religious institutions of non-Hindu groups) who dominated in the immediate postcolonial period as destroyers of this civilization's identity and greatness. Consequently, many of the problems seen in Hinduism from the medieval period onward, such as the presence of a rigid caste system and a decline in the status of women, are considered by Hindutva supporters to be the impact of Muslim rule and British colonialism and the corruption of Hindu ideals in this period, and not an inherent part of Hinduism. According to Hindutva supporters, only an openly and unashamedly Hindu state can right these historical wrongs. Hindutva ideology defines Hindus as those for whom India is their homeland and holy land, including groups like Sikhs, Buddhists, and Jains, whose religions originated in India (although these groups themselves generally resist this classification). Hindutva ideology, however, excludes Indian Muslims and Christians, who are often described as "foreigners" even though both groups are composed almost entirely of Indigenous members and both Islam and Christianity have existed in India for well over 1,200 years.

The Hindutva movement stresses the greatness of Hinduism and Hindu culture, the importance of Hindu unity, and the need to defend Hinduism and Hindus against discrimination, defamation, and the pressure to convert to other religions. The need for Hindu nationalism and Hindu self-assertion is justified by the argument (dismissed by most analysts) that due to the proselytizing activities of Muslim and Christian missionaries and the higher fertility rates of Indian Muslims, Hindus will soon be reduced to a minority in India (Kurien 2007a, 138). Competing Hindu and Muslim religious nationalisms developed during the period of British colonialism and eventually resulted in the partition of the subcontinent in 1947 into India and Pakistan.

The Hindu nationalist movement was suppressed in the immediate postcolonial period by secularist Indian leaders, and Hindu nationalist paramilitary organizations like the Rashtriya Swayamsevak Sangh (RSS, formed in 1925) were banned (a member of the RSS was responsible for assassinating Gandhi). But Hindutva resurged from the late 1980s with the *Ram* temple movement, which called for the erection of a temple to Lord Ram in a town in North India, on the site of a sixteenth-century mosque. Hindutva supporters claimed that the *Babri* mosque had been built over a temple commemorating the exact place of Lord Ram's birth. The Ram movement was spear-headed by the *Vishwa Hindu Parishad* (VHP, World Hindu Council), founded in 1964 as a transnational organization to promote Hinduism and Hindu unity among Hindus in India and abroad. The *Bharatiya Janata Party* (BJP, the Indian People's Party), established in 1980, was able to achieve a meteoric rise by adopting Hindu nationalism as its central plank in the late 1980s. There are a number of different, interlinked organizations at the core of the Hindu nationalist movement, which are all collectively referred to as the *Sangh Parivar* (the family of [Hindu] organizations).

Two watershed events define the public emergence of contemporary Hindu nationalism. The first was the demolition of the ancient Babri mosque in Ayodhya, North India, on December 6, 1992, by a mob of Hindus intent on building a Ram temple at that site, followed by violence against Muslims, leading to at least 1,000 deaths, mostly of Muslims. A second event took place in 2002 in Gujarat state when what several groups of independent investigators have characterized as an organized, state-sponsored pogrom against Muslims (ostensibly in retaliation against a Muslim attack on a train carrying Hindu activists and their families) took place, leading to over 2,000 deaths, again, mostly Muslim. After the violence was brought under control, Muslims in Gujarat were warned by members of the VHP that if they wanted to return to their villages, they should "do so as a subject, not an equal," and that they should learn to "live like a minority" (Waldman 2002). More generally, the rise of contemporary Hindutva mobilization in India has been marked by violence against Muslims, Sikhs, Christian missionaries and recent converts (mostly oppressed castes or tribals) to Christianity. The two incidents played an important part in mobilizing Hindu and Muslim groups in the United States, as well as anti-Hindutva groups composed of a coalition of progressive Hindus and South Asian Americans of Muslim, Sikh, Christian, and Dalit backgrounds.

After the coming to power of the Hindu nationalist Bharatiya Janata Party in 1998 (the BJP was in power from 1998 to 2004 as part of a coalition government), anti-conversion laws were put in place in around one-third of the states in India, and right-wing Hindu groups have been conducting *ghar wapsi* ("homecoming" or reconversion to Hinduism) crusades around the country, targeting oppressed caste Muslims and Christians. Hindu groups have also been working to introduce Hinduism to Indian tribals in different parts of the country through a variety of nongovernment educational organizations, with substantial funding coming from Hindu Americans (USCIRF

Annual Report 2018; SACW.net 2014).[1] Violence against Muslims and Dalits escalated after the BJP returned to power at the national level in 2014, and especially after 2019, when they returned to power with an even greater mandate. After an incident in December 2021 where Hindu religious leaders gathering at a Hindu conclave encouraged Hindus to take up arms against Indian Muslims and called for a genocide against them, without condemnation from BJP leaders or the prime minister, many international watchers have warned that a genocide against Muslims could take place in India (Chowdhury 2022).

Background to the Kashmir Imbroglio

The Muslim-dominated Kashmir region of South Asia is the location of one of the most intractable conflicts in the world today, an issue around which both Hindu and Muslim groups have mobilized in the United States. After five centuries (starting in 1343) under various Islamic dynasties from Central and West Asia and a brief period under a Sikh monarch (1819–1846), the state of Jammu and Kashmir was created in 1846 by the British East India Company. The company handed over the territory to the *Dogra* Hindu king Gulab Singh as a reward for his military help against the Sikhs, in return for a sizeable sum of money (Zutshi 2019, 48–49). The Dogras created an explicitly Hindu kingdom, claiming descent from the Hindu God Ram (Zutshi 2019, 50). They also marginalized and oppressed Muslims (Rai 2004; Behera 2006, 14–15). Kashmiri Muslims organized a movement beginning in 1930 to demand access to education and state employment, leading to widespread agitation across the princely state in 1931 and an incident where 22 protesting Kashmiri Muslims were shot dead by the police. Contemporary activists date Kashmiri Muslim mobilization against Hindu rule to this incident.[2]

Another "pogrom" or "ethnic cleansing" in the Jammu region in the latter part of 1947 is not acknowledged by many Indian historians but is burned into the psyches of Kashmiri Muslim American activists—a large-scale massacre against Muslims in the Jammu region by Dogra state troops and by Hindus and Sikhs (given weapons of Muslims who were forcefully disarmed by state troops), resulting in the death of around 200,000 (Copland 1991, 244; Rashid 2020, 221; Snedden 2001, 120). Consequently, many Muslims from the region fled to Pakistan (Rashid 2020, 221). As a result, the demographic composition of Jammu province changed from a Muslim-majority region (61.19 percent Muslim according to the 1941 census of India [Snedden 2001, 116]) to a Hindu-majority region in the next census of the region in 1961—Jammu and Kashmir was not included in the 1951 Indian census (Snedden 2001, 127).

Although the princely state of Jammu and Kashmir was a Muslim-majority region and should therefore have gone to Pakistan at the time of the partition, Maharaja Hari Singh, the Dogra Hindu king, tried to hold out for independence, refusing to join either Pakistan or India. He acceded to India only in return for Indian Army support when faced with a violent rebellion by Muslims in the northwestern region of Kashmir joined by armed tribal groups from Pakistan. Pakistan challenged the legitimacy of the accession, leading to a war between India and Pakistan (1947–1948). India took the matter to the United Nations, which asked for the demilitarization of the region, to be followed by a plebiscite to determine the wishes of the people. However, India argued that Pakistan never withdrew its forces from Kashmir and consequently refused to withdraw its forces and declined to hold a plebiscite. As part of Clause 7 of the instrument of accession that the Dogra king signed with India, the state could decide not to come under the constitution of India (Noorani 2011, 8). The Indian government gave the state of Jammu and Kashmir special autonomous status and instituted Article 370 to protect this guarantee (the only state to have this status). Another provision, Article 35A, linked with Article 370 protected the domicile status of members of the state. This provision was originally instituted in 1927 by the Dogra king due to the agitation of Kashmiri *Pandits* (Hindu Brahmins of Kashmir)[3] demanding "sons of the soil" rights, worried about the incursions into the state by Punjabi Hindus (Rai 2004, 253). In 2019, both articles were abrogated by the Indian government (see Chapter 5 for a discussion). Tensions between India and Pakistan over Kashmir led to three more wars.

A violent Islamic insurgency gained control over the Kashmir valley in the late 1980s, which led to an exodus of around a 100,000 Kashmiri Pandits from the valley. The Indian state brutally repressed the violence in Kashmir, putting the state under the Armed Forces Special Powers Act of the Central Government in 1990, with the Indian Army having the power to conduct searches, make arrests without warrants, shoot to kill, or destroy buildings on mere suspicion, leading to a variety of human rights violations. These suppression measures further strengthened the autonomy or *Azadi* (freedom) movement. Several tens of thousands of people were killed in the conflict (recent developments are discussed in Chapter 5). Due to the complicated history of Kashmir, many Muslim American activists from Indian Kashmir consider the region to be a territory under Indian occupation and have been active around the issue of Kashmiri autonomy and independence. Consequently, they do not identify as "Indian" but mobilize as Kashmiris or as Muslims.

Background to the Sikh Khalistan Movement

In the last years of the colonial period, Sikh leaders in India mobilized for a separate state for Sikhs as they realized that the Muslim demand for a separate state was being seriously considered. By 1946, this Sikh state was called *Khalistan*, land of the pure. However, the demand for Khalistan was not met. Indian nationalist leaders tried to pacify Sikhs. In 1946, Nehru was quoted as saying, "The brave Sikhs of Punjab are entitled to special consideration [and] I see nothing wrong in an area and a set up in the north wherein the Sikhs can also experience the glow of freedom" (K. Singh 2005, 291). Gandhi and Nehru are also said to have assured Sikhs that the Indian constitution would be framed in such a way that minority communities like Sikhs would be provided adequate protection. However, the final constitution document created a strongly centralized political structure, which the two Sikh representatives vigorously opposed (S. H. Singh 1949). Furthermore, Article 25 classified Sikhs (as well as Jains and Buddhists) as Hindus and refused to acknowledge that they were a separate religion. Consequently, the two Sikh representatives in the Constituent Assembly refused to ratify and sign the Indian constitution (P. Singh 2005, 914).

Sikhs as a group were particularly badly impacted by partition in 1947. Punjab was divided between India and Pakistan, with Pakistan getting a much bigger portion of the land than India. Sikhs living in the Punjab region of Pakistan had to move to Indian Punjab. Several sacred sites and sites important to Sikh history (such as the birthplace of Guru Nanak, founder of the Sikh religion, as well as the capital of the Sikh empire) remained in Pakistan. The partition of India came as a major blow to Indian nationalists of Sikh background in the United States who, as we saw in Chapter 1, had mobilized for an undivided India. Dilraj, descendant of a Sikh Ghadar activist, commented:

Even after the country got free, it was not according to their dreams because if they had their way there would be no division of India, there will be no Pakistan, there will be no Bangladesh [Bangladesh, originally East Pakistan, gained independence from Pakistan in 1971], it would still be probably the United States of India. That is what their dream was.

In the 1950s, Indian states were carved out based on language. However, the Indian government was reluctant to grant a separate Punjabi-language state for Sikhs given concerns about creating a state based on religion. Consequently, the Sikh party, *Akali Dal*, launched a Punjabi *Suba* (province) movement, and tens of thousands of Akali Dal supporters courted arrest (Chima 2010, 30–31). Finally, in 1966, after a victory for India in the 1965 Indo-Pakistan war, due in good part to the support of Sikhs (who continued to be overrepresented in the army), the Indian Punjab region was divided into three states and a Punjab-majority state was created. However, some of the specific ways that the division took place were not to the liking of Sikhs. The city of Chandigarh, capital of the undivided Punjab state, which the Sikhs had wanted as the capital of the newly reconstituted Punjab-majority state, became a union territory (under the control of the central government) and the capital of both Punjab and Haryana states. Again, some contiguous Punjabi-speaking areas were not incorporated into Punjab but went to neighboring states. The division of the Indian Punjab region into three states also resulted in tension about the division of the river water running through the region, with Sikhs arguing that the Hindu states of Himachal Pradesh and Haryana were favored over Sikh-dominated Punjab. These issues led to Sikh mobilization and a demand for "an autonomous region" within India where Sikhs and Sikhism could flourish. When the central government, by this time with Indira Gandhi as prime minister, proved intransigent on these demands, a secessionist Khalistan movement developed for a separate homeland for Sikhs. In the early 1980s some Khalistan leaders turned to violence and militancy.

Sikh discontent regarding discrimination against them and the Punjab region by the Indian central government came to a head on June 5, 1984, when Indira Gandhi ordered troops into their sacred Golden Temple (the center of Sikh spiritual and political authority) in Amritsar, North India, to rout out militants. Since the army invasion took place on the day of an important Sikh religious festival, there were several thousand Sikh pilgrims in the temple, and several hundreds, possibly thousands of pilgrims were trapped in the complex and killed in the attack. On June 15, visa restrictions were imposed on Sikhs living outside India, preventing them from visiting India (Howe 1984). On October 31, 1984, Indira Gandhi was assassinated by two of her Sikh bodyguards in Delhi, setting off anti-Sikh violence in Delhi and other cities in North India. Several thousand Sikhs were killed. There were allegations that key figures of the ruling Congress party were involved in the massacres and that the attacks were well organized, but no action was taken against the perpetrators. Political repression against Sikhs in Punjab suspected of being supporters of Khalistan continued for another decade, leading to the detention, torture, and disappearance of tens of thousands of Sikh men. Jugdep Chima (2010, 3), who has written on the Sikh separatist movement and the Indian government response to it, estimates that around 25,000 people (mostly Sikh) died in the violence between the early 1980s and 1993.

Close transnational ties between the diaspora and India have meant that events in India reverberate within the Indian American community. However, diasporas are not merely echo chambers. The religious and political context of the United States creates opportunities for groups and for particular types of advocacies and framing that are then transmitted to India and to the Indian diaspora in other countries. This will be discussed in subsequent chapters.

The Formation of Religious Advocacy Organizations in the United States

Hindu American Organizations

The VHP of America (VHPA), a branch of the VHP in India, was the earliest Hindu American umbrella organization (bridging sectarian, linguistic, and other internal divisions). It was founded in 1970 on the East Coast by four members of the RSS and was formally incorporated in 1974 (Lakhihal 2001, 59). Although the VHP in India is militantly nationalistic, perhaps partly because it is registered in the United States as a nonprofit, tax-exempt religious organization, which is forbidden from pursuing political activities, the VHPA has officially remained devoted to promoting Hinduism and pursuing cultural and social activities. However, unofficially, VHPA members and activists have been networked with a range of Sangh Parivar organizations and groups around the country and in India, including those that are more overtly political. The HSS (*Hindu Swayamsevak Sangh*), the overseas branch of another Sangh Parivar organization, the RSS in India, was established in New Jersey in 1977. There are also U.S. support groups for the Hindu nationalist party, the BJP (e.g., Overseas Friends of the BJP [OFBJP]). It is important to note that initially, none of these organizations were oriented toward engagement with wider U.S. publics. By the early 1990s Hindu nationalism was on the ascendancy in the United States. The demolition of the Babri mosque on December 6, 1992, energized American Hindu nationalist groups to come out more publicly within the Indian American community. The VHPA started to emphasize the need for Hindu unity and became more militant and more overtly political (Rajagopal 2001, 238–239). The Internet became a major site for Hindu nationalist propaganda and mobilization in the early 1990s. The Hindu nationalist message also began to be carried by several Indian American newspapers. The coming to power in 1998 of the BJP gave the Hindutva cause more legitimacy within Hindu circles both in India and in the United States. U.S. Sangh Parivar organizations and affiliates registered a "phenomenal growth" from the late 1990s (Lakhihal 2001, 59).

U.S. Hindu umbrella organizations began to use some elements of the Hindutva platform to unify and politically mobilize Hindu Americans. Some of this political mobilization began to be visible in the halls of the U.S. Congress. The control that Hindu groups were able to gain over Indian American politics as early as 2001 can be seen by the comment of Narayan D. Keshavan, special assistant to Congressman Gary L. Ackerman (former cochair of the Congressional Caucus on India and Indian Americans), who told *India Post* journalist Prashanth Lakhihal that "there are scores of Congressmen and dozens of Senators who clearly equate the growing Indian American political influence to the 'Hindu Lobby'—very much akin to the famed 'Jewish Lobby'" (Lakhihal 2001, 59).

The one-person *Infinity Foundation* formed in 1995 by wealthy Indian American entrepreneur Rajiv Malhotra focused on challenging the academic and popular portrayal of Hinduism from at least the year 2000 on, placing him in a good position to become a spokesperson of Hinduism and of Hindutva after the attacks of September 11, 2001. More recently, he has described his Infinity Foundation as a "Hindu Think Tank on Bharatiya (Indian) Civilization."[4] Through his efforts, and the mobilization of Hindu American supporters through his speeches and copious writing aimed at a mass Hindu readership (on the Internet and in book form with titles such as *Academic Hinduphobia, The Battle for Sanskrit, Breaking India: Western Interventions in Dravidian and Dalit Faultlines*, and *Being Different: An Indian Challenge to Western Universalism*), Malhotra became an influential, though often controversial, American Hindu spokesperson. He has also been conducting interviews with Hindu political and religious leaders in India, the United States, and the United Kingdom (uploaded on his YouTube channel), offering advice on everything from academic Hinduism to how to manage and co-opt Indian Muslims to how to compete with China. He has a large and apparently very devoted fan base from whom he periodically solicits donations in support of his "movement."

The *Hindu American Foundation* (HAF), formed in 2003 by "a band of young and savvy second-generation Indian Americans" to "provide a progressive voice" for the Hindu American community (Melwani 2009), is the best-known and most active U.S. Hindu umbrella organization. It is also the first Hindu organization to have a professional organizational structure and full-time staff. HAF leaders describe their organization as an "advocacy group" (S. Shukla 2008, 26). In 2006, they opened a full-time office in Washington, DC. Its location in the nation's capital allowed the HAF to become well-linked with governmental and policy offices and attain national visibility. Their website that year indicated that the organization "interacts with and educates government, media, think tanks, academia and public fora about Hinduism and issues of concern to Hindus locally and globally."[5]

Until the formation of the HAF, spokespersons for Hinduism in the United States had almost always been first-generation men who used their accomplishments in the professional and business world to legitimize their religious authority within the Hindu community. With the formation of the HAF in Washington, DC, this profile shifted—the HAF is led mostly by second-generation Indian American Hindu professionals (including doctors and lawyers), and both men and women are represented among its cofounders who continue to lead the organization to the present. More recently, cofounder Suhag Shukla, a lawyer (and a woman), has been the executive director and primary spokesperson. The cofounders indicated that they grew up in the United States in the 1970s at a time when the Hindu Indian community was small and there were very few if any other second-generation Hindu Americans in their schools. Many spoke about the negative perceptions of Hinduism they encountered in the wider society and in the media, as well as classes on Hinduism in school "filled with misconceptions, stereotypical images, misconstrued texts or outdated concepts" (Ishani Chowdhury quoted by Melwani 2009). It was only in college that they came to see the beauty and value of their heritage after encountering other young Hindus like themselves, often in Sangh Parivar–affiliated organizations such as the VHPA and the *Hindu Students Council* (Coalition against Genocide 2013a, 4–5). These experiences motivated them to form a Hindu advocacy organization. The influence of the Sangh Parivar can be seen clearly on one of the cofounders of the HAF, Mihir Meghani, a medical doctor who wrote approvingly of Hindutva (as "the Great Nationalist Ideology"[6]) and the demolition of the Ayodhya mosque in 1992 in an essay that became the ideological manifesto of the BJP and has been on the organization's website since the late 1990s (see Kurien 2017b, 145–146 for more details).[7] Other issue-based Hindu organizations led by members of the Sangh Parivar in the United States formed at various times and in different parts of the country, shape-shifting to meet particular needs. They will be introduced and their activities discussed in subsequent chapters. The return to national power by the BJP in 2014 brought the Hindutva voice to the fore within Hindu American communities.

American Dalit/Ambedkarite Organizations

Caste is not just about Dalits—all Indian Americans (and South Asian Americans more broadly) can generally be located within the caste hierarchy. As in the case of race where the focus is often on African Americans, caste is often mistakenly identified as a Dalit issue since the caste identity and privilege of "upper caste" Hindus is usually invisible and normalized. Until very recently, all major Indian American and South Asian American secular and religious organizations, including progressive ones founded by the second generation, were led by privileged-caste individuals. This is probably because most Indian Americans belong to privileged castes due to the elite nature of the migration to the United States. Privileged-caste leadership could also be due to the sense of confidence and entitlement that being from such a caste background confers. Despite constituting over 25 percent of the population of India, Dalits were estimated as making up a mere 1.5 percent of the Indian American population in 2003 (Chakravorty, Kapur, and Singh 2017, 68). Dalit Americans formed their own organizations to mobilize around issues of concern to them.

There was a small number of Dalit professionals who came to the United States in the 1970s as part of the early post-1965 immigrants or as students, but they were scattered around the country. Some worked to hide their caste identities and become part of the "upper caste" Indian American Hindu community in their localities so that they and their families would not be totally isolated in the United States. The first Dalit organization formed in the United States was *Volunteers in the Service of India's Oppressed and Neglected* (VISION), formed in the 1970s in New York by Dr. Shoba Singh of New Jersey, who had received a PhD in Physics from Johns Hopkins in 1957 and was working for AT&T and Bell Laboratories (Teltumbde 2017, 163). The first organized activity of VISION was a demonstration in June 1978, before the United Nations headquarters, when Indian prime minister Moraji Desai came to address the UN General Assembly. The demonstration, organized by Dalits in Canada and the United States, was to protest the way the Indian government had bungled an incident of caste violence against a Dalit group in North India, resulting in the arrest of the Dalits, not their attackers (Teltumbde 2017, 154, 163). The efforts of VISION in successfully transforming the Dalit issue into an international human rights issue, instead of a domestic issue, under the purview of the Indian government, will be discussed in Chapter 5. Due to the relocation of some of the members and internal schisms within the group, VISION disbanded in the 1990s.

Contemporary U.S. Dalit activists unify around the figure of Babasaheb ("respected father") Ambedkar and *mobilize as Ambedkarites rather than as Dalits* since a "Dalit" identity and the need to identify based on caste are not embraced by all. After VISION disbanded, a variety of Ambedkarite organizations started forming around the country, this time with a focus on Buddhism. The visit of Indian prime minister Vajpayee in 2000 mobilized U.S. Dalit groups to come together in a temporary anti-Hindutva coalition. On September 8, 2000, when Mr. Vajpayee was speaking at the United Nations, a multireligious Dalit coalition group, the *Federation of Ambedkarites, Buddhists, and Ravidasi Organizations of North America* (FABRONA), organized a protest in New York against the "atrocities and genocides of Dalits (Untouchables) of India" under the BJP government. The press release argued that the "BJP Alliance Government has been responsible for promoting Hindu Fundamentalism ... thus making living hell for Dalits, Christians, Muslims, Sikhs, Tribals and other minorities" (FABRONA 2000).

Raju Kamble, erstwhile founder of the best-known international Ambedkarite organization, the *Dr. Ambedkar International Mission* (AIM), formed in 2003 in the United States (it was founded in Malaysia in 1994), told me that his motivation for forming AIM was to "create a cultural identity for Ambedkarite Buddhists." As a Maharashtrian who had grown up in an Ambedkarite Buddhist family in India, he said that he had not been drawn to the ritualistic side of Ambedkarite Buddhism as a child, but

> today, I promote that as a cultural identity so that our people, the Ambedkarites, don't have to be drawn into Hindu culture or Hindu temples. Because Ambedkar created a distinct Buddhist identity so we must be proud about that.... Before Ambedkar International Mission came into being, all these families didn't know where to go. They were there in America and they didn't know where to go. They would go into the Hindu temple because at least there is some Indian culture there. There was no platform for the Ambedkarite Buddhist to practice or share their cultural identity.

Besides AIM, the other national organization is the *Ambedkar Association of North America* (AANA), formed in 2008, also around a strong Buddhist identity. In addition to these two organizations, there are a variety of local Ambedkarite organizations and reading groups. Some Ambedkarites in North America also purchased some land in the Washington, DC area to develop the Ambedkar International Center at the nation's capital. Thenmozhi Soundararajan, a charismatic, second-generation Dalit American woman with the Twitter handle "Dalit Diva," was one of the very few publicly visible Dalit rights activists in the United States at the start of my study of Dalit American activism in 2017 and the only full-time activist. As president of the AANA and founder of *Equality Labs* (an Ambedkarite technology organization formed in 2015 by Dalit feminists to mobilize on an anti-caste platform and around other axes of oppression), she engaged with issues in the United States and India in her multifaceted activism. Describing herself as a "proud Dalit-American," she urged Dalits to celebrate the resilience of their oppressed communities and their traditions of resistance and survival. She also argued strongly that the shame of the caste system should be on savarna (privileged) castes, who maintained and benefited from the system, and not on oppressed groups. Suraj Yengde, a more recently visible U.S. Dalit activist, had a PhD and a law degree and was a postdoctoral fellow at the Harvard Kennedy School affiliated with African American studies during the latter part of this research. He too wrote and spoke extensively about Dalit rights.

Ravidassia *sabhas* (worship centers) formed in several areas of the country with a large community including in New York City, several in the larger Bay Area and in central California, and some in Texas. Most Ravidassias are strong Ambedkarite supporters and work with Ambedkarite groups to mobilize around Dalit issues.

Since neither Christianity nor Islam is a uniquely Indian religion, Dalit Christians and Muslims in the United States often opt to join larger, mixed-race churches or mosques where their caste identity is hidden and they are just viewed as "Indians." Perhaps for this reason I did not find any Dalit Christian American advocacy organizations,[8] though I did locate a few individual Dalit Christian activists. Rachel McDermott, who conducted a study of Dalit Christians in the New York City area, was only able to talk to Dalit pastors serving non-Indian or "mixed" Indian and non-Indian congregations. These pastors were often open about their caste background as "a luxury or a necessity," but McDermott was told not to talk to Indian congregants since they would be uncomfortable revealing their family origins (McDermott 2008, 234). McDermott mentions that when a Dalit Christian leader appealed to U.S. Dalit Christians to help fundraise for Dalits in India, she was rebuked. They told her, "Why are you bringing Dalit issues up here? We came here to forget and get away from all this" (quoted in McDermott 2009, 96). Dalit American pastors have tried to support Indian Dalit groups by raising funds from White Christian congregations. Some also worked to lobby churches, Congress, and the United Nations. I did not find any Dalit Muslim advocacy organizations or activists, though I talked to some Indian American Muslim leaders who said their organizations (such as the *Indian American Muslim Council* [IAMC]) supported Dalit mobilization, particularly against Hindu nationalism.

Religion is probably the biggest barrier to the unity of the U.S. anti-caste movement, and an Ambedkarite identity may not easily dissolve religious differences. At an event organized in April 2017 by the AANA in the Bay Area (attended by a research assistant), a Ravidassia member in the audience pointed out that the Dalit community was very diverse, hailing from a variety of Indian regions, linguistic backgrounds, and religious traditions, including Buddhists, Ravidassias, Kabir panthis, Hindus, atheists, Christians, and Muslims. He raised the question of how they could come together in the United States to challenge the resources and the message of "high caste" Hindus who mobilized around the importance of "preserving Indian/Hindu culture" (which Dalits view as a code for maintaining "upper caste" privilege). Since 2020, after a momentous lawsuit in California around caste discrimination against a Dalit engineer, Dalit groups have managed to come together, gain powerful allies among Indian Americans and groups in the wider society, and lead important anti-caste initiatives to get caste recognized as a protected category in the United States (see Chapter 4).

Dalit Freedom Network

I learned about the formation of the *Dalit Freedom Network* (renamed *Dignity Freedom Network* in 2019) over lunch with two of its activists in the summer of 2018 and during a subsequent phone conversation with another activist. On November 4, 2001, at a mass conversion rally at Ambedkar Bhavan in New Delhi, between 20,000 and 50,000 Dalits (the exact numbers are in dispute) repeated the 22 vows that Ambedkar had taken in 1956 and converted to Buddhism. This was during the BJP's first term in power at the national level, and the party had tried to ban the rally and deployed police at train and bus stations to turn away tens of thousands of Dalits who wanted to enter New Delhi. The Dalit conversion rally was held with the support and cooperation of Indian Christian leaders of the All-India Christian Council (AICC). Dalit leaders such as Udit Raj who organized the conversion event invited Christians to educate Dalit children (many of the prestigious English-medium schools in India are run by Christian groups). Dr. Joseph D'Souza, president of the AICC, accepted the invitation on behalf of the Indian Christian community. Recognizing that vast funding would be necessary to build and run schools to educate Dalits, D'Souza, who had traveled extensively in the United States, asked his American contacts if they would start an American 501(c)(3) organization focused on educating Dalit children. This was how the Dalit Freedom Network was established.

DFN activists (mostly White Christians) recognized that to be successful in fundraising and advocacy they first needed to raise awareness of the plight of Dalits in the United States at a time when few people had even heard the term "Dalit." DFN activists reached out to a variety of American Christian organizations, church partners, foundations, aid organizations, and individual donors. After a year or two, DFN activists began to make some contacts in Washington, DC, especially with some members of Congress who were on various religious liberties committees (discussed further in Chapter 5). However, they realized that when they focused on advocacy, the fundraising went down considerably. Consequently, since 2014, the organization focused primarily on fundraising to support their work in India. However, D'Souza has been doing some advocacy in Washington, DC. The DFN hired a public relations consultant with experience on Capitol Hill to help D'Souza gain recognition on the Hill and network with a variety of congressional and Senate offices. Consequently, D'Souza got invited to a variety of meetings in Washington, DC (such as the National Prayer Breakfast) and was the only Indian who was part of the Congress of Christian Leaders, formed in 2018, described to me as "a group of high-level religious leaders who get together for dialogue on religious liberties issues."

Interestingly, even though Ambedkarite organizations and the DFN had many shared goals, such as the uplift of Dalit families and the education of Dalit children in India, there were almost no links between them, perhaps because Ambedkarites were suspicious of the agenda of White evangelical groups (the major supporters and activists associated with the DFN). DFN activists on their part do not reach out to Indian Americans or even Indian American Christian churches. They told me that when they had tried to do so, they had been rebuffed by (presumably privileged-caste) individuals who drew on their experiences in urban India to argue that caste was not an issue in India anymore.

Indian Muslim American Organizations

According to a 2017 Pew Research Center study of American Muslims, the largest group of foreign-born Muslims in the United States was from South Asia (35 percent, compared to 25 percent from the Middle East).[9] Indian Muslims made up 7 percent of foreign-born U.S. Muslims (Pew Research Center, 2017). Several Indian Muslims arrived in the 1950s and 1960s as students. The largest group hailed from the former princely state of Hyderabad in South Central India (Leonard 2001). Hyderabad state (called Andhra Pradesh in the postcolonial period), with a Hindu majority but a significant number of Muslims, remained under a *Nizam* (Muslim ruler) through the period of British colonialism and until 1948, when it was annexed by the Indian Army. After Hyderabad state was annexed, thousands of its elite Muslims emigrated first to Pakistan and then to the Middle East, England, and North America (Afzal 1991, 4). Another large group of activists of Muslim American background hailed from the Kashmir region.

The *Consultative Committee of Indian Muslims* established in 1967 in Chicago seems to be the first documented contemporary Indian American Muslim organization in the United States to draw the attention of American society to the attacks against Muslims taking place in India (Afzal 1991, 2). As the numbers of Indian American Muslims increased, and as Hindu nationalism was rising in the 1980s, leading to the rise in tensions between Hindus and Muslims in India, several other Indian American Muslim organizations were established in various parts of the country. The *Association of Indian Muslims of America* (AIM) was formed in Washington, DC in 1985, and the *American Federation of Muslims from India* (AFMI) was formed in Detroit in 1989. The *Indian Muslims Relief Committee* (IMRC) was also formed in the 1980s. While these Indian Muslim organizations were primarily focused on the uplift of Muslims in India, with a particular focus on improving their educational status, as Hindu nationalism continued to escalate, many of them took a stand in the U.S. public sphere to oppose Hindutva and to promote secularism and communal harmony in India.

A 1989 conference organized by the Indian Muslim Relief Committee (IMRC) at Stanford University, with papers being subsequently published as a book edited by Omar Khalidi (1991), led to the airing of a wide range of perspectives on the position of Muslims in India and what Indian American Muslims should do to help their coreligionists in India. For instance, Ahrari (1991, 26) floated the view, which also had support from some other authors in the collection, that India was a "paper democracy," with Muslims being treated as second-class citizens. Many conference participants agreed that it was important for Indian American Muslims to create and support a professional body that would become "an American lobby for Muslims in India" (Anisurrahman 1991). Some talked about how difficult it was to critique India's human rights record with respect to Muslims, due to the respect that India received in the United States for being "the world's largest democracy" (Hamid 1991, 44), the multi-million-dollar lobbying of the Indian government itself, the specter of Middle Eastern terrorism, and the "powerful Jewish influence" in the United States (T. Wright 1991, 53). Another contributor, Usama Khalidi, however, argued that the best strategy for Indian American Muslims to adopt was to "participate in the political process [in the United States] as nationalist Indians" (U. Khalidi 1991, 60) *and* as patriotic Americans, embracing pluralism, secularism, and human rights for minorities as important ideals for both India and the United States. Usama Khalidi (1991, 62) went on to argue that Indian American Muslims should emulate the Jewish lobby, whose "enormous success" in the United States was due to "the fact that it has always advanced its objectives by arguing that they were in the American national interest." As we will see, Indian American Muslims adopted both strategies.

In 1981, Dr. Sayyid Syeed, a Muslim from Kashmir who came to the United States to do his PhD, was one of the cofounders of the *Islamic Society of North America* (ISNA), an umbrella organization to unite and bring together Muslim Americans from a variety of backgrounds in the United States and Canada. ISNA continues to be the largest and most diverse Muslim American organization. Another American Muslim organization in which Indian Americans have taken key leadership roles is the *Muslim Public Affairs Council* (MPAC), formed in 1988. However, Muslim American mobilization around U.S. domestic issues is primarily conducted by the *Council on American Islamic Relations* (CAIR), formed in 1994. CAIR was founded by Palestinian activists, and Arab Americans still are a dominant force in the organization. Indian Americans have been part of some of the chapters of CAIR. Dr. Syeed took over as secretary-general of ISNA between 1994 and 2006 and successfully revived the organization. Subsequently, he worked as the national director of its interfaith efforts. He has also been involved in several other endeavors. Speaking at the Silver Jubilee function of the Association for Indian Muslims (AIM) in 2010 (https://aim-america.org/videos.html), Dr. Sayyid Syeed said that he had moved to the Washington, DC area in 1984 and had become interested in working

> to redefine Islam in a new context. We cannot turn to Saudi Arabia. We cannot go to Tehran or some other center that have served in the past as Islamic cultural centers. We were preparing for a new millennium where Islam, in a new contemporary situation, will be able to give new inspiration and sense of direction.... This is a gift of Indian American Muslims to India. Because Indian Muslims are themselves worried. What does it mean to be a Muslim in a democratic country? They are looking for models.

In this extract Dr. Syeed argues that Saudi Arabia is not the authority on modern Islam and that he wanted to understand what role Islam could play in multicultural, democratic societies like the United States. These models in turn would be of great relevance to India and would be the "gift" of Indian American Muslims like himself to India. Like Dr. Syeed, I found that many of the Indian American Muslim activists I interviewed challenged the common assumption that Saudi Arabia was the font of "real" or "authentic" Islam and critiqued some Middle Eastern Islamic practices. For instance, in my interview with "Salman," he shared:

> I am increasing upset with South Asians dressing like Arabs. It is due to their inferiority complex. They feel that they can look like a Muslim only that way. [One example is] women adopting Saudi type head covering as opposed to the dupatta [a long piece of cloth worn in many styles by South Asian women as a clothing accessory, which can be draped around the head and breasts].

Dr. Sayyid Syeed wrapped up his 2010 speech at the AIM Silver Jubilee function by pointing out to his audience the privilege they had as Muslims in the United States, where they had a much greater degree of freedom than in most Muslim countries. He exhorted his largely Indian American audience, "It is good to send money to support schools in India, but you have a bigger job. You live in a pluralistic country [the United States]. It is unparalleled. Out of the 57 members of the Organization of Islamic Cooperation, 54 have lived in a colonial environment. Hardly three or four are democratic countries." Looking at his audience, which contained many women, he remarked that Indian American Muslim women were full participants in the Indian American Muslim community and in the wider American society, whereas "if you are looking to Saudi Arabia, you wouldn't even drive." He talked about the fact that he had three daughters and had made sure each learned to drive well and also became full participants in American society. He remarked that all three now held leadership positions in the United States.

American Muslims of Indian origin have been civically active in both broader American Muslim organizations and specifically Indian American Muslim organizations. Some have been active in Indian American organizations as well. Their professional background, English fluency, and experience of living as a religious minority in a secular democracy gave Indian Muslims an advantage over many other Muslim groups and propelled them into leadership positions in broader American Muslim organizations (Leonard 2003). Being active in pan-ethnic American religious organizations is an option available to Indian American Muslims and Christians, unlike for Indian American Hindus and Sikhs, and this option impacts the patterns of activism of both Indian American Muslims and Christians, but in quite different ways, as we will see below (this section and the Indian Christian section). Not surprisingly, there are differences in the orientation of Indian American Muslims who are active in larger American Muslim organizations versus those who are active as Indian American Muslims.

An Indian American Muslim activist who was very open and helpful told me that several Indian American Muslims that I named to him who were active in larger American Muslim organizations (in most cases, I had read their biographies online and learned that they were of Indian origin) did not publicly identify as Indian Muslims except in interfaith contexts where being from a pluralistic country carried some cachet. He explained, "Indian Muslims [who are active in American Muslim organizations] have underplayed their Indian identity. They have bought into the project of an American Muslim. It is also due to their alienation from some of India's policies. Pakistanis on the other hand never relinquish their Pakistani identity."

Perhaps this practice of "underplaying" their Indian identity explains why several first-generation Indian American Muslims I talked to as part of this project (all male, all well educated, and all individuals who participated in American Muslim organizations) emphasized very early in their conversations with me that they considered themselves to be *American* Muslims and not *Indian American* Muslims. I was intrigued, since distancing from an Indian or even South Asian identity was not a sentiment I had heard expressed by first-generation Indian immigrants from other religious backgrounds whom I had interviewed up to that point. Granted, this could have been because I made clear to my interviewees that I was interested in talking to American Muslims of Indian background or ancestry (who cannot easily be distinguished by appearance or last names from other Muslims, particularly of Pakistani background) as part of my research on the activism of Indian Americans. Of course, it was also because these individuals were part of larger American Muslim organizations, but I was still piqued by their emphasis on an American identity. For instance, "Omar" told me:

> Basically, I define myself as an American Muslim. I take great pride in the fact that I was born in India, and I went to school in India. After I finished my college over there, I moved to the United States. And then I took the U.S. citizenship as most of immigrants do, and now I take a great pride in this, that I'm an American, I'm a Muslim, and you know, every single day, I take great pride in it.

Similarly, Salman said, "I don't identify as an Indian Muslim. Because I migrated here, I have been living here for more of my adult life than in India. I sold my house in India. In fact, I am part of an effort to create an American Muslim identity" (this effort and the role of Indian American Muslims will be discussed further in Chapter 4). In their interviews as well as their presentations at Indian American Muslim events (I accessed some via YouTube), they also emphasized their admiration for the United States and that they were patriotic Americans.

Omar criticized those who were active in Indian American Muslim organizations as being "so focused on India" that they do not get involved in their neighborhoods or their children's schools, an attitude that Omar, who was very involved with the wider community in his region, said he opposed. He explained that this was because most members of Indian American Muslim organizations tended to be recent immigrants who were H-1 visa holders or those with green cards. However, Omar may have drawn this dichotomy too sharply, since I found that many Indian American Muslims leaders who were active in larger American Muslim or other organizations also tended to be called on to help Indian American Muslim organizations as well.

Leaders of Indian American Muslim organizations such as AIM and AFMI, for their part, emphasized that they were in support of Indian interests by distancing themselves from Pakistani Americans and by stressing the multicultural and multireligious nature of India (Agarwala 2016; Kurien 2001). For instance, in an interview with sociologist Rina Agarwala, Kaleem Kawaja of AIM stressed, "We want to fight for human rights in India, but at the same time we do not want to be used by Pakistan [as an anti-Indian force]. So, we cooperate with the Indian government" (quoted in Agarwala 2016, 940). Consequently, they have lobbied U.S. policymakers on behalf of India in conflicts between India and Pakistan (Agarwala 2016, 938). In my earlier research on the AFMI branch in Southern California in the late 1990s, I found that AFMI leaders were trying to counter Hindu nationalist constructions of India as Hindu by emphasizing that current-day India is the result of a long interaction between Hinduism and Islam, and that India is a "multi-racial, multi-cultural, multi-lingual, and multi-religious country" (Kurien 2001, 273). I heard this discourse even in my interview with an Indian American Muslim leader in 2018. While telling me that the Indian government not protecting Indian Muslims against attacks in 1992 and 2002 "rankled" Indian American Muslims, "Hassan" made the case that "India has been a composite society, multi-religious composite society for thousands of years, and this kind of happening is against the spirit of India." To avoid the Hindu nationalist discourse of Indian Muslims as a threat, these organizations also pitched their efforts as being important for India as a whole, rather than just for Indian Muslims. For instance, Agarwala quotes a former president of AFMI as saying, "When we are trying to raise funds [from Indian American Muslims], we explain that a bad neighbor brings down the value of your house. Similarly, if one section of the community is educated, and another is not, it won't do anything for the country. People will fight and bring the country down" (Agarwala 2016, 939–940). In other words, he emphasizes the need for Indian Muslims to be educated so they can contribute to the progress of India. At their annual conventions, all these Indian American Muslim organizations invite prominent Indian politicians and public personalities from different religious backgrounds who have been working to promote secularism. Invited dignitaries also include representatives of the local Indian consulate and leaders of local Indian American organizations (all likely to be non-Muslims).

The anti-Muslim violence in Gujarat in 2002, however, led to considerable alarm and disenchantment on the part of Indian American Muslims. A new organization, the *Indian Muslim Council*, subsequently renamed *Indian American Muslim Council* (IAMC), was launched after this event. On their website, they indicate that this was because Indian Muslims in the United States realized that "it was time to act. Gujarat 2002 was clearly only the more visible tip of a dangerous iceberg [and] the poison of Hindutva-fascism had not only reached alarming proportions in India but had also insidiously infiltrated many institutions and individuals in the USA, particularly those related to India" (IMC-USA 2002). However, speaking to me, "Anwar," one of the leaders of the IAMC, adopted a different tone. Anwar told me that the IAMC was formed after 2002 since "at the time, the Indian Muslim community in the United States felt a need for a voice within the diaspora to represent not only Indian Muslims but also to join hands with other minorities within the diaspora and other like-minded individuals who were concerned about safeguarding pluralism and secularism in India." The IAMC formed alliances with Indian American Sikhs, Christians, Dalit Buddhists, and secularist Hindus to critique Hindu nationalism in India. Anwar emphasized his patriotism to India, telling me, "We want to make sure that we are not perceived as an anti-India group, we are not . . . what we are doing is our patriotic duty to safeguard India's pluralist and tolerant ethos." Similarly, speaking to sociologist Rina Agarwala (2016, 940), Shaheen Khateeb, founding member and former general secretary of the IAMC, emphasized, "We want India to be a more perfect country. What we want is India to flourish. We are proud to be Indian. And we don't want any part of the society to be left behind."

Kashmir and Opposing Muslim and Hindu Advocacy Organizations

The status of the (now former) Indian state of Jammu and Kashmir has been contentious in the diaspora, spawning opposing U.S. advocacy groups representing the interests of Hindus and Muslims, addressing themselves to policymakers in the United States and the United Nations. Until 2019, Jammu and Kashmir was a state at the northern tip of India on the border of Pakistan with a majority Muslim population but including regions with substantial Hindu and Buddhist populations (Jammu and Ladakh, respectively). One-third of Kashmir is held by Pakistan and the rest by India. From the Kashmiri Muslim side, there were two long-established U.S. organizations working to publicize human rights violations in the Kashmir Valley and to seek solutions: the *Kashmiri American Council* (KAC) and the *Kashmir Study Group* (KSG). The Kashmiri American Council was established in 1990 in Washington, DC by Ghulam Nabi Fai, of Muslim Kashmiri background (born in the Indian-administered portion of Kashmir). Its mission statement describes the organization as being "dedicated to raising the level of awareness in the United States about the struggle of the people of Kashmir for self-determination. It is also dedicated to the promotion of social contacts among families with Kashmiri ancestry settled across the country, regardless of their religious and political affiliations" (Pew Research Center 2011, citing "personal correspondence"). Kashmiri Muslim American activists maintain that Pakistan directly intervened in Kashmir only during the 1990–1994 period, but that for the rest of the time, the mobilization has been led by local Muslims fed up with the Indian military occupation of their homeland and the restrictions, oppression, and violence they faced.

In a 2019 interview, I spoke to an older Kashmiri Muslim American activist, "Raheem." Raheem arrived in the United States in the 1970s

> and at that time, the sense of us being a separate entity, being conscious of our heritage was becoming more and more manifest in our own thinking.

And we also had a sense of deprivation of our history because when we were in Kashmir ... the books were mostly India-centric.... We were not, for example, told about the massacres [in 1947] that took place in the city of Jammu where a quarter of a million people were wiped out.

He said that a group of them started getting active around the issue of self-determination for Kashmiris. Initially, it was composed of just a few hundred people, and they focused on educational activities, spreading some literature, and organizing meetings and annual conferences under an organization called the *Kashmiri Muslims of North America*. A turning point came when elections in Kashmir were rigged in 1987, leading to the development of protests and eventually an insurgency after 1989. The Kashmiri American Council (KAC), formed in 1990, began work as a lobby to bring awareness to human rights violations in Kashmir (the Indian central government–imposed governor's rule on the state in 1990, which lasted until 1996). Raheem emphasized to me that the goal was to create an independent Kashmir, "a place for everybody and [including] Hindus ... that it will be a pluralistic society not based on Islam."

Until at least 2011, the KAC used to hold regular press briefings as well as conferences, including an annual conference on Capitol Hill, with leading South Asian experts, Pakistani government officials (Indian government officials never attended), and members of Congress in attendance to discuss the human rights abuses in Kashmir perpetrated by the Indian military. Ghulam Nabi Fai, the executive director, also gave regular speeches in universities around the United States and at venues around the world, including at the United Nations Human Rights Council, and traveled to countries around the world to spread his message (Haniffa 2011). Describing the Kashmiri independence mobilization as an "indigenous movement," Fai drew parallels between the Kashmiri and Egyptian uprisings (Kashmiri American Council 2011). The Kashmir American Council also developed close relationships with American Muslim groups such as ISNA and CAIR, which supported their mobilization.

The Kashmir Study Group (KSG) was formed by Farooq Kathwari, a person of Muslim Kashmiri background (also born in the Indian-administered portion of Kashmir). Kathwari set up the Kashmir Study Group in 1996 to get a group of academics, former diplomats, and policymakers to work on peaceful solutions to the intractable problem in Kashmir. Kathwari, the CEO of Ethan Allen, one of the largest U.S. furniture chains, and a very wealthy man, financially supported the Kashmir Study Group himself. The group came up with the Livingston Proposal in 1998 and a revised version in 2005 based on feedback. The Livingston Proposal called for the creation of five geo-cultural self-governing entities, two in the Pakistani area of Kashmir and three in the Indian-controlled area, with open borders with each other and with India and Pakistan. Refugees would have the right of return (Kashmir Study Group 2005). Since the Indian government maintains that it does not welcome any outside mediation on what they see as an internal problem, the group could not play an official role in mediating the Kashmir crisis. However, at least two members came out with books drawing on the research of the KSG (T. Schaffer 2005; H. Schaffer 2009), and Kathwari met with officials in the prime minister's office in India after the report came out (Swami 2006).

On the Kashmiri Hindu side, the main U.S. advocacy organization was the *Indo-American Kashmir Forum* (IAKF), formed in 1991. The *International Kashmir Federation* (IKF) was another group that also rallied around the Kashmiri Pandit cause. The founder of that group, Jeevan Zutshi, was a co-founder of the IAKF and continued to be involved in its activities. Kashmiri Pandit activists in the United States argue that Kashmiri Hindus were "ethnically cleansed" from the Kashmir valley by Islamic fighters supported by Pakistan and that the Jammu and Kashmir state government (controlled by Muslims) had refused to provide help to allow the Hindu refugees to return. They were worried about attempts by the Jammu and Kashmir state government to change the Hindu names of various parts of Kashmir to Muslim names—in other words, "the systematic eradication of all rights and roots of Hindus in the valley." They also criticized the Indian government for its inaction in dealing with the plight of Kashmiri Hindu Pandits who were driven out of the valley, many of whom continue to live in refugee camps. Vijay Sazawal, an activist of the Indo-American Kashmir Forum from the 1990s, met with top leaders in India, Pakistan, and the United States and testified several times before the United Nations Human Rights Council (UNHCR) and at hearing rooms of the U.S. Congress and British Parliament (Sazawal 2013; Swami 2006).

On the Kashmiri Hindu side, I spoke in 2007 and 2009 with an activist, "Rajesh," from the IAKF about the struggles their organization had since its inception because it represented a small minority group and had little funding and clout. Rajesh told me that the Indian government was not supportive since it did not want the situation in Kashmir discussed, particularly in international forums. In contrast, Rajesh said "the other side" (i.e., the side representing Kashmiri Muslims, particularly the Kashmiri American Foundation) was getting large amounts of funding from the Pakistani government, which they were using to "penetrate U.S. legislators and the media." Some Hindu nationalist groups in the United States joined their cause, but these were groups whose support the IAKF did not want at the time. Rajesh described the faceoff between the Kashmiri Muslim and Kashmiri Hindu organizations as a "classic David and Goliath situation." He said that through a "laser-point strategy" whereby they identified key legislators around the country and their aides and worked to educate them, IAKF members were able to challenge or at least "inoculate" U.S. legislators to the Kashmir story of "the other side" by bringing up the refugee camps of the Kashmiri Hindus and the fact that they were not allowed to return to their homes. While Kashmiri Muslim advocates focused on violations of human rights taking place in Kashmir due to India's military presence in the region, IAKF advocates framed the issue of Kashmiri Hindus as one of "ethnic cleansing" (instead of an "exodus" out of the valley). They argued that what was really taking place was that "Islamic zealots were trying to implement an Islamic rule in the region, by using money gained from the narcotics trade." "We were the first to coin the term 'narco-terrorism,'" Rajesh told me, and while Americans were not too concerned with terrorism at that time, the narcotics angle grabbed their interest, "because they understood that they were the end-recipients of the narcotic trade in South Asia."

Rajesh told me that the attacks of September 11, 2001, brought a change in American concerns about militant Islam, Al Qaeda, and the Taliban, "and the concept of them [Muslim leaders in Kashmir] being freedom fighters went out of the window." Gradually, the issue of the Kashmiri Hindu Pandits gained recognition in the United States and in other international fora such as at the United Nations and the European Economic Community[10] and even in India, where a report in February 2009 presented to the upper house of the Indian parliament for the first time had a detailed account of the attacks against Kashmiri Pandits and the need for their rehabilitation. Acknowledging that the situation in Kashmir was intractable because of the conflicting interests of Pakistan and India, Rajesh mentioned that what

Kashmiri Hindus wanted was *Panum-Kashmir*, a separate area in the state of Jammu and Kashmir, governed by the Indian constitution, instead of Article 370, where Kashmiri Pandits could live harmoniously with other peace-loving religious groups. They were pushing for this since they didn't know when the larger Kashmir problem would be solved and did not "want to become extinct in the process." Rajesh added that these types of "people-centric" as opposed to "land-centric" solutions seemed more viable and that these solutions were the ones that were being explored by the different sides (including by Kathwari's Kashmir Study Group). "This shows how a small group of people who have lost their homeland, and don't have much money but a lot of passion can get things done," he concluded.

In June 2009, the International Kashmir Federation and the Hindu American Foundation cohosted a briefing on the situation in Kashmir, cosponsored by a variety of Indian American organizations such as the USINPAC. The briefing was to alert the audience (which included congressional staffers, members of the U.S. Commission on International Religious Freedom [USCIRF], and the media) to Pakistan's support for terrorism in Kashmir and the concern that aid from the United States to Pakistan might be diverted against India. Ishani Chowdhury of the HAF summed it up by saying:

> A cause for major concern is President Obama's recent promise made in Cairo last week for another $ 1.2 billion aid each year for the next several years to Pakistan. . . . Our demand as Hindu Americans and as U.S. taxpayers is that any aid mandate greater oversight and strict accountability so that U.S. taxpayer dollars are used by Pakistan in fighting the ongoing battles against the Taliban and improving the lives of Pakistanis, rather than continuing its six decade long cross-border, proxy war against India. (HAF 2009)

In 2010, Kashmiri Hindu leaders from across the country, led by Jeevan Zutshi of the International Kashmir Federation, met with U.S. administration officials and lawmakers to alert them to the plight of Kashmiri Hindu Pandits and ask for their help in solving the Kashmir problem. Apparently for the first time, in a departure from advocacy focused on alerting the U.S. administration to Pakistani-supported terrorism in the Kashmir Valley, they brought up the topic of "Panun Kashmir," "where Kashmiri Pandits can live in peace while holding onto their culture and traditions" along with "moderate and secular Muslim friends" since Pandits have coexisted in peace in Kashmir with Muslims for hundreds of years (Haniffa 2010).

Sikh American Advocacy Groups

While Sikhs started migrating to the United States at the turn of the twentieth century, most contemporary Sikh Americans are post-1965 immigrants. After the passage of the 1965 Immigration Act, Sikhs in the United States were able to sponsor their relatives from India. Others arrived for higher education or for work in professional fields. An early immigrant who came as a student in the 1960s described how the turban worn by many Sikh men made them stand out from other Indians. "When we came here, we were out and out Indians, you know. The identity of the Sikh was forced upon us when the local people looked on us turbaned people as different. So, we were Indians at heart, and Sikhs by our looks." Because of the turban, other interviewees told me that Sikh men faced some "hostility and backlash" during the Iranian hostage crisis (1979–1980) "because people associated Sikhs with Ayatollah Khomeini, because he wore a turban." Issues connected with the turban and beard led Sikh Americans to form an organization—the *Sikh Council of North America*—in 1979 to unite at the national level to combat discrimination.

Sikhs were the first Indian American religious group to lobby Congress. This was in response to the events of 1984 that stunned the Sikh community around the world and constituted a watershed moment, bringing together even those who had not been involved with the Sikh community until then. As one of my interviewees poignantly narrated, "We never thought, I never thought that a massacre [on us] would happen in India . . . we were part of India, we defended India, we spilt our blood in India for India, you know" (referring to the prominent role of Sikhs in the Indian Army). North American Sikhs held a large convention in Madison Square Garden in New York City on July 28, 1984 (this was after the invasion of the Golden Temple but before the large-scale anti-Sikh attacks in North India) with an estimated 2,500 in attendance and formed the *World Sikh Organization* to represent Sikhs in Canada, the United States, and Britain (at present the organization survives only in Canada). The leaders called for Sikhs supporting the Indian government "to disassociate themselves from that regime" (Howe 1984). There were many calls for Khalistan at the convention, but the final resolution defined it broadly as a place where Sikhs could "enjoy the 'glow of freedom'" promised by Nehru (Howe 1984). Sikhs in Canada and the United States mobilized to monitor events in India and to organize marches and protests in front of the Indian consulates and the United Nations in New York City. The *Sikh Foundation*, founded in the San Francisco Bay Area in 1967, hired a public relations team and prepared a full-page advertisement for newspapers in New York City, Washington, DC, San Francisco, and Los Angeles.[11] Through the help of the public relations team, Sikh commentators appeared on many radio and television shows and programs to discuss what was happening in India. Several Sikhs went to Washington, DC to lobby Congress "about the civil war against Sikhs happening in India" (the anti-Sikh attacks), in the words of one of my interviewees. Sikhs were successful in obtaining support from some Republicans in Congress, including Senator Jesse Helms (R-NC) and U.S. Representative Dan Burton (R-IN, founding member and cochair of the Pakistani caucus), who spoke about human rights violations in India in Congress on a regular basis. In the post-1984 period, a variety of Khalistani organizations formed in the United States, including the *Council of Khalistan* (founded in 1986) and the *Khalistan Affairs Center* (founded in 1991), both with offices in Washington, DC.

In the meantime, the Indian government undertook its own propaganda campaign. A book written by two well-known Toronto-based Canadian journalists on the investigation into the Air India disaster[12] makes the claim, based on reports from the reputed *India Today* magazine, that India had posted a number of "intelligence operatives" in North America from 1982 onward "to hijack" or discredit the Sikh separatist movement (Kashmeri and McAndrew 2005, 45). Several older Sikh men whom I interviewed seemed to be aware of this since they talked about "plants" by the Indian government being placed in Sikh communities. As one elderly man explained: "The thing is that, even before '84, I think, because of the Ghadar movement from USA, Sikhs have always been considered radicals by the Indian government. And so, it doesn't matter who is in Delhi [which party is in power], they always think that you know, anything that flares up [in India], flares up in United States." After the attack on the Golden Temple, the Indian government produced a video defending the raid and minimizing the damage on the temple and the casualties from the attack, as well as a glossy magazine praising the contributions of Sikhs to India and denouncing Sikh separatists. Around 50,000 video cassettes were sent to "every Singh [the last name of most Sikh men] they could find in North American telephone books, to every gurdwara [Sikh religious institutions] and Sikh society, and to key American and Canadian Hindus" at a cost of more than half a million dollars (Kashmeri and McAndrew 2005, 49). These efforts by the Indian government enraged Sikhs in North America. Geographer Thomas Lacroix (2016, 221) argued, based on his study of Sikhs in the United Kingdom, that the Indian government also used "the weapon of diplomacy" to make the case to countries where there were large Sikh diasporas (e.g., the United Kingdom, Canada, and the United States) that Khalistanis were terrorists to undermine their legitimacy in these countries and limit their migration.

Several Sikh interviewees mentioned that the events of 1984 created tensions with Hindus with whom they had cordial relations until that time. An older Sikh man from California told me, "I actually had a lot of Hindu friends . . . what happened in 1984 definitely created a wedge between the two communities . . . it took a long time to heal." Another issue that a large number of interviewees mentioned was that many Sikhs stopped identifying as "Indian" after the events of 1984. A second-generation man in his 30s said, "I was raised in a context, and this was part of my training earlier as a teen, where I was taught, we are Sikhs, we are Punjabis, we are not Indians, the Indian state has suppressed our community, and we ought to reject that identity." Another second-generation Sikh man similarly commented:

> I mean essentially . . . what's clear among most Americans [Sikhs] with whom I interact is that Indian identity is just not part of the equation . . . strangers come up to us in the streets all the time, especially with the turban and the beard, and they'll ask, you know, where are you from? Sometimes they'll say oh, are you from India? And I know many people including people in my own family who would say no, I'm not from India, I'm from Punjab. You know, just refuse to be identified with the Indian state.

A second-generation woman emphasized:

> For me, it was about my identity being primarily Sikh, and not Indian. I mean, I just always saw myself as Sikh. . . . I was well educated at a young age about the events of '84 and feel quite strongly about that to this day. I've always identified as Sikh, and as American. I have not identified with the Indian state.

In New York City, most Sikhs stopped attending the annual India Day Parade after 1984 and from 1986 on organized a separate Sikh Day Parade.

Indian Christian American Organizations

In 2012, Indian Christians constituted 18 percent of the Indian American population (Pew Research Center 2012).[13] This is far higher than their proportion in India, where they make up only around 2 percent. Syrian Christians from Kerala who are part of an ancient church from the Middle East trace their origin to the legendary arrival of Apostle Thomas on the shores of Kerala in 52 CE and his conversion of some locals, believed to be Brahmins, to Christianity. They constitute the largest group of Indian Christians in the United States (Williams 1996, 136). Syrian Christians are very proud of their Saint Thomas heritage, episcopal traditions, and "upper caste" status (see Kurien 2017a). Since Syrian Christians in Kerala are a well-integrated and prosperous minority with a very distinct sense of their identity and their caste status, they usually do not identify with oppressed-caste and tribal Christian converts in other parts of India (the majority of Indian Christians). This is the likely reason that Indian American Christians were so slow to form a national Indian American organization.

Even though Indian American Christians are substantially overrepresented in the United States, and many hail from the early wave of post-1965 immigrants, it was only in late 2000 that a national organization, the *Federation of Indian American Christians of North America* (FIACONA), was formed to represent all Indian American Christians. This was 30 years after Indian American Hindus, 16 years after Indian American Sikhs, and 11 years after Indian American Muslims had formed similar organizations. John Prabhudoss, an Indian American Christian activist who had grown up in an evangelical Christian family in South India, said he became concerned about the situation of Indian Christians as a young man, when Hindu nationalism was escalating in the 1980s. He moved to the United States in 1991 to "establish a base where I can network and create an awareness" about the threat facing Indian Christians. He was able to connect with a variety of U.S. Christian leaders working in the Reagan and Bush (Sr.) administrations. However, Indian Christians in the United States were uninterested in helping him.

For about, I would say about 10 years, until 2000, I had very little success in getting Indian American Christians to even understand the threat. So basically, I was working with mainly the [White American] Protestant and Pentecostal church in the U.S. on different issues and then when you talk about persecution of Christians, it resonates with them, so I was able to find allies among them. Within them. But I could not find even 4-5 leaders in the U.S. of Indian Christians.... Successful Indian American Christians could not really see it ... they were very uncomfortable even in thinking there should be an identity called Indian American Christians.

In the meantime however, the *Indian American Catholic Association* (IACA) had formed and was active in the Washington, DC area, meeting at the Catholic University of America, with the goal of installing a statue of *Our Lady of Good Health, Vailankanni* (the Marian deity in the Vailankanni shrine in Tamil Nadu state, known for her miracles of mental and physical healing, drawing over eight million devotees from all religious backgrounds every year) at the Basilica of the National Shrine of the Immaculate Conception in Washington, DC. In 1998, the year that the Hindu nationalist party, the BJP, came to power, there were a series of attacks against tribal Christians (mostly Catholic) in Gujarat state, leading to concern among the IACA. When the IACA and other Indian Christian leaders like John Prabhudoss in Washington, DC heard that the Indian prime minister, Atal Bihari Vajpayee, the head of the BJP-led government, was going to be making a presentation in front of the U.S. Congress in September 2000 during his official visit to the United States, they decided to organize an event to protest attacks against Christians in India. A coalition of Indian Christian organizations held a prayer vigil on Capitol Hill on September 14 while Vajpayee was addressing a joint session of Congress. John Prabhudoss told me that Prime Minister Vajpayee's visit received a lot of media coverage and that some members of Congress came over to the prayer vigil and started talking about their concerns regarding the violence against Christians in India. This was captured on live television and was rebroadcast twice. He continued:

> So eventually, at the end of this prayer vigil, on that particular day in front of the Capitol, [Indian American] people came from Chicago, from Houston, from West Coast, from New Jersey, New York, there were about 300 people—two busloads of people came from Chicago, we didn't even know

about them, that they were coming—but when they arrived in Washington, they heard about a group of Indian American Christians standing on the other side of the Capitol, they all came and joined. And they said, "We have to have a national umbrella organization." Now for me, it is nothing short of a miracle for even two Indians [to come to an agreement on anything]. And for about 40 different organizations to agree, I call it the second miracle that I have seen after Jesus walking on water! And that was the formation of FIACONA.

The Federation of Indian American Christian Organizations of North America (FIACONA) was formally launched on October 28, 2000, in Washington, DC. According to the press release announcing the formation of FIACONA, the organization was formed to

> counter the activities of [the] BJP-RSS-VHP-Bajrang Dal nexus. . . . We are fully aware that this neo-Nazi group has infiltrated many mainstream think tanks and political groups in the US particularly in Washington and in New York under the cover of cultural organizations or political educational forums. . . . We are particularly concerned about their increasing assault on the Christian Churches and members of the defenseless Christian communities in India. (FIACONA 2000)

I asked one of the long-time FIACONA leaders, "Prakash," why there were no second-generation Indian American Christians involved in FIACONA, unlike the case of Hindu and Sikh American organizations, which were often led by the second generation. Prakash's response was very interesting. He argued that the difference was because most second-generation Indian American Christians are integrated within local American churches (i.e., they do not remain in "ethnic" Indian American churches like their parents), and so they

> do not see themselves as a group of alien people who are not fitting into the society. Whereas, in the case of Indian American Hindus, Sikhs, and Muslims, professionally, they are okay, they interact, but when they go home, they go to a cocoon . . . they don't feel that they are part of the mainstream society. . . . In Washington and New York City, it's different. But you go to West Virginia, you go to Indiana, you go to Kentucky, they find it very difficult to identify themselves with the mainstream society, community.

He continued saying that while American-born children of Indian American Hindu, Sikh, and Muslim immigrants did not see themselves as "Indian," they also did not see themselves as part of the wider "Anglo-Saxon Protestant community." It was this insecurity "that propels the second generation to be active. And that is not the case with Indian Christians."[14]

To further make the point about the insecurity felt by these groups, Prakash told me about an Indian American Hindu friend, a Trump supporter who had brought some of Trump's children to visit a local Hindu temple. When Prakash asked him why he was supporting Trump and why it was important to bring Trump's children to visit a Hindu temple, the friend replied:

> This guy [Trump] is making all this noise about Muslims. It [the United States] is fundamentally, at the end of the day, it is a Christian nation. You may constitutionally say it is not and all those things, but practically speaking, at the end of the day, it is a Christian nation. And leaders like that raising supporters by talking about Muslims that way, it is [only] a matter of time before you start talking about Hindus. So, we want to make sure that we have a bridge, a connection to him.

In other words, the Hindu friend was articulating a sense of insecurity in the United States as a religious minority and the fear that anti-Muslim sentiment could easily be turned against Hindus as well. While it is not clear that all or even most Hindus would agree with this sentiment, it is nevertheless one that I have heard occasionally.

Conclusion

In this chapter, I show how and why religion became a central organizing principle among Indian Americans, shaping their political formation and mobilization from the 1980s on. Religious tensions and conflicts in India (built on groundwork laid during the colonial and immediate postcolonial period) triggered religious group mobilization and the formation of advocacy organizations for the major Indian American religious groups. The historical legacy of religion becoming the receptacle for ethnicity and the political success of Jewish organizations provided an opportunity structure for contemporary U.S. immigrants to mobilize through religious organizations. Having separate religious organizations also shaped the characteristics of groups differently. Initially, most Indian American religious organizations were formed by immigrants and oriented around transnational citizenship, or concerns around coreligionists in India. Since Hindu nationalism is based on a definition of Indian identity and culture that marginalizes or excludes Sikhs, Muslims, Christians, and Dalits, these groups formed religious organizations in the diaspora that individually and in coalition attempted to oppose political Hinduism. In fact, groups such as Indian Christians united to develop a national organization only in response to the Hindutva threat. Khalistani and Kashmiri Muslim groups frequently allied to discuss the human rights violations committed by the Indian state in Punjab and Kashmir (for instance, the U.S. House Subcommittee met in May 2004 to hear testimony from both groups). Over time, as we will see in subsequent chapters, second-generation leaders developed new organizations focused on cultural citizenship to obtain rights and recognition in the United States.

Notes

1. See https://www.uscirf.gov/sites/default/files/Tier2_INDIA.pdf and http://www.sacw.net/IMG/pdf/US_HinduNationalism_Nonprofits.pdf (both retrieved January 4, 2022).
2. However, at different periods, a unified Kashmiriyat (Kashmiri) identity was also articulated, which knit together various religiously defined groups in the region (Rai 2004; Zutshi 2019).
3. Most other Hindu castes in the valley converted to Islam beginning in the fourteenth century (Rai 2004, 37).
4. https://rajivmalhotra.com/infinity-foundation/ (retrieved November 18, 2018).
5. www.hinduamericanfoundation.org (retrieved March 3, 2006).
6. https://groups.google.com/g/soc.culture.indian/c/d49vB38zNjs?pli=1 (retrieved April 16, 2022).
7. In an April 2006 statement, Mihir Megani disavowed the essay—"I do not stand by what is written"—which he claimed he had written as a history major at the University of Michigan in the early 1990s. https://www.hinduamerican.org/blog/letter-to-editor-india-abroad-mihir-meghani-april-2006 (retrieved April 29, 2022).
8. Except for the *Dalit Solidarity Forum*, which became active in the U.S. public sphere in 2020 as part of a human rights coalition mobilizing around Hindu nationalist attacks against minorities in India.
9. But in the study, Iran is defined as being part of Asia. When Iranian Muslims (11 percent) are included in the Middle Eastern category, Muslims from the Middle East are the largest group from any single region.
10. The Baroness Nicholson Report of 2007 to the European Parliament overrode the position of the Pakistani ambassador to the European Union.
11. http://www.sikhfoundation.org/wp-content/uploads/2011/07/Preserving_Lives_1984/1984_Full_Page_advertisement.pdf, discussed in the archived interview http://www.1984livinghistory.org/2014/02/28/narinder-singh-kapany (retrieved November 28, 2016).
12. An Air India flight originating in Canada was blown up in 1985, allegedly by Sikh Canadian Khalistan supporters, killing all on board.
13. In 2022–2023, this fell to 15 percent (Pew Research Center 2023).
14. In an earlier book (Kurien 2017a), based on research among an Indian American Christian group, I noticed that second-generation Indian American Christians were turning away from their parents' "ethnic churches" and were orienting themselves to wider American, particularly evangelical, churches.

3

Ethnic versus Pan-Ethnic Mobilization

Indian American versus South Asian American Groups

A section of financially powerful and politically well-connected Indian Americans has emerged during the last decade. They have effectively mobilized on issues ranging from the nuclear tests in 1998 to Kargil Conflict, played a crucial role in generating a favourable climate of opinion in Congress and defeating anti-India legislation there.

—Government of India (2001, xx–xi)

The issues that we are addressing—primarily civil rights—those issues impact many groups from South Asia in the U.S. in exactly the same way. Issues like immigration, anti-discriminatory issues, hate crimes, the issues are roughly the same. [Also] our focus is primarily on younger people and the future of our community in our country. If you examine what is happening in the younger community, they don't view themselves within the narrow nationality-based identification that the first generation does. A lot of times they refer to themselves as South Asian or simply Desi because the nationality distinctions don't mean anything for them. I think the backgrounds in terms of growing up are very, very similar. We all come from roughly similar cultures.

—Debashish Mitra (*South Asian American Leaders of Tomorrow*, 2003 interview)

For a long time now, I have been unhappy about the "South Asia" fixation a lot of US-based Indians exhibit. . . . [I]t makes much more sense to push the "Indian" brand forward. We lose by pushing "South Asia."

—Srinivasan (2000)

Even though the Indian American community began to fragment with the rise of religious divisions, attempts to form unified Indian American advocacy organizations continued. In part this was due to the power of the "ethnic" paradigm in U.S. politics where groups are expected to unify and mobilize around their ancestral national identity. The "ethnic" model of mobilization and identity draws on the experiences of European immigrants arriving in the United States who experienced some hostility, discrimination, and exclusion but eventually became integrated into the U.S. "mainstream" (Kibria 2002, 2). As we have seen, the "ethnic" model homogenizes ethnic groups and their political interests. The Indian government, through U.S Indian embassies, also played an important role in encouraging and shaping this mobilization.

Over time, a new type of mobilization began to develop among a section of "progressive" Indian Americans, mostly from the second generation: the formation of a "South Asian" identity and South Asian American organizations, which "took off" after the attacks of September 11, 2001. Pan-ethnicity, or the forming of broader coalitions among ethnic groups that are lumped together, is another basis of identification and mobilization in the United States in addition to national origin and religion. Dina Okamoto and Cristina Mora (2014) discuss the variety of factors that led to the development of new pan-ethnic categories such as "Asian American" and "Hispanic or Latino American" including (1) state policies toward groups from a particular region as well as state classification schemes; (2) common processes of racialization of groups that "look alike"; (3) the discovery of cultural similarities as groups, particularly second and later generations, encounter each other in colleges; and (4) the efforts of ethnic entrepreneurs to create larger solidarities so that the group has more political clout. We will see that all these factors played a role in the development of the "South Asian American" category, but also that the South Asian American mobilization was an outcome of frustrations with the pan-ethnic "Asian American" model that seemed to exclude South Asian Americans. Those who mobilized as South Asian Americans draw on the "racial" instead of the "ethnic" model, on the experiences of racial minorities in the United States such as Blacks and Latinos for whom race has continued to be a barrier to full integration into

U.S. society, even after several generations (Kibria 2002, 2), unlike Indian American groups that drew on the "ethnic" model of White ethnic groups (e.g., Jewish organizations). For the most part, Indian American and South Asian American organizations have had very different goals and strategies.

After a section on the development of the India caucus as well as a contemporary India lobby and the role of the latter in financially supporting and advocating to U.S. policymakers for India's nuclearization, this chapter focuses on two models of mobilization embraced by Indian Americans. Those who were active as "Indian Americans" were largely from the immigrant generation and used the normative ethnic lobby group model of mobilization. The constant highlighting of the success of Indian Americans and parallels with Jews were probably attempts to sidestep racial categorization or perhaps to embrace the "common ancestry" Aryan theory. Immigrants who mobilized as "Indian Americans" generally identified with the nationalist ideology of India. Consequently, their focus was primarily on foreign policy, against Pakistan and Islam, and had Hindu underpinnings (almost all members of such organizations were of Hindu background). Second-generation progressives who mobilized as South Asian Americans, on the other hand, used a pan-ethnic, racial solidarity model. They preferred to confront and challenge racialization as well as the religious divides of their parents' generation instead of side-stepping these issues like immigrant activists. As American-born individuals, they had much greater interest in domestic issues and civil rights activism than issues connected with India. Generational differences also shaped gendered patterns of mobilization. Women were very prominent as leaders in South Asian American activism, unlike in Indian American activism, and South Asian organizations like SAALT have been sensitive to women's issues. Most second-generation organizations also have leadership rotation built into their structures, preventing the formation of organizations around one male leader as in the immigrant generation (see Table 3.1).

First, let's continue the story of the development of Indian American advocacy organizations from Chapter 1. We saw how advocacy groups formed by early post-1965 immigrants mobilized around the variety of racial restrictions they faced. Speaking to me in 2007, Dr. Manoranjan Dutta (who was instrumental in forming the *Association of Indians in America* [AIA] in 1967) chuckled as he described how diplomats at the Indian embassy were not happy about the political mobilization of Indian Americans around domestic U.S. issues. Dutta said they told the Indian American activists, "You should help with Indian government policy and not [focus on] U.S. policy."

Table 3.1 Ethnic versus pan-ethnic mobilization.

Basis of Mobilization	Characteristics of Groups	Main Focus	Nature of Mobilization	US Models Used	Ally Groups
Indian American identity	Largely immigrants	Foreign policy	Hindu-centric	Ethnic paradigm	Hindu and Jewish
South Asian American identity	Largely second generation	Domestic policy	Secular/Multi-religious	Racial paradigm	Sikh, Muslim, Dalit, non-white immigrants

In the immediate postindependence period, Jawaharlal Nehru, India's first prime minister, rolled out a policy where Indian immigrants naturalized in other countries were viewed with indifference or suspicion by the Indian government (Naujoks 2013, 44; Varadarajan 2010, 51–52). However, this changed over time. Facing a foreign exchange crisis in 1980, the Indian government created new bank accounts that permitted "nonresident Indians" (NRIs) to invest their money in India.[1] Rajiv Gandhi, Nehru's grandson, who became prime minister in 1984, took a different approach to Indian Americans than his grandfather. Ramesh Kapur, a pioneer post-1965 activist who became politically active in Democratic politics through his involvement in the Dukakis campaign, told me that he had been at one of Rajiv Gandhi's U.S. press conferences when Gandhi declared, "Indian Americans are our ambassadors in the U.S." Ramesh said that Rajiv Gandhi was the first Indian prime minister to see Indian Americans as a catalyst for the United States–India relationship and that P. K. Kaul, the Indian ambassador to the United States between 1986 and 1989 (when Rajiv Gandhi was prime minister), was the first to reach out to the Indian American community to help India. In response, the *National Federation of Indian Americans* (NFIA) mobilized Indian Americans in 1987 and successfully lobbied Congress against the sale of AWACS planes to Pakistan (A. Sharma 2017, 103).

The Formation of the India Caucus and a Contemporary "India Lobby"

The India caucus was formed in 1993 in the House of Representatives. To set the context for this development, some background to the relationship between India and the United States is important. Trying to stay neutral in the escalating Cold War, Prime Minister Nehru announced in 1954 that India would pursue a policy of "nonalignment" and would not ally with either the United States or the Soviet Union, instead pursuing an independent policy. India became one of the leaders of the Non-Alignment Movement (NAM), creating a "third bloc" of around 120 newly independent "developing" countries. At the same time, India pursued some socialist policies and signed a friendship treaty with the Soviet Union (trying to offset the alliance that Pakistan was cultivating with the United States and China) and received aid from the USSR for several infrastructure projects (Talbott 2006, 10). NAM countries, including India, periodically criticized the United States and its European allies for some of their policies. India's nonalignment, overtures toward the Soviet Union, and criticisms of the United States alienated American leaders, and "key players" were "anti-Indian" for much of the Cold War period (A. Sharma 2017, 176). When the Soviet Union invaded Afghanistan in December 1979, Pakistan became a key U.S. ally to defeat Soviet forces in Afghanistan and to prevent the spread of communism, further marginalizing India. The collapse of the Soviet Union in 1989, which had provided aid for India, triggered an Indian economic crisis, necessitating the intervention of the International Monetary Fund and the liberalization of the Indian economy as a condition for the funds. The end of the Cold War also allowed for a reset in the U.S.-India relationship. Speaking at a reception for members of Congress organized by the NFIA in October 2007 that I attended, Congressman Jim McDermott (D-WA), an Indian American ally, referred to this change, declaring, "In the 1980s it was hard to find anyone in the State department with a good word for India. It was our relationship with Pakistan that had everyone's attention. When the Berlin Wall collapsed, things changed" (see also Talbott, 2006, 12; Rubinoff 2001).

Stephen Solarz (D-NY), a nine-term Democratic congressman first elected in 1974 and a key player in the House Foreign Affairs Committee, was India's sole supporter in the U.S. Congress in the 1970s and 1980s (Hathaway 2001, 27). At that time Dan Burton (R-IN), a friend of Pakistan, used to speak against India on a regular basis and every year would introduce "anti-India amendments" over human rights issues to try to reduce foreign aid to India. A representative of the *Council of Khalistan* would frequently contact Dan Burton and other members of Congress asking them to censure India for the harsh policies pursued against Sikhs in Punjab. Those supporting independence for Kashmir would attack India. The anti-India group also succeeded in stopping U.S. aid to India in 1987 until financial assistance had been restored to Pakistan (Rubinoff 2001, 47). Stephen Solarz (D-NY) was defeated at the end of 1992, leaving India without any supporters in Congress. This was the context in which the India caucus was formed. Its main goal was to counter the activities of Dan Burton and the anti-India group and to improve the image of India on the Hill. The India caucus grew to become the largest ethnic caucus on the Hill. A Senate "Friends of India" caucus was formed in 2004, the first country-focused caucus in the Senate.

Congressman Frank Pallone from New Jersey, who, due to redistricting, suddenly had a lot of Indian Americans in his district, took the initiative to form the India caucus. In March 2007, I talked to Kapil (Kap) Sharma, Frank Pallone's former staffer and a second-generation Indian American from Pallone's newly created district in New Jersey. Kap Sharma was invited to work for Frank Pallone to help him launch the bipartisan Congressional Caucus on India and Indian Americans, "one of the first congressional caucuses devoted to promoting relations with a single country" (Hathaway 2001, 27). Kap told me that Pallone asked him to go to Washington, DC to run the campaign to start the caucus, saying, "This is going to fall on your shoulders since I can't as a White man tell Indian Americans what to do." Kap collaborated with three other Indian American activists in New Jersey to come up with an agenda for the caucus and urged Indian American donors to ask their congressional representatives to join. India's economic liberalization lured many American businesses seeking its large market of middle-class consumers, and many members also wanted to support India as a potential "hedge" against a rising China. Consequently, they saw "no downside to enlisting in the Caucus" and readily joined. By the middle of 1999 the caucus had 115 members, more than one-fourth of the House of Representatives (Hathaway 2001, 28).

Kap told me that the first goal for the caucus was educating Congress about India. To this end, they organized the first congressional trips to India and to Punjab to meet Sikhs so they could see that Sikhs in Punjab were not badly treated nor as anti-India as Burton painted them out to be. The trips were a success. According to Kap, "When people came back from India, they loved it. They could see the warmth and hospitality and there were cases when even some who had been critics would return from their trip all gung-ho about India." Robert Hathaway (2001, 28), a long-time observer of the caucus who had been senior congressional staffer for Stephen Solarz and later the director of the Asia Program of the Woodrow Wilson International Center, argued that "under Pallone's leadership, the Caucus provided India, for the first time, with an institutional base of support on Capitol Hill." Hathaway pointed out that Dan Burton's annual anti-India amendment was soundly defeated starting from 1996. After a second defeat in 1997, Burton stopped offering the amendment, recognizing that India supporters "had organized too overwhelming a force to warrant submitting his amendment; they would 'beat me into the ground' he admitted" (Hathaway 2001, 29).

Nuclearization, Indo-Pakistan Tensions, and the India Lobby

In 1998, the Bharatiya Janata Party (BJP), the party promoting Hindu nationalism, came to power in India for the first time as part of a coalition government after winning national elections. In a public acknowledgment of the support the BJP received from the Hindu diaspora, particularly in the United States, the party presented a budget in June 1998 that had several special provisions for nonresident Indians (NRIs) willing to invest dollars in the country, including a Person of Indian Origin (PIO) card entitling the holder to several benefits. Shortly after taking over the reins of leadership in the country, the BJP embarked on a nuclearization program that culminated in the historic nuclear tests of May 1998 (followed a few weeks later by Pakistan), in violation of the nuclear Non-Proliferation Treaty, which India had refused to sign since it found the treaty discriminatory in not pushing for universal disarmament, instead allowing some countries, but not others, to have nuclear weapons.

American Hindutva groups had long been advocating nuclearization for India (P. R. Singh 1996, A26; 1997, A26). Although the initial support for the nuclearization program within India evaporated in the wake of the explosions in Pakistan and increasing prices consequent to the sanctions (leading to protests around the country), the BJP government's actions dramatically increased its popularity among Indian Americans. Large sections of Hindu Indian Americans, including those who had been relatively apolitical, came out strongly in support of the Indian government's actions with jingoistic assertions of nationalistic pride and fervor. The BJP wasted no time in harnessing the enthusiastic response to its nuclearization program. The government launched a *Resurgent India Bond* to enable NRIs to help the Indian government tide over international sanctions. The response to the scheme was so positive that the government exceeded its target of $2 billion in just a few weeks (Rekhi 1998). A State Bank of India Report dated August 18, 1998, indicated that the scheme was expected to procure the Indian government foreign exchange reserves worth $4 billion by the time of its close on August 24, 1998. With its large pro-liberalization Hindu Indian American business constituency in the United States, the BJP hastily abandoned its nativist *swadeshi* platform (to manufacture and buy Indian goods) and came out strongly in support of liberalization. Hindu Indian American organizations had also been pressing the BJP government to grant NRIs dual nationality and for representation in the Indian parliament. Under such pressure, the prime minister announced that a separate department would be created within the External Affairs Ministry to act as a link with NRIs and to deal with their concerns (*India Journal* 1999).

In 1999, India and Pakistan got into a conflict over the incursion of Pakistani troops into Kargil on the Indo-Pakistani border. The nuclear test and the incursion by Pakistan into Kargil brought about a significant change in the level of engagement of the Indian government and Indian Americans with the United States: there was a dramatic increase in mobilization and lobbying (Hathaway 2001, 24; A. Sharma 2017, 207–208). The Indian government dispatched senior statesman Jaswant Singh for a series of talks, lasting for over two years, with Strobe Talbott on the American side, to explain India's position on nuclear disarmament and the Pakistani threat to India (Talbott 2006). Indian American computer professionals using their technological expertise organized an email campaign (likely one of the earliest email lobbying campaigns launched on Capitol Hill) inundating congressional offices with hundreds of emails, which "startled" congressional staffers (Hathaway 2001, 24). This mobilization yielded results: while the nuclear tests automatically triggered sanctions on India and Pakistan, by the fall of 1999, members of Congress were calling for lifting of the sanctions and some were lifted (Hathaway 2001, 22). All sanctions were lifted in 2001.

The Kargil conflict was resolved only when President Clinton intervened and urged the Pakistani president to withdraw his forces. According to a front-page article in the *Washington Post* on October 9, 1999, it was the pressure that Indian immigrants put on Congress members that forced Clinton to intervene on behalf of India. The *Post* article went on to conclude that it was the generosity of Indian Americans in political campaigns that had been responsible for the growing support for India in the earlier pro–Pakistan American administration and that Indian Americans had become a powerful domestic lobby (Lancaster 1999). Similarly, political scientist Arthur

Rubinoff (2001, 57) argued that this transformation in the attitude toward India on Capitol Hill "confirms the necessity that a foreign country have a strong domestic base of support in the American political system if it intends to be influential in Washington." In September 2000, Bill Clinton hosted Indian prime minister Vajpayee at the White House and Vajpayee addressed a joint session of the U.S. Congress. The Clintons organized a huge banquet for Vajpayee with around 700 guests, mostly Indian American, in attendance (Talbott 2006, 207). One Washington, DC policy expert that I spoke to described this event as "the biggest state dinner in history," a "love fest," and a "turning point" in the political visibility of Indian Americans.

At the same time, it is important not to overstate the power of Indian American lobbying and advocacy during this period. As several people (including the policy expert) pointed out, in many cases, members of Congress supported pro-India measures due to their own domestic or foreign policy interests. In other words, these were situations when Indian Americans were "pushing at an open door." For instance, farm-belt members of Congress such as Sam Brownback (R-KA) were strongly in support of waiving the sanctions on India imposed by the 1998 nuclear test since "lifting sanctions would help farmers in his home state sell wheat" to India (Talbott 2006, 127). The U.S. pivot to India at the expense of Pakistan was also short-lived. With Afghanistan regaining strategic importance because of the attacks of September 11, 2001, Pakistan came to be viewed, for the second time, as an important U.S. partner, this time in the "war on terror." In 2004, much to India's displeasure, Pakistan was designated by Secretary Powell as a "Major Non-NATO Ally" of the United States, a designation that entailed a variety of military and financial benefits and that India did not receive (Talbott 2006, 222).

Recognizing the importance of the Indian diaspora for India, in 2000 the Indian Ministry of External Affairs set up the High-level Committee on the Indian Diaspora to study homeland-diaspora relations. The 2001 report of the committee acknowledged important economic and political contributions that Indian Americans were making to India, including the quote that began this chapter. In December 2003, India passed a law to grant dual citizenship (*Overseas Citizen of India* [OCI] status) to a person, their children, or their grandchildren who had been a citizen of India from 1950 (when India became a republic) or after. However, individuals who had ever been a citizen of Pakistan or Bangladesh or had parents or grandparents from Pakistan or Bangladesh were denied this status. While the OCI status does not allow individuals to vote in Indian elections, it entitles visa-free travel and stay in India for any length of time and some property, business investment, and educational rights in India.

We see that contemporary Indian American mobilization on behalf of India, beginning from its early days in the 1980s when the NFIA rallied against the U.S. sale of AWACS planes to Pakistan, has been deeply intertwined with the tension and rivalry between India and Pakistan. The bloody history of partition that gave birth to the countries of India and Pakistan, the disputes over Kashmir that have led to two wars between India and Pakistan and a near war in 1999 over Kargil, India's entry into the 1971 war between West and East Pakistan (now Pakistan and Bangladesh) on the side of East Pakistan, and ongoing conflicts, border incursions, and military standoffs have contributed to this situation. Indian American organizations and immigrant Indians (particularly older-generation members from Indian states bordering Pakistan who remember some of the Indo-Pakistan wars) are inheritors of this legacy. Even though there are more Muslims in India than in Pakistan, it is easy for tensions between India and Pakistan to slide into religious hostility (on both sides) since Pakistan was formed based on religion. However, these subcontinental tensions mean little to many in the American-born generation. Instead, many second-generation South Asian Americans, whatever their nation of origin, find that they have a lot in common, an important reason for the rise of South Asian American groups and organizations.

The Generational Divide and the Formation of South Asian American Organizations

In the 1980s, some pioneer immigrant-generation Indian American activists joined Asian American political coalitions. However, several subsequently got disillusioned and pulled out. Two older men told me that they felt they were being "used" by Chinese Americans to add numbers to the Asian American group but were cut off when it came to divvying up the benefits (e.g., political appointments for those active in electoral campaigns). One such individual involved with an Asian Americans for Reagan-Bush group shared that he decided that Indian Americans should go their separate ways for future elections because Chinese Americans were "hogging it" (leadership positions in the coalitions) and not giving Indian Americans a voice.

While the immigrant generation broke away from Asian American political coalitions to form Indian American organizations, similar experiences of marginalization by activist Indian and Indian American students within Asian American college groups led to the formation of South Asian American campus organizations in the late 1980s and the 1990s (Prashad 1998, 107).

As South Asians encountered each other on college campuses, they discovered how much they had in common—from their historical, social, and cultural heritage to their experiences of racialization in the United States as Brown-skinned individuals (Kibria 1998; Prashad 1998, 114). It made them come together to challenge the exclusion of South Asian voices within Asian American studies and to mobilize as a progressive coalition against the religious and nationalist bigotry that seemed to be sweeping through their communities (Prashad 1998, 112). This background explains the concern of South Asian groups for social justice issues, their emphasis on inclusivity, and their secular or multireligious orientation. People of Indian American ancestry who gravitated toward "South Asian" rather than Indian American organizations (as mentioned, Indian Americans have made up over 85 percent of the South Asian American population for the last several decades) consisted of two primary types of individuals: (1) a small group of immigrants who were educated in U.S. PhD programs in the humanities and social sciences from the late 1980s and (2) many second-generation Indian Americans (as well as the 1.5 generation—those who had come to the United States when they were young) who obtained their undergraduate and graduate degrees in the United States. Most activists in national South Asian American organizations are in this second group. This is not to say that *all* second-generation Indian American activists turned to South Asian American organizations. For instance, national Hindu and Sikh advocacy organizations were founded by second-generation Indian Americans, and some second-generation Indian Americans were active in Indian American political and trade organizations. However, it is fair to say that identifying as "South Asian American" instead of as "Indian American" is largely a "made in the USA" second-generation phenomenon.

All the individuals I talked to who were part of national South Asian American advocacy organizations, both civic advocacy and partisan organizations (all second-generation members), told me that they had grown up in families that identified as "Indian" or "Indian American" but had developed a "South Asian" perspective in college in the United States. As one young activist exclaimed with a laugh, "I don't think I ever heard the term South Asian until I got to college." She continued, "That's where I became really cognizant of using that [South Asian] versus Indian, because, you know, our community . . . as young college students, wasn't just Indian, it was Indian, Pakistani, you know, Sri Lankan, there was whatever else. So . . . I think we became more cognizant of it, and, and tried to consciously use South Asian." Jayesh Rathod, cofounder of the Washington, DC-based *South Asian Americans Leading Together* (SAALT), the leading national South Asian American organization in the country, explained:

> I think growing up, to be honest, I didn't have that much exposure to non-Indian South Asians because . . . there were some Pakistani friends I had growing up but you know, Sri Lankan, Bangladeshi, umm I can't even think of anyone I knew when I was in high school or younger from those backgrounds. It's possible that they were there, and I just didn't have the awareness, but it wasn't really until I got to college that I developed more of consciousness of kind of a shared history of the different national origin groups and cultural similarities and differences. . . . I think where I really became the most politicized and most aware of the South Asian identity was when I went to law school in New York. . . . And I think it was partly a function of just being in New York City and being exposed to all the immigrant rights issues and also seeing the injustices that our, my own community was facing [referring specifically to the mobilization around the rights of South Asian taxi drivers and domestic workers in New York City].

The generational cleavage came up several times in my discussions with those who identified as South Asian Americans since they always contrasted their inclusive orientation and focus on domestic American issues with the obsession of immigrant-generation "uncles" and "aunties" (in Indian culture, men and women of the parents' generation are addressed as "uncle" and "aunty") with the competition and conflict between India and Pakistan. In addition, they emphasized that there were growing subgroups of South Asian Americans—besides Pakistanis and Bangladeshis, also Indian Muslims, Christians, Sikhs, Bengalis, Indo-Caribbean people, Dalits, and working-class Indians—who all felt alienated from the upper-class, "upper caste" Hindu-centric vision of many of the Indian organizations and favored a more inclusive South Asian identity. Consequently, South Asian American organizations, while serving and advocating for South Asian Americans of all backgrounds, have been particularly aware of the need to help the more disadvantaged members of these communities. This makes them different from the Indian American organizations that tend to focus on wealthier and more elite groups.

South Asian Americans Leading Together (SAALT), based in Washington, DC, was, until early 2023, when it went into a hiatus (see below, Updates section), the leading South Asian American national organization in the country. It was originally formed as the *Indian American Leadership Center* in February 2000 and became a South Asian American organization (at that time called South Asian American Leaders of Tomorrow) in 2001 to broaden its scope. I interviewed one of the cofounders of SAALT, Debashish Mishra, in 2003. At that time, the organization did not have a full-time staff person, but in 2004, civil rights attorney Deepa Iyer. who was already involved with SAALT as a board member, was hired as the executive director. She led the organization for the crucial first decade, laying its groundwork and activities and building its visibility in Washington, DC and around the country before stepping down to pursue other social justice passions.

Debashish told me that SAALT had started from a conversation between some first- and second-generation Indian Americans concerned about "the absence of a national organization" focused on the problems faced by the community in the United States such as civil rights and discrimination issues. The founding members of the organization and their board of trustees at the time included senior-level corporate executives from several Fourtune 500 companies, and their mission was to develop leadership and foster civic engagement among the younger generation. Once the organization was formed, Debashish said that there were two reasons they decided to broaden the organization into a South Asian American organization. First, they realized that civil rights issues "impacted many groups from South Asia in the United States in exactly the same way." Second, they saw that second-generation South Asian Americans do not

> view themselves within the narrow nationality-based identification that the first generation does. A lot of times they refer to themselves as South Asian or simply Desi because the nationality distinctions don't mean anything for them. I think the backgrounds in terms of growing up are very, very similar. We all come from roughly similar cultures. So, by remaining an Indian American organization we were in danger of being out of touch with the group that we were most concerned with.

In the first two years, while they were still an Indian American organization, their primary activity consisted of organizing a national Gandhi day of service involving "hundreds of student and community groups around the country to perform community service such as park clean ups, working in soup kitchens, refurbishing homes for indigent clients," as one activist told me. SAALT had also been reaching out to South Asian American organizations around the country to get a grassroots perspective on the needs of the community. The attacks of September 11, 2001, propelled the organization into the limelight.

A short-lived South Asian American organization, the *Subcontinental Institute*, also based in Washington, DC and led by Indian Americans, was formed in 2002 with a goal of providing a forum for the development of an inclusive South Asian American political identity representative of the various perspectives that prevail within the community. Its central activity was the production and distribution of a journal, *The Subcontinental*, targeted primarily at politically active South Asians and policymakers in Washington, DC. Besides the need to be inclusive and to address common concerns of the community, Nirav Desai, the editor, indicated in a 2003 interview that there were two additional reasons that motivated the founders (all Indian Americans) to make the institute a South Asian organization: (1) they realized that policymakers often "wanted to talk about issues in terms of South Asia," and (2) they wanted to show that their loyalties were not split with another government. That being perceived as a patriotic American can sometimes be an important motivation for politically active Indian Americans adopting a South Asian identity is a point that was also made by journalist Sarah Wildman. In a 2001 article on South Asianness, she quoted Kris Kolluri, an Indian immigrant and senior policy adviser to then–House minority leader Dick Gephardt, as saying, "What you're seeing is not only a movement to stand up for our civil rights but also a movement to ensure that the larger society knows that we are Americans" (Wildman 2001).

The Watershed of 9/11: South Asian American versus Indian American Responses

In her article on the development of a South Asian identity, Sarah Wildman quoted Professor Madhulika Khandelwal as saying that the concept of South Asianness had "taken off" in the post-9/11 period "because to American bigots, Pakistanis, Indians, Bangladeshis, Muslims, Hindus, and Sikhs all look the same—brown—many victims are deciding they have a lot more in common than they had previously realized" (Wildman 2001). The development of a "post-9/11 Brown" racial category of people—South Asians, Muslims, Sikhs, and Arab Americans who were viewed as "Muslim looking" and who became the target of hate crimes—has been noted by several activists and scholars (e.g., Iyer 2015; De 2016; N. Sharma 2016). In general, South Asian groups around the country mobilized to present a united front against the hate crimes that followed in the aftermath of 9/11, to challenge government policies like the special registration required of immigrants from predominantly Muslim countries, and to protest violations of civil rights in the Patriot Act. Debashish Mishra told me that 9/11 had catapulted SAALT into the public arena since they put out a "very authoritative report" on hate crimes one week later[2] (which they had been working on even before 9/11) and a documentary on hate crimes in 2002, both of which "spread like wildfire" through student, community, law enforcement, and advocacy groups around the country. The organization formed coalitions with Arab American and Muslim groups and took up the cases of the families of South Asian victims of hate crimes, including that of a Pakistani American, who was shot and killed in Texas in the wake of 9/11, whose family was about to be deported. However, many Indian American groups and organizations reacted differently to 9/11 and its aftermath.

Beginning in the year 2000, many immigrant Indian Americans had taken to the Internet in large numbers, forming discussion groups and writing copiously in global Indian e-zines (Internet magazines) like Sulekha.com and Rediff.com. I monitored several of these Internet forums in the early 2000s in connection with my earlier research (see Kurien 2007a). The topic of Indian Americans embracing a "South Asian" identity roused the fervor and indignation of many in the immigrant generation. Perhaps the first salvo was fired by Rajeev Srinivasan, an IT specialist and columnist, in March 2000 on Rediff.com. He started his piece with a lament on the "South Asia fixation" of many "progressive" Indian Americans and argued that he objected on three grounds: (1) it sullied "brand India," (2) it pandered to the mistaken American tendency of using the term "Indian" to mean "Native American," and (3) it emphasized a commonality between people from South Asia where none existed (Srinivasan 2000). This piece let loose a volley of attacks against the concept of a South Asian identity, mostly in online forums, with critics describing themselves as patriotic Indians trying to build community solidarity and inculcate individual and collective pride based on an identity and culture that was thousands of years old. They maintained that it was disadvantageous for India to be lumped together with the other countries in South Asia, since "India's geographical size, economy, and progress are far ahead of these countries." They further argued that the cultural and political gulf between members of these countries was too vast to bridge and that instead of trying to ignore these cleavages, Indian Americans ought to educate their children and the wider American society about these fundamental differences and not buy into the "artificial" U.S. State Department construct of a homogenous subcontinent (Rao 2003; see Kurien 2003 for a discussion).

After the attacks of 9/11, many of these critiques emerged in the public sphere, mostly articulated by those who mobilized as Hindu Americans. This will be discussed in the next chapter, but here I will briefly mention four articles written by Rajiv Malhotra (2003b, 2003c, 2004a, 2004b) of the Infinity Foundation between December 2003 and January 2004 on Rediff.com. The articles attacked South Asian studies programs around the country for being run by scholars hostile to India's interests, which undermined "brand India" and India's unity, promoted internal conflicts and cleavages, and could lead to the "Talibanization" of India (see Kurien 2007a, 206–207 for more details).

The Jewish Model and Generational Differences in Indian American Activism

An issue that came up in many of my interviews was a reference to the Jewish model of political organization and mobilization as a touchstone for Indian American activism. As we will see, the discussion of the Jewish model often intersected with generational differences. This model was brought up several times in my early interviews with Indian American activists but also came up in one of my interviews with a policy expert and in an interview with a journalist who covered Indian American issues. In later interviews, I sometimes brought up the comparison to get the reaction of my conversational partners. The Jewish comparison was also a frequent topic for discussion at the Indian American political conferences and events I attended. In one of my first interviews for this project (early 2007), an older immigrant activist, "Ram," lamented, "Unfortunately, we have nothing like the AIPAC—a united, democratic, effective organization, not based on individual agendas." Jewish American organizations, and particularly the AIPAC, were an aspirational model for many in the immigrant generation. Immigrant activists like Ram emphasized that like Jews, Indian Americans were (mostly) religious minorities in the United States and were also a small, dispersed, well-educated, and successful group. Again, they argued that Israel and India were democratic nations surrounded by nondemocratic countries and that both countries were subject to terrorist attacks from their neighbors (in the Indian case this referred to Pakistan, but also to China, which had fought a war with India in 1962).

In an article on the "new" strategic partnership between Indian Americans and Jewish Americans, Robert Hathaway (2004, 70) quotes Kumar Barve, then majority leader in the Maryland state assembly and the highest elected Indian American official at the time, as saying in a 2003 interview with the *Washington Post*, "Indian Americans see the American Jewish community as a yardstick against which to compare themselves. It's seen as the gold standard in terms of political activism." Kumar Barve is a second-generation Indian American, probably one of the oldest of his generation (born in Schenectady, New York, in 1958). However, several younger second-generation activists I talked to, particularly those who had held positions as interns or staffers on the Hill or had worked closely with members of Congress, were more likely to point out the many ways that the comparison was not appropriate and was "like apples and oranges," as one of them, "Arjun," put it. Arjun pointed out that Jewish Americans are a long-established group in the United States, that they had worked hard for decades to make sure that Americans recognized the importance of Israel for the United States, and that Israel was very dependent on the United States for its existence, all of which made it different, "apples and oranges," when compared to the Indian American case. Another activist, "Vinay," said:

> Jews are ... one of the most unique ethnic communities on the planet, with an incredibly unique history. We don't have a holocaust to talk about. We don't have a homeland that we're trying to protect.... We might have some border skirmishes with China and Pakistan, but who the hell cares? I mean, there's very little relevance to our life as Indian Americans. However, the homeland they're trying to protect and define, is very fundamental to the Jewish American experience. And, you know, the Jews come from a religious tradition that has a lot in common with the Christian faith. But we come from several religious traditions, none of which [laugh] have much at all in common with the Judeo-Christian tradition.... So, I mean, all these things kind of lead me to believe that it's kind of a strange place for us to be looking for any kind of guidance.

The argument that Jewish Americans were a "single-issue constituency," focused on the survival of Israel, in contrast to Indian Americans, who were diverse, with many different interests, was a point that practically all second-generation activists mentioned when they discussed the contrast. The disagreement was about whether Indian American diversity was a political strength or a weakness, with individuals taking different positions on this issue. "Ravi," another second-generation Indian American who had worked on the Hill, brought up other differences:

> Number one, although they are democratic countries, Israel is a very, very small country population wise, compared to India. India has a billion people, the second largest country in the world. So, Israel is surrounded by much larger populated countries, India is the largest country, surrounded by smaller countries in South Asia. Second thing is, even though they've [Jewish Americans] been very small, they've shown great political dexterity, great political strength, because even though they're such a small community, there are dozens of Jewish members of Congress, there are hundreds of Jewish American people elected at the local, state, and federal level across the United States.

Ravi added that he did not see "the same kind of political smarts" among Indian Americans, particularly in the immigrant generation. These types of discussions invariably turned to a critique of the immigrant style of activism by second-generation members, particularly those who worked within congressional circles.

While a few second-generation activists emphasized that the "old guard" had faced real struggles and barriers and that their efforts should be appreciated, others like Ravi tended to be very critical of the immigrant generation "uncles" who were trying to get involved in lobbying. Ravi and others critiqued the "uncles" for forming organizations just to claim the title of "president" or "chairman," for getting involved in politics and making donations to candidates just for the "photo ops," and for remaining India focused despite having lived in the United States for over three decades. Ravi talked about his experience while working on the Hill:

> When I was at the White House briefing for the nuclear deal last year, there were a hundred American-Indians in the White House briefing room, and ... when they asked, you know, please give your name and identify who

you're with, well, every single Indian uncle stood up and they're all either the founder, or the chairman, or the past chairman, or the past president, or the future chairman, or the next president of an organization. Every single one. I mean, there were a hundred people, and there were a hundred different organizations. So that's an example where, you know, diversity can be a weakness, where you have no strength in unity.... All these uncles, in some ways, they're competing against one another to be the head person.

Ravi also talked about the way the immigrant generation would charge toward politicians to get photographs with them:

It's really embarrassing, the first generation, they'll rush towards politicians, Congressmen, and just take pictures. I've had a friend in the White House say he's never seen anything like it. And they work with a lot of other ethnic communities, and he's said he's never seen people react [in this way] with their cameras around Congressmen.... Someone gave the comparison, it was like teenage girls spotting Brittney Spears, they basically like swarmed the Congressman, they all were just, like bees on a honey hive or whatever.

Again, second-generation activists with experience in Washington, DC congressional circles felt that the immigrant generation did not understand how politics worked in the United States, how Congress worked, how legislation was passed, how to lobby, and how to be strategic about their donations. As "Dipak" explained, for the longest time Indians were known as easy money since they had no demands and were pacified with a few words about the greatness of India and photo opportunities. He added, "It is crucial that everybody needs to know what the agenda is and that this is communicated out. Because when someone holds a fundraiser and the staffer calls to ask what your issues are, you should know what to say." He told me that this was beginning to change.

Another complaint was that the immigrant-generation "uncles" were so focused on getting a meeting with members of Congress that they did not understand, as "Lekha," a young woman who worked as a fundraiser for Democratic congressional campaigns, shared, "that it is the staff and the ongoing relationship [with them] that is the most important thing because the member [of Congress] doesn't know anything." She continued, saying that the immigrant generation believed that the members of Congress tell staffers what to do when it was often the reverse. "Everything happens on the staff level so it's just a matter of us as a community understanding it." Lekha also talked about the difficulties she had in coaxing wealthy immigrant Indian Americans to donate to support candidates:

> Indian Americans are inherently not trained to write checks to candidates. It's a hard, just a very difficult concept for them to get you know.... I mean they'll write $1,000 to go see you know Sonu Nigam [an Indian singer] but the idea of writing a check to a person trying to win an elected office is just not something... that's ingrained in us. And a lot of it has to do with I think, the generational stuff.... I talk to these uncles all day long and they're like, just tell me who is going to win, and I'll write a check, one check to whoever is winning. And I'm like, we don't know. I'm like, nobody is going to win if you don't write a check. Just write a check.

Several of the second-generation political activists also felt that for Indian Americans to gain political clout they needed to have at least one permanent, professionally staffed organization with the necessary infrastructure and advocacy at the national level to represent the community. However, they emphasized that this should be an organization led by the second generation since the immigrant generation did not have the training or the experience to run such an organization. Speaking to me in December 2007, Ravi explained:

> The best way to do it is take the money from the first generation, which they have, funnel it to an Indian-American association that's based in D.C. that's headed up by second-generation Indian Americans that have legislative, political experience, financial, fundraising experience, and they'd be the ones who pound the pavement, they'd work full time to lobby the House, lobby the Senate, the Administration, they'll make the political appointments, that'll be the right model.

Jewish Links and the Formation of USINPAC

In October 2002, the four major Indian American organizations that were in existence at the time—the National Federation of Indian Americans (NFIA), the Indian American Forum for Public Education (IAFPE), and the trade organizations representing Indian American doctors (AAPI) and hotel owners

(AAHOA)—came together to "present a joint front" to represent Indian Americans. The Coordination Committee with two representatives from each of the four organizations was set up (Rangarajan 2002). However, this unity did not last very long and imploded with a contentious election.

In late 2002, the immigrant-led United States India Political Action Committee (USINPAC) was formed to create a "political brand" to represent Indian Americans in Washington, DC. USINPAC opened an office in New Delhi in 2005. In 2007, I talked to the founder and chairman Sanjay Puri, then probably in his 40s. At the time, Sanjay had also launched another organization, USIBA (*United States-India Business Alliance*, later renamed the *Alliance for US International Business* (AUSIB), to promote U.S. trade with India, and both USINPAC and USIBA functioned out of the same office in Washington, DC. USINPAC participated in an annual U.S. business delegation to India to meet with Indian businesspeople and politicians. In our 2007 conversation, Sanjay Puri told me that his goal in founding USINPAC was to give voice to the Indian American community so they could have a say in shaping "the decisions that are about us or that affect us." While there were several Indian American organizations that would organize an event once a year on the Hill, he felt that it was important to have an organization that would be on the Hill on a day-to-day basis, building relationships with members of Congress. So, when an issue came up, they could contact the members of Congress and vice versa—members of Congress had a representative of the Indian American community to contact. As a bipartisan, registered political action committee, USINPAC has been active around U.S. elections, holding fundraisers for candidates around the country. The organization "bundles" Indian American campaign contributions and contributes them to candidates (although these amounts are not very large, as Sanjay Puri himself mentioned). They also supported Indian American candidates running for state and national offices in a variety of ways.

Sanjay Puri brought up the Jewish model in his conversation with me, telling me that what motivated him to establish the organization was his experience of attending an Indian American fundraising event for a gubernatorial candidate in 2002 where there was "no talk of issues" at all. He also saw that the candidate's staff did not take the Indian American community seriously and were laughing at them. He felt strongly that it was important for the organizers of fundraisers to talk to candidates about the challenges faced by Indian American businesses, but also how Indian Americans were well placed to contribute to various sectors of American society. "The Jewish community does this," he told me. He said he had a good friend who was Jewish with whom he had been talking for a long time about setting up an organization to promote the interests of India and Indian Americans. I later talked to this friend, "Noah," who had been involved with NACPAC, "the nation's largest pro-Israel political action committee" (http://www.nacpac.org/), and had helped Sanjay develop a legal structure for USINPAC to mirror the NACPAC structure. Noah had been working with USINPAC from its inception and gave them suggestions based on the Jewish community experience. Noah told me that as early as 1994, Sanjay would comment on how well organized the Jewish community was and ask why Indian Americans could not organize in similar ways. When his business was more settled and secure, Noel said, Sanjay was able to start USINPAC. Robert Hathaway (2004, 69) writes that USINPAC is "widely credited with a leading role in deliberately reaching out to American Jews for the purpose of promoting a sustained partnership" and that it had worked closely with a variety of Jewish groups such as AIPAC, the American Jewish Committee (AJC), and the Jewish Institute for National Security Affairs (JINSA) to "promote ties between Indian-Americans and US Jews." In July 2003, USINPAC organized a Capitol Hill reception with AIPAC and AJC, attended by "an impressive number of legislators" who showed up because of the clout of the Jewish groups. Hathaway (2004, 70) writes that "by all accounts" it was the AJC that initiated the outreach to Indian Americans and that JINSA on its part had been working to promote a "trilateral" cooperation between India (specifically focusing on Hindus), Israel, and the United States. As we will see, this Hindu-Jewish alliance is a contentious issue among some Indian American subgroups, since it is often viewed as an anti-Muslim partnership and often presented that way by both Hindu and Jewish activists.

In his conversation with me, Sanjay Puri mentioned the role of USINPAC in the nuclear deal (on that, more below, see U.S.-India Nuclear Deal section) but also talked about other issues that he felt were important for the Indian American community such as the H-1B visa, telling me, "We can't just leave it to Microsoft and Intel, or Bill Gates to go to Congress to make the arguments [for the visa].... They have their own mission and agenda. Sometimes it may overlap with ours and we can collaborate. At other points it may not overlap with our agenda." He also mentioned the enormous length of time it took for someone from India to get a green card (due to country quotas on green cards that penalize high-immigration countries like India) and how long it took for a spouse of a green card member to be allowed in (which then was around five to six years). He continued passionately: "Green card members pay taxes, social security, can contribute to political campaigns. But they are denied the basic right to have their spouse join them. [Whereas] those on H1 and F1 visas can bring their spouses with them without any problem. This boggles my mind." He said this is why Indian Americans "need an organization, we need a brand."

He told me that he had started USINPAC by "tramping through the halls of Congress" talking to a range of members of Congress about the Indian American community. In the next phase, Puri targeted individuals who were on committees that focused on core issues (e.g., the U.S.-India relationship, trade, immigration, and small business) that were of importance to the community. I asked him what his general pitch had been. He said he would emphasize that the United States had a growing Indian American community that was economically successful and that contributed to American society in many ways. "There is probably no hospital without at least one Indian American doctor, no University without at least one Indian American professor. If you go to the South, there are so many motels owned by Indian Americans. This community is now ripe and ready. They have fulfilled the American dream. They are now ready to give back." He emphasized that he did not just mean financial contributions. Indian Americans were widely traveled and had a global perspective, which would be helpful to have in contemporary discussions. Indian Americans also had a unique perspective on economic issues because of their involvement in small business in the United States. Similarly, because of their experience in the health care sector, they had a unique perspective on health care issues.

Another Indian American active in USINPAC, "Ishan," whom I interviewed in 2010, talked about their early days on the Hill:

> And it was interesting, back then Indian American activism in Washington, it was so new, so many of the Congressmen had never even met an Indian . . . before. It was you know so very different from what it is today. And we would actually have to you know argue our case and we had some pretty rude responses.

I asked Sanjay Puri about the first big achievement of USINPAC, and he referred to the fact that in 2003 they were able to get language inserted in a bill for an aid package for Pakistan making the aid conditional on Pakistan not supporting terrorism in Kashmir. He told me gleefully that this got a lot of attention in the Pakistan embassy and press. In listing what USINPAC had been able to achieve in its first four years, he again mentioned that they were able to push back against Pakistan and make it more accountable. During our 2010 conversation Ishan laughed when he mentioned that putting conditions on U.S. aid to Pakistan had since become standard, referring particularly to the strong provisions imposed on Pakistan by the October 2009 Kerry-Lugar bill for the $7.5 billion U.S. aid provided over a five-year period. But he emphasized that USINPAC was not against Pakistan, telling me, "At the time we were considered to be very anti-Pakistan, which we—which we reject quite strongly. We're actually not anti-Pakistan; we were just—we're anti-terrorism."

Regarding domestic policy issues, Sanjay Puri mentioned that USINPAC had engaged with issues of concern to small businesses and with immigration issues. USINPAC also worked to support Indian American candidates at the state and national levels. He told me that he was also trying to get state governors to bring Indian Americans into their cabinets. In my discussion with Noah, he said that earlier, politicians used to feel that there was no political risk in ignoring Indian American issues but that was not the case after USINPAC was established. He emphasized that due to strict limits on PACs, members of Congress do not receive a lot of money from USINPAC, so USINPAC's influence was not primarily because of the money they donated to campaigns but because members of Congress use these donations as an indicator of whether they were doing right by the community. Politicians also knew that if they were out of line with USINPAC, there was a very good chance that they were out of line with the community, something they did not want to risk. Noah also said that many people on the Hill went to USINPAC as their first source of information.

In November 2008, 10 members of a terrorist organization based in Pakistan carried out a series of coordinated shooting and bombing attacks across different sites in Mumbai, India (including two hotels and a train station), lasting four days, killing over 160 individuals and injuring over 300. Ram Narayanan who was one of the early Indian American activists to use the Internet and email to regularly inform and educate Indian Americans, organized the *Indian American Task Force on Terrorism*, and a group of 150 Indian Americans from across the country, representing a variety of Indian American advocacy organizations, arrived in Washington for *Washington Chalo* (Let's go to Washington) Day, January 27, 2009, to meet members of Congress and the Obama administration to urge them to put pressure on

Pakistan to take action against the perpetrators of the Mumbai attacks (L. Jha 2009). Since USINPAC was based in Washington, DC, the organization was able to take care of organizing the arrangements for the meetings. Perhaps partly because of these efforts, the Senate and the House adopted a resolution condemning the attacks and praising India for its restraint (*Economic Times* 2009).

In our 2010 conversation, Ishan mentioned that by then (2008) people knew what USINPAC was since it had been in existence for so many years. "You know, so I didn't know anybody at the Indian embassy, the people there. But they came up and introduced themselves, oh you're USINPAC? Yeah, we know who you are." Ishan talked about how USINPAC went through an evolution to what he described as USINPAC 2.0 in 2009, trying to push more of an American policy angle to their advocacy. Consequently, their National Security Committee worked on a short policy document titled "US National Security and US-India Strategic Relations." Ishan shared:

> Everything in that [document] was deliberately done. We talked about U.S. national security and then India's role within that. And our point was we're not talking as Indian Americans. We're speaking as Americans; that's number one. Number two... our basic point is that the security threat has moved to Asia and as Asian Americans and Indian Americans we understand that part of the world and we think India happens to have a very key role in that [region]. As opposed to you know [saying] we're Indians and we want—we want close relations [between India and the United States]. Here we're saying these are the challenges that the U.S. faces and here's how we think this country [India] can really play a part in those challenges. And you'll note that we really talked about a lot of things from direct military engagement, [nuclear] proliferation, terrorism, economic security, and climate change.

The document argues:

> India's strategic location between East Asia and the Middle East, combined with its growing economy and longstanding commitment to democratic values make it America's most natural partner in the region... given these shared values and interests, and given the central role it can play in achieving America's security goals, we recommend a "special relationship" be established between the US and India, akin

to America's existing relationships with Britain, Australia and Japan. (USINPAC 2009, 2)

USINPAC's position in the document is linked to the "dehyphenation" argument that Indian Americans had been advocating for several years, from at least the time that Bill Clinton had been president (1993–2001). As articulated in 2008 by Ashley Tellis, a senior policy analyst of Indian American background, a dehyphenated U.S. policy toward South Asia would mean that instead of bracketing India and Pakistan together and viewing South Asia as a region where the United States had to carefully balance the competing demands of the two rival countries, the United States would instead recognize the differences between the two countries and pursue independent policies toward each of them. In the Indian case, this would mean recognizing that India had the potential to emerge as a "great power,"[3] which warranted a strong level of support and engagement from the United States (Tellis 2008).

Perhaps not surprising, given the divisions within the Indian American community and the rivalry and competition between community leaders, USINPAC came under attack in its early years for attempting to project itself as a moderate and pragmatic organization representing Indian Americans. Hindu groups criticized the organization's support for the candidacy of Bobby Jindal, the first Indian American elected to Congress in the contemporary period, since he had converted from Hinduism to Christianity in his teens. They also attacked USINPAC for not presenting the Hindu perspective on the 2002 Hindu-Muslim riots in the state of Gujarat and on other sensitive communal issues and for not speaking out against South Asian studies scholars who they claim undermined "brand India." South Asian groups, on the other hand, criticized USINPAC for allying with groups like AIPAC on an anti-Muslim platform and for not speaking out against the post-9/11 Patriot Act but only asking for Indians to be exempted from the special registration.[4] USINPAC also came under attack from conservative Americans worried about outsourcing and the impacts of H-1B workers on American jobs, as well as the influence of the India caucus on U.S. foreign policy (e.g., Sanchez 2004). While all those I talked to who worked for USINPAC praised the group, as did some other Indian American activists, critiques about the leaders in the group having "no standing in the community," the lack of leadership rotation and it being a "one-person show" (Sanjay Puri's) driven by his personal agenda due to his business interests, and the organization's lack of grassroots connection and professionalism were common among Indian

American activists in the early years of USINPAC's existence. At the same time, USINPAC received praise from independent political analysts.[5]

The U.S.-India Nuclear Deal

I have mentioned that when I started this research in 2007, the nuclear deal was the talk of the town. Consequently, I started out by spotlighting Indian American activism around the nuclear deal and talked to many activists and policy experts in Washington, DC about mobilization around this issue. But the focus of my research shifted a great deal after that. There have also been several academic publications on the nuclear deal (Kirk 2008; Mistry 2013) and many newspaper articles, so I will not go into the details here. The nuclear deal activism has been regarded as a watershed moment in Indian American political activism, bringing the Indian American community to the attention of politicians and policymakers. Several commentators started referring to the power of the "India lobby" after this agreement. For instance, in his 2008 article in *Foreign Policy Analysis*, Jason Kirk of the Virginia Military Institute argued that the nuclear deal portended the emergence of Indian Americans as a major power in foreign policy: "An increasingly professional and well-funded 'India lobby' among Indian-Americans was critical in pressing members of Congress to support the nuclear agreement . . . this episode may portend its emergence as one of the most important ethnic communities seeking influence over U.S. foreign policy in the 21st century" (Kirk 2008, 275).

The Henry Hyde United States–India Peaceful Cooperation Act was a civilian nuclear agreement between the United States and India, signed by President George W. Bush in December 2006, following a joint declaration made by Indian prime minister Manmohan Singh and President Bush in July 2005. The agreement was historic since it required an amendment of the U.S. Atomic Energy Act to enable the United States to sell nuclear fuel and technology to a country that had not signed the Nuclear Non-Proliferation Treaty. In return, India promised to separate its civilian and military nuclear facilities, to open the civilian nuclear facilities for international inspection, and to place them under permanent safeguards. Before getting to President Bush's desk in December, the legislation had to make its way through Congress, where it faced a great deal of opposition, with nonproliferation experts concerned about breaking the norms of the nonproliferation regime.

A bipartisan Indian American mobilization around the civilian nuclear issue began in 2005, when it became evident that the deal would go before Congress. Indian American leaders around the country started to mobilize and to contact their senators and members of Congress to win them over to support the deal. The Indian embassy reached out to Indian American activists around the country and held regular meetings with them. One such activist, Swadesh Chatterjee (see Chapter 6 for more on how he forged ties to Jesse Helms, a powerful Republican member of Congress), an entrepreneur from North Carolina, emerged as the leader of this group and was able to form the *U.S.-India Friendship Council*, uniting eight different Indian American groups—IAFPE, NFIA, GOPIO, AAHOA, AAPI, PANIIT (a group of alumni from the famous Indian Institute of Technology engineering schools), FIA Tri-State area, and a group that called itself the *National Organization of Indian Associations* (the AAPI dropped out of the council in 2006 and after that there were seven organizations)—around support for the civilian nuclear agreement. Under the auspices of the council, Chatterjee was also able to coordinate the activities of around 15 to 20 well-connected first-generation Indian American activists around the country. Some other Indian American–led organizations did not join the council but conducted their own lobbying efforts to promote the nuclear deal. USINPAC was one of these organizations. Another was *Bridging Nations*, an organization founded in 2000 by Washington, DC–based entrepreneur Dr. Prakash Ambegaonkar to promote strong Indo-Chinese relations, which organized educational events on the Hill. Ramesh Kapur of Boston formed the bipartisan *Indian American Security Leadership Council* (IASLC) to mobilize veterans' groups in support of the deal with the argument that a strong India would be good for American national security interests. "We believe that India, the world's largest democracy with over half a century of electoral stability, is a growing military and economic force in the region and can help safeguard American security in a way that no other country in the region can," he is quoted as saying in a July 2006 IASLC press release.

Swadesh Chatterjee discussed the work that went into the mobilization in a 2007 conversation with me and went into even more detail in his 2015 book *Building Bridges: The Role of Indian Americans in Indo-U.S. Relations*. When the Indian ambassador contacted him for help, Chatterjee suggested that they form a new group just to mobilize around the nuclear deal, instead of working with existing organizations. "From the start, the group that we formed, the U.S.-India Friendship Council, was conceived as temporary and virtual—not a formal organization, weighed down by bureaucracy" (Chatterjee 2015, 143). In our conversation, he said that he got together a group of around 20 Indian Americans and told them at the first meeting, "As you know [in] the Indian American community, there are 2 million people but 10 million egos. The only way this will work is if we put our egos in cold storage for a year" (see also Chatterjee 2015, 140). The council set up a website, which was updated frequently, and kept in touch with each other through weekly conference calls (Chatterjee 2015, 149). With the help of Ram Narayanan's *US-India Friendship Net*, they launched an email campaign updating Indian Americans of the progress of the legislation. They had Indian Americans "jam the Internet and fax machines" in the offices of key members of Congress and senators by sending thousands of emails and faxes. They also launched signature campaigns in many states. The group took out advertisements in Indian American papers but also in the *Washington Post* and the *Roll Call* before key hearings. On May 3, 2006, around 200 Indian Americans from around the country descended on the Hill in a *D.C. Chalo* (Let's go to DC) campaign orchestrated by Chatterjee, met with 150 members of Congress and the Senate during the day, and held an evening reception, which around 75 members of Congress and the Senate attended. Chatterjee wrote (2015, 160), "Like American Jews, we conveyed to politicians that we could be a great asset. We vote, we raise funds, and we organize. And this—the U.S.-India civil nuclear deal—was our issue." Over lunch, the group had talks with the U.S. India Business Council, which had formed the *Coalition for Partnership* with India to coordinate the lobby efforts of all the groups supporting the deal. Speaking to me, Chatterjee said, "All in all this created a buzz on the Hill. Before May 2nd [2006] there were only nine co-sponsors of the bill. From nine it increased to 35. At that point, people felt they were missing the boat and so said, I have to join the boat." The council was in constant touch with staffers and members of Congress during the entire process and monitored the votes closely. There was continuous follow-up and they also kept in touch with the U.S. Chamber of Commerce, which was mobilizing to support the deal on behalf of several U.S. businesses such as Boeing, AIG, and Westinghouse.

Since the 2006 elections were around the corner, Indian Americans also held several fundraisers around the country, at which they made clear to the candidates that the community expected support for the deal in return for getting the financial contributions of the community. Influential Indian Americans around the country including in Nevada, Massachusetts,

Texas, Mississippi, Indiana, and North Carolina who had developed close personal relationships with members of Congress from both parties "called upon [them] to help in our cause" (Chatterjee 2015, 169). They also worked closely with the American Jewish Committee (AJC), which helped them recruit Jewish lawmakers to support the deal (Chatterjee 2015, 148). Recognizing that Democrats could win in the midterm elections, the Friendship Council held a conference call with Nancy Pelosi, where they emphasized the number of jobs the agreement would create, "how it would reduce India's dependence on oil from the Middle East, how it would reduce greenhouse gases, and how U.S. companies could earn billions of dollars by building and supplying nuclear reactors in India—which would create jobs for Americans" (Chatterjee 2015, 164). Pelosi seemed persuaded, particularly recognizing how a large group of Indian Americans had united behind the nuclear deal. In November, the Democrats won the elections and Pelosi became the Speaker. After several twists and turns, the bills made their way through the two houses and were then combined for President Bush to sign in December 2006. Supporters of the bill on the Hill have acknowledged that the mobilization of Indian Americans was crucial in getting the deal through Congress. Norman A. Wulf, Clinton's special representative for nuclear nonproliferation, declared that "the India lobby, if I can use that phrase, is, some have suggested, perhaps the second most powerful, shall we say, foreign lobby in the U.S. Congress. The first being Israel or AIPAC" (Arms Control Association 2006, 14). Commentators and policy experts agree that most Indian American supporters did not follow the details of the agreement but backed it because it was viewed by them as a sign of the emergence of India as a global power and an important partner to the United States (W. Andersen 2006; McIntire 2006). The passing of the legislation in Congress was an important watershed moment and helped Indian Americans realize the power of organized efforts.

However, the legislation was challenged in the Indian parliament by the BJP (the opposition party at the time) and the Left Front (part of the ruling coalition government), both concerned that the deal would compromise India's sovereignty and foreign policy. The stalemate was only resolved in July 2008 when the ruling Indian party (Congress) decided to stake its future and call for a vote of confidence, which they won narrowly. In August 2008, the International Atomic Energy Agency, representing international nuclear groups, approved the deal. The agreement then had to make another round through the U.S. Congress and again Chatterjee and his Friendship

Council mobilized to organize resources to support the passage of the agreement. The final agreement was signed by President Bush on October 8, 2008. Swadesh Chatterjee took more than 50 trips to Washington, DC during the three-year campaign (Chatterjee 2015, 195).

Green Card Backlogs and Immigration Voice

In 2007, I also talked to an activist with *Immigration Voice*. The organization was founded in 2005 by Aman Kapoor to find a solution to the green card backlogs due to the per country caps (of 7 percent of the total visas) on employment-based green cards. In 2006 and 2007, most members and all the core organizers of Immigration Voice were from India. In 2019, 12 of 13 team members that were listed on their website (http://immigrationvoice.org) were of Indian origin; the 13th was Chinese. The cap on green cards meant that immigrants from countries with many individuals who were immigrating to or being recruited for employment in the United States such as India and China had to wait for decades. Indians were the country-group with the longest wait. In 2011, the wait for a green card for an Indian-born professional was estimated as being as long as 70 years (S. Anderson 2011). In 2018, this had gone up to 150 years (Bier 2018)! While the green card is being processed, the worker cannot change employers or even be promoted, in effect creating a class of "bonded" workers for the company.

The Immigration Voice activist I spoke to, "Rudra," talked to me about the founding of the organization. He said that Indian workers interested in green cards had long been active through an immigration web portal. At the end of 2005, a budget reconciliation bill was being discussed on the Hill that had a provision that would have allowed for the green card quota to be exceeded. High-tech workers on the portal were closely following its progress. However, the provision was thrown out. At that point, Aman Kapoor decided that they needed to organize themselves under Immigration Voice to lobby for the issue and organized a conference call. A group met in Washington, DC in early 2006 and started to raise funds. Since members (estimated at around 15,000 in 2007) did not have green cards, they could not vote or even contribute to political campaigns in the United States. Consequently, they hired Patton Boggs, a top U.S. lobbying firm, to represent them. They kept in touch with their membership through web-based activism. Rudra claimed that they were the first within the Indian American community to mobilize politically through web activism. He also talked about how they found it difficult to navigate the complex American political process "since we are computer programmers, and we are completely out of our element when it comes to politics. In our work we deal with 1 and 0. But in politics it is always grey."

Rudra complained that established Indian Americans and their organizations were reluctant to take up their cause. I was surprised to hear this since, as in the case of my conversation with Sanjay Puri (earlier), immigration issues came up in almost all my discussions with Indian American activists. Rudra told me that a few Indian American leaders had connected Immigration Voice activists to congressional offices but had not been willing to push the issue themselves. I brought this issue up with some second-generation activists whom I spoke with after my conversation with Rudra. I think "Navin" provided the best explanation for the reluctance of even well-meaning immigrant-generation "uncles" to make the green card issue their cause. Navin explained that this was because Indian American leaders recognized the political sensitivity of the issue for members of Congress (due to opposition from American companies and workers) and the high price they would have to pay from their constituents if they supported the issue. "So, if you have a friendship with the Congressman and you ask him to support the green card issue and he says no, and Immigration Voice says help me please, how much pressure do you think the uncle is willing to put on the Congressman? I think not much." In other words, this is not a case where they would be pushing on an "open door" but a door that was almost shut.

SAALT and South Asian American Advocacy

In my 2007 conversation with Deepa Iyer, executive director of SAALT, she told me that SAALT was in regular contact with staffers from the Congressional Asian Pacific American Caucus and with individual members of Congress, mainly those who had large South Asian constituencies. They also worked with government agencies such as the Justice Department and Homeland Security. Since Sanjay Puri had made it clear that his "pitch" on the Hill was to emphasize the wealth and accomplishments of Indian Americans, I was curious about how SAALT made its case. Deepa told me that she did not approach members of Congress saying, "This is what we can give you." It was always, "These are groups and organizations in your district and so you are accountable to them." How successful had this been? I asked.

Deepa was modest, saying that it was "somewhat" successful considering that the organization had only moved to full-time staff status (with two staff) in 2004. But she pointed out that they had held a South Asian American briefing on the Hill in March that year (2007) as part of a three-day South Asia summit, the first national South Asia summit and South Asia briefing that had taken place, at least as far as they knew (subsequently, SAALT held these summits every two years). Around 20 staffers from the India, Pakistan, and Bangladesh caucuses; the Asian Pacific American caucus; and the immigration subcommittee attended the event and Deepa told me that they had responded very positively. The staffers told SAALT that they wanted to hear more about the domestic issues of South Asian Americans since all they normally heard about was foreign policy (i.e., issues regarding South Asia). Deepa added, "So this is our goal [to be available to address the domestic concerns of the South Asian American community]. We are not trying to be hugely powerful. It is more about moments where we can exercise power." She told me that the focus of SAALT was on the factors that prevented South Asian Americans from being engaged in civic society and politics in the United States, whether this was class, immigration status, racism, English proficiency, or marginalization. Their goal was to erode and eliminate these barriers. In a 2009 meeting she further clarified the focus of SAALT, saying that they worked on behalf of a range of groups:

> We advocated the Federal hate crimes bill that was just passed, and this affects everyone—whether it is a doctor or a waiter. But there are other sets of issues where we focus on members who may be of lower socio-economic status. For instance, in our advocacy for access to health care, we talk about how it is important that those who have limited English are able to access health care. We emphasize that our community comes in many stripes and forms and that there are gaps in terms of what services are reaching which groups and that we have to be aware of this.

At the March 2007 meeting, South Asian American groups from around the country asked SAALT to be their national representative and voice on the Hill. In 2008, the National Coalition of South Asian Organizations (NCSO) was formed with 34 groups (in 2014 there were 49 groups), coordinated by SAALT, and they held biennial summits, organized and led by SAALT. In our 2009 conversation Deepa constantly emphasized that SAALT was very careful to not claim to be speaking on behalf of all South Asian Americans but only for their dues-paying members and the groups served by their coalitional partners, and that they expressed only the interests that they heard through their town hall meetings and from the people who turned to their coalition partners since "we want to avoid being a shell." When I asked Deepa how the organization handled divisive issues (such as the Mumbai attacks that had mobilized the Indian American community), she told me that they had several groups that had contacted them interested in putting out a public response that was not "demonizing" Pakistan or asking for a cut for funding to Pakistan.

Civil Rights Advocacy, Outreach Activities

SAALT was involved in a variety of activities around the civil rights of South Asians in the United States. This included engaging in activities to support the civic and political engagement of South Asians in the country such as putting out guides for elections; conducting voter registration, election monitoring, and exit polling; and ensuring language access to ballots. They also worked to educate South Asian Americans about the importance of filling out the census forms and to ensure that census advertisements were translated into South Asian languages. Another of their activities was to support South Asians who were detained. According to their website, between 2014 and 2018, over 17,000 South Asians (with the numbers tripling between 2017 and 2018), mostly Indian, were arrested by Customs and Border Protection for crossing the border and sent to detention facilities, where they were held in very poor conditions without proper language access or support for religious or dietary needs. SAALT members provided legal and other types of support (including help to raise bond funds) and contacted journalists and members of Congress to demand investigations into the conditions under which detainees were being held (saalt.org/detainee-support). Gender rights and gender equity were of concern to the organization. SAALT partnered with South Asian American domestic violence organizations and contacted members of Congress when laws with an impact on South Asian women went through Congress (such as the problematic revision to the Violence against Women Reauthorization Act in 2012 or issues around the H-4 visa for dependents of H-1 visa holders). Racial and religious profiling and surveillance (e.g., in the post-9/11 period by New York City police) was another issue around which SAALT was very active. They mobilized with

Sikh American organizations to protest the mass shooting attacks against Sikhs in 2012 and 2021. They also partnered with Equality Labs to hold a congressional briefing on caste discrimination against oppressed-caste groups in the United States on May 22, 2019. With the deterioration of the situation of minorities in India, SAALT occasionally publicly commented on India-based issues dealing with human rights violations (starting in 2020), reversing its earlier policies. Finally, the organization compiled and put out demographic data on South Asian Americans, an important resource for journalists, policymakers, researchers, and others.

Recent Indian American Advocacy

It has been 20 years since USINPAC was founded to "represent the interests of the Indian-American community" (http://www.usinpac.com/about/), and until at least 2020, the organization was the only consistent Indian American voice on the Hill. Sanjay Puri continues to be the face of USINPAC. Since their online sites (website, Facebook, Twitter) are not updated regularly and they do not send out regular bulletins or newsletters (unlike some of the other advocacy groups), it has been harder to keep up with their activities. However, it was clear that USINPAC had become an important advocacy group on behalf of the government of India, particularly after the BJP came to power in 2014.

It is possible that USINPAC's position in this respect fits in with the members of the Indian diaspora with whom they engage, but Sanjay Puri also had a close connection with Narendra Modi even before Modi became prime minister. In 2010, Congressman Faleomavaega (D-American Samoa), who served in the House of Representatives from 1989 to 2015, visited Gujarat on the urging of USINPAC and introduced a statement in the Congressional Records in 2012 on behalf of USINPAC congratulating Modi on his re-election as chief minister of Gujarat. The congressman also had the American flag flown over the U.S. Capitol in honor of Modi on April 7, 2014, the day the national elections in India began, "to mark victory's dawn" (Faleomavaega 2014a), and again, on behalf of USINPAC, in honor of the BJP president Rajnath Singh on April 30, 2014, when voting was held in Lucknow, where Rajnath Singh was running as a candidate (USINPAC 2014). After Modi was elected as prime minister of India, Congressman Faleomavaega, likely again on the behest of USINPAC, waxed eloquent in a

Businesstoday.in opinion column on Modi's "stand for inclusive growth and development for all, and his Vibrant Gujarat brand," and about Sanjay Puri's efforts "to bring Vibrant Gujarat to the attention of US lawmakers at a time when Modi was Chief Minister" (Faleomavaega 2014b). Since Faleomavaega was the ranking member of the House Foreign Affairs Subcommittee on Asia, the Pacific, Central Asia, and Nonproliferation, it is not surprising that USINPAC, which focuses largely on foreign policy issues, forged a strong relationship with him. Although flying the flag over the U.S. Capitol in honor of Indian politicians might be dismissed as a symbolic gesture of little significance, framed certificates of the accompanying effusive statements (see Faleomavaega 2014a) from the U.S. Congressional Record can provide legitimacy and clout to leaders in India.

USINPAC's support of Hindu nationalism was also seen in 2013–2014. In November 2013, Indian American Muslim and secularist groups were successful in getting a resolution introduced in Congress by Congressmen Joseph Pitts and Keith Ellison (D-MN), the first Muslim member of Congress. House Resolution 417 focused on the 2002 human rights violations in Gujarat, called for the revoking of anti-conversion laws that exist in several Indian states, and asked that religious freedom be included in the U.S.-India Strategic Dialogue. Through their visits to Congress offices, the Hindu American Foundation and USINPAC activists succeeded in preventing the House resolution from being considered in the House (Janmohamed 2014; Faleomavaega 2014b). But the U.S. Congress went ahead with a hearing on the plight of religious minorities in India on April 4, 2014, just before the national elections in India. All panelists raised concerns about the situation of religious minorities in India and claimed that there had been many reports of religious violence over the past year. The only dissenting position at the hearing came from Congresswoman Tulsi Gabbard (D-HI, of Hindu background, who had been closely associated with Hindu American groups) and Congressman Faleomavaega, who both raised concerns about the timing of the hearing, just before the national elections in India. Congressman Faleomavaega also introduced the USINPAC statement in order, he said, to promote a "fair and balanced view" of the issue (Congressional Hearing 2014, 69). USINPAC's statement was shorter than that submitted by the Hindu American Foundation, but more than one-third of it repeated that of the HAF verbatim. Whether the USINPAC was repeating the words of the HAF or vice versa is unclear. However, several parts of the document make it clear that the statement was written on behalf of Hindus. For instance, USINPAC brought up the issue of the timing of the hearing and indicated,

"The Hindu American community clearly sees it as an attempt to influence the elections." A little later they referred to the composition of the panel, complaining that it had "no Hindu representation" (but did not mention the lack of Muslim or Sikh representation). The concerns of Hindus were mentioned two more times in the same paragraph (Congressional Hearing 2014, 82) This clear bias toward Hindus was despite USINPAC's claim to represent all Indian Americans and the fact that Hindu Americans then only constituted a little more than half of Indian Americans (also see Therwath 2007 for a similar point).

USINPAC also continued to oppose funding for Pakistan. In a letter to U.S. secretary of treasury Steve Mnuchin in March 2019, USINPAC asked for U.S. support in opposing any International Monetary Fund (IMF) loans to Pakistan until Pakistan ended "state-sponsored terrorism." On October 16, 2019, USINPAC, along with some regional Indian American organizations and an organization representing Kashmiri Hindus, hosted a Capitol Hill briefing on the situation in Kashmir (on August 5, 2019, the Indian government removed the articles that gave Kashmir autonomous status, clamped down on communications and mobility in the region, and also pre-emptively arrested a large number of Kashmiris) to present the Indian government's position: "On August 5, 2019, PM Modi's government took historic action to promote peace and reintegrate India-administered Jammu and Kashmir (J&K) by removing Articles 370 and 35A."[6] On October 22, 2019, the U.S. House of Representatives Foreign Affairs Subcommittee on Asia, the Pacific, and Nonproliferation held a briefing on the situation in Kashmir. USINPAC included a statement on Kashmir for the record. Their press release declared that their goal was to "counter any false narratives put forward." Their statement repeated that the goal of the removal of the articles of autonomy was to bring peace. It continued, "No one should use the removal of Article 370 to faith-bait. India is against terrorism, not religion." USINPAC also reiterated "that India is the largest democracy on Earth and PM Modi is a freely elected leader. He was elected in a landslide victory, as was his Party. The vast majority of Indian and Indian Americans stand with the Party and the PM."[7]

Indian American versus South Asian American Advocacy

This section provides further examples of the opposing goals of Indian American and South Asian American organizations around a variety of issues.

Immigration Reform

On May 22, 2007, at a time when there was a discussion about comprehensive immigration reform, the congressional India caucus organized a briefing session on the Hill on "Comprehensive Immigration Reform: What It Means to the Asian Indian Population in the U.S." The organizations that were invited were Immigration Voice, the AAPI (representing Indian American physicians), the AAHOA (representing Indian American hoteliers), and SAALT. I found it interesting that SAALT was invited to speak on the impact of the immigration bill on Indian Americans and not USINPAC. SAALT was also invited to participate in a hearing in the afternoon organized by the House Subcommittee on Immigration as the representative of South Asian Americans. In both presentations, SAALT representatives emphasized the diversity in the economic and immigration status of Indian Americans, pointing out that in terms of immigration status, members included citizens, legal permanent residents, skilled and unskilled workers on short-term visas, students, and a sizeable proportion of undocumented immigrants (at the time Indians constituted the fourth-largest and fastest-growing undocumented population in the United States). SAALT's emphasis on the diversity of Indian Americans contrasted with the focus of other Indian American organizations, which usually advocated just for a small group of the population. For instance, during the same period, USINPAC emphasized the importance of H-1B visas and family-based immigration, and Immigration Voice stressed green card backlogs. In 2007, when the abuse of over 500 Indian welders and pipe fitters (many of whom were Dalit) held in slave-like conditions by Signal International (a marine construction company that used the H-2B guest worker program to hire workers to repair oil rigs and other facilities damaged by Hurricane Katrina) came to light, SAALT was the only Indian/South Asian American organization to take up their cause.[8] SAALT also mobilized in support of DACA and the DREAM Act (both programs supported individuals who had been unlawfully brought into the country as young children, making them eligible for a work permit, and in the case of the DREAM Act, for permanent residency, under certain conditions), again unlike USINPAC and other Indian American organizations.

The issue of green card backlogs and attempts to remedy this situation has been periodically raised in Congress (e.g., between 2012 and 2014, when the issue of a comprehensive immigration reform plan was brought up again, and in 2017). In July 2019, the House of Representatives passed a law—the Fairness for High-Skilled Immigrants Act of 2019—eliminating the country caps on employment-based immigrant visas. It was sponsored by Zoe Lofgren, a Democrat from the Silicon Valley area of California, and Ken Buck, a Republican from Colorado (Indian American congressman Raja Krishnamoorthy was a cosponsor). Top Silicon Valley companies who likely pushed for the bill welcomed it, as did the U.S. Chamber of Commerce (perhaps in the face of research and reports indicating that well-qualified immigrant engineers from the United States were leaving for Canada due to the green card paralysis and Trump's hardline attitude on the H-4 visa for spouses of H-1B holders). The bill was introduced to the Republican-controlled Senate, where Kamala Harris was one of the sponsors (Mozumdar 2019a). Since most of the 800,000 individuals caught in the green card backlog were Indian nationals, Immigration Voice played an important advocacy role in gathering support for the bill (Hauslohner 2019). The bill almost passed the Senate but Senator Richard Durbin (D-IL) blocked it, arguing that it would unfairly penalize non-Indian nationals, and proposed a new bill, the Resolving Extended Limbo for Immigrant Employees and Families Act (RELIEF), which would raise the overall number of green cards (and consequently the number of immigrants), thus obviating the need to deal with country caps, leading to a standoff between the two versions of the green card bill.

Immigration Voice activists such as Aman Kapoor responded with fury protesting the bill, since they argued that it had no chance of passing a Republican-controlled Senate in this period of strong anti-immigrant sentiment. Immigration Voice led a campaign against Durbin "calling him a 'racist' and accusing him of 'ethnic cleansing' for stopping the Fairness for High-Skilled Immigrants Act" (Hauslohner 2019). However, SAALT opposed the Fairness for High-Skilled Immigrants Act. Lakshmi Sridaran, interim executive director of SAALT, criticized the "model minority" framing of Immigration Voice (which emphasizes the importance of highly skilled immigrants for the United States) and argued that the bill was "dangerous" because while countries like India would benefit, countries like Bangladesh, Pakistan, Sri Lanka, and Nepal would be badly affected with much higher wait times (Sridaran 2019). Instead, SAALT allied with the National Iranian American Council, United We Dream, and United Chinese Americans in supporting Senator Durbin's alternative legislation.

Hate Crimes

While USINPAC occasionally took up the issue of hate crimes (in 2013, it supported a new measure to expand the FBI's tracking categories of hate crimes to include Hindus and Sikhs), tracking hate crimes continued to be one of SAALT's regular activities. They put out a report in October 2010 on the "rise in xenophobic and racist rhetoric" attacking South Asian American political candidates and more generally on rhetoric against South Asians, Muslims, Sikhs, and Arab American communities portraying them as threats to American national security. This was followed by two reports in 2012 and 2013 on racial and religious profiling of South Asian American communities and three more reports in 2014, 2017, and 2018 on hate violence and xenophobic rhetoric directed against South Asian Americans. The 2018 report documented "record attacks since the election of President Trump in November 2016" and that "one in five perpetrators invoked President Trump's name, his administration's policies, or his campaign slogans during attacks" (SAALT 2018). The one time there was a concerted mobilization by USINPAC and SAALT around a hate crime was after an incident when Senator George Allen (R-VA) repeatedly called a second-generation Indian American man "macaca" during a 2006 campaign rally in southwestern Virginia (see Chapter 6 for more details).

Affirmative Action

Affirmative action is another issue where South Asian organizations and Indian American organizations tend to take opposing positions. In 2014, the U.S. Supreme Court upheld a law in Michigan (approved by voters) that banned affirmative action, one in a string of affirmative action lawsuits around the country. Indian American organizations such as the Educators' Society for Heritage of India, National Federation of Indian Associations (NFIA), and Global Organization of Persons of Indian Origin (GOPIO) supported the decision, while SAALT (along with groups like the Asian American Legal Defense and Education Fund[AALDEF]) opposed the decision (G. Joseph 2014a).

Overall, while many immigrant-generation Indian American activists I talked to were wary about or critical of SAALT because of their South Asian American platform and their advocacy of undocumented immigrants, many second-generation Indian Americans active on the Hill praised the professionalism of SAALT and their support for the 25 percent of Indian Americans (the disadvantaged members) that other Indian American organizations tended to ignore. In recognition of her contribution to the community, Deepa Iyer received the 2013 Person of the Year Award from *India Abroad* (a long-established weekly Indian American newspaper, and a prestigious award for Indian Americans) "for being a champion of immigrant rights; for her commitment to South Asian communities; for working towards creating a just and more welcoming America."[9]

Updates on USINPAC and SAALT

With the rise of new organizations such as *Indiaspora* (formed to make the diaspora "a force for good" through collaboration and community engagement) and the 2018 establishment of its Washington, DC office, and *Indian American IMPACT* (formed by second-generation men publicly launched in 2018 to help Indian Americans run for office and to elect politicians that support the progressive domestic interests of the community), USINPAC has been less visible as "the voice" of the Indian American community on Capitol Hill since around 2020. For instance, there was a strong, public mobilization by IMIPACT, Indiaspora, and other organizations in 2021 around COVID support and vaccines for India. USINPAC was not visible around this effort.

On March 2, 2023, SAALT made a dramatic announcement on their website (https://saalt.org/saalt-enters-period-of-organizational-transformation) to say that the organization was entering a period of "chrysalis" until late 2024 to "build an analysis of caste" and to change its leadership structure to a "co-stewardship model." It appears that this move was prompted by a recognition (perhaps pointed out by Ambedkarite activists) that the organization and leadership were not adequately sensitive to issues of caste. The statement continues:

> If we simply continued the work of SAALT as is, we would overlook the essential first step—to build an analysis of caste—through which we understand our South Asianness, and navigate the other values we hold dear. By not understanding caste, we lack a true understanding of ourselves and our peoples' histories....

Throughout our twenty-year history, SAALT's advocacy, policy, and programming have lacked this core foundation and at times have even been caste supremacist in nature as a result. This focused, intentional time to build a caste analysis is what is needed for us to be truly transformative as South Asian Americans and as a South Asian American serving institution.

This heartfelt and honest appraisal shows how the acknowledgment of caste and caste privilege has been a challenge even for progressive second-generation leaders and organizations attuned to race and religion. The next two chapters will demonstrate the importance of integrating caste into the discussion of race and religion.

Conclusion: Contrasting Patterns of Mobilization

This chapter examined the mobilization of those who were active as "Indian Americans" and those who were active as "South Asian Americans." As professionals and members of a U.S. group that has high levels of education and income, immigrant leaders who mobilized as "Indian Americans" used an ethnic model and wanted to distance themselves from "problematic" U.S. racial minorities. Indian American organizations articulated the interests of successful, elite Indian Americans involved in entrepreneurship. They were also Hindu centric. The organizations were mostly led by immigrant-generation, male entrepreneurs with strong ties with Indian businesses and, consequently, were also focused on trade issues. Indian American organizations primarily allied with Jewish and Hindu groups.

Second-generation leaders who mobilized under the "South Asian American" umbrella used a racial solidarity model—"SAALT is committed to racial justice through structural change" (https://saalt.org/about/about-saalt/). Even though the executive directors of SAALT and other key leaders (particularly in the initial founding period) were from Hindu backgrounds, they emphasized a pluralist, multireligious model of advocacy; operated from a social justice framework; and articulated the interests of the full range of South Asian Americans, concentrating primarily on the more disadvantaged and on domestic policy issues—"centering and prioritizing the demands of those most marginalized" ((https://saalt.org/about/about-saalt/). They allied with immigrant rights coalitional organizations; Asian Pacific American, Sikh, and Muslim organizations; and Equality Labs around caste discrimination. Yet, they were tripped up by their own caste-privileged position.

We see the importance of generational status (immigrants versus the American-born generation) in shaping how racial identity and racialization as well as the history of religious tensions in the homeland are perceived. The American-born generation was also more interested in domestic policy issues, while immigrants continued to be centered on homeland and foreign policy concerns. Perhaps because of their greater ease in the American system, second-generation activists were also comfortable publicizing the problems that their communities were dealing with, unlike the immigrant generation, which wanted to project an idealized version of their group to outsiders. All these differences worked together to give rise to fundamentally different patterns of mobilization on the part of Indian American versus South Asian American activists. However, some of these patterns may be fracturing in the current period (see Chapter 6) and should continue to be monitored.

While those who mobilized as South Asian Americans were using a pan-ethnic model, the development of South Asian American groups was a result of not only racial lumping as Brown-skinned individuals, the commonalities that these groups perceived among themselves in the American context, but also, very importantly, anger about marginalization within Asian American circles. In the United States, "Asians" are generally believed to be a racial group who are phenotypically East Asian (Nadal 2019). South Asians are excluded as Asians by mainstream discourses, by media such as the *New York Times* (e.g., see Ramakrishnan 2023), by other Asian American groups, and even by Asian American scholars and programs. As two leading Asian American scholars, Jennifer Lee and Karthick Ramakrishnan (2020, 1748), write, based on their analysis of the 2016 National Asian American Survey, "South Asians... perceive themselves as Asian but other groups [including other Asians] are significantly less likely to perceive [them] as Asian." Thus, Asian American pan-ethnicity only holds up for East Asian groups, and perhaps for some Southeast Asian groups (but see Nadal 2019). This is something that scholars writing about pan-ethnic Asian American groups (Espiritu 1992; Okamoto 2014) have overlooked.

There are several reasons for the gendered patterns of leadership that we saw in the immigrant versus the second generation. First, with a few exceptions,[10] the migration patterns of Indian Americans have been primarily male led (see Kurien 1999). Immigrants also tended to follow

Indian cultural and gendered norms emphasizing male dominance (see also Agarwala 2022, 206; Jones-Correa 1998b, on the male-dominated nature of immigrant organizations). These two factors resulted in immigrant-generation organizations being headed by men, often individuals who formed or got involved in Indian American organizations as a way to further their business interests, or those who did so to achieve community status *after* becoming financially secure. On the other hand, the American-born generation, both men and women, developed an interest in careers in political or civic engagement in college and sought training to further this interest (primarily in civil and human rights law or public policy) before getting involved in advocacy organizations. This is probably why we do not see the stark gendered differences in leadership that we do in the immigrant generation. The second generation is also much more sensitive about including women in leadership positions—this came up many times in my discussions with both men and women. The female leadership of organizations such as SAALT also made them proactive around gendered issues. It is also possible that the dominance of women in the nonprofit advocacy arena is because the compensation offered by nonprofit organizations is lower than in the private sector, making it less likely for men to opt for these positions. This is merely speculation since I did not ask about pay scales and this factor was only alluded to indirectly.

This chapter brought together a variety of debates and discussions about the factors promoting new ethnic activism and has shown how they link together. We see how and why individuals from the same ethnic group can mobilize in substantially different ways, challenging the idea that ethnic groups share common political interests and perspectives. Finally, the chapter presents a clear picture of how generational status can play a role in impacting mobilization patterns and strategies and can map onto other dichotomies in the literature: ethnic versus pan-ethnic mobilization, foreign policy versus domestic policy focus, an ethnic versus a racial model, the impact of religion on mobilization, and gendered patterns of leadership.

Notes

1. India has received the largest amount of remittances among countries in the world for several years in a row recently. In 2018, it received $79 billion, followed by China at $67 billion (https://economictimes.indiatimes.com/nri/forex-and-remittance/india-highest-recipient-of-remittances-at-79-bn-in-2018-world-bank/articleshow/68788815.cms).
2. See http://saalt.org/wp-content/uploads/2012/09/American-Backlash-report.pdf.
3. Condoleezza Rice had made this argument in 2000 (Rice 2000).
4. For the Hindu perspective, see Chhibber (2003) and Mehra (2003). For the South Asian point of view, see Farees (2004) and Ravishankar and Chandra (2004).

5. See W. Andersen (2006), Forsythe and Trehan (2006), and McIntire (2006).
6. http://www.usinpac.com/press-release/usinpac-jointly-holds-capitol-hill-briefing-on-kashmir/ (retrieved December 13, 2019).
7. http://www.usinpac.com/press-release/usinpac-on-the-record-with-us-house-of-representatives-regarding-kashmir/ (retrieved December 13, 2019).
8. In 2008, the Southern Poverty Law Center and other organizations filed a suit against the company on behalf of the workers, resulting in a $14 million verdict against the company in 2015.
9. Also see https://www.rediff.com/news/slide-show/slide-show-1-winners-gallery-india-abroad-person-of-the-year-2013/20140621.htm.
10. Among Indian American Christians from Kerala, female nurses were often the primary migrants, and husbands followed later (see Kurien 2017a).

4
Enacting Cultural Citizenship

Majority versus Minority Religious Status and Contemporary Mobilization around Domestic Issues

In the previous chapter we saw how Indian American and South Asian American groups drew on U.S. archetypes of activism—ethnic and racial—to model their own advocacy. This chapter focuses on how religious-minority Indian American groups initially adopted a different archetype of American activism: primarily of Jewish organizations. After September 11, 2001, most also drew lessons from U.S. civil rights organizations of racial minorities and melded religious and broader rights activism together. In the following sections we see the variety of ways in which Indian American religious advocacy organizations "perform" cultural citizenship and demand inclusion in the nation.

Religion has been a blind spot for multicultural citizenship policies in Western Europe and the United Kingdom since secularism has been a bedrock principle (Modood 2010). However, religious diversity was constitutive of American pluralism. Consequently, unlike in Europe, contemporary U.S. immigrant groups had precedents to follow. European literature centers Muslims since they are "the most prominent source of rights claims" (Koopmans 2013, 158) compared with other religious groups such as Hindus, Buddhists, and Confucianists, even relative to their proportions in the population (Koopmans 2013, 151). A focus on Indian Americans shows how other religious groups besides Muslims have become active in the United States. This chapter also explains why religious-minority status in the United States propels strikingly similar patterns of mobilization by Hindu, Sikh, and Muslim advocacy groups (very different from Indian American Christian organizations) around domestic policy issues, even though these religions and their U.S. religious communities are quite distinct. Briefly, "institutional isomorphism" (DiMaggio and Powell 1983), or the tendency for the organizational structures and strategies of successful groups to be adopted by others, is responsible for the many similarities among the advocacy organizations of Hindus, Sikhs, and Muslims in the United States. At the same time, there are also some differences, reflecting the characteristics of the particular group and the needs of its members.

The attacks of September 11, 2001, brought about a big change in the religious dynamics and mood of the country. While South Asian American organizations such as SAALT mobilized against hate crimes targeting South Asian Americans overall, several new organizations representing South Asian religious minorities were formed. Others were transformed. The backlash of 9/11 coincided with the coming of age of the second generation, and women and men of this generation played a leadership role in the formation of these new organizations. The immediate goal was to bring the hate crimes to the attention of authorities and to provide support and legal assistance for those attacked. As the organizations became more established, they also mobilized around longer-term goals. These post-9/11 organizations modeled themselves not just after Jewish organizations, but also after U.S. racial organizations such as the NAACP and its legal arm, the NAACP Legal and Defense Fund (LDF), as well as the many civil rights organizations of U.S. racial minorities (e.g., the Japanese American Citizens League [JACL], particularly its activism around reparations for Japanese internment; the League of United Latin American Citizens [LULAC]; the Mexican American Legal Defense and Education Fund [MALDEF]; and the Asian American Legal Defense and Education Fund [AALDEF]) and their mobilization around domestic policy (see Table 4.1).

As we will see, although their activism is based on minority religious status, or religious and cultural difference from the American mainstream, the groups highlight how their religions embody central American values

Table 4.1 Religious minority status and host country activism.

Basis of Mobilization	Characteristics of Groups	Main Focus	Nature of Mobilization	US Models Used
Religious Minority status in host country	Largely second generation	Domestic Policy	Around discrimination and for positive recognition	Minority US religious and racial groups and civil rights activism

and the ways their members contribute to American society and culture. In other words, cultural citizenship claims constitute a dialectical process: claims making is an attempt to reshape America to include and recognize new groups, but the groups emphasize forms of religion that fit American values (Bloemraad 2018; Ong 1996). This chapter will also discuss activism around caste discrimination in the United States, often led by Ambedkarite (Buddhist) organizations and leaders, supported by Hindu groups like Sadhana and Hindus for Human Rights on the one hand, and opposed by Hindu groups such as the Hindu American Foundation (HAF) on the other.

Activism before September 11, 2001

As a highly successful group integrated into mainstream American society while still maintaining religious and cultural distinctness, close community ties, and connections with the home country, American Jews are viewed as a group that has been able to "fit in" while remaining different. This is the route that Indian Americans also want to follow. Following the pattern of the Jewish Anti-Defamation League formed in 1913, the first organizations established by Muslim, Sikh, and Hindu Americans that were oriented toward the wider American society focused on prejudice and anti-defamation concerns. The *Council on American Islamic Relations* (CAIR) was formed in 1994 by three Arab Americans (later some Indian American Muslims joined CAIR) to address the negative portrayals of Muslims and of Islam. In 1996, Sikhs formed the *Sikh Media Watch and Resource Task Force* (SMART) to combat negative stereotypes about Sikhs in the media. In 1997, the Hindu umbrella organization, Vishwa Hindu Parishad of America (VHPA), formed *American Hindus against Defamation* (AHAD), with the goal of defending Hinduism against defamation, commercialization, and misuse. Subsequently, several other Hindu anti-defamation groups were formed around the country, including the *Hindu International Council against Defamation* (HICAD) based in New Jersey. As civil rights and discrimination issues started coming to the fore after the attacks of 9/11, each of these anti-defamation organizations went on to either develop other foci (e.g., CAIR), to morph into other types of organizations (e.g., SMART), or, in the case of Hindu umbrella groups, to give rise to other national organizations such as the Hindu American Foundation in 2003.

The Watershed of September 11, 2001: New Mobilization around Domestic Issues

Muslim Mobilization

While there is no specifically Indian American Muslim organization mobilizing around U.S.-based concerns, Indian American Muslims have been important American Muslim leaders who have founded institutions to promote interfaith dialogues, to explain Islam, and to advocate for the American Muslim community. We have seen in Chapter 2 that some of this activism began before the attacks of 9/11. However, for the most part, pre-9/11 activism focused on issues in India or on American Muslim immigrants, attempting, as Dr. Sayyid Sayeed did, to redefine Islam in a pluralistic and democratic context. In the post-9/11 period, attention shifted to engaging the wider American society as representatives of American Muslims.

Three immigrant Indian American Muslims, Dr. Sayyid M. Sayeed, then secretary general of the Islamic Society of North America (ISNA) based in Indiana; Dr. Muqtedar Khan, then a political scientist at Adrian College, Michigan; and Dr. Parvez Ahmed, an academic then at Penn State University in Harrisburg, emerged as important leaders of the Muslim American community in the 9/11 aftermath. Sayeed was one of the first Muslim American leaders to publicly condemn "the attacks as contrary to Islam." He also urged American Muslims to raise funds for victims and their families. He was commended for his efforts to educate Americans about Islam and for his interfaith work in the aftermath of 9/11 by Indiana governor Frank O'Bannon in January 2002 (Whittle 2006). Khan posted a "Memo to American Muslims" on his website on October 5, 2001, criticizing American Muslims for their silence and hypocrisy. He wrote, "Muslims love to live in the U.S. but also love to hate it" and went on to argue that American democratic values were "aligned with the highest values in Islam—peace and tolerance" (Soulsman 2006). Subsequently, Khan published *American Muslims: Bridging Faith and Freedom* in 2002. In the foreword, well-known Islamic scholar Akbar S. Ahmed described Khan as a "leading spokesman of the Muslim community" (M. Khan 2002, ix). Dr. Parvez Ahmed talked to me about how the attacks of 9/11 prompted him to get involved in Muslim institutions in the United States. He had been a student in Texas when the 1995 bombing of the Murray Federal Building in Oklahoma City had taken place (perpetrated by two White-power activists) and "there was a backlash on the Muslim community even though the Muslim community had nothing to do with it." Even before the identity of the 9/11 perpetrators was confirmed, his 1995 experience made Ahmed sensitive to the fact that the 9/11 attacks could result in a rash of hate crimes directed against Muslims.

> And I kind of participated in those conversations, what to do next, how to help the community, how to prepare the community. And I guess because . . . I had the ability to speak in public, members of the community wanted me to go out and speak to other institutions who were looking to hear from Muslim representatives in their community. So that kind of started me on this path . . . [although people like us had] never envisioned ourselves in this position of representing Muslims of this country.

This experience of being called to speak as a representative of American Muslims also prompted Ahmed to become active in a local CAIR chapter to encourage American Muslims to become more active in the wider society. Declaring that "my Islamic values require me to be of service to broader humanity," Parvez Ahmed went on:

> Post-9/11, the Muslim community was not only suffering from a variety of draconian policies and attitudes but also, I felt that there was a need to help the Muslim community open up to embracing a robust interfaith dialogue, a robust broader civic engagement, which I did. I used my platform at CAIR to push for greater interfaith dialogue and greater civic engagement.

For second-generation South Asian Muslim Americans, the attacks of September 11, 2001, were a "formative moment" as Fatima explained, pushing many into legal careers. Fatima, who was of Indian ancestry, described how her Muslim identity "was more invisibility and sort of a blissful anonymity" while growing up. But after 9/11, while the rest of America was "becoming unified and sort of dealing with the healing process together as a nation," she realized that Muslims had suddenly become "the other." At the time, Fatima was involved with the Bay Area Association of Muslim Lawyers (a chapter of the *National Association of Muslim Lawyers* [NAML]), which started organizing "know your rights" presentations in the

Muslim community trying to be a bridge between Muslims and those in the civil rights legal community. Several members of NAML (which included Indian American board members like Asifa Quraishi), who were based in Washington, DC, saw that there was no strong Muslim voice to challenge the provisions of the Patriot Act passed right after 9/11 on October 26, 2001. The act heavily targeted Muslims, leading to indefinite detentions, searches of homes and businesses, and FBI surveillance at mosques. Originally set to end in 2005, it was subsequently revised and extended. Concern over the act and its violation of the civil rights of Muslim Americans led members of the NAML to form a charitable organization, *Muslim Advocates*, in 2005. Based in the San Francisco Bay Area, the organization at the time comprised largely younger, legally trained South Asian American Muslims who, in the aftermath of 9/11, got involved in legal action to challenge the Patriot Act and racial and religious profiling. I asked Fatima (who was active in Muslim Advocates) why the organization was composed largely of South Asian Americans, and she replied that it may have been because South Asian Americans were "ahead" of other Muslim groups in terms of class and educational background. Also, she felt that there was a bigger divide between Muslims who were religious and those who were secular among Arab and Iranian communities, whereas "as a South Asian Muslim, you were friends with people who didn't practice at all, and also those who were much more conservative. There was kinda more fluidity in those identities." According to her, Muslim Advocates was founded by individuals who identified as Muslim but were generally progressive in their outlook. "And I think it's kind of the ability to be in that middle which maybe made South Asians more prominent in groups like Muslim Advocates."

Sikh Mobilization

Turban-wearing Sikhs became particularly vulnerable to hate crimes after September 11, 2001, since they were often mistaken for Osama Bin Laden followers. Balbir Singh Sodhi of Arizona was a Sikh who was killed on September 15, 2001, by a man who thought Sodhi was a Muslim. This was the first fatality and one of the 645 incidents of violent backlash targeting individuals of South Asian or Middle Eastern descent in the week after the 9/11 attacks (SAALT 2001). In describing how Sikhs were affected right after 9/11, a young activist from the Richmond Hill locality of Queens (an area with a large Sikh settlement, which he noted "had become pretty much our neighborhood") spoke of a Sikh man walking down the street who was beaten up by a bunch of young White men with baseball bats. "So that was a shocker to everybody. We thought we were safe in Richmond Hill after India [a reference to the anti-Sikh attacks in India] and now this was happening to us." Another young Sikh told me of hearing about "someone getting shot on 57th street because of their turban and the police not registering a case. And the community was not taken seriously by law enforcement and also the media and politicians." The "horrible, burning platform of 9/11" led to the formation of a new Sikh advocacy organization in the United States and the refocusing of others. The *Sikh Coalition*, one of the major U.S. Sikh advocacy organizations, was formed in the weeks after 9/11. Discussing its founding, "Amrita," a second-generation Sikh woman, one of the founding members, argued that the need had been urgent

> because it was such a big tragedy that occurred. And Sikhs were being impacted and targeted so, so deeply and so violently, that, you know, people took six months off work, and . . . stopped going to school . . . they spent a lot of time addressing these issues because they just felt like they couldn't do any other work.

Another Sikh Coalition activist, "Gyanpreet," also a second-generation woman, indicated that they had been able to get invited to meetings in Washington, DC in the early post-9/11 days through their contacts with Asian American civil rights leaders like Karen Narasaki,

> and it was people like her who were able to sort of say to the government, these people are really having a problem, and you need to give them a seat at the table . . . and so it was through those contacts that we were able to essentially meet with government officials and get invited to meetings to discuss what people were seeing, you know, as this emerging backlash.

The Sikh organization SMART changed its focus to civil rights issues after 9/11 and renamed itself the *Sikh American Legal Defense and Education Fund* (SALDEF) in 2004. Yet another Sikh American organization, *United Sikhs*, which had originally been created in 1999 to help the underprivileged in

New York City's borough of Queens, also changed its mission after 9/11 to focus on international issues of concern to the Sikh diaspora and to provide help during humanitarian crises around the world.

Hindu Mobilization

In 2001, Hindus did not have a national advocacy organization, and Hindus were generally overlooked in the several interfaith events that were organized in the wake of 9/11. In the days after 9/11, America's "Judeo-Christian" sacred canopy seemed to stretch into an "Abrahamic" one that included Muslims, as Muslim clerics (who repeatedly emphasized that they were part of the same tradition as Christians and Jews) were incorporated into the numerous interfaith services organized in different parts of the country. Hindu Americans viewed the development of the "Abrahamic" American sacred canopy with alarm, fearing that it would further marginalize non-Abrahamic religions such as Hinduism. Hindu International Council against Defamation (HICAD) and several hundred individual Hindus sent a petition to President George Bush, "Why Do You Exclude Hindus from Your Prayers?," a reference to the fact that Hindu leaders were not invited to be part of the national prayer service on September 16, 2001 (Kurien 2003). They emphasized that Hindus were a numerically and professionally significant part of the United States and were model citizens who needed to be included within "America's pluralistic and multicultural traditions." The petition referred to Hinduism being a monotheistic religion (worship to the "One Almighty God") that is over "8,000 years old"; it also emphasized exemplary intergenerational and gender relations among Hindus ("We are a family-oriented people with low divorce rates . . . we save for our children's education and support our elders and extended families") and repeatedly stressed the tolerance and pluralism of Hindus (describing them as "peace-loving," upholding "nonviolence, pluralism and respect" as central tenets). The petition also drew attention to the difference between Hinduism and Islam, for instance, by pointing out that Hindus "never threaten violence against our host country" and that there was "no worldwide Hindu network of terrorists."

As mentioned, the Hindu American Foundation was formed in 2003. Since the organization was led by American-born Hindus, they argued that they brought a "paradigm shift" to national and international advocacy on behalf of Hindus by adopting a "wholly US-centric approach" (S. Shukla 2008, 26). One of the cofounders of the organization told me in a 2007 interview that unlike the other Hindu American organizations run by Indian immigrants focused only on issues in India, the Hindu American Foundation wanted to represent all Hindu Americans, including Hindus of Indian ancestry from other parts of the diaspora like Fiji and Africa, Hindus from Bangladesh and Pakistan, and Anglo-American Hindus (e.g., belonging to the International Society for Krishna Consciousness [ISKCON], an American Hindu organization founded in New York City in 1966). She continued saying that the HAF also wanted to speak on behalf of Hindus in countries around the world. "So, we want to be like the AJC (American Jewish Committee) or CAIR (Council on American-Islamic Relations)." It is significant that she referenced the foremost Jewish and Islamic advocacy organizations in the United States. While HAF leaders emphasized that the organization was not affiliated with any religious or political organization or entities, most of their members and their "high-end donors" were first-generation Indians (Melwani 2009), likely individuals affiliated with Sangh Parivar organizations, which undoubtedly had an impact on the HAF platform.

Sadhana: Coalition of Progressive Hindus was formed in October 2011 in New York City by an Indian American and two Caribbean American Hindus. They were motivated by the lack of a progressive Hindu voice in the United States, including at interfaith meetings and discussions, and by the apparent absence of individuals who got involved in social justice causes as Hindus, motivated by their Hindu values. Initially they focused on issues in New York City but later expanded their scope to other parts of the United States. An important difference between Sadhana and the HAF was that Sadhana did not just advocate for Hinduism or Hindus. Instead, they advocated for a variety of marginalized groups including Muslims and Dalits based on "the values at the heart of Hinduism." These values included a deep emphasis on the oneness of all people (*Vasudhaiva Kutumbakam*, or the "world is one family," is a Sanskrit phrase found in several ancient Hindu texts that they quoted) that motivated their social justice activism. During my 2015 interviews with three Sadhana activists, I learned that they had received overtures from the HAF in their early days to which they had responded cordially and had worked with the HAF on some projects. However, my 2020 interview with a Sadhana activist made clear that Sadhana was no longer working with the HAF. As we will see, Sadhana and HAF activists have sometimes ended up on opposite sides of several mobilization campaigns.

Ambedkarites: Mobilization around Domestic Issues Primarily after 2015

The Dalit community in the United States was very small in 2001 and there was no visible Dalit organization mobilizing around domestic U.S. issues. Ambedkarite organizations started forming a few years later as more Dalit immigrants arrived on H-1B visas to work in the IT sector. Equality Labs was the first Ambedkarite organization to publicly mobilize around U.S.-based caste discrimination.

Christians—Lack of Mobilization around Domestic Issues

At the time of the September 11, 2001, attacks, I was conducting research in an Indian Christian parish in the United States and examining adjustments that members and clergy were having to make to traditional ideologies and practices in the American setting (see Kurien 2017a). Through the people I was in touch with at the time, I heard about several Indian American Christian men who shaved off their beards and moustaches after 9/11 to avoid being viewed as Muslim and targeted in a hate crime, and how several stuck American flags on their cars to show their patriotism. Some women also avoided wearing Indian clothes in public. However, these actions remained at the individual level and did not translate into any type of group mobilization. In fact, there has not been any organized effort on the part of Indian American Christians to mobilize around domestic, U.S.-based issues. Second-generation Indian American Christians in particular (also some immigrants) stressed commonalities with White American Christians, quite unlike other Indian American religious groups. Though interviewees sporadically referred to experiences of racial discrimination, they framed it as an outcome of a few prejudiced individuals rather than any larger structural reasons (see Kurien 2017a).

Education and Awareness

Due to the lack of understanding and negative stereotypes of Islam, Hinduism, and Sikhism in the United States, and the absence of a required religious education curriculum in American schools, an important task facing Muslim, Hindu, and Sikh American organizations has been to educate Americans about their respective religions. In the aftermath of 9/11, SALDEF, CAIR, and MPAC, representing Sikhs and Muslims who were most under attack, developed programs to educate and train law enforcement personnel about the cultural and religious heritage of their communities and to create a relationship with their communities, who were often viewed with suspicion. CAIR, MPAC, the Sikh Coalition, and SALDEF also worked on educating the Transportation Security Administration (TSA) at airports about the rights of Muslims and Sikhs around their symbols of faith, including the Muslim *hijab* and the Sikh turban and *kirpan* (ceremonial dagger carried by initiated, *Khalsa* Sikhs), to ensure that Muslim and Sikh air travelers were not harassed. In a 2011 interview, an MPAC activist described how she conducted a TSA training. "I trained 2,200 officers at LAX [Los Angeles International Airport], and I'm trying to just revamp my cultural training and make it even tighter." She talked about how some of the TSA officers were initially hesitant

> because some were like, are they gonna try to convert us? [Laughs] But then they realized this is way more about culture than religion. It's to help you out, because LAX [Los Angeles] is such a diverse city. So . . . so it's all about like when I framed it like that, I think they were more accepting of it. When they saw that I'm not really touching on religion so much as I am on culture, I think they really accepted it!

More recently (e.g., in 2019), the Sikh Coalition was also holding awareness sessions for National Park Service security personnel (e.g., at the Statue of Liberty National Monument on Ellis Island).

Working with Media Organizations

The Muslim Public Affairs Council (MPAC), based in Los Angeles, had a Hollywood bureau that worked with television networks, film studios, and production companies to ensure "that audiences see Muslims as vital contributors to creating social and cultural change in America and around the world."[1] Sikh advocacy organizations also worked with media organizations to educate Americans about Sikhs. Based on a 2013 report, "Turban Myths," prepared by SALDEF and Stanford University, which showed that

70 percent of Americans misidentified turbaned Sikhs, SALDEF developed a short video public service announcement media message, first aired in July and August 2014 via Comcast. Comcast provided a $2 million donation to enable SALDEF to create the message and provided substantial funding to enable the message to be broadcast every year since 2014. The PSA featured Sikh American model and actor Waris Singh Ahluwalia, who wears a turban. After several images of turbaned Sikhs participating in a range of activities in the United States, Waris ends the PSA saying, "For over 125 years, Sikhs have been part of the American culture. My name is Waris, and I am proud to be American."[2] The National Sikh Campaign (NSC), an organization created in 2014, based in Washington, DC, whose goal is to educate American society about Sikhism and the positive contributions of Sikh Americans, launched a series of "We Are Sikhs" commercials that aired nationally on CNN and Fox News as well as on TV channels in Fresno (home to one of the largest concentrations of Sikhs in the country as well as one of the areas where Sikhs suffer the most hate crimes).[3] The commercials focused on Sikhism and its progressive values, how Sikh Americans shared common values and interests with other Americans, and why Sikhs were proud to be Americans. Another series of advertisements targeted PBS children's programs to educate children about Sikh practices and answer questions children might have about their Sikh friends.[4] The campaign won the top 2018 *PRWeek* U.S. Public Cause award for its portrayals of Sikhs "as neighbors and everyday Americans who face discrimination due to ignorance of their faith" (Louis 2018). The NSC organization also formed We Are Sikhs chapters in areas around the country with significant Sikh populations to engage with the wider society in a variety of ways, including through participation in July 4th parades and baseball games.

The Sikh Coalition's media and communication team organized a traveling photography exhibit on the Sikh turban and identity starting in New York City in September 2016, and from there it moved to Maryland, Illinois, Texas, and Los Angeles (at the Museum of Tolerance in the fall of 2019). Through their networking and advocacy, they were able to get Sikhs featured in television programs such as a 2016 segment with Hasan Minhaj on "Confused Islamaphobes Target American Sikhs" (part of Trevor Noah's Daily Show) and the CNN docuseries *The United Shades of America with W. Kamau Bell* in May 2018. Sikhs were also one of the three groups (along with Jews and Muslims) included in the 2019 CBS Religion and Culture's special "Religion and Identity in Young America." In the 2016 humorous segment aimed at teaching Americans about the Sikh faith, Manhaj, himself a Muslim, joked that he dealt with Islamophobia by working hard at blending in by acting "super White" and asked his Sikh panelists why they did not distance themselves from Muslims when they were mistaken for being one. The Sikh leaders responded that this was not an option for them since their faith enjoined them to "treat humanity with care and kindness." Despite being mistaken for Muslims and becoming targets of hate crimes and the TSA after the 9/11 attacks, second-generation Sikh leaders have consistently emphasized that this did not mean that they should join Islamophobes in attacking Muslims.

Sikh Americans participated in major U.S. parades—including around Memorial Day—to highlight the contribution of Sikh soldiers fighting as part of the British army in the two world wars. Sikh American groups have also sponsored a float at the New Year's Rose Bowl Parade in Pasadena, California, since 2014. Finally, Sikh Americans also organize their own parades in cities around the country to celebrate Sikh festivals. Thousands of Sikh men in colorful turbans and Sikh women in vibrant, brocaded Punjabi clothing participate in the Annual Sikh Day Parade in New York City that Sikh Americans have organized since 1987. A similar annual parade is also held in Los Angeles. Sikhs have organized an annual parade in Indianapolis since 2015. The Sikh parade in Yuba City, California, with several large floats is the oldest (begun in 1979) and most famous. Over 100,000 people attend every year (based on estimates provided by newspaper articles covering the parade over a period of several years). In the summer of 2020, Sikh communities around the country got involved in serving free community meals at pandemic hotspots (at a time when soup kitchens and food banks were running out of food) and at racial justice protests around the country, drawing on their experience of cooking and serving the langar (community meal provided to all visitors at the gurdwara). On June 8, 2020, the *New York Times* ran a long piece, "How to Feed Crowds in a Protest or Pandemic: The Sikhs Know,"[5] with several pictures of turbaned, masked, gloved Sikh men and women preparing, packing, or distributing plastic containers of food. The story focused on how cooks in "at least 80 gurdwaras" around the country were serving hot meals to anyone who wanted food, since "an essential part of Sikhism is langar, the practice of preparing and serving a free meal to promote the Sikh tenet of seva, or selfless service." It provided much more information about Sikhism and Sikh Americans and about the hate crimes that the community faced after September 11, 2001.[6]

Activists from Muslim, Sikh, and Hindu organizations gave innumerable talks and presentations around the year in a variety of venues. They also wrote media articles to educate Americans on the positions of the religious tradition or the group on various current issues. HAF activists were active contributors to online publications such as the *Huffington Post*, Patheos.com, the "On Faith" section of the online edition of the *Washington Post/Newsweek*, and Beliefnet.com for some years until around 2011. For instance, Aseem Shukla, cofounder of the HAF, described the contrast between Abrahamic traditions and religions like Hinduism as that between "exclusivists and pluralists" (A. Shukla 2010c). He also contrasted the Hindu view of homosexuality "as an external trait that cannot taint the immortal and immanent divinity ensconced in every being" (A. Shukla 2010a) with the perspective of some "Semitic" religious groups that oppose same-sex behavior based on their understanding that lesbian and gay individuals are denied entry into heaven and are condemned to everlasting hell. In 2010, the HAF launched a "Take Back Yoga" campaign with Aseem Shukla's article in the *Washington Post*'s "On Faith Blog" titled "The Theft of Yoga." In the article, Shukla pointed out that yoga originated in ancient Hindu texts, making it a Hindu practice, and that it consisted of more than just physical exercises. The campaign received coverage in articles in the *New York Times* and CNN. Shukla's claims were rebutted by Deepak Chopra, who argued that yoga's roots long predated that of modern Hinduism.[7] Scholar of religion, writer, social media influencer, and Sikh Coalition leader Simran Jeet Singh was, until 2017, an active contributor to HuffPost, writing about the Sikh tradition, and since 2018 has become a columnist for Religion News Service.

Education about Caste

Caste has been a sensitive issue for the HAF since they recognize that this is one of the few things that Americans know about India and that caste is one of the cudgels people use to attack Hinduism. In 2011, the organization released a report, *Hinduism: Not Cast in Caste: Seeking an End to Caste-Based Discrimination* (this report was first released in December 2010 and resulted in a torrent of protests from Hindus in India; in response, the HAF revised the report and published it in July 2011—see Chapter 5 for more details), where they made the arguable claim that caste was not mentioned in the central sacred texts of Hinduism, but only in secondary texts, which meant that it was not intrinsic to Hinduism. HAF activists wrote media articles to publicize their position (e.g., see S. Shukla 2011).

Raising awareness among Indian Americans about how caste advantage and disadvantage work was an important goal of anti-caste activists like Soundararajan and her Equality Labs associates. Similar to White privilege discussions, they launched discussions of caste privilege in the diaspora. In a 2015 article they pointed out that caste migrated along with South Asians and argued, "It is time that those who are Savarna, or Upper-caste, begin **to learn to name and own** their privilege and take on the burden of educating and dismantling caste in your own families and social networks" (emphasis in the original). They critiqued the "I don't see caste" stance of privileged-caste Indian Americans and continued, "Privilege provides you the opportunity to unsee caste and with it also your own caste heritage . . . this is caste privilege 101" (Soundararajan and Varatharajah 2015). Thenmozhi Soundararajan and Yashica Dutt challenged the HAF position on caste and wrote about caste discrimination in Silicon Valley (Y. Dutt 2020; Soundararajan 2020) and the battle over the portrayal of caste in California textbooks (Soundararajan 2016)—see the following sections for details on both. Ambedkarites in the Boston area were able to get WGBH, the Boston Public Radio station, in collaboration with PRI's *The World* and the Pulitzer Center, to run a four-part series on "Caste in America" in the spring of 2019 with interviews with several Ambedkarite activists in the Boston area who talked about the insidious ways caste operated on U.S. university campuses.

Education through Their Websites

The websites of the organizations are a very important site providing education about the groups as well as information about their activities. I conducted a systematic analysis in August 2020. This was while Donald Trump was in office, after the coronavirus pandemic had hit the United States, and in the middle of the racial justice protests. Some organizations had sections of their websites dedicated to the media (e.g., the "For the Media" section of the Hindu American Foundation website and the "Newsroom" section of the Sikh Coalition and Muslim Advocates websites). Besides educating the wider American society, the websites also provided resources for their own communities, including educating them on their rights and providing contact information to report discrimination and hate crimes. The Sikh

Coalition, SALDEF, and United Sikh websites had detailed information about the 2020 census, which had become an important point of mobilization for Sikh Americans (see more below, A Political Voice). Sadhana also provided detailed information about the census since the Indo-Caribbean community tended to be undercounted. The Hindu American Foundation had a brief mention about the census, urging people to fill out the form, while the Muslim Public Affairs Council's website featured a statement about the unconstitutionality of Trump excluding undocumented immigrants from the census.

Muslim Advocates provided resources on denaturalization (when the federal government strips naturalized citizens of their citizenship, which they indicate had significantly increased under the Trump administration) and had a "Take Action" section listing issues of concern that they wanted the community to mobilize around such as stopping anti-Muslim violence on Facebook, urging Congress to do more to end police violence, and demanding justice for an unarmed Black Muslim man in Phoenix who was killed by police pressing their knees on his neck, in much the same way as George Floyd. Muslim Advocates prominently highlighted their role in working for the defeat of Trump's "Muslim ban," resulting in the U.S. House of Representatives voting to reverse this ban on July 22, 2020, and showcased the impressive range of work the organization had engaged in to "halt bigotry" against Muslim Americans. This included advocacy for religious freedom for Muslims such as their right to build mosques in the United States, to practice Islam in prisons, and to be free from discrimination in the workplace. Under their mission to end law enforcement bias toward Muslims, they included an eye-opening 2011 report detailing the extreme surveillance that Muslims and Arabs were put through during the 10 years after the passage of the Patriot Act. Muslim Advocates described how they had been pressuring hotel chains (with some success) to ban the holding of hate group (primarily White nationalist) events on their premises. They also documented Islamophobia on Twitter and Facebook and indicated that they had filed a brief (June 2, 2020) to challenge the new rule of the Trump administration that visa applicants had to disclose their social media information.

In the summer of 2020, most Muslim, Hindu, and Sikh organizations, as well as Equality Labs, provided COVID-19 informational and support resources for their communities on their websites. In August of 2020, SALDEF's website also featured a link to a national survey of Sikh Americans, "the first ever survey of the Sikh American community in the United States" to provide a profile of the Sikh community as a resource for the community and for policymakers. On their website (http://hinduamerican.org), the Hindu American Foundation offered an "About Hindus and Hinduism" link featuring a Hinduism 101 lesson and providing resources on Hinduism to schoolteachers and others. In 2020, the HAF launched a podcast series, "That's So Hindu," with interviews and conversations with prominent Hindus in a variety of fields. The website also had information distancing Hinduism from caste as well as a critique of the Equality Lab survey of casteism in the United States[8] (see below this section and also The Battle Over California State Textbooks) for being biased and based on "non-randomized population samples" primarily among immigrants. On their website, Sadhana also featured information about a "Progressive Priests Network" that they had access to, of Hindu priests who were willing to perform interfaith and same-sex marriages. Their website also featured a Hindutva 101 feature, "a guide for discussing Hindu nationalism with your parents, friends, colleagues." It emphasized their belief that Hindutva "violates the core teachings of Hinduism," that it was also an "American problem" since Hindutva activists "have a significant presence" in the United States, and that Hindus "have a special responsibility to speak out against Hindutva." Their "Hindu Apology for Caste and Untouchability" was directed toward Hindu Americans, pointing out, for instance, that Hindus should stop justifying the caste system as being "a creation of foreigners" (i.e., of Mughal and British rulers, a favorite Hindutva argument) since caste existed since at least 400 CE—fifth-century Chinese pilgrim Fa-Hsien discussed untouchability as a practice in India.

Equality Lab's website indicated that their mission was to "fight the oppressions of caste apartheid, Islamophobia, White supremacy, and religious intolerance" and that their membership "includes Dalit and Bahujan (caste-oppressed communities), Adivasi (indigenous people of South Asia), Muslim, Buddhist, Sikh, and Christian South Asians."[9] Most prominent was information from their online survey on caste in the United States conducted in 2016, taken by over 1,500 individuals. Among the key findings was that one out of two Dalits lived in fear of their caste being "outed," two-thirds of Dalits in the United States reported being treated unfairly in their workplaces due to their caste identity, one in three Dalit students reported being discriminated against, and one in four reported facing verbal or physical assault based on their caste identity.[10]

Virtual Programming around Race

While Dalit, Muslim, Hindu, and Sikh organizations in August 2020 all carried statements in support of Black Lives Matter (BLM) activists who were organizing protests around the country after the killing of George Floyd, against the rash of murders of unarmed Black men and women, Dalit and Sikh organizations went the furthest in developing programming that explained the stakes involved and why it was important for their communities to understand the issues so they could become good allies in the BLM struggles. Both groups also drew parallels between the historical and contemporary position of Black Americans with that of Dalits and Sikhs in India. Equality Labs had several virtual events including South Asians in solidarity with Black Lives Matter, queer South Asian poets, and the Quran as a liberating text for social justice activism. The Sikh Coalition conducted a week-long, virtual summer series in August 2020 with one session on race and solidarity (with W. Kamau Bell). SALDEF went even further. Between August 15 and September 15, 2020, it organized a six-part webinar series, "Demystifying U.S. History and Activating Sikh Action for Black Justice Movements," led by cofounder Dr. Jaideep Singh, a scholar of American history. Featuring African American scholars in discussion with SALDEF activists, the series was intended to educate Sikh Americans about the history of race in the United States so they could understand their location as U.S. religious and racial minorities and could be allies in the struggle for racial equality.

American Academia and School Textbooks

American Academia

Members of minority religious traditions in the United States feel that their religious traditions are not adequately understood and portrayed by American academia. This has motivated them to fund programs and endowed chair positions to teach their religions. The *Sikh Foundation*, a California-based organization founded in 1967 by Narinder Singh Kapany, a Sikh physicist and founder of a successful Silicon Valley optics company, focused on showcasing Sikh art (sponsoring exhibitions at the San Francisco Asian Art Museum, the Victoria and Albert Museum in London, the Royal Ontario Museum, the Smithsonian, and the Rubin Museum of Art in New York City) and establishing Sikh studies chairs at several California universities starting with the University of California, Santa Barbara (1999) and then expanding, with community support, to the University of California, Riverside (2006); California State University East Bay (2007); and the University of California, Santa Cruz (2010). In 2015, a Sikh studies program was started at the Graduate Theological Union in Berkeley with the support of the Sikh Foundation.[11] Other Sikh philanthropists set up a Center for Sikh Studies at Claremont Lincoln University in California (2013), a Sikh studies endowed chair position at the University Michigan, Ann Arbor, in 2006 and at the University of California, Irvine, in 2017. On the East Coast, two endowed chair positions (one in Sikh studies in 2000 and another in Sikh musicology in 2011) were set up at Hofstra University, New York.

Hindu American leaders like Rajiv Malhotra of the Infinity Foundation have long argued that the academic study of religion in the United States has been based on the model of the "Abrahamic" traditions and that this model is not applicable to religions such as Hinduism. Related to this critique is their condemnation of the study and presentation of Hinduism by American scholars (see Kurien 2007a, 192–204 for details about the claims and mobilization around the academy by Hindu American activists). The Infinity Foundation has sponsored scholarship from a Hindu-centric perspective, including the 2007 book *Invading the Sacred: An Analysis of Hinduism Studies in America* (http://invadingthesacred.com), and Rajiv Malhotra, who retired early from a career in the software industry, has himself written and published several books, including *Academic Hinduphobia: A Critique of Wendy Doniger's Erotic School of Indology* (2016).[12] Hindu groups also endeavored to sponsor endowed chair positions, but with less success than Sikh and Muslim organizations. The California-based *Dharma Civilization Foundation* (DCF) raised community funds to set up a Hindu and an India studies chair at the University of California, Irvine. However, the university returned the multi-million-dollar gift to the DCF due to concerns "about the [right wing] ideology of the donors and the influence they sought to exert in the search process" (Redden 2016). The DCF also raised funds for another Hindu studies visiting professorship at the University of Southern California. This position was filled by Dr. Rita Sherma for two years (2012–2014), after which she moved to the Graduate Theological Union at Berkeley to take up a position as director of Hindu studies, where the DCF was able to work with Bay Area philanthropists Mira and Ajay Shingal to fund the Center for

Dharma Studies. Ajay Shingal, director of the Hindu Swayamsevak Sangh (HSS, counterpart to RSS in India) in the Bay Area from 2004 to 2006, indicated that he was interested in developing a center for Dharma studies after his involvement in the California textbook controversy in 2006 (see below, The Battle Over California State Textbooks) when he realized that Hinduism was presented "badly" in the school textbooks and that there were no Indian Hindu scholars of Hinduism studies with degrees from U.S. universities. "There are a few who claim they are scholars but I think they are not." He said that he decided to fund a whole center instead of just a chair since that would provide the greatest assurance that the teaching of Hinduism studies would continue into the future (R. Jha 2016).

Ambedkarites, for their part, have been concerned about South Asian studies being dominated by a "caste Hindu" perspective, leading to the neglect of the everyday realities of lower castes. They have also been keen on making sure that Dr. Ambedkar's life and work is taught at American universities. Several Ambedkarite activists asked me why there were so many courses on Gandhi but none on Ambedkar. Raju Kamble set up an annual Dr. Ambedkar Memorial Lecture at Columbia University beginning in 2009 in collaboration with their South Asia Institute, along with a conference in 2013 to commemorate the arrival of Ambedkar to Columbia University 100 years earlier, and another conference in 2016 to commemorate the 125th anniversary of his birth. The Boston Study Group (BSG), an Ambedkarite organization, was able to encourage Brandeis University to initiate an annual international conference on the Unfinished Legacy of Dr. B. R. Ambedkar starting from 2015 (the fifth conference was held at The New School in 2019). A BSG member who had helped to initiate the conference told me, "This is a three-day conference. Even in India there is no place that a three-day conference on Ambedkar happened anytime. So ... we really are proud of making that happen." Ambedkarites also installed busts of Ambedkar at several universities (Columbia, Brandeis, University of Massachusetts, Amherst), with speeches at the installation ceremony to explain his contributions. Several of these universities have since been holding regular events around Ambedkar's birthday with the support of local Ambedkarite groups. That these efforts seem to be paying off can be seen by the title of an article (July 19, 2019) in *India Abroad*, a weekly newspaper, titled "Ambedkar Lives in America: There Is a Resurgence of Interest in the U.S. Academia." Along with publicizing Ambedkar and his work, some Ambedkarites also mobilized to criticize Gandhi (as mentioned in Chapter 2, Gandhi opposed Ambedkar's attempt to give political power to Dalits). In 2017, riding on a wave of scholarship documenting Gandhi's racism toward Zulu Africans in South Africa (e.g., Desai and Vahed 2015) as well as earlier accounts (including Gandhi's own autobiography) detailing his celibacy tests with young female relatives, Dalit activists organized a social media campaign against Gandhi with the hashtags #Dumpgandhi and #Gandhimustfall. Thenmozhi Soundararajan also wrote an Internet article, "Why It Is Time to Dump Gandhi," citing his "insidious legacy of Casteism, racism, and sexual predation misogynism" as reasons to do so (Soundararajan 2017).

There are several programs, centers, and departments focusing on Islamic studies—for example, at Harvard, Duke, Georgetown, and San Diego State Universities and the University of Michigan—some of which were funded through community or donor support (Prince Alwaleed, a member of the Saudi royal family, donated funds to support the Islamic studies program at Harvard and the Islamic Studies Department at Georgetown, and an Indian Muslim man, Salim Shah, was the primary fundraiser for the Center for Islamic and Arabic Studies at San Diego State University). There are also several Islamic chair positions, for instance, at Harvard, George Mason, American, and Claremont Universities, as well as a chair of Shia studies at Hartford Seminary, and again, at least some of these were funded through community support.

School Textbooks

Muslims, Sikhs, Hindus, and Ambedkarites have been active around challenging the delineations of their religious histories and traditions in U.S. school textbooks. An Indian American Muslim man in California, Shabbir Mansuri, founded the *Council on Islamic Education* in 1990 to assess the portrayals of Islam in American school textbooks and to recommend changes. In 2009, the Sikh Coalition began a campaign to get the Texas Board of Education to include information about Sikhs and Sikh practices as part of the statewide curriculum, and in 2010, they were successful in getting Sikhism included in the social studies state standards. Following this victory, the organization worked with textbook publishers to correct errors and to train teachers until the textbooks were released in 2015. Here is a Sikh Coalition leader in a 2010 interview, explaining why they chose to focus on textbooks in Texas:

> Well, as it turns out, Texas is the biggest and largest [market] for textbook manufacturers, school textbook manufacturers.... And what these textbook manufacturers do as a matter of efficiency is just look to the Texas standards for determining what to include in the social studies textbooks. And for that reason, Texas has a lot of clout, and if their state board of education decides that students also learn about an aspect of history that hasn't been included in the standards before, that may influence textbook manufacturers to include that information in all of the textbooks which are sold to all schools in all the states. So, the idea was, if we can get the state of Texas to agree to incorporate information which is correct about the Sikh religion into its standards, derivatively, we will have accurate information about Sikhs included in social studies books which are sold and used nationally. And we were successful! ... And then hopefully, if all goes as planned, within the next, several years, students throughout the country, certainly in Texas, but perhaps even throughout the country, will have, access to accurate information about Sikhs, for the first time ever.

In other words, the selection of Texas for their textbook activism was a strategic choice since Sikh Coalition activists had learned the "rules of the game" about textbooks and decided to focus on the largest textbook market first. That they were successful in their first attempt in a conservative state like Texas speaks to their shrewd calculation and hard work. This victory laid the foundation for the Sikh Coalition to serve as consultants to the largest textbook publishers in the country, providing the publishers with scholars knowledgeable in Sikh history who corrected many errors and distortions in the textbooks. As of November 2023, the Sikh Coalition had been able to get Sikhs and Sikhism integrated into state standards in 18 states around the country.[13]

The Hindu American Foundation and other Hindu groups also mobilized to demand a positive portrayal of Hinduism in school textbooks on parity with those of other religions. Hindu American mobilization against school textbooks began in the fall of 2004, when the school district in Fairfax, Virginia, put forward a new set of world history textbooks for public review. Hindu parents mobilized and were relatively successful in making some changes in the way Indian history was taught in their district. Encouraged by this success, Hindu American groups decided to organize and turn their attention to school textbooks in other regions of the country. They got involved in a long-drawn-out legal battle against the California State Board of Education. In November 2014, they were successful in getting changes implemented in textbooks in Texas.

The Battle over California State Textbooks

In 2006, the California State Board of Education opened its process of textbook review for sixth-grade social studies to the public. Due to the size of the state textbook market and the fact that the state of California has the largest number of Hindu Americans in the country, Hindu groups were interested in getting involved in the textbook review process. Two Hindu American groups—the *Vedic Foundation* (VF), a group based in Austin, Texas, and the *Hindu Education Foundation* (HEF), a group made up of members from around the country and India—participated in the review process. The VF and HEF were backed by the Hindu American Foundation (HAF). Some edits corrected blatant errors or gratuitous insults. But others became controversial, including the changes they proposed around caste and around the treatment of women in ancient India, and a group of scholars and a multireligious Indian American group including Ambedkarites, mobilized under a South Asian umbrella to challenge these edits. The South Asian group traced the links between the VF-HEF-HAF and Hindutva groups in the United States and India and denounced the changes as trying to promulgate a sanitized version of history and deny oppression, much like the changes that Hindutva groups in India had been implementing in Indian school textbooks during the time the BJP was in power (1998–2004). Supporters of the VF-HEF-HAF combine on their part argued that they were merely demanding that Hinduism be treated with the same consideration and respect in U.S. school textbooks as other religious traditions and denounced the South Asian critics as "anti-Hindu". Members of the California State Board of Education found themselves caught in the crossfire between the Hindu and South Asian groups and overturned most of the contentious changes proposed by the Hindu groups while keeping the changes agreed to by both sides. In response, the HAF and HEF filed a lawsuit against the California State Board of Education. In September 2006, the judge presiding over the case ruled that the textbooks complied with the legal standards but also that the California board had not followed some of the regulations governing the textbook approval process (see Kurien 2007a, 204–206 for more details).

In 2016 (the textbook review process takes place every 10 years), the Hindu American Foundation and allies (including *California Parents for the Equalization of Educational Materials* [CAPEEM] and the *Uberoi Foundation*) worked to provide guidelines for the history–social history framework dealing with the social science curriculum of the California Board of Education for the sixth and seventh grades. These Hindu groups wanted to remove any references to caste being a product of Hinduism and of the caste system being a birth-determined hierarchical pyramid, and any comparison between the caste system and African American slavery. Instead, they wanted to portray caste as a social system like occupational guilds, which brought stability to India but had become rigid under British colonialism. They maintained that most Indians in India and the United States no longer identified in terms of caste. They pressed the point that negative portrayals of Hinduism impacted the self-esteem of Hindu children and led to their being bullied and teased in school.[14] A HAF activist in California, and a mother to a teenage son, explained:

> What we were really looking at, we were looking at from kind of equality and dignity in the representation. So, the kids who are of Hindu origin who are studying it, along with the kids who come from all religions and backgrounds and ethnicities, they have something to take home to. They feel proud. And also, the other kids can relate to the subject better, understand the core essence of Hinduism.

This activist from a Brahmin background also thought that downplaying caste would be beneficial to students from oppressed-caste backgrounds to ensure that they were not made to feel ashamed about their caste origins.

> In public schools, we have Hindu students, Hindu kids who come from all different caste[s]. And we don't want people to feel alienated just because, you know, their ancestors were born in a certain time and were marginalized. We want to bring that unity and structure in a modern era so that everybody is kind of proud of their sense of belonging.

Ambedkarite activists who mobilized around the attempts of Hindu groups in the United States to erase discussions of caste inequality and oppression, however, had a different perspective on their history. Instead of viewing it with shame as the Brahmin activist implied, they viewed it with pride since it showed the resilience and strength of their communities. Consequently, they wanted details of caste oppression documented, as well as their long history of struggle and resistance against this oppressive system and the heroic work of anti-caste activists through history. They joined a South Asian organization, South Asian Histories for All (SAHFA) to protest the edits. Progressive Hindu organization Sadhana supported Ambedkarite groups and endorsed SAHFA's "Don't Erase Caste" petition, opposing the HAF and its allies.

California is an important place for Sikh American history, and like Hindus, California is the state with the largest number of Sikhs in the country. Consequently, Sikh Coalition activists also joined SAHFA to prevent the HAF and allied groups from deleting references to Sikh immigrants in California (replacing Sikh with the phrase "South Asian" immigrants) and from rewriting Sikhism by leaving out the fact that the religion was founded in opposition to the caste system and idolatry. A Sikh activist, Kaur, was quoted as saying, "Their edits run a lot deeper than just textbook edits. They want to usurp Sikhs back into Hinduism" (Chari 2016).

SAHFA was greatly outnumbered by Hindu groups. Also, while SAHFA was a volunteer group, the Hindu side was represented by professional organizations that had spent several millions of dollars on the effort, including bringing in busloads of children to give emotional testimonies at the hearings, accusing the SAHFA group "of 'Hinduphobia' and robbing them of selfhood" (Medina 2016). The Hindu organizations may also have been able to raise the threat of lawsuits. Perhaps for these reasons, the board sided more with the Hindu groups. Ambedkarite activists with whom I spoke were furious. Kishore, a software entrepreneur based in the Bay Area who had participated in the mobilization, said, "The Hindu religious groups ... I can't believe how vicious they have become. ... They can't even admit [to caste] ... it's like telling [saying that] the Holocaust never happened." "Mukta," one of the women I spoke to, argued:

> You want to show only a rosy picture, which is incorrect ... [in this way a] superiority complex is always maintained. It is never questioned. Tell me, in American history, don't they talk about slavery? Tell me, in German history, don't they talk about Hitler? ... They are just trying to deny the history so they can carry forward their superiority.

This experience, particularly the argument of Hindu groups that caste did not matter in the United States, was the impetus for Soundararajan and her Equality Labs associates to conduct the online survey in 2016 on caste discrimination in the United States.

Ambedkarite Activists Promote Ambedkar as the Martin Luther King Jr. of India

Dr. Laxmi Berwa was the second president of the Dalit American organization VISION. Speaking with me in 2018, Dr. Berwa described his experience as a Dalit student in India where he faced "humiliation in college" and was called "derogatory names" and his turn to Ambedkarism as he was introduced to Ambedkar's work as a student. "And I became so inspired that I became his devotee.... Till today, I pray in front of him.... I pray for him and for his inspiration to me." Berwa converted to Buddhism after arriving in the United States in 1971. Berwa was one of the first contemporary Dalit American activists to reach out to African American groups through speaking on radio programs targeting African Americans in the Washington, DC area (Omvedt 2004, 188) and at an event at Howard University in 1998 to celebrate the 107th anniversary of Ambedkar's birth. In a speech titled "Two Leaders and One Message," Berwa described the event as "a new beginning in the human rights movement of Dalits and Afro-Americans" and drew a parallel between the efforts of Dr. Bhimrao Ambedkar and Dr. Martin Luther King Jr. to obtain rights for oppressed groups in India and the United States (Berwa 2000, 61–63).

Ambedkarites have been passionate about getting Dr. Ambedkar, their hero and leader, more widely known. While Dr. King is considered the "American Gandhi" (e.g., Jackson 2007), Dalits want to make Americans aware that the parallel is erroneous and that India's Dr. King was really Dr. Ambedkar. They want Dr. Ambedkar to obtain the same international name recognition as Gandhi and Dr. King. In the 2012–2013 period, a group of Dalit Americans formed a group and registered as an organization with the goal of acquiring some property in the Washington, DC area and building a memorial for Ambedkar. As one of them explained, "You talk about Dr. Martin Luther King, everybody pretty much knows him in the world. And if you think about in terms of social transformation, Dr. Ambedkar's contribution is much, much, more and beyond. But people don't know him." A few months later, the group came to know of a suitable 13-acre property in Maryland and bought the property. "Within the span of one week, we pooled in $100,000 roughly." There were 26 individuals in that first group (in 2017 there were 50 to 60 contributors) and they inaugurated an Ambedkar International Center in 2013. There was a small building on the property and the plan was to demolish it and raise funds to construct a museum and a memorial for Ambedkar "like the Lincoln memorial."[15] Their goal was "to promote the name of Babasaheb and to increase awareness in the United States and worldwide about human rights violations [in India] and Dalits." They felt that having a Washington, DC location would help them engage with policymakers and allow them "to raise their voice [on behalf of Indian Dalits] at the international level." The New York City Ravidassia temple had been sponsoring an Ambedkar float at the annual India Day Parade in the city since the year 2007 with a large picture of Ambedkar and several of his quotations pasted on banneris. As the float moved through the streets of New York City, his speeches were played and copies of Ambedkar's "Annihilation of Caste" were distributed. Other U.S. Ambedkarite organizations and reading groups worked to spread Ambedkar's ideas to Indian Americans and the wider American society.

Advocacy around Civil Rights

Mobilizing around the civil rights of their groups is another important task of the advocacy organizations of Hindus, Muslims, Sikhs, and Ambedkarites. Since its formation, the Hindu American Foundation has been active in mobilizing against hate crimes targeting Hindus, and they have a list of documented hate crimes against Hindus and temples as well as anti-Hindu prejudice (now described as "Hinduphobia") in the media on their website.[16] The organization also took part, along with other religious groups, in court cases challenging the public display of the Ten Commandments in Texas and a state-funded Christian-themed license plate in South Carolina, in both cases arguing that such public displays expressed an inherent government preference for Christians and Christianity over all other citizens and faith traditions that make up the United States (S. Shukla 2008, 28). They also participated in amicus briefs against Christian prayers in public settings, arguing that such prayers were against the separation of church and state and would make non-Christians feel unwelcome (G. Joseph 2014b). The HAF also participated in other amicus briefs including for the right to financial compensation for violations of religious freedom under the Religious

Freedom and Restoration Act and the right to have contraceptives covered under health insurance plans (both in 2020, information from HAF website). In 2018, Sadhana joined with activists at a march in San Diego to protest Trump's planned border wall as part of their migrant justice platform.

Muslim Advocates activists spoke about rising anti-Muslim sentiments and incidents in 2010 and testified at the Capitol Hill Hearing on Protecting the Civil Rights of Muslims on March 29, 2011. As hate crimes against Muslims escalated under the Trump presidency, with threats and attacks against mosques and Muslims, Muslim Advocates joined with other faith groups and civil rights advocates to ask the FBI director to take action against White nationalism. Muslim Advocates also mobilized to protect the rights of Muslims to build mosques and other religious buildings (including developing a detailed guide for religious communities to navigate the process of obtaining land for religious use, available on their website), to advocate for the rights of Muslim prisoners and immigrants detained by ICE, around workplace discriminations faced by Muslims (including helping workers at Amazon file a federal case against the company for discriminating against some Muslim employees), and around fighting law enforcement bias against Muslims, including the Countering Violent Extremism (CVE) program, which, they argued, was a ploy to target Muslims using troubling and innocuous activities as indicators of radicalism. Muslim Advocates also filed lawsuits around many of these issues.

Hate crimes against turban-wearing Sikhs have been an acute problem long after the initial 9/11 backlash. In addition to frequent attacks against individual Sikh men, a 2012 shooting attack on a Sikh temple in Oak Creek, Wisconsin, by a White supremacist killed six Sikhs (a seventh victim died of his wounds in 2020) and wounded four others. Sikh American advocacy organizations who had been mobilizing to bring attacks against Sikhs to the attention of authorities even before the 2012 shooting increased their efforts after the Oak Creek incident.[17] In 2013 the FBI agreed to track incidents against Sikhs (as well as Hindus and Arabs). Hate crimes against Muslims have been tracked by the FBI since 1990. In an email on December 10, 2013, the Sikh Coalition laid out what steps it had taken to change this federal policy, indicating that they had worked for over two years to raise the issue at meetings with Justice Department members, mobilized supporters to send 8,448 petitions to Congress, motivated over 135 members of both parties in Congress to send letters to the Justice Department, and coordinated over 150 organizations to support the demand of the Sikh Coalition for a Senate hearing in response to the Oak Creek shootings. On August 25, 2020, SALDEF was part of a meeting with FBI director Christopher Wray along with representatives of national faith organizations (which they indicate included representatives of the Baptist, Catholic, Episcopalian, Muslim, and Mormon communities; interestingly, Hindus were not part of this meeting). The meeting was held to discuss hate crimes, the security of places of worship, and how COVID-19 was affecting religious communities.[18] Sikh organizations also joined and supported other groups that were the victim of hate crimes. In the spring of 2015, three Muslim college students belonging to one family were murdered in a hate crime in Chapel Hill and the Sikh Coalition joined with Muslim Advocates in holding a briefing on Capitol Hill for lawmakers about the hate crimes that both communities faced. A few months later, in the summer of 2015, nine African American worshippers were gunned down by a White supremacist in Charleston, South Carolina. Sikh Coalition leaders wrote op-eds in American news outlets to show their solidarity with the families in Charleston.

Caste as a Protected Category in the United States

Ambedkarite groups have been mobilizing to get caste recognized as a protected category in the United States since without that, it is difficult for individuals who experience caste discrimination in the United States to obtain any legal recourse. In December 2019, Brandeis University became the first American university or college to ban caste discrimination on its campus (in addition to the standard American protected categories of discrimination based on race, color, ancestry, religious creed, gender and sexual identity and orientation, and national and ethnic orientation). This prohibition came about due to the activism of Ambedkarite organizations and students and the leadership of Professor Larry Simon, of Brandeis's Heller School of Social Policy and Management, an expert on caste. Since then, many other colleges and universities around the country, including the entire California state university system, has also banned caste discrimination on their campuses.[19]

The June 2020 lawsuit against Cisco Systems by California's Department of Fair Employment and Housing (CDFEH) on behalf of a Dalit employee was a particularly momentous occurrence in the attempt to obtain legal recourse for caste discrimination in the United States. The lawsuit claimed that a Brahmin supervisor who knew the employee from engineering school in

India revealed the employee's caste background to some other Indian Cisco employees in 2016 and that the employee had availed of affirmative action at the engineering school. Along with a second Brahmin supervisor, the first supervisor then retaliated against, and demoted the employee when he objected. The employee approached the human resources and employee relations office claiming caste-based discrimination and two internal investigations were conducted. But it appeared that despite uncovering evidence of discrimination and harassment, HR did not take any corrective action since they did not consider casteism a form of discrimination falling under the Civil Rights Act (CDFEH 2020, 10). Further extending its significance, the lawsuit was subsequently supported by the Alphabet Workers Union (Alphabet Inc. is Google's parent company). One of the news articles covering this case pointed out, "For decades this silent discrimination had remained hidden, as Dalits have been terrified of speaking out over fears of losing their jobs or their visas" (Gilbert 2020).

Emboldened by the Cisco lawsuit, Equality Labs received more than 250 further complaints about workplace caste discrimination from Dalit employees in dozens of major Silicon Valley companies, including Facebook, Google, Microsoft, Amazon, and Cisco itself (Gilbert 2020). U.S.-based Ambedkarite organizations came out immediately in support of the Cisco employee. A Bay Area–based Ambedkarite group, the Ambedkar King Study Circle, swung into action, organizing a signature campaign directed at U.S. companies to "recognize caste, as operating similarly to race and gender as a source of discrimination and harassment and incorporate caste practices as an unfair and punishable practice in their Human Resource polices."[20] They also organized a weekly Zoom series on caste in the United States (including experts on caste in India and the United Kingdom in addition to the United States) and devoted a section of their website (http://akscusa.org) to the case, including the actual case complaint and media coverage. The Cisco case received a great deal of coverage in mainstream U.S. media (*New York Times*, *Washington Post*, CNN), as well as in outlets like Vice.com, The Wire, Aljazeera, and several Indian newspapers and programs. There were also several audio and video programs focused on discussing this case. In audio and video discussions, Thenmozhi Soundararajan spoke repeatedly about why Dalit groups wanted caste to become a protected category in the United States at the federal, state, and local levels, arguing that since caste discrimination was a structural problem, it needed a structural remedy. Obtaining legal protection would mean that people who work in corporations, schools, and universities will have to be trained in the contours of caste and caste discrimination practices so they can prevent caste discrimination and harassment. Since Silicon Valley corporations have hundreds of thousands of employees in India, they will have to monitor and prevent caste discrimination in their Indian offices as well.[21]

Hindus for Human Rights (HfHR), a sister organization of Sadhana (formed in 2019 to mobilize against Hindutva), signaled its strong support for the lawsuit, saying, "As progressive Hindus who have seen discrimination based on caste throughout our lives—including, in more subtle but undeniable ways in the United States—we applaud the Dalit complainant for coming forward." They indicated that they had played an "ally" role in supporting the amicus brief against Cisco. HfHR also rejected the argument that the caste system is not "intrinsic to Hinduism," pointing to statements in ancient Hindu scriptures mentioning caste and to the presence of "untouchable" castes in the ancient period (Viswanath and Rajagopal 2021). However, the Hindu American Foundation seemed alarmed by the Cisco lawsuit and put out a statement that it "uniquely endangers Hindus and Indians." The statement argued that existing U.S. federal and state laws protecting against discrimination on the basis of national origin and ancestry should take care of any caste discrimination that might be validated. They were particularly concerned that the lawsuit would prompt anti-immigrant bigotry against Indians and Hindus since the case falsely "conflated caste-based discrimination with Hinduism and Hindus," and that it "amplifies misleading claims of an anti-Hindu group"[22] (i.e., Equality Labs, referring specifically to some statements its leaders have made against Hinduism). They also argued as they did earlier (see above, Education through Their Websites) that the Equality Labs survey had numerous "methodological" problems. In their statement, dated August 23, 2020, the HAF indicated that they had "written to the CDFEH demanding redactions and revisions of the complaint."[23] A January 22, 2021, article in *India Post*, a California-based Indian American weekly, indicated that the HAF filed a legal motion on January 2, 2021, to intervene in the case, arguing that "California's actions are unconstitutional and violate the rights of Hindu Americans. If California succeeds, ALL people of Indian origin will be presumed to be bigots." The HAF also argued that the caste system "is rooted ... in colonialism, not in Hinduism" (*India Post* 2021, 23). CDFEH dropped the charges against the supervisors in April 2023, but the case against Cisco is ongoing at the time of writing. In 2023, Ambedkarite groups mobilizing with Sikh, Muslim, and progressive Hindu organizations such as HfHR, and with gender, racial, and labor activists, together with civil rights organizations and associations representing different legal groups (in opposition to the Hindu American Foundation and several other Hindu groups), were successful in getting caste as a protected category included in the cities of Seattle and Fresno, and in getting the California legislature to overwhelmingly pass a bill to make caste a protected category in the state. However, some weeks later, in a surprising move given the support the bill had received in the legislature, the California bill was vetoed by Governor Gavin Newsom, echoing the argument of Hindu groups that the bill was unnecessary since caste was already covered under California's "ancestry" clause. Newsom, who is believed to have presidential ambitions, apparently did so at the urging of two major Hindu American Democratic fundraisers (Kindy 2023).

Accommodation of Religious Practices

Obtaining accommodation for their religious practices has also been an important focus for organizations representing Muslims, Sikhs, and Hindus. From its founding, CAIR has had to deal with cases where women wearing the hijab have faced discrimination, and this issue continues to be important to the organization (Nimer 2002, 133–134). In her book on religions in America, Diana Eck refers to a brochure published by ISNA and offered to schools, "You've Got a Muslim Child in Your School," which describes some of the basics of Islam and some of the restrictions that Muslim children have to observe, including food restrictions, dress codes, and Islamic prayers (Eck 2002, 285). Similarly, CAIR has a brochure, "An Educator's Guide to Islamic Practices." The Hindu American Foundation promotes vegetarianism and has been involved in several events to advocate for a plant-based diet.

Sikh advocacy organizations have been particularly active around religious accommodation rights. They have put a lot of energy into gaining accommodations in the U.S. Army since it is the largest U.S. employer and they feel that if the army permits them to maintain their articles of faith, as a Sikh Coalition activist told me, "it gives a strong signal to the corporate world and others that this discrimination must end." Another Sikh Coalition leader explained, "Our strategy is to take very high impact cases that will change policy or set precedence overall." Although turbaned Sikhs have been banned from joining the U.S. Armed Forces since the 1980s, due to the activism of second-generation Sikh leaders, individual exceptions were made in 2009 for three Sikhs who were allowed to join the army and maintain their beards, turbans, and kirpans so they did not have to choose between serving their country and being Sikh. One of these included Major Kamaljeet Singh Kalsi, a Bronze Star winner who campaigned for the U.S. Army to stop putting restrictions in the way of Sikhs who wanted to join, arguing, "We should be in the army not as exceptions but as freely as other minorities" (Pais 2013). Four other Sikh men were granted religious accommodations in 2016 and allowed to serve with their articles of faith. In early 2017, the U.S. Army made it easier for religious accommodations to be provided for new recruits by allowing them to be approved at the Brigade level. In 2020, the U.S. Air Force updated its uniform code to allow Sikhs and Muslims to serve while wearing their turbans and hijabs.

Sikh activists also mobilized around the right of Sikhs to maintain their symbols of faith in the workplace and were able to get the Workplace Religious Freedom Act introduced in New York City and California. In 2015, the Sikh Coalition, working with the ACLU, successfully got Walt Disney World to "desegregate" a Sikh mail carrier who had until then been kept hidden from public view due to his turban and unshorn beard. The kirpan (small sword) is another article of faith for which Sikhs need to get accommodations or exceptions. Here again Sikh advocacy organizations, particularly United Sikhs and the Sikh Coalition, mobilized to educate officials, police forces, corporations, schools, and other institutions and worked with legally trained individuals to get individual accommodations or exceptions for a small, blunt kirpan usually hidden under clothing from particular institutions, which they then parlayed into wider policy—getting accommodations for all observant Sikhs in similar situations. In 2015, when Pope Francis visited the United States, Sikhs were welcomed at the Ground Zero interfaith service with their kirpans (unlike at earlier papal visits) due to the advocacy efforts of United Sikhs.

Recognition and Inclusion

As we have seen, citizenship is not just about legal status but also about recognition and inclusion by policymakers and the wider society. Hindu, Sikh, and Muslim advocacy organizations have worked to have their religious traditions acknowledged as "American religions," part of the multireligious and multicultural fabric of the United States. Obtaining acknowledgment and recognition for their religions from the White House and the U.S. administration has been a strategy followed by advocacy groups of Muslims, Hindus, and Sikhs. The White House now holds an annual *Iftar* dinner (begun in 1996) to celebrate *Ramadan*, an annual Diwali celebration (from 2003) to honor an important Hindu festival (there has also been a Diwali celebration at the Pentagon since 2003), and an annual event to commemorate the birth of Guru Nanak, the founder of the Sikh religion (from 2009). In 2014, SALDEF hosted the first langar (a traditional shared meal of Sikhs) on Capitol Hill for members of Congress and their staff. Introducing resolutions in Congress to honor their religious celebrations is another way that Hindu, Sikh, and Muslim organizations have tried to spread awareness of their religions and obtain recognition. In the fall of 2007, on the urging of the Hindu American Foundation, the Senate and the House of Representatives passed resolutions (written with the input of the Hindu American Foundation) recognizing the significance of the festival of Diwali (S. Shukla 2008, 27). In 2015, Sikhs were able to have Vaisakhi, an important Sikh festival, recognized through a resolution in the U.S. Congress through the activism of the Sikh Coalition.

In September 2000, despite some opposition from conservative Christians, Indian American lobby groups were successful in having a Hindu priest open a session of Congress (this was a joint session of Congress when Prime Minister Vajpayee was giving an address) for the first time, an achievement reported with great pride in Indian American newspapers and websites. In 2019, a Sikh priest (*granthi*) offered Sikh prayers to open a Senate session of the U.S. Congress to mark the 550th anniversary of Guru Nanak's birth. In 2011, a Hindu woman, Pratima Dharm, was named as the first Hindu chaplain of the U.S. Army. While President Bush overlooked Hindus in the prayers organized in Washington, DC after 9/11, President Obama, perhaps partly as a result of Hindu American activism and the rising public profile of Hindu Americans in administrative circles, included Hindus under the American religious canopy in his inaugural address in 2008 when he described the country as "a nation of Christians and Muslims, Jews and Hindus, and nonbelievers," a description that overjoyed Hindu Americans since this was the first time they were included.

Being included in interfaith activities and events has been another important way that U.S. religious traditions have been acknowledged. While Islam has been included for a long time, Hinduism and Sikhism had been left out, but they have been included with greater frequency more recently. For instance, the opening events of the Republican National Convention since 2012 have included Sikh prayers (but apparently not Hindu), and Sikh prayers have been included in the opening events of the Democratic National Convention since 2016. The opening events of the Democratic National Convention in 2020 included both Sikh and Hindu prayers.

Indian American Muslims have initiated a variety of interfaith programs. I have mentioned the efforts of Professors Muqtedar Khan, Parvez Ahmed, and Dr. Sayeed M. Sayeed in civic engagement and interfaith dialogues in the aftermath of 9/11. There have been many others. For instance, Mike Ghouse established a Foundation for Pluralism in 1996, renamed as the Center for Pluralism in 2014, in the Washington, DC area; Islam Siddiqui is the founder and chairman of the Washington, DC-based American Muslim Institution, launched in 2015 with the mission of building "a greater understanding between American Muslims and fellow Americans by working together to create a more just, inclusive, and harmonious society";[24] and Frank Islam has been active around interfaith dialogue and education, also in the Washington, DC area. Zafar Siddiqui, cofounder and past president of the Islamic Resource group in Minnesota (whose goal is to educate Americans about Islam and Muslims), has participated regularly in interfaith dialogues, as has Muzammil Siddiqui, former imam of the Islamic Society of Orange County in Southern California. Eboo Patel, a second-generation Indian American Muslim man, is the founder of the Interfaith Youth Core and strongly emphasizes the importance of religious pluralism in his books and speeches. Two Muslim American women of Indian backgrounds, Azra Nomani and Daisy Khan, who both describe themselves as "progressive" or "modern" Muslim women, are prominent though somewhat controversial figures who speak at interfaith events. Nomani, a journalist, is author of the book *Standing Alone: An American Woman's Struggle for the Soul of Islam* (2006) (where she criticizes the Arabization of Islam, particularly the dominance of Saudi Wahhabi Islam in American mosques), and an activist for Muslim reform and for women's rights in Islam. She was one of the main organizers of the women-led Muslim prayer in New York City in 2005. She became controversial for her support of the racial and religious profiling of Muslims and her support of Donald Trump and his "Muslim ban" (Harvard 2017). Daisy Khan is the executive director of the Women's Islamic Initiative for Spirituality and Equality and an interfaith activist. She was listed on *Time* magazine's 100 Most Influential People and has received numerous awards for her activism. Like Nomani, Khan is an activist for Muslim reform and promotes women's rights in Islam. She and her husband proposed the building of the Cordoba House mosque and community center close to the site of the World Trade Center, which sparked protests.

On May 21, 2020, California Assembly member Ash Kalra (on the behest of the HAF) introduced a resolution to designate October 2020 as California Hindu American Awareness and Education Month.[25] In the resolution, Hindu Americans are described as people who "promote the ideals of tolerance, pluralism, and religious freedom, which are inherent to their beliefs," which leads them to "respect the diversity of all faiths."[26] This is an example of how Hindu American like to portray themselves. As seen in the article by Aseem Shukla (2010b) and in many other public pronouncements by Hindu American leaders and the earlier article by Rajiv Malhotra (2003a), Hindu American leaders often contrast Hinduism with Abrahamic traditions, particularly Islam and Christianity, which they describe as exclusive and intolerant. Sikhs on their part emphasize that fighting injustice is a central value in Sikhism. The "We Are Sikhs" initiative probably has the most clearly articulated discussion of Sikh values. After stating that Sikhism is a religion that "stands for the equality of women and men and denounces any discrimination pertaining to gender, race, caste, creed, religion, or color," they assert, in a section titled "Sikh Values Are American Values":

> We feel at home in America, a nation that traditionally celebrates diversity and religious liberty. Sikh communities foster love, equality, and acceptance of all. Like the U.S. Bill of Rights, Sikh scripture promotes ideals of equality and the freedom to pursue paths of peace and prosperity. And like the United States, Sikhs stand against injustice and inequality wherever it exists.

A Political Voice: Shaping National Policies and Laws

In a 2008 article, "Hindu American Political Advocacy," Suhag Shukla, cofounder of the Hindu American Foundation, argued for the importance of a Hindu voice in key national dialogues that other religious groups have long been participating in. She said that the HAF was filling this void by "working the halls of Congress every day, voicing the concerns of Hindu Americans and educating our nation's leaders on Hinduism" (S. Shukla

2008, 26). As articulated by Ash Kalra, then San Jose City council member, speaking to *India Abroad* at a 2012 HAF Northern California panel discussion on "Emergence of a Hindu Political Voice in America," building this political voice was important so Hindus could "become part of the decision-making process regarding issues that all Americans care about—like education, health care, and the economy" (R. Jha 2012). In this chapter, I have mentioned several policies that the HAF has advocated for including hate crimes legislation, recognizing Diwali on the Hill, preserving the separation of church and state, and arguing against Christian prayers at public places and events. The HAF launched their annual Capitol Hill reception in 2004 where leaders and volunteers would meet with members of Congress to discuss issues of concern, followed by a reception. The religious worker visa program to permit priests to get visas to work at Hindu temples in the United States was one of the issues of concern to the HAF in 2007 when I was able to attend some of the events on the Hill in which they participated. In 2010, I attended the HAF's annual reception. A HAF representative I spoke to indicated that they had spent a full day on the Hill discussing legislation, including pushing for more plant-based food in schools and the Texas school textbooks issue, trying to advocate for a national body to develop standards for social science textbooks. Under President Obama, Hindu faith-based social service organizations were included under the Faith Based and Neighborhood Partnership initiative in 2009 (the White House Office of Faith-Based and Community Initiatives was established by President George W. Bush in 2001; under the Obama administration the initiative continued but was renamed) and the Hindu American Seva (service) Charities (HASC) under the direction of Anju Bhargava, a Hindu American who had made a name for herself through her involvement in interfaith activities, was formed.[27]

A group of Sikh Americans was able to get a Sikh caucus formed in Congress in 2013 to advocate for Sikh American interests (in 2016 it had 48 members). In a 2017 interview, "Jaivir," a California-based Sikh American activist, talked about the background work involved to form the caucus and to get a Democrat (Judy Chu, California) and a Republican (David Valadao, California) to agree to be cochairs. Jaivir laughed and told me that although the caucus was primarily to focus on domestic issues of discrimination and hate crimes that Sikhs face, there had been "a lot of pushback" from the Indian government—he said the Indian ambassador had "walked the halls of Congress" to argue against the caucus, alleging that some Khalistani separatists were behind the effort. This effort by the Indian government was not successful and the caucus was launched on May 8, 2013. In another sign of influence, on September 14, the Sikh Coalition was able to get a resolution (H. Res. 5317) passed in the U.S. House of Representatives to name a post office in Houston, Texas, after a Sikh policeman, Sandeep Singh Dhaliwal, who was killed in the line of duty. Both the Sikh Coalition and SALDEF sent emails (Sikh Coalition on September 15, 2020, and SALDEF on September 16, 2020) taking credit for this achievement. A SALDEF representative described the naming of a federal building in honor of a Sikh man as a recognition that "reconfirms that Sikh Americans are part of the fabric of this country" (group email, September 16, 2020). In June 2023, Congressman Shri Thanedar announced the formation of a congressional Hindu caucus at the first-ever Hindu American Summit held in Washington, DC. Facing criticism for excluding Dalit and other Hindu groups, the caucus was subsequently expanded to be a Hindu, Buddhist, Sikh, and Jain (HBSJ) congressional caucus to combat religious discrimination and ensure inclusion. But apparently several organizations such as Hindus for Human Rights, Dalit Hindu organizations, and the major Sikh advocacy organizations were not consulted. Hindus for Human Rights along with the Sikh Coalition and SALDEF put out a statement expressing concern about the intended goals of the organization (October 3, 2023, statement received via email).

Since the United States does not include religion in the census, accurate figures of the number of adherents of particularly smaller American religions are hard to come by. The Pew Forum on Religion and Public Life has conducted surveys and statistical analyses to estimate these numbers. In the case of Sikhs, Pew's estimate is that there were 200,000 adherents in the United States in 2012 (Pew Research Center 2015).[28] This low number has been a source of anger since Sikh American organizations feel that it considerably underestimates the number of Sikh Americans. As I have mentioned, the Sikh parade in Yuba City draws over 100,000 participants every year. These numbers, as well as the numbers of people they have on their mailing lists and the information about gurdwara membership from around the country, have led Sikh leaders to argue that there are at least 500,000 Sikhs in the United States. This is one of the factors that led to a movement by Sikh American organizations to have Sikhs classified as a separate ethnic group, distinct from Indian Americans, in the 2010 U.S. census.

In Britain, the House of Lords ruled in 1983 that Sikhs were an ethnic group and could therefore receive legal protection against discrimination for their articles of faith under the Race Relations Act of 1976 (G. Singh and Tatla

2006, 133). Using that precedent, United Sikhs, with the support of SALDEF, the Sikh Coalition, and other Sikh organizations, petitioned the U.S. Census Bureau to create a separate Sikh category in the census and to count them as an ethnicity, challenging the Census Bureau practice of counting Sikhs as "Asian Indians" even if they marked the "Other Race" category and wrote "Sikh" on the census form. Sikh organizations argued that this change was important because American Sikhs fit the classification of a minority under international law, the U.S. category of "race" should also include ethnicity and the right to self-define that ethnicity, the U.S. Sikh population remains invisible and undercounted due to the lack of a separate census category, and finally, Sikhs have been victims of hate crimes and discrimination, particularly after 9/11, but these issues could not be properly documented or prosecuted unless Sikhs were recognized as a separate ethnic group.[29] This campaign was not successful for the 2010 census, but in January 2020, the U.S. Census Bureau announced that Sikhs would be counted as a separate ethnic group in the 2020 census (Louis 2020). United Sikhs, which had been working on this initiative for the last two decades, hailed this decision. Sikhs could check off "Other Asian" in the census form and then write in "Sikh." This milestone for Sikh Americans was viewed with concern by some members of the Indian American community, including the fear that it would further encourage Sikh separatists (Mozumdar 2020a). In the end, only a relatively small minority of Sikhs, 119,018, checked off this box in the 2020 census.[30]

On May 22, 2019, Equality Labs, in partnership with South Asian Americans Leading Together (SAALT), presented data from their caste survey at a congressional briefing sponsored by Indian American member of Congress Pramila Jayapal (D-WA). Ro Khanna (D-CA), an Indian American Congress member representing the Silicon Valley region, had initially agreed to cosponsor the session but abruptly pulled out two days before. "Sources on the Hill" attributed this about-face to pressure from Hindu groups (Salim 2019). During their public debriefing session after their congressional session, Thenmozhi Soundararajan described how they had wondered whether the congressional briefing would even take place since several briefings about the position of religious minorities in India had been canceled at the last minute due to calls received by members of Congress from Hindus threatening consequences in their districts.[31]

The Muslim Public Affairs Council (MPAC) indicates that an important part of their advocacy work for Muslims includes seeking "to inform and shape policy" and connecting their members to policymakers. MPAC provides testimony at congressional hearings around issues of concern to Muslims. Similarly, the Council on American-Islamic Relations (CAIR) has a government affairs department that monitors legislation and government activities. Besides fighting against the "Muslim ban," "no fly lists," unconstitutional "watch lists," and illegal surveillance of Muslims, they also have an Islamophobia watch program. Muslim Advocates also mobilizes against Islamophobia, including by politicians. The Islamic Society of North America (ISNA) has advocated for affordable health care and in 2019 joined with other faith groups to call for the implementation of the Affordable Care Act. They have also advocated for the DREAM Act and federal funding for poverty assistance (in 2011) and gun violence prevention (2013).

The major Washington, DC-based advocacy organizations for Hindus, Sikhs, and Muslims (HAF, SALDEF, Sikh Coalition, MPAC, CAIR) have internship programs in Washington, DC to educate and train the younger generation in advocacy and community engagement and to work in congressional offices. Several have additional leadership development programs (e.g., MPAC has the Congressional Leadership Development program; SALDEF has the Sikh Lead program; the Sikh Coalition has the Sikh Advocate Academy, Sikh Coalition Ambassadors, and Junior Sikh Coalition programs; and the HAF has the Dharma Ambassadors program).

Conclusion: Lessons from Minority Religious Group Activism around Domestic Policies

This chapter demonstrates how religious organizations of minority religious groups from the Indian subcontinent have been mobilizing around cultural citizenship in the United States, melding models of religious and racial activism together. Though the literature focuses on how ethnic groups claim cultural citizenship, or the right to maintain culture and difference, we see here that religious minorities also demand assurance that their unique identities and needs are recognized and respected in Western countries. Most of the organizations discussed in this chapter were led by the American-born generation, primarily individuals with legal and policy backgrounds, which meant that they understood the political opportunity structures in the United States and the strategies to adopt for political incorporation. They followed clear scripts, as can be seen by the commonalities between the groups. A fundamental need they confronted is to educate members of Western societies about their religions, including emphasizing commonalities and similarities with dominant Western religious and cultural traditions. Consequently, they were concerned about the portrayals of their traditions in school textbooks and within the American academy. They also demanded protection from hate crimes, school bullying, and job discrimination based on their identities as visible racial minorities as well as their religious accoutrements or practices. They wanted to be recognized and included as American religious groups by the administration (both state and federal) and were interested in shaping policies that impacted them directly or indirectly.

At the same time, there were some differences in their strategies, depending on the profiles and requirements of the group. Muslims must combat Islamophobia, which has often been legally codified, as in the Patriot Act and the Muslim ban. They are also not a uniquely Indian group. In fact, Indian American Muslims are often overlooked in the United States and within Muslim American circles, which they tried to counteract by emphasizing their experience of living as a minority in a democratic, multireligious society and by leading interfaith efforts. Sikh organizations worked to educate Americans about their turbans, so they focused on visual sources such as Hollywood films, television programs, photographic representations, and parades. But they endeavored to do this without using the distancing strategies from Muslims adopted by some Hindu and Christian groups. The hate crimes they experienced were one reason that Sikhs were seeking to have a separate category in the U.S. census so their community could be more accurately counted and recognized. Sikhs also tried to use their traditional communal kitchen, or langar, to provide help to various American communities in times of crisis and to gain positive visibility and recognition as a religious and racial group. Ambedkarites and Sikhs were more likely to demonstrate solidarity with Black and Islamic groups, since they felt that there were commonalities between the marginality and state discrimination these groups experienced in the United States and their own social location in India.

As a major religious group excluded from the Abrahamic umbrella, a strategy used by Hindu leaders has been to position Hinduism as superior to and more progressive than Abrahamic traditions. Groups like the Hindu American Foundation also mobilized around how caste is depicted and to ensure that Hindus and Hinduism were not blamed for caste discrimination, bringing them into conflict with Ambedkarite organizations, as well as with

Sadhana and Hindus for Human Rights, both Hindu groups with a strongly anti-caste platform. While Ambedkarite organizations do not publicly mobilize around Buddhism, they have been critical of Hinduism and have been publicizing caste discrimination in the United States. They have also been promoting the life and work of Ambedkar to get him acknowledged as a great international social justice leader for oppressed groups, like Dr. King. By learning about Ambedkar, Ambedkarites understand that Americans will also become aware of the brutality of the caste system (Ambedkar suffered great humiliations as a Dalit in India despite being one of the most educated people of his day), the Dalit rights movement, and Ambedkar's role as the architect of the Indian constitution, resulting in his achievement in getting caste discrimination and the practice of untouchability legally banned in 1950 and instituting affirmative action provisions in India. Americans will also learn of Ambedkar's critiques of Hinduism, privileged castes, and Gandhi, and the reasons for his conversion to Buddhism. In other words, once this information becomes more widely available, Dalits believe that many Americans will become allies in the anti-caste movement, which is one of their goals.

In contrast to many Indian American Muslims, Hindus, and Sikhs, second-generation Indian American Christians do not adopt a racialized discourse and have not participated in political activism. Consequently, their organizations (the best known being the Federation of Indian American Christian Organizations of North America [FIACONA]) remain first generation led and homeland oriented, focusing on attacks against Christians in India. The reasons for these differences between Christian and non-Christian Indian American organizations are discussed in the concluding chapter.

Notes

1. https://www.mpachollywoodbureau.org/ (accessed August 6, 2020).
2. https://saldef.org/comcast-invests-two-million-dollars-sikh-american-community/#.VNFGKGc5CM8 (accessed August 20, 2020).
3. View them at http://www.sikhcampaign.org/wearesikhs (accessed August 20, 2020).
4. http://www.sikhcampaign.org/pbs (accessed August 20, 2020).
5. https://www.nytimes.com/2020/06/08/dining/free-food-sikh-gundwara-langar.html (accessed September 9, 2020).
6. In a June 10, 2020, email titled "Sikh Coalition Continues Working to Highlight Seva in U.S. Media," the Sikh Coalition discussed how they worked with the *Times* reporter to ensure accurate reporting. The email also provided a long list of other positive coverage that Sikh American communities around the country had received for their large-scale charitable work during the pandemic.
7. https://www.hinduamerican.org/projects/hindu-roots-of-yoga (accessed August 20, 2020).
8. https://www.hinduamerican.org/blog/equality-labs-social-hierarchy-survey-misdirected-at-hindus/ (accessed August 20, 2020).
9. The exclusion of (privileged-caste) Hindus from this list is something that, as we will see below, The Battle Over California State Textbooks, the Hindu American Foundation picked on to argue that they are an anti-Hindu organization.

10. https://www.equalitylabs.org/castesurvey/#key-findings (accessed September 9, 2020).
11. http://www.sikhfoundation.org/our-story/ (accessed September 9, 2020).
12. Professor Wendy Doniger is a well-known scholar of Hinduism at the University of Chicago.
13. https://www.sikhcoalition.org/our-work/creating-safe-schools/including-sikhism-in-state-curriculum-standards/
14. See https://www.hafsite.org/hindu-americans-take-significant-steps-towards-equitable-education-california for the HAF perspective and http://www.southasianhistoriesforall.org/about-us/ for the SAHFA perspective (accessed April 7, 2019).
15. In October 2023, a large statue of Ambedkar was unveiled at the Ambedkar International Center. https://ambedkarinternationalcenter.org/2023/10/aic-unveils-dr-ambedkars-largest-statue/
16. https://www.hinduamerican.org/projects/hindu-hate-watch (accessed September 11, 2020).
17. In April 2021, a mass shooting at a Federal Express facility in Indianapolis, where many Sikhs worked, led to the death of eight people, four of them Sikhs. The shooter, a 19-year-old White man who was fired from the FedEx facility in 2020, took his own life at the scene, and partly for this reason, a motive was never clearly established. However, Sikh advocacy organizations argued that the shooter knew that the facility was "overwhelmingly staffed by Sikhs" and, consequently, that the mass shooting could well have been a hate crime targeting Sikhs (Holcombe and Kaur 2021).
18. Information received via email on August 26, 2020.
19. Colby College; the University of California, Davis; Colorado College; Claremont College; Carleton University; the Harvard Graduate Student Union; Brown University; and the California Democratic Party have also recognized caste as a protected category.
20. https://akscusa.org/solidarity-statement-to-end-caste-practices-in-silicon-valley-and-the-usa/ (accessed September 9, 2020).
21. *Open Doors with Rahul Dubey*, Asiaville, August 23, 2020. https://www.youtube.com/watch?v=CHZAnLv2jv0 (accessed August 28, 2020).
22.. https://www.hinduamerican.org/blog/california-cisco-lawsuit-uniquely-endangers-hindus-indians/ (accessed September 9, 2020).
23. https://www.hinduamerican.org/blog/california-cisco-lawsuit-uniquely-endangers-hindus-indians/ (accessed September 9, 2020).
24. www.americanmusliminstitutions.org/about (accessed June 3, 2020).
25. The designation of October as Hindu American Awareness and Education Month in California was first achieved in 2015; Sikhs were able to have November declared as Sikh Awareness and Appreciation Month in California starting from 2011.
26. http://leginfo.legislature.ca.gov/faces/billTextClient.xhtml?bill_id=201920200ACR194 (accessed September 11, 2020).
27. https://berkleycenter.georgetown.edu/interviews/a-conversation-with-anju-bhargava-founder-hindu-american-seva-communities-washington-d-c (accessed September 14, 2020).
28. The 2022–2023 Pew survey, however, indicated that Sikhs made up 8 percent of the Indian American population, or around 352,000, based on the Indian American population being 4.4 million.
29. http://www.unitedsikhs.org/petitions/Memo%20re%20Sikh%20Ethnicity.pdf (accessed January 5, 2017).
30. Email update sent by the Sikh Coalition on September 28, 2023.
31. https://www.facebook.com/talktosaalt/videos/680780749058479/?eType=EmailBlastContent&eId=4a1f6b8b-c2ca-4656-83bd-76eab5e3a741 (accessed September 15, 2020).

5

Enacting Transnational Citizenship

Majority versus Minority Religious Status and Contemporary Mobilization around India-Centered Issues

The Indian American Muslim Council (IAMC) ... has called on the Government of India as well as various state governments to take note of the 2011 Annual Report of the United States Commission on Religious Freedom (USCIRF) that has placed India on a "Watch List" for the third year in succession. . . . IAMC firmly believes that the recommendations of USCIRF are based on factual information. They represent genuine concerns about the treatment of religious minorities in India.

—IAMC (2011)

[There were 158 anti-Christian attacks in India in 2010 with no arrests]. FIACONA strongly condemns all these acts. . . . FIACONA Board supports the decision of USCIRF to put India on its watch list.

J. Malhotra (2011)

Putting India on the watch list by USCIRF is a step which will spread international awareness regarding the plight of religious minorities and the continuous denial of justice to members of religious minorities who suffered violence in India. In November 1984, Sikhs were killed with the complicity of senior members of the Congress Party ... none have yet been convicted.

—Statement by legal advisor to Sikhs for Justice (H. Singh 2011)

The Hindu American Foundation (HAF) strongly criticized the listing of India, the world's largest secular democracy, with the likes of Russia, Afghanistan, and Cuba, on a U.S. State Department Advisory group's "watch list" of violators of religious freedom.

—HAF (2011b)

As these quotes show, advocacy organizations of Indian American Muslims, Sikhs, and Christians (as well as Ambedkarite groups) exhibit similar patterns of activism and sometimes even mobilize together around India-based issues, whereas Hindu advocacy groups have been the outlier (see Table 5.1). This pattern of mobilization is a reversal from the group configuration we saw in the last chapter where Indian American Christian groups were the outlier with respect to domestic policy concerns.

As we see in these quotes, the release of the annual report of the U.S. Commission on International Religious Freedom (USCIRF), which is often critical of India's religious freedoms record, is one example of the opposing patterns of mobilization. The report sparks off the competing mobilizations of Hindu American groups, which have attacked the commission for its Christian bias, and of Muslim, Sikh, and Christian Indian American groups, which have supported the commission's decision to place India on the list of "Countries of Particular Concern" after the Gujarat anti-Muslim pogrom (2002–2004), on its "Watch List" (2009–2011), on its list of "Tier 2 Countries" (2013–2019), and back on its list of "Countries of Particular Concern" between 2020 and 2023.[1]

Recall that the term "transnational citizenship" is used to recognize the bond that immigrants and their descendants continue to have with their ancestral homeland. The concept of "long-distance nationalism" coined by Benedict Anderson (1998) refers to a similar idea: loyalty to the homeland by members of its diaspora and willingness to "take whatever action the

Table 5.1 Home country activism of Indian American Organizations.

Basis of Mobilization	Characteristics of Groups	Main Focus	Nature of Mobilization	US Models Used
Religious minority status in home country	Largely immigrant but also second generation	Foreign policy	Around attacks by majority group	US racial minorities
Religious majority status in home country	Immigrant and second generation	Foreign policy	Defending majority group and/or the state	Emphasize pluralism, also parallels with Israel

homeland requires" (Glick Schiller 2005, 571). This loyalty in turn has been cultivated and deployed by politicians and homeland governments for financial, political, and foreign policy gains through the "diaspora strategies" of sending states (Ho 2011). Diasporic groups on their part may partake in "diaspora diplomacy" to promote their homelands in their new countries (Ho and McConnell 2019). Glick Schiller (2005, 573) points to how new communications technology has greatly expedited the ability of governments as well as diasporic groups to "organize social movements around homeland politics from afar." In Chapter 3, we came across examples of both "diaspora strategies" and "diaspora diplomacy." We saw how the Indian government changed its attitude toward Indian Americans over time and started to cultivate them to be "ambassadors" for India in the United States. The enthusiastic involvement of a variety of Indian American leaders and groups around the nuclear deal is an example of Indian American "diaspora diplomacy."

If homelands try to harness the political, economic, and social capital of their former citizens, and emigrants continue to feel a sense of identity with their home countries and are willing to mobilize to further its interests, what explains the very different patterns of mobilization toward India manifested by Indian American Muslims, Sikhs, Christians and Ambedkarite organizations on the one hand, and most Hindu (and de facto Hindu) organizations on the other? This chapter shows that the reason is because understandings of ethnic identity and attachments toward the homeland, particularly toward the homeland state, are often religiously inflected even in secular democracies. In other words, it is important to make a distinction between the bond diasporas feel toward their *home community* and the *government* that is in power. Consequently, there are differences in the concerns of groups that are in the majority versus in the minority in the home country (Dowley and Silver 2000; Horowitz 2000; A. Smith 1986; Staerklé et al. 2010). These differences continue, or are even magnified in the diaspora, in turn shaping the injustice frames, mobilization patterns, and strategies of majority and minority groups with respect to homeland events. In short, manifestations of transnational citizenship by citizens of a globally powerful country may not just mean advocacy *on behalf* of their homeland governments. It may mean advocacy *against* particular ruling regimes in the homeland. It is crucial to examine how religion affects the political mobilization of immigrants around homeland issues. To date, the bulk of this research has focused on European Muslims (Fetzer and Soper 2005; Hunter 2002; Laurence 2012; Modood 2005). Since Indian Americans are a politically active group from a variety of religious backgrounds, we get a broader understanding of how religion shapes the political goals and strategies of immigrant interest groups by examining their patterns of mobilization around India-based concerns.

Hindu American and de facto Hindu American advocacy organizations have generally explicitly or implicitly supported a Hindu-centric or Hindu nationalistic perspective and have been particularly active when a Hindu nationalist government has been in power in India. On the other hand, Muslim, Sikh, Christian, and Ambedkarite Indian American advocacy organizations have mobilized to publicize attacks on their communities by Hindu-majority groups in India, to emphasize India's multireligious and multicultural society, to seek U.S. intervention to safeguard India's secularism, and to end caste segregation and discrimination. The focus here, as in Chapter 4, is to show that despite big differences between each of the groups, there are distinct, patterned forms of mobilization, in this case around foreign policy issues, based on majority and minority religious background in India (see Table 5.1). This is corroborated by a report examining how "Indian Americans view India," based on a 2020 Carnegie survey, released on February 9, 2021 (Badrinathan, Kapur, and Vaishnav 2021). It showed that 69 percent of Indian Americans of Hindu background approved of the performance of Indian prime minister Narendra Modi, compared with 20 percent of Indian American Muslims and 34 percent of Indian American Christians (Sikhs were not mentioned). Similarly, 40 percent of those who identified as Hindus versus 67 percent of non-Hindus viewed Hindu majoritarianism (Hindutva) in India as a threat. The survey showed that Indian American religious groups are not monolithic but that there are significant differences between Hindus and non-Hindus when it comes to support for Modi and for Hindutva. Over time, as we will see, the division became one between supporters and opponents of Hindutva instead of between Hindus and non-Hindus since some progressive Hindus joined the mobilization against Hindutva.

This chapter will look at four examples of mobilization around India-based issues that demonstrate fundamental divergence in the goals of organizations supporting the interests of Hindu Americans (and even some ostensibly secular Indian American organizations), the dominant religious group in India, and those representing minority Indian religious groups (Muslim, Sikh, Christian, and Ambedkarite). The examples include mobilization around the status of religious minorities in India; caste discrimination, particularly the position of Dalits; and the political situation in Punjab and in Kashmir.

It is important to underscore that the lack of support for government policies does not necessarily mean that Indian American religious minorities are anti-India. Recollect from Chapter 2 that Indian American Muslim leaders emphasized that they were doing their patriotic duty toward India by working to "safeguard India's pluralist and tolerant ethos." After telling me that Indian American Muslims were shocked by the anti-Muslim pogrom in Gujarat in 2002, "Hassan" of the Association of Indian Muslims of America (AIM) went on to argue, "But, you don't give up your home because something bad has happened.... It is your home, you rebuild.... In America, we are citizens, but besides America, India is our country and a lot of our traditions and way of life, everything is Indian." He continued, saying that activists like himself were motivated by the belief that their mobilization around secularism was necessary for "our survival, the survival of our community, and [the] survival of India as a composite nation ... we are convinced that India's welfare lies in being a composite nation, a composite society." Many immigrant-generation Indian American Muslim activists with whom I talked, including Hassan, spoke with regret about how Indian society seemed to be turning away from the secularism and pluralism that had characterized their upbringing. Hassan indicated that he did not experience any "division" between Hindus and Muslims in India in the 1960s and 1970s. "When I went to school in India, I never saw anything like that, and I have a lot of Hindu friends there, and I never saw that.... I was often the only Muslim [in college] in a class of 40. I never came across any teachers or students making any comment that made me feel conscious that I am a Muslim." He even mentioned that earlier BJP leaders such as Atal Bihari Vajpayee, prime minister from 1998 to 2004, were not against Muslims, saying that Vajpayee had admonished Modi after the 2002 anti-Muslim riots in Gujarat (Modi was chief minister of Gujarat state at that time). His point was that the intense and public anti-Muslim agenda of many BJP leaders was a relatively new thing, which led to increased concerns among Muslims in the diaspora.

The Status of Religious Minorities in India

Attacks against religious minorities in the homeland by the state or by the dominant religious group is one obvious issue where we can expect to see differential mobilization by majority and minority religious groups. This is also the case in the Indian American diaspora. In Chapter 2 we saw how

Sikhs, Muslims, Hindus, Christians, and Ambedkarites formed organizations in the United States to mobilize around homeland issues due to such attacks. In this chapter we will see how Indian American secularists/religious pluralists and religious minorities have come together to form a platform against Hindu nationalism and its attacks against religious minorities in India.

Indian American Muslim leaders Hassan of AIM and Amin of the IAMC talked about how their organizations had collaborated with secularist groups and other Indian American minorities to publicize attacks on minorities in India, starting with the demolition of the Babri mosque in 1992 and the ensuing violence against Muslims, and the violence against Muslims in Gujarat in 2002. In a 2018 interview, Amin said that during the founding of the IAMC in 2002 after the "pogrom in Gujarat,"

> the Indian Muslim community in the U.S. felt a need for a voice within the diaspora to represent not only Indian Muslims but also to join hands with other minorities within the diaspora and other like-minded individuals who were concerned about safeguarding pluralism and secularism in India ... the *Coalition Against Genocide* [CAG]... was formed as a result of that effort.

Hindu nationalist supporters for their part realized the need to "develop a presence in the halls of US Congress so as to tell its side of the story" (Friedrich 2020b). The 2005 denial of a visa by the U.S. administration to Narendra Modi (see The U.S. Congress section below for more), then chief minister of Gujarat, who was held responsible for the 2002 anti-Muslim violence in that state, served as a wakeup call for Hindu nationalist supporters. Modi had been invited by the Asian American Hotel Owners Association (AAHOA, an organization dominated by Indian Americans, mostly from Gujarat state) as chief guest for their 2005 annual convention. This is when the Coalition against Genocide (CAG) mobilized against Modi's visit and urged the AAHOA to withdraw their invitation (CAG 2005). As Hindu nationalists came to form the Indian government in India in the recent period (from 2014 to the present), group alignments in the diaspora hardened. Amin told me that the IAMC also participated in a different multireligious progressive coalition, the *Alliance for Justice and Accountability* (AJA), formed in 2014 in anticipation of Modi's visit to the United States that September, where he was to speak at a huge event in Madison Square Garden. He said that a key partner in this alliance was the Dalit Coalition (including Equality Labs and several other Ambedkarite organizations from around the country). Additionally, the group included Indian American Christians, Sikhs, and secularists or pluralists. The AJA and several other similar organizations organized protests during Modi's 2014 visit, and a month-long #ModiFail campaign around Modi's 2015 visit to Silicon Valley, to raise awareness against the rising tide of intolerance in India and attacks against minorities. Some Indian American minority activists also filed a lawsuit through the American Justice Center in New York City based on the Alien Tort Claims Act (which allows lawsuits against violators of international law) and the Torture Victim Protection Act in 2014, just before Modi arrived, for committing crimes against the Muslim community in Gujarat in 2002 (Haniffa 2014). This was for symbolic effect since sitting heads of government have immunity from suits in American courts.

The U.S. administration as well as the legislative and policy community on Capitol Hill is an important focus of mobilization. The AJA and other organizations organized an event on Capitol Hill along with human rights activists such as Jennifer Prestholdt, director of the International Justice Program of the Advocates for Human Rights, on May 23, 2017, where they released a report on "Minority Rights Violations in India." An article on this event in *India Abroad* cites an unnamed Dalit activist as saying that the overlooking of human rights abuses in India by the U.S. administration more recently was due to the "heavy lobbying by forces of the Hindu Right ... [and the] infiltration of Hindu supremacist forces at all levels of the United States advocacy process" (Haniffa 2017b). On November 29, 2018, the Indian American Muslim Council (IAMC), with practicing Hindu Ajit Sahi as its advocacy director, organized a briefing on Capitol Hill on religious freedom in India, at which they also drew attention to and protested some militant Hindu nationalist speakers in Chicago as part of the World Hindu Congress in September 2018 (the Hindu American Foundation was one of the organizers, along with the Vishwa Hindu Parishad). The Alliance for Justice and Accountability and other progressive groups had been successful in getting Congress members such as Tulsi Gabbard and other U.S. politicians to back out of the event (Sirohi 2018). Organizations that were part of this broader coalition also mobilized separately to bring attention to attacks against their group. For instance, FIACONA organized a campaign on Capitol Hill in March 2015 to bring attention to attacks against Christians and Christian churches in India (Haniffa 2015). In 2017, the AJA, along with other organizations (e.g., the

South Asia Solidarity Initiative in New York City and *Multifaith Voices for Peace and Justice* in San Jose), organized rallies in several cities around the country to protest mob violence against Indian Muslims.

On its part, the Hindu American Foundation expressed concern in 2016 about Keith Ellison's candidacy for DNC chair, arguing that the Muslim American congressman had long shown a bias against Hindus in India, portraying them as aggressors against religious minorities, and had also not supported the rights of Hindus in Bangladesh and Pakistan (Haniffa 2016c). The HAF's protest led Ellison to hold a conference call with Hindu and Indian American leaders and to release a detailed statement addressing their concerns (HAF 2016). In 2017, the Hindu American Foundation supported India's move to end the U.S.-based Christian charity Compassion International's work to serve impoverished communities in India (an organization working in India for over 50 years) despite protests from U.S. lawmakers. The HAF argued that the organization was conducting religious conversions under the guise of its poverty programs, a charge denied by the organization and lawmakers. The HAF's Suhag Shukla argued, "The consequences of predatory proselytization are so harmful and so expansive that we welcome the Indian government's move" (Haniffa 2017a).

The U.S. Congress and the Plight of Religious Minorities in India

In a December 2013 article, Zahir Janmohamed, who worked in Washington, DC between 2003 and 2011 (including as an aide for Congressman Keith Ellison [D-MN]), indicated that he was part of the campaign to get the administration to deny the visa to Modi in 2005. He argued that John Prabhudoss, leader of FIACONA, played a key role in mobilizing evangelical Christian support against Modi and in getting Republican Joe Pitts (PA) who, together with Prabhudoss, had visited Gujarat in the aftermath of the 2002 violence) and Democrat John Conyers (MI, who had a large Muslim constituency) to introduce a resolution in the House in 2005 criticizing Modi for his inaction in Gujarat and condemning violations of religious freedom in India. This resolution led the State Department to deny Modi a visa to the United States (Janmohamed 2013). The Hindu American Foundation, on their part, called the resolution "Hinduphobic" and expressed frustration that the congressmen "made India a focus of a resolution condemning religious persecution in South Asia while Pakistan and Bangladesh escaped mention" (HAF 2005a).

On November 18, 2013, Congressmen Joe Pitts and Keith Ellison introduced another House Resolution (HR 417) in Congress. The resolution focused on human rights violations in Gujarat in 2002, called for the revoking of anti-conversion laws that existed in several Indian states, and asked that religious freedom be included in the U.S.-India Strategic Dialogue. The HAF immediately criticized the resolution for "attacking India's record on religious freedom, targeting only Hindus as instigators of violence, and ignoring the impact of Islamist and Maoist terrorism in the country." The HAF also claimed that the Indian American Muslim Council (IAMC) and the Coalition against Genocide (CAG) had hired a lobby firm, Fidelis, to lobby Congress members before the resolution was introduced and that they were disappointed to "see Indian Americans hiring an American lobbying firm to advocate for a deeply flawed and insulting American resolution critical of India" (E. Dutt 2013). The IAMC and CAG responded on December 6 accusing the HAF of having "existential links to the Sangh Parivar—an ideological conglomerate of organizations that seek to subvert the secular moorings of India's Constitution and relegate religious minorities to the status of second-class citizens," and called on "all Indian Americans and people of conscience" to support HR 417 (IAMC 2013). On December 15, they released a report on connections between the HAF and the Sangh Parivar (CAG 2013a). The HAF responded the same day with a report on CAG arguing that many of its leaders and member organizations "espouse Marxist ideology or fringe Islamist positions openly advocating anti-American, anti-Israel, and anti-India (and anti-Hinduism) views" (HAF 2013). According to Janmohamed (2014), who said he used his contacts with congressional staffers to obtain the information, the HAF, working with the United States India Political Action Committee (USINPAC), went to work visiting the offices of congressional members who had signed the resolution and was successful in getting some key members to withdraw their name from the resolution because of their visits. The sparring between the HAF and the Coalition against Genocide (CAG) continued with the CAG releasing another report on December 22, 2013, further documenting the links of the leaders of the HAF to Hindutva organizations as well as the close alignment of their positions with Sangh Parivar ideology (CAG 2013b). With respect to the situation in Gujarat, they argued that the account of the HAF "sharply diverges" from the reports of Human Rights Watch, Amnesty International, and many Indian investigations, and that the HAF was presenting the "RSS [the Hindu nationalist group] line on the Gujarat carnage." Despite the mobilization of the Indian American Muslim Council (IAMC) and their hiring of a lobby firm, however, the HAF and USINPAC were successful in preventing the House from considering HR 417 (Faleomavaega 2014b).

On April 4, 2014, the U.S. Congress held a hearing on the plight of religious minorities in India with Congressman Joseph Pitts presiding. It included testimony from representatives of the USCIRF, Human Rights Watch, a Minnesota-based group called Advocates for Human Rights, and John Dayal, a well-known Indian Christian human rights advocate who flew in from India. The HAF, USINPAC, and the Sikh Coalition submitted statements that were placed on record. The HAF report was placed before the hearing by Congressman Brad Sherman as one that promoted the "pro-Indian Government view" (Congressional Hearing 2014, 26). Panelists raised concerns about the situation of religious minorities in India and claimed that there had been many reports of religious violence over the past year. Robin Phillips, representative for Advocates for Human Rights, stated, "The Indian diaspora groups with whom we work have consistently expressed concern about religious freedom in India" and went on to list religious violence, lack of prosecution of perpetrators of violence, anti-conversion laws, anti-terrorism laws, and police practices that target Muslims (Congressional Hearing 2014, 10–11). Her repeated mention of Muslims (the only religious group she specifically referred to in her statement) was not accidental. Advocates for Human Rights had worked with the IAMC in the past (see IAMC 2012), and clearly this was the Indian diaspora group that was the primary constituency of the organization. The only dissenting positions at the hearing (see Chapter 3) came from Congresswoman Tulsi Gabbard (D-HI, of Hindu background) and Congressman Eni Faleomavaega—see Chapter 3 for more details about the relationship between him and USINPAC (Congressional Hearing 2014, 69).

Not surprisingly, the HAF statement presented a strong defense of the religious rights record of India. The HAF maintained, contrary to Sikh groups, that Sikhs were not socially and economically marginalized in Punjab and that there was no evidence that attacks against Sikhs had been religiously motivated. They referred to "aggressive proselytizing" by Christian missionaries as being the cause of some of the violence against Christians and that conversions of "vulnerable populations" through force and fraud were responsible for the introduction of laws restricting conversion that exist in some of the Indian states (Congressional Hearing 2014, 71–79). The statement by the Sikh Coalition was also not surprising. In contrast to the HAF description of the events of 1984 as a "riot," the Sikh Coalition referred to the events as anti-Sikh "pogroms" and argued that successive governments (i.e., both Congress and non-Congress governments) had not brought the main instigators of the violence to justice (Congressional Hearing 2014, 80). They urged the Human Rights Commission to support efforts to obtain justice for Sikh victims. As mentioned in Chapter 3, more than one-third of USINPAC's statement repeated that of the HAF verbatim. This, together with the Congressman Brad Sherman's reference to the HAF statement as the "pro-India view," shows how Hindu groups have been able to hijack the definition of "Indian" in the U.S. Congress.

Hindutva and Attacks against Religious Minorities in 2019 and After

In 2019, as they did in 2014, Modi's U.S. supporters began to mobilize, calling friends, family, and acquaintances in India, urging them to vote for Modi in the upcoming Indian elections (Mozumdar 2019b). As mentioned, Modi won a resounding victory in May 2019 with an even greater mandate than in May 2014. Showing the functioning of the HAF as an "India lobby" since the BJP's rise to power in India, the HAF along with the India caucus held a briefing on Capitol Hill on June 7, 2019, entitled "India's Democracy in Action: A Post-Election Analysis," with Suhag Shukla of the HAF opening the panel discussion and another HAF board member moderating the panel discussion. On September 22, 2019, both Modi and Trump greeted an audience estimated to be more than 50,000 strong at a Howdy Modi rally in Houston, with the HAF being one of the co-organizers of the event, along with the Texas India Forum affiliated with the RSS (see Chapter 6 for how this event impacted Indian American support for the Republican Party). Members of the multireligious organization the Alliance for Justice and Accountability (AJA) demonstrated outside (Kumar 2019).

In 2019, the BJP set about fulfilling several of its Hindu nationalist promises. On August 5, 2019, the government of India nullified Article 370, established in 1954, which had granted special status and limited autonomy to Jammu and Kashmir, and Article 35A, which had given special domicile rights to long-term citizens of the state (recall from Chapter 2 that this provision was originally instituted in 1927 to protect Hindu Kashmiri Brahmins against Punjabi Hindus). Prior to this, a curfew was imposed on the state, large numbers of security troops were moved in, local Kashmiri leaders were arrested, and a total blackout of communications was imposed, including landline and cellphone services, the Internet, and cable TV (4G Internet services were only restored six months later, on February 5, 2021). Local and foreign journalists and fact-finding teams were not allowed access to the state. The state was also partitioned into two "union territories" (under the direct control of the central government). On December 12, 2019, the Citizenship Act Amendment (CAA) amended the 1955 Citizenship Act by providing a way for *non-Muslim* migrants and refugees from South Asian countries (specifically Pakistan, Bangladesh, and Afghanistan) to obtain Indian citizenship. In other words, it was a citizenship act that was explicitly based on religion, in this case, excluding Muslims.

The CAA gained broader significance beyond the question of migrants from neighboring Indian countries for a variety of reasons. First, many Indians saw a link between the 2019 CAA and the National Register of Citizenship (NRC) implemented in Assam state starting in 2013, which the BJP planned to implement in the whole of India in 2021 (this link was also emphasized several times by the Indian home minister). Second, Indian Muslims worried that the CAA could be used to provide an escape clause for non-Muslims in India who did not have proper documents (a lot of Indians do not have these documents: for instance, registration of birth only became a legal practice in 1969) since they could claim to be refugees from neighboring countries who left their documents behind when they fled, an option not available to Muslims. In other words, the fear was that implementation of the CAA along with the NRC could lead to Muslims being systematically excluded from Indian citizenship on grounds that their documents were inadequate (Haniffa 2020d).

In response to these developments and others in India targeting religious minorities and Dalits, *Freedom House*, an international watchdog of democracy, demoted India from "free" to "partly free" in 2020 (Varshney 2021). It is these events that motivated the USCIRF to classify India as a "country of particular concern," a status reserved for the worst offenders (including countries like China, Myanmar, North Korea, Iran, Pakistan, and Saudi Arabia). Groups representing Indian minorities like the IAMC and FIACONA welcomed this designation for India, as did Hindus for Human Rights (HfHR). The HAF, on the other hand, fulminated against the report, characterizing the USCIRF chairperson as "anti-India" (Free Press Journal 2020).

The events of 2019 in India led to huge protests around the United States. Campaigns for and against the CAA were waged in early 2020 (protests about changes in the status of Kashmir will be discussed later). On January 19, 2020, groups like the South Asia Solidarity Initiative, the IAMC, and Equality Labs organized a National Day of Action in cities around the country against the CAA and Hindutva to emphasize the importance of upholding the secularism enshrined in the Indian constitution (Kulkarni 2020a). On India's Republic Day, January 26, 2020, the *Coalition to Stop Genocide*, comprising some of the same organizations such as the IAMC, Hindus for Human Rights (HfHR), Equality Labs, and many others, organized protests in several cities across the United States. Thenmozhi Soundararajan of Equality Labs is quoted as saying, "This project may start with Muslims but all caste-oppressed communities are at risk as we are the communities in the crosshairs of Hindu nationalists" (Kulkarni 2020b, 18). The next day, January 27, 2020, the IAMC and HfHR organized a Capitol Hill briefing on "Implications of India's Citizenship Law." One of the speakers, Harrison Akins, policy analyst for the South Asia region of the USCIRF, argued that the NRC and CAA together "could become a weapon to target millions of Indian Muslims, potentially leading to their disenfranchisement." Another panelist, John Sifton, the Asia advocacy director of Human Rights Watch, pointed out that the CAA violated two international treaties that India had signed and ratified (in 1967 and 1979) that had explicitly warned against deprivation of citizenship on the basis of national and ethnic origin (Haniffa 2020a). Critics also pointed out that the CAA law[2] only included non-Muslims from Muslim countries, did not even mention religious persecution or ask for proof of such persecution, and excluded religious minorities from countries such as Sri Lanka, China, and Myanmar who also experienced religious and ethnic persecution. On February 1, 2020 (two days after the anniversary of the death of Mahatma Gandhi on January 30), the Association of Indian Muslims (AIM) and the Young India Association (YIA) organized a "sit-in-satyagraha" in front of the Gandhi statue opposite the Indian embassy in Washington, DC to protest the repeal of Article 370 in Kashmir and the CAA and to warn that dividing India on the basis of religion was a fundamental violation of the Indian constitution. Kaleem Kawaja of AIM led participants in reading the preamble of the Indian constitution and in singing several Indian patriotic songs, and Rohit Tripathi of the YIA spoke about the importance of mobilizing through nonviolence (satyagraha). The event ended with the singing of the Indian national anthem (Haniffa 2020e). As protests spread through the country, several U.S. cities including Seattle, Cambridge, Albany, St. Paul, and San Francisco passed resolutions against the CAA and NRC.

The Hindu American Foundation (HAF) came out in strong support of the Citizenship Act Amendment (CAA), discussing it without any mention of the NRC, disregarding the fact that Amit Shah, India's home minister, had repeatedly linked the CAA and NRC and reassured non-Muslims that the CAA would help them maintain their citizenship if they could not produce the necessary documents for the NRC requirements (Venkataramakrishnan 2019). The HAF argued that the CAA was similar to the Lautenberg Amendment (1990) in the United States, meant to fast-track the resettlement of Jews from the former Soviet Union and later expanded to include persecuted religious minorities from Iran (S. Shukla 2020). The HAF also strongly criticized the March 4, 2020, hearing held by the USCIRF on Capitol Hill on "Citizenship Laws and Religious Freedom" with a specific focus on India, arguing that it presented a distorted account of the CAA (Haniffa 2020b). Other BJP supporters distributed Indian government–produced brochures to Indian Americans. Several groups (including the *Indian American Heritage and Cultural Foundation* and the *American India Public Affairs Committee*) organized rallies, seminars, and panel discussions around the country to show support for the CAA (Mozumdar 2020b).

President Trump visited India in March of 2020, and during his visit, there were several right-wing mob attacks in northeast Delhi in response to peaceful CAA protests, with the violence mainly targeting Muslims, their homes, and mosques, which President Trump did not condemn or even remark on. In another sign of the close links between Modi supporters and President Trump, on December 22, 2020, in an event that did not receive much attention or publicity, President Trump presented America's highest military decoration, the rarely awarded Legion of Merit, to Prime Minister Modi for "exceptionally meritorious service as the Prime Minister of the Republic of India from May 2014 to August 2020.... Prime Minister Modi's personal engagement expanded U.S.-India ties across all facets of the relationship" (IANS 2020).

The events of 2019 also led to the formation of new organizations such as Hindus for Human Rights (HfHR), a sister organization of Sadhana, and *Students Against Hindutva Ideology*, a group formed initially in Ivy League universities in the Northeast, which then spread to other universities. I spoke to a cofounder of HfHR in 2020, "Meena," who was also involved with Sadhana (mentioned in Chapter 4). Meena mentioned that as a person who was born and raised in India who was a "progressive Hindu" (which she defined as "somebody who connects their faith to social justice and stands against oppression of people and stands against all injustice"), she had been deeply concerned about the rise of Hindutva in India but had been unsure what to do about it. Finally, after the re-election of Modi in 2019, she said, a group of Indian American Hindus had formed HfHR to "have a platform to talk about India and address Hindutva in India and address human rights in India." Like Sadhana, HfHR members were mobilizing as Hindus to defend the values of pluralism and justice that they believed were inherent in their religion. Like Sadhana, HfHR was not mobilizing on behalf of just Hindus, but on behalf of the human rights of all groups. This is what makes them very different from the HAF. While the HAF did sometimes protest attacks on other groups in the United States and globally, their primary role was as an advocacy group for Hindus. Meena indicated that HfHR and its anti-Hindutva mission seemed to fill a void, since very soon many Indian Americans who were "deeply concerned about the insanity of what's happening in India" found them. The group also quickly became connected to "very high-profile people in India" who were also concerned about the rise of Hindutva. They then worked to combine and connect these people together to "make a Hindu force that can really respond and debate and take on Hindutva." HfHR has also been working closely with the IAMC and the Dalit Solidarity Forum. Meena told me:

> We think this is a moment that all of us—Hindus, Muslims, all the nonreligious people, Dalits, all of us who care about human rights and democracy need to stand together and defeat Hindutva. And then, if we succeed in that, then, we can go back to all the many, many, many things that could divide us... but right now the house is on fire. We don't check where the water comes from.

By early 2021, HfHR was able to raise enough funds to have an advocacy director, Nikhil Mandalaparthy, based in Washington, DC. Nikhil described the goal of the organization in a YouTube video on May 7, 2021:[3] "to advocate on issues of pluralism, civil rights and human rights in South Asia and North America from a Hindu perspective and to provide a Hindu voice of resistance to caste, to Hindutva, to racism, and all the forms of bigotry and oppression."

Recall that Sadhana had done some work with the HAF in the early years but had stopped that collaboration later. Meena explained it as being a result of "too much misalignment" over time. Specifically, Meena referred to the misalignment between the HAF and HfHR. She mentioned that the HAF was part of the organizing committee for the huge Texas Howdy Modi September 2019 event, while HfHR "was outside protesting." In my 2018 interview with Hassan from the IAMC, he too suggested that the HAF had changed over the years:

> When it was founded . . . its objective was very good. They wanted to protect Hindus from discrimination, you know. Because in this country, there are some right-wingers, racist people, and they attack Muslims, Hindus, anybody who is not like them. . . . But what has happened in the last few years . . . political groups from India like Vishwa Hindu Parishad and RSS, they are trying to control them or infiltrate them [HAF], and they are trying to tell them what to do.

In August 2020, groundbreaking for a Hindu temple on the site of the Babri Masjid mosque (razed by Hindu nationalists in 1992) took place. Hindus mobilizing as the *American India Public Affairs Committee* celebrated by organizing a Times Square event with images on the huge billboards there. However, the Coalition to Stop Genocide, consisting of more than 100 Indian American and other U.S. civil rights organizations, wrote to advertisers and Mayor Bill de Blasio asking them to prevent the planned billboard images and organized protests at the event (Beaty 2020). After Biden was elected to become president, a broad coalition of 19 Indian American progressive organizations (including HfHR, Students against Hindutva Ideology, the IAMC, AIM, SAALT, and several Ambedkarite organizations) wrote a letter to president-elect Biden in December 2020 asking him to vet Indian American appointments to his administration for RSS-BJP links. They wrote that "certain Indian-American individuals who are proximate to your Presidential administration [later specifically mentioning Sonal Shah and Amit Jani] . . . purport to uphold the values of the Democratic Party in the context of American politics; however they also advance the ideology and political interests of violent, extremist Hindu nationalist groups in India, essentially serving as their foreign agents" (see Chapter 6 for more details).

The letter also urged support for pending House bills supporting religious freedom in Kashmir and for including caste as a protected category under the Civil Rights Act (Sahni 2021).

These examples demonstrate the opposing U.S. mobilization patterns of Hindu groups like the HAF, on the one hand, and secularist, progressive Hindu, Muslim, Christian, Sikh, and Ambedkarite groups on the other around the status of religious minorities in India. We see how each side cultivated alliances with influential members of Congress and with other American groups whose interests might align with their own. Both sides framed their arguments to resonate with the American context and to show the convergence of their agenda with U.S. national interest (DeWind and Segura 2014, 24), with the HAF referring to their CAG opponents as "Marxists" and "Islamists," and Christian and Muslim groups emphasizing that the BJP was undermining India's secular constitution and appealing to human rights groups to support the rights of religious minorities in India. The CAA was defended by the HAF as being like the Lautenberg Amendment providing special status for Jews from the Soviet Union to immigrate to the United States, while religious minorities pointed out that it violated India's secular constitution by discriminating against Muslims.

Activism around Caste Discrimination in India

The Racial Paradigm and Anti-Caste Mobilization

U.S. Dalit activists have been very active around the issue of caste discrimination in India. They are aware that they could organize and mobilize in the United States in ways they could not in India. As one noted, "We enjoy a unique advantage.... We are outside the clutches of what happens to people when they open their mouths in India." They told me that particularly after the coming to power of the BJP in 2014, "people there in ground zero are in a very casteist space . . . it's very challenging for people because they have to keep up their jobs, they have to bring food to their home, provide shelter to their families." "Asha" said that after the coming to power of the BJP in 2014, things had changed so much that even "Dalits in the U.S. are afraid to speak out because often their bosses are people who are involved with the RSS [Hindu nationalist organization] and they are afraid of the impact it will have on them. People are really scared now."

Dalit American activists have close links with Dalit organizations in India and are directly involved in efforts to ameliorate the position of Indian Dalits. However, due to the magnitude and entrenched nature of the problem and resistance from caste-privileged groups and the Indian state, Dalit Americans recognize that the only way to bring about significant change is by obtaining the support of the international community. U.S. anti-caste activists work to propagate information about the position of Dalits in India, a group that few in the United States or the international community know about (see Kurien 2023).

Gail Omvedt (2004, 189) argued that the first "world level Dalit organizing" was initiated by Dr. Laxmi Berwa, an Indian American physician based in the Washington, DC area, in 1975, when he organized a protest against caste atrocities in India during the visit of then–prime minister Indira Gandhi to the United States. Berwa was also the first contemporary Dalit activist to use a human rights discourse for the Dalit cause (P. Mehta 2013, 74). He testified about the situation of Dalits before the UN Commission on Human Rights in 1982 and 1995, before the Congressional Human Rights Caucus in 1993, and in a wide variety of other venues arguing that although untouchability was abolished by the Indian constitution, the Indian government had failed to implement the laws and that as a human rights violation, it was not an internal problem but a problem that came under the purview of international organizations (Berwa 2000). The Indian government viewed this as a public shaming attempt.

Dalit rights activists in India picked up the use of human rights language and the comparison to racial discrimination (recall from Chapter 4 that Berwa had reached out to African American groups making this comparison and had likened Dr. Ambedkar to Dr. King), recognizing that "race was the most universal language of condemnation. Race moved mountains like the UN, the foundations and the corporations" (Visvanathan 2001, 2513). Dalit activism around human rights and the racial paradigm led by members of VISION and some Indian Dalit activists led eventually to caste being recognized by the UN Committee on the Elimination of Racial Discrimination (CERD) in 1996 as a matter that fell within their mandate (P. Mehta 2013, 82). It also led to a groundbreaking 1999 Human Rights Watch report highlighting the dehumanization of Dalits and the continuation of practices such as manual scavenging (where Dalits clean dry latrines with bare hands and minimal tools), the devadasi system (dancing girls dedicated to a temple deity who work as prostitutes for priests and elite temple patrons), and the range of violence Dalits faced.

In the early years, the Dalit Freedom Network did some advocacy work around Dalit rights on Capitol Hill, explicitly drawing parallels between race and caste. In October 2005, the DFN held a conference in Washington, DC entitled "Racism and Caste Based Discrimination in India: Implications for the US-India Relationship." This was followed by a House hearing on "caste abuses in India," and in 2007, the U.S. Congress passed a resolution (HR 139) urging the United States to address the problem of untouchability in India. The Hindu American Foundation retorted that the hearings were deliberately biased against India and Hindus and that they included individuals who were known for their "anti-Hindu activism" (HAF 2005b).

In response, the HAF put together a report, "Hinduism: Not Cast in Caste," released in December 2010. In an email to a group of Hindu supporters, they said that they had been working on the report for five years and that it was important to speak out on misconceptions regarding caste because caste had "become a major international issue." Putting out the report would allow the HAF to get involved when there were discussions in the U.S. media about Dalits or when there was a vote on a bill submitted by the Dalit Freedom Network in Congress (Rajan 2011). In the last paragraph of the executive summary, the HAF argued that many Christian organizations (often funded by the West) had started supporting and working with the Dalit movement in India over the past 10 to 20 years, likely "driven primarily by conversion agendas." The HAF made the case that missionary organizations were able to carry out their agendas because of "caste-based discrimination in Hindu society. This is why we argue that Hindu society has a great moral burden to act in a more determined and concerted fashion to end caste-based discrimination" (HAF 2010, 10). The HAF asserted that caste was not intrinsic in Hinduism because caste was not mentioned in the central sacred texts of Hinduism, only in secondary texts (this is arguable, as even the HAF notes in their 2010 report, p. 34). Consequently, they concluded triumphantly, "Hinduism can be the solution to the problem if Hindus follow key Hindu scriptures and the teachings of Hindu saints" (HAF 2010, 62). They called for rejecting passages in the Hindu scriptures that mentioned caste and for working within a Hindu framework to combat caste prejudice and discrimination.

The release of the report led to a firestorm of protests from Hindus in India and in other parts of the world who questioned the authority of people who had never lived in India to speak on behalf of Hindu Indians and to make the argument that Hindu society in India needed to be reformed (see Jain 2010; also see Kalyanaraman 2011; Rajan 2011). Some Hindu leaders and scholars who had endorsed the report withdrew their endorsement (Kalyanaraman 2011). In response, the HAF retracted the December 2010 document. A revised version was uploaded in July 2011 with a much more strongly worded executive summary supporting the Indian government's position, including the following statement:

> There have been recent attempts to pass resolutions and legislation on the issue of caste-based discrimination in international fora, including the United States Congress, United Kingdom, European Union, and the United Nations. These efforts should be firmly rejected as they are often lobbied for by the same international organizations that seek to carry out aggressive conversion campaigns. These efforts are also significantly misguided as they often equate caste-based discrimination with racial discrimination of the kind that existed in apartheid South Africa. Not only have modern genetic studies shown conclusively that caste is not the same as race, but caste-based discrimination is certainly not the policy of the GoI [Government of India] as racial discrimination was in apartheid South Africa. Indeed, the GoI, an avowedly secular institution comprised predominantly of Hindus, has instituted one of the most extensive and far-reaching systems of affirmative action quotas anywhere in the world. Interference by any external agency in the internal affairs of the sovereign state of India, a vibrant democracy, is thus unacceptable and unwarranted. (HAF 2011a, 17)

The sparring between the HAF and the DFN continued after publication of the report. In October 2012, the HAF's executive director presented a summary of the report at the Religion Newswriters Association's annual conference after a press briefing about a film, "Freeing the Untouchables," sponsored by the Dalit Freedom Network (HAF 2012). On January 15, 2014, on the 85th birthday of Martin Luther King Jr. (who in a sermon in 1965 had drawn a parallel between the situation of African Americans and Dalits), the DFN along with African American Congresswoman Eleanor Holmes Norton and other U.S. congressional members joined several prominent African American legacy families in organizing an event at the U.S. Capitol, described as a "milestone" in the contemporary abolition movement. Attendees signed

"The Declaration of Empathy" to show that African American families "stand in solidarity with the oppressed Dalit people in India." The DFN representative indicated that the event was "the culmination of a tremendous commitment on all our parts to bring the Dalits' plight into the public square" in the hope of developing an "international groundswell of support for their freedom" (Dalit Freedom Network 2014). A few months later (May 2, 2014), Congresswoman Eleanor Holmes Norton introduced a resolution "condemning Dalit Untouchability" and "the practice of birth-descent discrimination against Dalit people" in the U.S. Congress. A representative of the HAF wrote a HuffPost blog in response, criticizing the DFN for being an evangelical organization working to convert non-Christians. The writer argued that caste and race cannot be equated since caste divisions in the Indian subcontinent have absolutely nothing to do with skin color, a specific religion, or even economic status. Consequently, he argued that comparing caste discrimination to Jim Crow belittled the brutality and abuse faced by African Americans (Balaji 2014).

In subsequent years, DFN leaders told me that they had become concerned about the variety of restrictions on religious freedom in India such as anti-conversion laws and India's Foreign Contribution Regulation Act (FCRA) requiring charitable groups receiving funding from overseas sources to be registered and to comply with opaque and changing rules. Foreign Christian workers were also denied visas to work in India even though Hindu priests obtained religious visas to serve in the United States. Likely motivated by the Indian case, at a July 2019 State Department conference on religious freedom, D'Souza of the DFN made a broad argument (referring specifically to Saudi Arabia, Yemen, and China but not India) in favor of the importance of the United States "including international reciprocal religious freedom laws in bilateral relations."[4]

As mentioned, Equality Labs, formed in 2015, became publicly active around the situation of Dalits. Thenmozhi Soundararajan frequently drew parallels between apartheid and the practice of untouchability in her presentations, using the term "caste apartheid." When addressing international audiences, she often braided ideas from Black feminism and Ambedkarism together, criticizing the Hindu nationalist Indian state for its violence against Dalits, particularly Dalit women.[5] Addressing international women's rights activists at a packed New York City Women in the World Summit in April 2014, Soundararajan and an Indian Dalit activist explained that the experience of rape (generally by "upper caste" men) was very common for Dalit women in India, who usually had no recourse to report the violence or have the perpetrator convicted since police, doctors, and judges, generally caste Hindus, believed that Dalit women were sexually immoral and did not take their word that a rape had occurred.[6] Speaking before another group of international women's activists in December 2015, Soundararajan described India as one of the largest violators of human rights and also the "largest [religious] fundamentalist country in the world." She argued that at the core of its violence was "the vicious system of apartheid which is the caste system." She continued, describing how atrocities "honed on the bodies of Dalit women" were being used against other groups in India (referring to Muslim women).[7]

Soundararajan also initiated several types of technology-based anti-caste activism. In 2015, she, along with some Indian Dalit women activists, built on an idea floated by Indian Dalit activists more than a decade earlier to introduce a Dalit History Month (in April, Ambedkar's birth month) modeled on Black History Month. In April 2015, Equality Labs started a Dalit history timeline and posted articles online every day over the month to focus on key Dalit leaders and events, disseminating this information through Twitter, Facebook, and Instagram (http://www.dalithistory.com/). Their goal was to create Wikipedia pages showcasing important Dalit contributions through history, to "de-brahminize" knowledge about Dalits, and to challenge savarna narratives about caste and Dalits. This project continued with Dalit activist groups organizing "Wikipedia hackathons" to train people to create Wikipedia entries. Equality Labs was also involved in getting Twitter and Facebook to deal with caste abuse on their platforms in India. Equality Labs also successfully prompted progressive U.S. Hindu organizations like Sadhana and Hindus for Human Rights to adopt anti-casteism along with anti-Hindutva as their central planks. Here, Sunita Viswanath, cofounder of both Sadhana and Hindus for Human Rights, argues for the important role of progressive Hindus in both anti-caste and anti-Hindutva efforts: "how can we annihilate caste without Hindus, and how can we defeat Hindutva without Hindus?"[8]

From the Racial Paradigm to a Descent-Based Discrimination Policy Framework

The June 2001 UN subcommission report arguing that discrimination based on "work and descent" violated human rights law was followed by another working paper two years later focusing on caste-like groups in Africa and Yemen. Initially, these types of discrimination were equated with racial discrimination (Bob 2007, 183). However, over time, the concept of "work and descent-based discrimination" gained a degree of independence from "race" to refer to caste-like practices around the world. Japanese Burakumin leaders, later joined by Dalit rights activists and other groups, working through the UN Sub-Commission on the Prevention of Discrimination and Protection of Minorities, developed a new norm of "descent-based discrimination" to refer to caste-type discrimination.

A good example of a U.S. organization that uses the descent-based discrimination framework is the International Commission for Dalit Rights (ICDR) formed in 2006 in London by a Nepali Dalit rights advocate, D. B. Sagar, and established in Washington, DC in 2008. The main goal of the ICDR is to "eliminate Caste or Work and Descent-based Discrimination (CWDD), inequality and injustice" (http://icdrintl.org/about-us/). Impacting policy was central to the focus of the ICDR. Sagar explained that they had moved their office from London to the United States "because we thought having an office in U.S. would be more influential than keeping it there [London]. Because World Bank is here, United Nations is here, so of course the United States has a huge role to play in international policy and development." The ICDR developed the Caste Freedom Index (CFI) across six domains as a tool to help policymakers and NGOs measure and address caste inequality. Some of their other activities included lobbying to include caste or descent-based discrimination in the UN's post-2015 development agenda. For several years, the organization had also been advocating that the U.S. Congress pass a binding resolution against caste-based discrimination. Sagar explained to me that if this resolution passed, "it will affect the foreign policy of the U.S. government. That includes how to regulate the foreign aid, how to work with the foreign countries where the caste system exists." In other words, foreign aid would be conditional on the countries improving their anti-caste record and some percent of the aid would be directed toward caste-oppressed groups. The ICDR was also trying to get the U.S. government to pass a law against caste discrimination in the United States.

Other policy-oriented Dalit rights activists in the United States also advocated to international human rights organizations and the U.S. Congress using the descent-based discrimination frame, seeking support to deal with caste violence. For instance, Raj Cherukonda, former president of the AANA, testified at a congressional hearing before the Tom Lantos Human

Rights Commission in June 2016 on behalf of the Dalit American Federation (a temporary coalition of Dalit organizations across the country) about caste atrocities and discrimination in India. Cherukonda called for human rights and freedom to be part of the U.S.-Indian Strategic Dialogue and for agencies such as USAID to channel some of their resources to support marginalized groups in India, particularly Dalits and tribals. He also asked for the UN Sustainable Development Goals to include the elimination of discrimination based on work and descent (Cherukonda 2016).

This section shows how Dalit rights groups, on the one hand, and the Hindu American Foundation, on the other, worked to bring their respective positions on caste discrimination in India into the U.S. public sphere. In the HAF case, we also see that pressure from Indian groups led them to tone down their initial position that caste discrimination was a serious problem in Indian society that needed to be addressed, and instead to highlight the programs that the Indian government had developed to address the issue and emphasize that outside interference was unwelcome. While Dalit groups define caste as "birth-descent discrimination," which made the position of Dalits comparable to that of Black groups in the United States and South Africa and allowed them to forge alliances with these groups, the HAF emphasized that caste is not based on color or class to reinforce their argument that due to the unique nature of the caste system, international interventions are misguided and an impediment to solving the problem.

Mobilization around Khalistan and Farmers' Protests

As the anti-Sikh violence abated in India in the mid-1990s, support for an armed Khalistani movement among immigrant Sikhs in North America gradually dwindled, though some pockets of support remained. Consequently, scholars refer to Khalistan in the contemporary period as a "deterritorialized imagined community" (Shani 2008, 143) or as "political critique" (Mahmood 2014). Some of my respondents seemed to agree with this characterization. An older Sikh man described it this way: "this demand for Khalistan and our disowning India, it's, it's really a form of protest." However, from my interviews it seemed that Khalistan meant different things to different people. Here is a Sikh graduate student articulating in 2017 what he thought Khalistan meant for the U.S. Sikh community today:

> I think a better way to think about the Khalistani movement is that... most Sikhs think that they got dicked over when partition happened, and that Sikhs didn't get their fair share. And I think in general they would like to see a space in which Sikhism would be able to flourish in India. I don't think people are super-crazy about wanting their own nation-state, but they understand that because of the historical processes around post-colonialism, that Sikhism has been corrupted. And the Punjab is not a place in which Sikhism is allowed to flourish and spread its wings as far as it can go. So, in that sense most Sikhs are Khalistani in that they wish for a space in which Sikhism can flourish.

Many of my interviewees who talked about Khalistan (the issue did not come up in all interviews) did seem to see it as a protest movement against the Indian state that emphasized Sikh self-determination rather than an actual separatist movement. These individuals, mostly second-generation Sikh Americans, pointed to the variety of ways that organizations formed by individuals of their generation had been mobilizing around discrimination against Sikhs by the Indian state without mentioning the issue of Khalistan.

For instance, *Ensaaf*, formed in 2004 by second-generation Sikh Americans in the Bay Area, had been working in Punjab to "end impunity and achieve justice for mass state crimes ... by documenting abuses, bringing perpetrators to justice, and organizing survivors" (Ensaaf.org). The organization's oral history and video testimonies project had collected 200 oral histories about disappearances and extrajudicial killings in Punjab between 1984 and 1995. There was a mobilization around the 30th anniversary of the events of 1984 by a variety of Sikh American organizations formed by second-generation Sikh Americans. An organization called *Saanjh* in the Bay Area came up with the idea of creating a video archive of interviews with Sikhs around the world about their memories and experiences of 1984, The 1984 Living History Project (http://www.1984livinghistory.org). Another organization, *The Surat Initiative*, collaborated with Ensaaf to create the 2014 Remembrance Project, posting a historical item linked to 1984 every day through the whole of 2014.[9] In September 2014, when Narendra Modi was visiting the United States, the Sikh Coalition (which had until then focused on domestic issues) and Ensaaf organized a congressional hearing focusing on the alleged collusion of Indian politicians from the Congress Party in the 1984 anti-Sikh violence and the lack of indictments against the perpetrators of that violence. All these organizations seeking justice for the victims have kept the issue of anti-Sikh violence and discrimination alive, educating the younger generations and some members of the wider society.

In contrast to the interviewees quoted above who argued that Khalistan was a form of protest and not about an actual Sikh state, others felt the Khalistan movement continued to be about establishing a Sikh political territory. Another Sikh graduate student who had read Shani's (2008) book on Sikh nationalism, for example, said it was "absurd" to argue that Sikh nationalism was no longer tied to territory. "Because how could people be shouting these slogans [for Khalistan] at the Sikh Day Parade, and then not pointing to Punjab?" He felt that Khalistan was still a simmering issue within the Sikh American community although not a focus of many Sikh American organizations in the post–September 11 period. The young man, however, pointed me to a Sikh American organization, *Sikhs for Justice*, that was working with the United Nations for Khalistan.

I interviewed an activist with Sikhs for Justice and learned about the organization. It was established in 2009 in New York City (and later formed offices in Canada and the United Kingdom) largely by immigrant Sikh lawyers in response to the lack of justice for the "genocide" of Sikhs in India after the death of Prime Minister Indira Gandhi. The organization gained publicity within the Indian American community by filing human rights violations lawsuits under the Alien Tort Claims Act (eventually dismissed by U.S. courts) against prominent Indian politicians alleged to have been involved in the anti-Sikh attacks of 1984 who were visiting the United States. In 2015, influenced by the Scottish independence referendum of the previous year, the organization launched a referendum 2020 movement, seeking to build support from Sikhs around the world for "India-occupied Punjab" to become an independent country (Nibber 2015). The goal was to hold an "unofficial" referendum in 2020 (subsequently postponed to 2022 due to the pandemic) among Sikh communities in India and around the world to find out the level of support for Khalistan. If the majority supported Khalistan, the organization planned to work with the United Nations to hold an official referendum and, the group hoped, to achieve independence. In a YouTube video of a Sikh community event held in Toronto on April 9, 2015, to educate people about the referendum, a second-generation activist for Sikhs for Justice from Toronto speaking in English and some Punjabi (most speeches were by immigrants and were in Punjabi) addressed the "youth," explaining the goals and rationale of the referendum: "Sikhs for Justice's goal is an independent Punjab, whether it is called Khalistan, whether it is given any other name, we want a state that is based on Sikh principles that looks out for Sikh issues, and Sikh people. We want our home, and we want our home back, which we *chose* to give to the Indians in 1947."[10] Describing India as "the occupying power," he argued that every year, Indians "steal 80 billion dollars from Punjab [referring to the river waters], I want to make it clear, steal 80 billion dollars every year from your pocket." At the end of his speech, he introduced Karen Parker, a U.S.-based attorney specializing in human rights law, as a person who had liaised with the United Nations to help a variety of groups achieve independence, and who had "single-handedly brought the world's most oppressive regimes to their knees." Parker outlined the five principles of self-determination of the United Nations, advised her audience on how Sikhs could make a case under each of the five principles, and promised her support to Sikhs for their self-determination movement.[11] A similar event with many of the same speakers (including Karen Parker) was held in California on August 17, 2015.[12] Sikhs for Justice was banned in India in July 2019. In 2020, its digital distribution system (Google Play) was removed, and its websites were blocked (Rohatgi 2020). Its main activists were charged with sedition and secession (Nanjappa 2020). Sikhs for Justice piggybacked on the Indian farmers protests (see below, this section) to continue mobilizing Sikhs in Punjab in 2020 during the pandemic. The referendum was conducted in some Western countries (including Canada and the United Kingdom) in 2022 and 2023. All this took place within the Sikh community, but the issue of diaspora-initiated Sikh separatism and the Indian government's alleged attempts to eliminate its leaders burst into the North American public sphere in late 2023. In September 2023, Canadian prime minister Justin Trudeau alleged that the Indian government had been behind the June 2023 assassination, in Surrey, British Columbia, of a Khalistani leader associated with Sikhs for Justice, Hardeep Singh Nijjar. The allegation was denied by the Indian government and led to a major diplomatic standoff between Canada and India. In November 2023, however, American news media carried details of a thwarted "murder-for-hire plot" in New York City, also in June 2023, linked to the killing of Nijjar. The plot was allegedly directed by an Indian "official" and was against Gurpatwant Singh Pannun of Sikhs for Justice, the person who had initiated the referendum movement. It was foiled because the assassin recruited (for a promised payment of $100,000) was an undercover agent. The Indian government promised to investigate (Hong 2023). Sikh American organizations that had been calling the Biden administration to ensure the safety of the Sikh American community in the wake of the

September 2023 Canadian allegations expressed deep concern about "the continuing threat of transnational repression" and asked the Biden administration to sign the Transnational Repression Policy Act, a bipartisan bill introduced in Congress in March 2023 to protect U.S. citizens from repression from foreign governments and to hold foreign governments responsible for such repression (Sikh Coalition email, November 30, 2023).

The Indian farmers' protests began in response to three new agricultural laws passed by the BJP government in September 2020, trying to wean farmers away from a guaranteed minimum price for their produce (a practice in the states of Punjab and Haryana, both close to India's capital, Delhi) and deregulate the agricultural market. When state protests asking for a repeal of the laws did not yield results, tens of thousands of farmers drove to Delhi on tractors and encamped there for months. Since Punjab is a Sikh-dominated state, and many Sikhs are farmers, Sikh men with their colorful turbans were very visible in the protests, with their langar or community kitchen tradition serving to sustain them during their encampment. The Indian police frequently turned to violence against the farmers. The farmers' protest was supported by the Sikh diaspora in Canada, the United States, and the United Kingdom and garnered international attention. On December 12, *India West* reported that three members of the American Sikh caucus sent a letter to the Indian ambassador to ask India to stop "brutally suppressing the voices" of the Indian farmers. The caucus members said that many of the farmers had children and relatives in the United States who had reached out to them (*India West* Staff Reporter 2020). The three major Sikh American advocacy organizations, the Sikh Coalition, SALDEF, and United Sikhs, all rallied in support of the farmers and to protest state violence against them. They contacted members of Congress and other policymakers on the issue (emails received from the organizations over the period). On December 24, 2020, Sikh organizations in Northern California mobilized thousands of protesters to block traffic on Highway 50 in Sacramento to draw attention to the plight of the Indian farmers. Hindu American Foundation leaders, however, criticized the unnecessary "religionizing" of the farmer's protests (discussions on Twitter, December 2020). As the farmers' protests went into March 2021, the Sikh Coalition sent a letter on March 4 to acting secretary of state Lisa Peterson, offering to organize a briefing for the Department of State on the issue (news received via Sikh Coalition email, March 13, 2021). The Indian protestors and their supporters in the diaspora were jubilant when Modi suddenly backed down and repealed the three farm laws in November

2021. Protestors departed from Delhi in December 2021, after more than a year. Undoubtedly diasporic financial and lobbying support helped sustain the long encampment. Journalists attributed the about-face from Modi to the pressure of upcoming elections in Punjab and Haryana (Shih 2021).

The Khalistani case and the farmers' protests demonstrate the transnational nature of diasporic activism and the ways in which events in the diaspora and the home country are closely linked. The fact that citizens of Canada and the United States were targeted in assassination plots, allegedly by Indian officials, meant that North American government representatives got involved, showing how diasporic activism can impact countries of settlement. Mobilization around the farmers' movement by U.S. Sikh organizations educated policymakers and the wider society about the issue, leading to expressions of support by members of the Sikh caucus and international celebrities including Rihanna and Greta Thunberg, likely putting pressure on the Indian government.

Recent Mobilization around Kashmir

Recall from Chapter 2 that the Kashmir issue had seen U.S. mobilization by Kashmiri Muslim groups (until 2019 the majority population of the state of Jammu and Kashmir), particularly the Kashmiri American Council (KAC), and by Kashmiri Pandit (Hindu Brahmin) groups, primarily the Indo-American Kashmir Forum (IAKF). In a dramatic development in July of 2011, Ghulam Fai of the Kashmiri American Council was arrested, charged with participating in a long-term conspiracy to act as an agent of the Pakistani government in the United States without disclosing the affiliation as required by law (Rana 2017). The FBI said that Fai had received between $500,000 and $700,000 a year from the Pakistani government in support of his activities and had consequently transferred millions from the government of Pakistan and the ISI to support his lobbying over Kashmir for 20 years (FBI 2011). The arrest of Ghulam Fai provided credibility to the claim of Hindu American groups that Pakistan had been sponsoring both the militancy in Kashmir and anti-Indian propaganda in the United States. Lalit Koul, president of the Indo-American Kashmir Forum, declared, "It was always clear that this [Fai's] group was following the official Pakistani version of the Kashmir story. In all instances, the truth was obfuscated by misinformation provided by our opponents masquerading as Kashmiri freedom fighters." He continued, saying that he now hoped "U.S. lawmakers would get an opportunity to listen to the true stories of real victims of terrorism ... including our story of being 'refugees in our own country'" (Rajghatta 2011). In October 2011, the issue of Hindu Pandits in Kashmir was again discussed at the U.S. Capitol at a briefing. The panel comprised representatives from the HAF and the IAKF along with a U.S. expert on South Asian affairs, Lisa Curtis of the Heritage Foundation. Discussing the briefing, Suhag Shukla of the HAF argued that thanks to Pakistani propaganda, the "insurgency in Kashmir is commonly understood as an indigenous movement by Kashmiris for independence, but in reality, it was a planned and orchestrated campaign by Pakistan's military and Inter-Services Intelligence to destabilize India and promote global jihad" (Haniffa 2011). The imprisonment of Fai (he was sentenced to two years in prison but subsequently released in November 2013 after 16 months) led to a temporary lull in the activity of KAC (another group, the *World Kashmir Awareness Forum*, formed in 2005 in Ohio, remained active).

By 2017, Kashmiri Muslim group activity had picked up, led again by Fai, at the time the secretary-general of the World Kashmir Awareness Forum, who achieved a comeback as "the undisputed campaigner-in-chief of the Kashmiri separatist movement in the U.S." (Haniffa 2017a). "Raheem," the older Kashmiri Muslim immigrant I interviewed in 2019, told me that Kashmiri Muslims still regarded Fai highly and saw him as a victim of India's political campaign since India had similarly funneled funding to members of Congress through Indian Americans. Despite the "legal problem" that Fai got into, Raheem told me, "morally he stands very tall still." Raheem argued that Fai and the Kashmir freedom movement continued to remain very "Kashmir-centric," emphasizing the need for Kashmiris to have the freedom to decide their future, but that Fai was willing to accept funding from anyone willing to support this cause, including Pakistan.

When India abruptly revoked Articles 370 and 35A on August 5, 2019, the Kashmiri Hindu American community celebrated the decision, and the Hindu American Foundation described the abrogation as an important step in integrating the former state into India (Kulkarni and Mazumder 2019). However, the move and the forced conversion of the state into two union territories, ruled directly by the central government, were viewed with tremendous shock and alarm by Indian American Muslims and progressives, who declared the actions illegal (Haniffa 2019a).[13] Kashmiri

Pandit organizations in the United States along with USINPAC held a congressional briefing on October 16 to lay the groundwork for the upcoming congressional hearing on "Human Rights in South Asia" on October 22, 2019. They emphasized the "genocide" and "ethnic cleaning" faced by Kashmiri Hindus and argued "that Kashmiri Hindus have a 5,000-year documented civilizational legacy" and that "the Hindu ethos is very secular" (Haniffa 2019c). Despite this effort, leading congressional members castigated India at the congressional hearing. Covering the session, seasoned *India Abroad* journalist Aziz Haniffa (2019b, 10) argued that it was particularly significant that these attacks were coming "from longtime and time-tested friends of India, including many founding members of the Congressional Caucus of India and Indian America." These Congress members, mostly Democrats (who, according to Haniffa, were responding to their Muslim American constituencies, mobilized by Kashmiri Muslims) also severely criticized the Trump administration for not "standing up" to India (Haniffa 2019b).

Taken aback by the "India bashing" in Congress, the Indian government hired a second lobbying firm, Cornerstone (they were already working with Barbour Griffith and Rogers to focus on Republicans in Congress), to help them with their congressional PR battle (Haniffa 2020a). With these additional resources and new determination, journalists Kumar and Lacy (2020) alleged that the Indian embassy launched a "full-court press of lobbying initiatives" against a bipartisan resolution condemning Modi's actions in Kashmir introduced in December 2019 by Indian American Congress member Pramila Jayapal (D-WA), cochair of the Progressive Caucus in 2020, with 65 cosponsors. The resolution did not make it to the schedule for a markup in the House Foreign Affairs Committee in March 2020 despite a promise by committee chair Eliot Engel that it would be brought up for debate. The Hindu American Foundation (HAF), which had sent a message to its supporters to stop Jayapal's "anti-Hindu, anti-India bill," indicated in a newsletter that their message had resulted in over 2,500 emails to Congress, and that it was this outpouring that had resulted in the defeat of the resolution—"You spoke. Congress listened" (HAF newsletter linked in Kumar and Lacy's 2020 article). Kumar and Lacy (2020) allege that the HAF was "at the forefront of reinforcing the embassy's efforts . . . and masquerading as a liberal representative of the Indian American community."

While KAC and other Kashmiri Muslim advocacy groups were led by immigrant activists, second-generation Kashmiri Muslims formed two new advocacy organizations in 2019, *Americans for Kashmir* to work on the Hill (including with Representative Jayapal on her resolution criticizing Modi's actions in Kashmir, and with Representative Tlaib [D-MI] on another resolution supporting Kashmiri self-determination, which ended up being tabled), and *Stand with Kashmir* to educate and mobilize the Kashmiri diaspora and the wider American public. I spoke to "Daneen," an activist with Stand with Kashmir, at the end of 2019. She told me about moving from Kashmir to Buffalo, New York, when she was a young child. Buffalo had a community of Kashmiri Muslim doctors and engineers at the time and was "a stronghold" for KAC, which had regular meetings. Being part of this Kashmiri community in Buffalo, she said, "so much of what we ate, breathed, and talked was about Kashmir and things that were going on back home... and there would be political debates that I would hear from like a young age." Daneen described the older-generation activists in KAC as people who had "a particular idea of how politics gets done, and it's through the main power brokers," so that is what they focused on. She contrasted this approach with a grassroots approach "to change American perceptions of what's happening in Kashmir," which is what second-generation activists of Stand with Kashmir were trying to achieve. "We realized that it was really important to move away from this framing of India versus Pakistan. It should be about Kashmiris and what they want and what they had to undergo all of these years." Daneen remarked that she and others in Stand with Kashmir hoped that their movement would "eventually become something like the Palestine Solidarity Movement or Black Lives Matter where there would be enough of a groundswell of support in the United States to raise awareness about what's happening in Kashmir and why it matters." Daneen also emphasized that part of their effort was to train and educate second-generation Kashmiris "who didn't necessarily know their own history or weren't as informed." Then came the events of August 2019, which "totally kind of shook us to the core." After August, they organized several teach-ins and other educational events in cities like New York and Chicago, as well as online webinars. They emphasized that what was happening in Kashmir "is not a conflict, it's an occupation." Their events after August were disrupted by "Indian jingoistic types," their websites and social media were trolled, and they were attacked as a Pakistani ISI (Inter-Services Intelligence) group. Daneen remarked that this was what happened to Kashmiris who spoke out against India. They were always called Pakistani agents and "their agency is just completely erased." She also talked about the Hindu nationalist rhetoric that they found particularly offensive, that "a genocide has been happening [in Kashmir] for seven centuries, that all Kashmiri Muslims are invaders... and also that we're foreigners in a Hindu land, that Kashmir is a Hindu space." Stand with Kashmir activists also worked closely with Americans for Kashmir to connect Kashmiri Americans with elected officials. Both Raheem and Daneen told me that despite their efforts and intent to be inclusive and to create a secular Kashmiri mobilization and identity, it had been hard for immigrants and even second-generation Kashmiri Muslims to create common ground with Kashmiri Hindu Americans, particularly in the post-1990 period after the uprising in Kashmir and the rise of contemporary Hindu nationalism. They were also not successful in forming an interfaith U.S. coalition group to deal with the Kashmiri imbroglio.

Even though Jammu and Kashmir started out as an exception, a Muslim-majority state where Hindus were a minority and were initially overpowered by a Muslim lobby, we saw from Chapter 2 that the attacks of 9/11 began the attempt to reframe the Kashmiri situation as a case of Islamic terror. The coming to power of a Hindu nationalist party in India in 2014, and particularly the re-election of the party to a second term in 2019, resulted in an almost unimaginable scenario of the central government taking over and carving up an entire state that had been guaranteed special protections in the constitution as part of its accession. How much of that was due to a feeling that they could get away with it because of a strong U.S. Hindu lobby and because Trump was in power and was not interested in the United States interfering with foreign policy issues is unclear. To connect with their American audiences, second-generation Stand with Kashmir activists drew parallels with the Palestinian Solidarity Movement and Black Lives Matter. They also mobilized with these groups, and these groups in turn supported the Kashmiri Muslim mobilization after 2019.

Conclusion

Most countries around the world are composed of ethnic majority and minority groups. This chapter demonstrates the powerful ways in which majority and minority status can shape diasporic nationalism and the political activism of immigrant groups around homeland-oriented issues. While the focus of scholarship has been on Muslims who are the dominant group in their home countries but become religious minorities in Western countries, there has been little research on how religious status in the homeland can shape immigrant political activism. With religion emerging as a powerful global force, it is important to understand how religious groups can impact countries of birth or ancestry as well as countries of settlement. Religion and national identity are often closely related for many immigrants who were part of the dominant group in their home countries, and many view their religion as the basis of national culture and cohesion. Majority religious groups thus usually identify with the homeland state and mobilize in support of the state. Minority religious groups that mobilize politically in support of the interests of coreligionists in their homeland often do so in response to attacks or perceived discrimination against the group by the majority group or the state. As a result, majority and minority religious groups often have diametrically different interests and agendas when they mobilize around homeland concerns.

Religious background can be linked with perceptions of racial identity in complicated ways. In the case of Indian American organizations, both sides in the advocacy wars frame their grievances using religious and racial models that resonate with U.S. and Western audiences and forge different sets of alliances to achieve their objectives. For instance, Sikhs and Muslims often make the case that they are discriminated against in India like Black and Latino groups are in the United States. Kashmiri Muslim advocates draw parallels between the conflict in Kashmir and that in the Palestinian territories and demonstrate solidarity with Black Lives Matter activists. We have seen that Dalit advocates ally with African American anti-slavery advocates to argue that Dalits in modern India experience "harsh and inhumane treatment that rivals the worst aspects of historical [American] slavery" (Dalit Freedom Network 2014), or "caste apartheid" in Soundarajan's words. Hindu groups like the HAF, on the other hand, argue that U.S. and South African racial paradigms are not applicable to the Indian context and point to high-profile Indian politicians from Muslim, Christian, and Sikh backgrounds to make the argument that India practices religious pluralism (HAF 2011c). They also draw similarities between the situation of Hindus in India and Jews in Israel.

On March 25, 2021, *India West* carried an article indicating that the Chicago City Council had rejected a resolution condemning the CAA, the NRC, and the Indian government's actions in Kashmir on March 24 because of "intense pushback from members of the Indian American community." The article stated that the resolution had been first presented to the council in June 2020. However, the U.S.-India Friendship Council branch in Chicago had mobilized against it and claimed to have pushed it back six times. The U.S.-India Friendship Council alleged that the resolution had been sponsored by the Council on American-Islamic Relations (CAIR) and backed by Pakistan. They also claimed that seven other U.S. cities had passed similar resolutions "behind closed doors under the quiet of the COVID-19 crisis" (*India West* Staff Reporter 2021). In another incident, the India Day Parade in Edison, New Jersey, in 2022 featured a bulldozer along with a picture of Hindu hardliner Yogi Adityanath, chief minister of Uttar Pradesh state, and a sign describing him as "Baba Bulldozer" (father bulldozer). In India, bulldozers had become a symbol of Hindu nationalism since they had been used by Adityanath and others to raze Muslim homes and businesses. Indian American Muslims and their allies protested to lawmakers in New Jersey, and a representative of the Indian American Muslim Council (IAMC) told journalist Atul Dev that they were hurt to see hatred against Muslims in India "migrating" to the United States and appearing "in our backyard" (Dev 2022). These examples show how homeland-based conflicts and the opposing mobilizations of advocacy groups can lead to tensions in countries of settlement as both sides recruit allies to support their causes. The Sikh Khalistani movement and the attempt of the Indian government to suppress it and target its leaders demonstrate transnational repression where "foreign governments stalk, intimidate, or assault people in the United States," which the FBI considers a crime,[14] and which U.S. policymakers had become concerned enough about to introduce a congressional bill in 2023. Sikh diasporic support of the year-long farmers' movement led to the unprecedented situation of a powerful government backing away from its demands, exhibiting the influence of transnational networks.

Finally, this chapter demonstrates the importance of second-generation leadership in mobilization around human rights violations in their ancestral home country, something that has been overlooked in the literature, since the assumption is that it is primarily immigrants who are concerned about homeland matters. We have seen that the HAF, Sikh organizations like the

Sikh Coalition and SALDEF, and the post-2019 Kashmiri Muslim organizations have been led by the second generation, who were raised in the United States and were better equipped to "work the system" and felt empowered to do so. There are other reasons that second-generation activists come to demonstrate an interest in policy surrounding their ancestral homeland. In 2007, panelists at an *Indian American Leadership Initiative* (IALI) conference (primarily targeting second-generation Indian American Democrats) I attended had a passionate discussion about why the American-born generation should be concerned about issues impacting India. Two second-generation activists made the case that they had come to realize that often politicians did not differentiate between India and Indian Americans. "As the relationship with India goes, we go," said one of them, which was also echoed by Ro Khanna (now D-CA), who had not yet won elected office at that time. Sanjay Puri from USINPAC argued that the previous five years had seen a change "in the paradigm" where politicians had come to recognize that concerns about India were no longer a "foreign policy issue" but had become a "constituent issue" as members in their constituency showed interest in these matters and pressed politicians for support. In Chapter 6, we will see how Hindu nationalism and opposition to it, as well as generational differences, have played an important role in Indian American partisan politics.

Notes

1. Since 2011, the Indian government has refused permission for USCIRF commissioners to visit India on fact-finding missions. The U.S. Department of State under both Trump and Biden has refused to designate India as a country of particular concern or to make attacks against minorities in India an issue since it is eager to court India as a bulwark against a rising China. At a September 2023 India hearing, USCIRF Commissioner David Curry was quoted as saying, "I've become convinced that India has the most sophisticated, systematic persecution of religious minorities by any democratic government. And I don't say that lightly" (email from IAMC, one of the organizers of the event).
2. https://www.thehinducentre.com/resources/article30327343.ece
3. https://www.youtube.com/watch?v=UMU6TTYJ74k
4. https://www.foxnews.com/opinion/joseph-dsouza-religious-liberty-ministerial-pompeo-washington?fbclid=IwAR0Z8qa2ZtZqw7w0Q2PHeskjY8NYPonj8oASmWT26o7-MpjfrKnCYKoLPO8
5. It is important to note that while Ambedkarites strongly opposed Hindu nationalism (since it goes against Ambedkar's secular constitution and is supported by privileged-caste Hindus), some emphasized to me that they were not anti-Indian, unlike some other diasporic Indian minorities, but simply wanted their constitutional rights upheld.
6. The horrific Hathras case is just one example: https://time.com/5900402/hathras-rape-case-india-violence/ (accessed October 20, 2020).
7. Bodies of Revolution, https://www.youtube.com/watch?v=2gvaqfs8thA (accessed August 8, 2018).
8. Statement by Sunita Viswanath, June 29, 2020, webinar, https://www.youtube.com/watch?v=Fk3j_lnZqZM&feature=youtu.be.
9. http://www.thesuratinitiative.com/social-justice-project/1984-remembrance-project (accessed December 27, 2016).

10. Elsewhere he refers to the fact that since the Sikh representatives did not sign the Indian constitution, Punjab was never a part of India legally.
11. https://www.youtube.com/watch?v=tbXQr3lx_cI (accessed January 3, 2017).
12. https://www.youtube.com/watch?v=tbXQr3lx_cI (accessed January 3, 2017).
13. Kashmiri Muslim activists emphasized that Article 370 was linked with accession and that "without Article 370, there is no accession"—in other words, that the region does not belong to India if the article is revoked. Article 370 could only be revoked by the Constituent Assembly of the state, but since this assembly was dissolved, the article was deemed to be permanent. However, the provisions of this article were gradually whittled away over time (Rai 2019).
14. https://www.fbi.gov/investigate/counterintelligence/transnational-repression#:~:text=Transnational%20Repression%20When%20foreign%20governments%20stalk%2C%20intimidate%2C%20or,intimidate%20their%20own%20citizens%20living%20in%20the%20U.S

6
Race, Religion, Generation, and Activism around U.S. Partisan Politics

It wasn't the Indian-specific background that was driving the organization, rather [it was] the issues we face here, which I think are ... very similar to the issues that other South Asian Americans, not necessarily Indian Americans, face here in terms of acculturation, you know, language issues, hate crimes, civil rights, things like that.

—Activist, *South Asians for Obama*

Mosques should be monitored completely, vetting should be taking place.... I am totally for profiling.
—Shalabh Kumar, Republican Hindu Coalition founder, July 2016 interview with *The Hill* newspaper (Swan 2016)

President Trump has the potential of ushering in a true Ram Rajya[1] in US that could be followed by other countries.
—Kumar postelection February 2017 interview with *The Times of India* newspaper (David 2017)

I am literally surrounded by Asians and when I found that that we were not going to the polls as we should have ... it was heartbreaking to me ... because I thought, my goodness, if we had turned out maybe Trump wouldn't have been elected.
—Indian American activist in Georgia with *They See Blue* formed in 2018 to get out the Democratic vote among South Asian Americans

The U.S. press has started to pay attention to Indian American partisan behavior. In an October 2020 article in *Foreign Policy*, "Why Indian Americans Matter in US Politics," the authors outlined two main reasons for the outsized influence of Indian Americans: as a donor base because of the affluence of the group (Governor Newsom's veto of the caste bill being a good example of this outsized influence)[2] and the significant numbers of Indian Americans in key swing states, enough to flip close races (Ghori-Ahmad and Salman 2020). Another article, published around the same time in Politico, "How Hindu Nationalism Could Shape the Election," detailed how Hindu American activists and donors were using the Hindutva ideology as a "wedge issue" in elections to mobilize Indian Americans to support particular candidates (both Republican and Democratic), to form a few Republican political action committees (e.g., *Indian Voices for Trump* and *Americans for Hindus*), and to put pressure on Indian American candidates to support the policies of Prime Minister Modi (S. Paul 2020a).

Drawing on primary and secondary material, this chapter describes and explains the voting patterns and partisan behavior of Indian Americans and focuses on how Indian American groups such as the ones mentioned in the four quotes above mobilized to support Democratic or Republican candidates at the federal level over the past several elections. Based on interviews with 27 Democratic activists and 10 Republican activists, and secondary data sources, I unpack several puzzles regarding the partisan mobilization patterns of Indian Americans, viewed as "unusual" by some commentators. One puzzle is the strong support for the Democratic Party by most Indian Americans despite high income levels. A second question is why Hindu political organizations mobilized around Trump in the 2016 and 2020 elections even though he was a strong supporter of, and was strongly supported by, the Christian Right. A third issue has to do with generational differences in how and why individuals become activists and fundraisers for either the Democratic or Republican Party. I show how race and religion, sometimes working together and other times in opposing ways, interact to shape the partisan behavior of Indian American groups and to provide the answer to these three puzzles. We see how the fault lines discussed in earlier chapters—the mobilization of some under an Indian identity versus the mobilization of others under a South Asian umbrella and the political interests and activism of immigrants versus second-generation Indian Americans, of religious minorities in the United States versus Indian Christians, and of Hindu nationalist supporters versus opponents—all come together to shape Indian American mobilization around U.S. partisan politics in complex ways. The chapter also examines new groups that developed around the 2020 elections targeting Indian and South Asian American voters as the numbers of South Asian Americans across the country increased dramatically. These new groups worked to flip swing states to get a Democratic majority or to increase the numbers of Indian Americans in elected and administrative positions.

Factors Shaping Partisan Politics

There has been much discussion about the "hyperpolarized" and divisive nature of U.S. partisan identities (Iyengar 2016; Layman, Carsey, and Horowitz 2006). Scholars find that race, class, education, religious background, and gender are all significant factors shaping partisan divisions (Brown and Brown 2015; Layman, Carsey, and Horowitz 2006, 88, 94). Most of this research focuses on the "third-plus" generation of American voters. Yet, immigrants and their children made up 26 percent of the U.S. population in 2017 (Pew Research Center 2019), and it is important to apprehend how they view partisan politics, and the factors shaping partisan affiliation among first- and second-generation voters. Since Asian Americans are the fastest-growing group in the United States, expected to overtake Hispanics as the largest ethnic group by the middle of this century (Budiman and Ruiz 2021), it is crucial to understand how they imbibe American partisan politics and develop their own political identities. As the largest Asian American group, a study of Indian American partisan behavior and identities can provide insights into these issues.

There is a debate about whether political party selection is based on a rational assessment of policies, performance, and individual candidates (Fiorina 1981; Erikson, MacKuen, and Stimson 2002), conservative or liberal ideological preferences (Abramowitz and Saunders 2005), or social identities based on social class, race/ethnicity, and religion (Green, Palmquist, and Schickler 2002). While these are cross-cutting categories (e.g., the conservative/liberal division cuts across racial categories and across religions), African Americans have been the exception in that they tend to be Democrats regardless of ideology, religious background, and, to some extent, even class. Clearly, racial background trumps other factors when it comes to African Americans.

The role of race in shaping partisanship has traditionally been viewed through an "African-American-politics archetype" (T. Lee 2008, 465). However, scholars question whether this archetype is relevant for groups such as Latinos and Asians (Segura and Rodrigues 2006; T. Lee 2008). Because the "Black-White" paradigm dominates the study of race and politics, we do not clearly understand how other minorities identify with parties and whether it is for the same reasons as White and Black Americans (Hajnal and Lee 2006). While Latino voters (except for Cubans) are largely Democratic, we do not know what issues are of particular importance to Latino and Asian subgroups and what role ideology and other factors play in shaping their party preferences.

Research on Latino groups shows the growing development of a Hispanic or Latino social identity, which then can lead to a cohesive political outlook (Huddy, Mason, and Horwitz 2016). It also appears that sociopolitical factors such as orientation toward affirmative action and immigration policy (which differs by subgroup) are more important in shaping partisanship among Latino voters than economic factors (Alvarez and Bedolla 2003). Unlike Hispanics, Asian Americans are heterogeneous not just in terms of language and religion but also with regard to culture in addition to national history, in turn leading to ethnic cleavages in political outlook among Asian American voters (Wong et al. 2011, 155). The 2008, 2016, and 2020 National Asian American Surveys provide information about Asian American partisan politics. For the 2020 elections, there was also a survey of party and voting preferences among Indian Americans (Badrinathan, Kapur, and Vaishnav 2020).

The rise of the religious Right since the late 1970s gave expression to White racial anxieties and brought religion into the mainstream of contemporary American politics. The alliance between the Christian Right and the Republican Party started with the Reagan presidency and has continued to the present, led by a new set of evangelical leaders and organizations in each decade (Jones 2016). Since then, religion has been strongly related to partisan identities, with evangelical and fundamentalist Christians being overwhelmingly supportive of the Republican Party, while Jews, liberal Christians, and the nonreligious are associated with the Democratic Party.[3] Donald Trump emerged victorious in 2016 due largely to the mobilization of White Christian evangelicals who voted overwhelmingly for him (Wong 2018).

Both race and religion can explain the support for the Democratic Party by new ethnic groups. The Democratic Party has traditionally been viewed as the party of immigrants.[4] It has also been more supportive of issues of racial and economic inequality that are important to racial minorities. In addition to the Republican Party becoming aligned with the Christian Right, it has also been perceived as a party that is against minorities and immigrants since the 2012 elections. Consequently, many minorities and immigrants tend to vote Democratic, and even immigrant evangelical Christians are wary of voting for Republicans. However, when it comes to support for immigrants running for office, the picture may be somewhat different. Since many contemporary immigrant destinations are Democratic strongholds, there is little incentive for the party to reach out to newcomers and to allow immigrants to run for office (Aptekar 2008; Rogers 2006). On the other hand, Republicans realize the need to incorporate more racial minorities into the party. These issues also came up in my interviews.

Asian American Partisan Politics

In their comprehensive study, Wong et al. (2011) point to several paradoxes in Asian American political behavior. First, Asian Americans have relatively low voting rates relative to their educational levels (p. 27). Despite relatively high economic income levels, they lean Democratic (except for Vietnamese) and have been becoming more so over time (pp. 126–127).[5] This may indicate that like Hispanics, Asian Americans are more swayed by noneconomic factors. However, a large proportion still tend to identify as independent or nonpartisan (p. 29), showing that they do not have entrenched or stable partisan identities. Consequently, their vote choice may not necessarily be an indicator of partisan identity. Parties have also not shown interest in trying to reach out to Asian Americans (Wong et al. 2011, 29–30).

Recent research has shown that although a majority of Asian Americans support the Democratic Party, "different intersections of religion and race influence political preferences in different ways" (Jeung, Jiminez, and Mar 2020). While Asian American Christians were likely to be socially conservative in terms of issues like abortion and gay marriage, they were often progressive when it came to racial issues, supporting the role of the government in addressing racial inequalities (Wong, Rim, and Perez 2008). Asian Americans who identified as Protestant or Christian had a greater likelihood of identifying as Republican compared with those who did not claim a religious affiliation (Wong, Rim, and Perez 2008, 291–292). With respect to race, how Asian Americans interpreted pro- or anti-minority messages by candidates or political parties depended on the way they perceived their racial identity and whether they identified with perceived "White opportunities" or "non-White opportunities" (Samson 2015; Jeung, Jiminez, and Mar 2020, 216). Specifically, Asian Americans who perceived that they were marginalized and discriminated as a racial group were much more likely to identify as Democrats (Kuo, Malhotra, and Mo 2017). Again, generational status also shaped partisan identities, with second-generation Asian Americans who identified with a religion but were not evangelical Christians more likely to support the Democratic Party, perhaps because they were more aware of experiences of religio-racial marginalization. However, U.S.-born Asian American evangelicals were more likely to support Republicans, particularly Trump in 2016 (Jeung, Jiminez, and Mar 2020, 219; Park and Tom 2020).

Indian American Partisan Politics

While this chapter focuses on Indian American organizations mobilizing around U.S. partisan politics, I start with a discussion about Indian American partisanship and voting, how Indian Americans develop a partisan identity, and generational differences, to provide context and to show how the organizations and cleavages discussed in previous chapters map on to partisan politics.

As in the case of Asian Americans overall, survey studies (see Tables 6.1 and 6.2) have found that there is a disjuncture between partisan identities and actual voting patterns among Indian Americans. Indian American voters have overwhelmingly voted for Democrats in recent elections (2012, 2016,

Table 6.1 Indian American Partisan Affiliations
PARTISAN IDENTITY (%).

	Democrat	Republican	Independent
2008	39	7	21
2016	53	7	37
2020	54	7	24

2008 and 2016 figures from National Asian American Survey Reports.
2020 from AAPI Data.

Table 6.2 Indian American voting patterns.

	Democrat	Republican
2012	84% (Obama)	16% (Romney)
2016	77% (Clinton)	16% (Trump)*
2020 (intended vote)	66% (Biden), AAPI 72% (Biden), Carnegie	28% (Trump), AAPI 22% (Trump), Carnegie

* In an October 5, 2016, pre-election National Asian American Survey, only 7% said they would vote for Trump.

2012, 2016 figures from the National Asian American Survey 2012 pre-election and 2017 postelection reports. 2020 figures from pre-election AAPI and Carnegie Endowment Studies, September 2020.

2020) though a large proportion identified as independent or nonpartisan. The 2020 Indian American Attitudes Survey (Badrinathan, Kapur, and Vaishnav 2020) found that Muslim Indian Americans were most likely to support Biden (82 percent), followed by Hindus (67 percent) and Christians (49 percent).[6] My research showed that the perception that the Republican Party is dominated by conservative White Christians who negatively stereotype racial minorities, as well as Hindus, Muslims, and Sikhs, seemed to be an important factor (also see Kapur 2012; Haniffa 2012c).

Indian American Republicans tried to counter this perception by arguing that their party is more welcoming than Democrats to racial minorities (citing the example of former Indian American governors Bobby Jindal and Nikki Haley) and to "individuals of faith" belonging to any religious tradition. They also contend that the conservative social and economic platform of the Republican Party fits better with the moral values and fiscal beliefs of most Indian Americans (Chougule and Subramanian 2013; Dhume 2012). The fact that the first two Indian Americans with the highest political positions—Governors Jindal and Haley—were converts to Christianity and played down their Indian ancestry was discussed extensively (e.g., at Indian American political conferences and events I attended in 2007 and 2010), as was the issue of whether non-Christians could be elected to high political office in the United States. In a 2010 *Washington Post* article, Aseem Shukla, cofounder of the Hindu American Foundation, expressed frustration about a possible "religious litmus test" in U.S. politics. He argued that while Obama's election as president and Nikki Haley's and Bobby Jindal's elections as governors of two U.S. southern states (Haley in South Carolina and Jindal in Louisiana) might be an indication of a "postracial" era in politics, Jindal's and

Haley's constant references to their Christian faith (Jindal converted from Hinduism to Catholicism as a teenager and Haley was brought up as a Sikh but joined the Methodist church of her husband upon marriage) seemed to indicate that "Christian faith is a foregone criterion for electability" for high political office (Shukla 2010b). Some Hindu Indian American state-level candidates who ran for office from largely White, rural areas also claimed that religion mattered more to their constituents than race (discussions at the 2010 Indian American Leadership Initiative Conference). However, the perception that only Christians were electable to federal office may have begun to change when Tulsi Gabbard, a practicing Hindu and Samoan American representing Hawaii, was elected to Congress in 2012, and in 2016 with the election of four more Indian Americans to Congress in addition to Ami Bera, at least two of whom, Ro Khanna and Raja Krishnamoorthi, publicly identified as Hindu. In 2020, another Indian American who identified as Hindu, Shri Thanedar, was elected to Congress.

My research indicated that while most Indian Americans were not strongly moved by issues of abortion (except Catholics and evangelical Christians) or LGBTQ rights (here too except for many Christians and Muslims), they emphasized "family values," and many wealthy Indian Americans and small business owners tended to be fiscally conservative and to want less government regulation in economic matters, making them lean Republican on these issues. However, because of their minority racial and immigrant status, Indian Americans were concerned by the anti-minority and anti-immigration messages of the Republican Party. In short, the contradiction between the overwhelmingly Democratic voting patterns of Indian Americans and the large numbers who do not identify with either party can be explained by the fact that while neither party fully matched the needs and interests of many Indian Americans, many found themselves particularly repulsed by the racial and religious exclusivity of the Republican Party. This was particularly the case after the election of Trump and the rise of xenophobia in the United States. At the same time, India-based factors caused some shift toward the Republican Party since 2016. The election of Modi as prime minister at the head of the BJP party in 2014, the support shown to Modi and Hindu nationalism by Trump and leading Republicans such as Steve Bannon, and the fact that Republicans have ignored attacks against minorities in India (including the events of 2019 discussed in the previous chapter) while Democrats have been more critical of these developments have led to this shift (see Tables 6.3 and 6.4).

Table 6.3 Factors shaping Indian American partisanship, 2004–2012.

Main Factors	Positive or Negative Orientation	Party
Race (non-white racial identity)	Positive	**Democratic** (perceived as more racially and immigrant inclusive)
Religion (non-Christian identity)	Positive	**Democratic** (perceived as more religiously inclusive or secular)
Race (non-white racial identity)	Negative	**Republican** (perceived as White-focused)
Religion (non-Christian identity)	Negative	**Republican** (perceived as Christian-focused)

Table 6.4 Factors shaping Indian American partisanship, 2016 and after.

Main Factors	Positive or Negative Orientation	Party
Race (non-white racial identity)	Positive	**Democratic** (perceived as more racially and immigrant inclusive)
Religion (pro-Modi/ Hindu nationalist)	Negative	**Democratic** (perceived as less supportive of Hindutva and Modi)
Race (non-white racial identity)	Negative	**Republican** (perceived as White-focused)
Religion (pro-Modi/ Hindu nationalist)	Positive	**Republican** (perceived as more supportive of Hindutva and Modi)

The Evolution of Indian American Partisan Politics

Immigrant Partisan Activists

National-level Indian American (and South Asian American from 2004) Democratic and Republican organizations and partisan fundraising bodies were formed at least from the early 2000s. Well before that, there were immigrant men—generally wealthy professionals or entrepreneurs with successful businesses—who were active in U.S. partisan politics. Through my discussions with several such men, I learned that some had been politically engaged in India in student politics or had hailed from politically involved families. Others began their engagement with politics in the United States. In either case, most were drawn into partisan politics by first getting involved in regional Indian American organizations. Sometimes their reaching out to

U.S. politicians was due to an issue of personal importance (e.g., wanting a green card) or of community importance. The latter included India-centric matters but also hate crimes and discrimination in jobs and in admission to universities. Others were invited to fundraise for a local politician because they had come to be known as leaders of a wealthy ethnic community. But in all cases, immigrant leaders got involved through state-level politicians and their partisan identities were formed by which political group or politician got them into politics. Two second-generation Indian American political activists, both Republicans, corroborated my observation. According to "Nora," "What happened was, they got recruited by either a member of Congress, or a Governor. And whoever recruited them, that's the party they belong to." "Ravi" said much the same thing: "I think it just depends on . . . how they were received by people in the party. If someone was really welcomed by a Democrat 30 years ago, they're typically a life-long Democrat for that reason." Since many Indian Americans lived in blue (Democratic) states, Democrats were more likely to reach out to them.

At the same time, five Republican activists (both first- and second-generation Indian Americans) told me that the Republican Party was more welcoming to Indian Americans than the Democratic Party. In a 2013 interview, "Manan," an older immigrant male Republican activist from the U.S. South, told me that he had started out wanting to be a Democrat, "since that is the natural orientation of Indians coming from socialistic India at that time" (in the 1970s). But the Democrats rebuffed him: "They would not invite you or they would not accept you." He explained that it was because

> they don't need us. Democrats have Blacks, Black Democrats to offset their issues. . . . Republicans, they have no African Americans or Black Americans to supplement them. So, they will easily accept you as a minority. A White Democrat or American will not accept you. . . . They will not offer you any place or participation in any party or any post or anything like that. . . . Republican Party, will very easily accept [Indian Americans] in the South. If you go to Mississippi or to Texas or Florida, Louisiana, there are more Indian American Republicans.

I heard this explanation—that Republicans needed Indian Americans to add "a touch of color" to their party—many times during my research.

"Hegde," another immigrant Indian American, was viewed as a Republican activist, but he told me that his big concern was, "who does good things for

India? I am for that party, and I am for that President." The emphasis on U.S.-India policy above everything else was a common sentiment among many immigrant activists and could explain the large proportion of independents among Indian Americans. Since the majority of Indian Americans are foreign born, we can see why so many declared themselves independents and did not have a clear U.S. partisan identity. Hegde added that his generation was "very patriotic ... I feel every day for India. ... I may be a U.S. citizen ... but on my part, I am trying to repay [my debt to India]." He talked about how he tried to promote the interests of India at every opportunity. He also told me that there were many "closeted Republicans" among Indian Americans due to the perception that the Republican Party was anti-minority and elitist, something I also heard multiple times. But Hegde felt that this was precisely why Indian Americans needed to join the Republican Party. "You have to get involved, if something is wrong, you have to change [it], that is leadership."

The story of how Swadesh Chatterjee, a wealthy Indian American Republican activist, "converted" Senator Jesse Helms (R-NC) from being virulently anti-India to an India supporter is a good example of how immigrant partisan activists were able to influence members of Congress. As chair of the Senate Foreign Relations Committee, Senator Jesse Helms was a "powerhouse" in Washington, DC but was considered an arch conservative and a racist. Chatterjee, then president of the North Carolina chapter of the Indian American Forum for Political Education (IAFPE), received a call from Jesse Helms's campaign manager in 1995, requesting the support of the North Carolina Indian American community for Helms's re-election campaign. Chatterjee took the opportunity to meet with Senator Helms and educate him about India. He also asked Helms to meet with the Indian ambassador, to do a long interview with *India Abroad*, and to attend several IAFPE events (including as keynote speaker of the 1997 IAFPE annual convention) in return for getting support from the Indian American community. Over time, Chatterjee developed a warm relationship with Helms, which helped him to get the senator's support for India at key points, such as in 1998, when India conducted nuclear bomb tests, infuriating U.S. leaders, including Helms. Chatterjee was able to persuade Helms to initiate a dialogue with Jaswant Singh, India's foreign minister. The dialogue that Jaswant Singh initiated with key American leaders, including Helms, about India's nuclear interests eventually led to the lifting of sanctions against India three years later (Chatterjee 2015, 89–103) and laid the foundation for the U.S.-India civil nuclear deal that Chatterjee played a key role in (see Chapter 3).

The situation in the U.S. Northeast was different for Indian American Republicans. Another immigrant based in the Northeast said that while he was attracted to the Republican Party because of its values, he found it "difficult to break in." He was only able to take a leadership role in local politics after the proportion of Indian immigrants grew significantly in the region. Other immigrant activists (interviewed before the Trump presidency) indicated that they got involved with the Republican Party because they supported its values, specifically mentioning limited government, low taxes, free markets, free trade, and strong national defense, along with traditional family values. "Onkar," an Indian American of the immigrant generation, articulated why he thought the Republican Party is the "natural home" for Indian Americans: "We're a community that tends to work hard, believe in education, we don't come to this nation to seek entitlements, we come to contribute to society. And I think that that's much more in line with what the Republican Party stands for, which is individual liberty, economic freedom, don't overtax people."

As we can see from this quote, Onkar makes an implicit contrast with groups perceived to be those that might not value education in the same way, may not work as hard, and may come to the United States seeking "entitlements." Another immigrant Indian American Republican activist interviewed in 2021 who was a Trump supporter said that one of the things that attracted him to the Republican Party was their policy on immigration: "I just hated people pushing through the border and trying to come here, and then not having the proper credentials, not having the proper etiquette, not having proper skills, and not even integrating."

At the same time, most immigrant Indian American Republican activists were strongly against the GOP turn toward White Christian nationalism. In 2012, after Mitt Romney's defeat, several Indian American Republicans who were credited with having raised $15 to 20 million for Romney's campaign (Hoft 2012) called for the party to become more inclusive. Dr. Zachariah P. Zachariah of Fort Lauderdale, characterized by *India Abroad* journalist Aziz Haniffa as "arguably the most influential Indian-American Republican," was quoted as saying, "Romney lost because he alienated the women and Hispanics. When you alienate these two groups, there is no way you can win." Several other Indian American Republicans also echoed similar sentiments (Haniffa 2012d). Bobby Jindal, then the Republican governor of Louisiana, was one of the two prominent Indian Americans in elected positions who criticized Romney for claiming that President Obama had won the election because of his "gifts" to women, minorities, and students and emphasized that it was imperative that "a concerted effort be made [for the Republican Party] to be more inclusive of minorities, women and young voters" (Haniffa 2012e). In media interviews conducted in 2012 and later in 2016, many older-generation Indian American Republican activists defined themselves as "Reagan Republicans." This meant that they were middle-of-the-road Republicans and did not support far-right Christian nationalism.

Older immigrant Democratic activists, on the other hand, lauded the diversity and multiculturalism of the Democratic Party and the promotion of immigration, economic fairness, and family reunification. Some told me that their orientation to the Democratic Party originated in India where there was admiration for Presidents John F. Kennedy and Lyndon B. Johnson (possibly due to their support for immigration law reform that made it possible for Indians to enter the United States as immigrants). An early activist in the Democratic Party, "Chauhan" told me that he got involved with the Democratic Party because he was interested in participating and having his voice heard. He said he "agreed with the policies of the Democratic Party," specifically "their openness. They were much more open to different ethnicities than any other party that I had known. They were much more open, much more friendly, and so it was natural attraction there." An Indian American Muslim who was a Democratic activist provided a different reason for involvement with the Democratic Party. He shared that he and his wife "got very actively involved in the Kerry campaign because we were very strongly against the politics of the Bush administration—against the Iraq war, attack on civil liberties, and the Patriot Act. We raised a lot of money for Kerry along with the Indian American Leadership Council of the DNC [Democratic National Committee, the governing body of the Democratic Party]." "Hassan" was another Indian American Muslim immigrant activist who was involved with a major Indian American Muslim organization. He gave yet another explanation for why Indian American Muslims "have been mostly involved with the Democratic Party." He acknowledged that there were some Indian American Muslims including those who were wealthy businessmen or who had startup companies who supported the Republican Party for financial reasons, but he said that the majority of Indian American Muslims supported the Democratic Party since "they have more of our issues" (supported more of their concerns). Addressing my question regarding whether he believed that the Republican Party was more open to people of faith than the Democratic Party, he admitted that the Democratic Party was more secular, and the Republican Party was more "conservative in religious terms." However, while most Indian American Muslims "are not sympathetic to LGBTQ issues," making them closer to religious Republicans in that regard,

> that alone is not enough, bread and butter issues are very important, you know, for survival in America, our children doing well, jobs, and things like that, and not having discrimination in jobs or glass ceiling, those things are more important, because you can observe your religion and all, you can protect the children from LGBTQ issues, but if you're not going ahead, if your children are not going ahead in their careers, then that's a very bad break on us, it's very frustrating.... We can observe our religion at home. But the more important thing is, why we came to this country, you know? We came to this country to succeed, to work hard, to improve our lives, and if we cannot do that, if there is a break on that overall, the glass ceiling in our jobs, then that's very discouraging. So, most of our people, ... the American Muslims I know, most of them really are pro-Democratic Party.

Even though Hassan mentioned "bread and butter issues," he did not mean the economic platform of Democrats per se, but instead their support of immigrants and Muslims through anti-discrimination workplace policies that allowed Indian American Muslims and their children the opportunity to succeed in their jobs.

We see from this discussion that older-generation immigrant activists offered a variety of reasons for their involvement in partisan politics. However, the second generation felt that "uncles" got involved in partisan politics only for "photo ops." "Suresh," an immigrant activist, also mentioned the same thing in a 2007 interview:

> For the first twenty years (1984–2004), the Indian Americans who wrote checks did so principally to get their picture in the paper. There was no agenda. Not—I'll do this if you do this. Or my issues are such and such. It was mainly, I have the money and I can use it to get a candidate to come to my house. This was very naïve and simplistic but also useful. Candidates used to say, "I have Indian American friends and contributors."

Suresh went on to say that immigrant activists had become more sophisticated from 2004 on, largely due to the involvement of the second generation.

Second-Generation Activists and Organizations

The first second-generation political organization, the *Indian American Leadership Initiative* (IALI), was formed in 2000 after the "election debacle" when George Bush lost the popular vote to Al Gore but was declared the winner by the U.S. Supreme Court. Initially, it was founded by Varun Nikore to be bipartisan and to form a national network of donors to support Indian American candidates for state- and local-level races as well as political appointments. However, in 2005, the organization switched to only supporting Democratic candidates. I learned in a 2007 interview that this switch came about because Bobby Jindal's candidacy (probably his successful run for Congress in 2004) became "a litmus test" of Indian American values and many people were uncomfortable with his positions, particularly his support for the religious Right. An IALI activist also stressed that unlike immigrant-generation organizations, the second generation believed in a "network model [of leadership] that did not revolve around one male President" and that many women were involved. In 2008, IALI held a well-attended reception during the Democratic National Convention, at the height of enthusiasm and mobilization around Obama, and formed a political action committee (PAC) in 2009 so they could support Indian American candidates running in federal races. I attended IALI conferences in 2007 and 2010 in Washington, DC, along with a large, enthusiastic, mostly young-adult audience.

In March 2003, Reshma Saujani, an Indian American lawyer by training, launched *South Asians for Kerry* (SAKI) around Senator John Kerry's presidential candidacy, with chapters around the country. SAKI was the first South Asian American political organization. Saujani wrote that SAKI "was born of a provocative idea that there was an alternative avenue of political organization that moved beyond traditional, narrowly constructed paradigms. SAKI's team was a response to a culture of fear where exclusion and marginalization inspired unity and togetherness" (Saujani 2004). By "alternative avenue of political organization," she was referring to a pan-ethnic South Asian American political organization, and by the "culture of fear," she meant the intimidation experienced by South Asian Americans in the post-9/11 period. In a 2009 interview for this project, Saujani (who hails from a Hindu background) indicated that she was motivated to create a South Asian American organization when she was going to work (in New York City) and saw a large number of men "looking like my father" waiting in lines for the special registration required by the Patriot Act of those from predominantly Muslim countries (Pakistanis and Bangladeshis in New York City were greatly impacted by this act). She talked about having to face much resistance from "Indian uncles" who did not want to work with Pakistanis because many of the older generation remembered the trauma of partition. However, the American-born generation was much more open, and they made up most of SAKI's volunteers. Donors came from both generations. Through focus groups, Saujani brought different groups together to educate them and to learn about the issues they were concerned about. She spoke with pride about how she was able to overcome resistance and bring the South Asian American community together, organizing hundreds of thousands of people, and raising a lot of money. Saujani was interviewed by several news channels and SAKI gained national visibility. SAKI paved the path for the formation of South Asian American organizations in subsequent elections such as *South Asians for Obama* and *South Asians for McCain* in 2008.

South Asians for Obama (SAFO) was launched in 2008 by another second-generation Indian American (also of Hindu background), Hrishi Karthikeyan, to rally second-generation South Asian Americans. In an article in *The Indian American*, Hrishi Karthikeyan mentions the importance of the "macaca incident" in setting the stage for the development of SAFO (Karthikeyan 2009). As mentioned in Chapter 3, this refers to an incident when Senator George Allen (R-VA) repeatedly called an Indian American man "macaca" (Portuguese for monkey) during a 2006 campaign rally. Second-generation South Asian Americans took to social media, publicizing the incident widely by posting the video on YouTube and inundating the blogosphere with discussions. Shekar Narasimhan, the young man's father, was a prominent Democratic fundraiser in Virginia and helped to mobilize funds for Allen's Democratic challenger, James Webb. Narasimhan was also able to convince Howard Dean, Democratic National Committee (DNC) chairman, that Webb had a chance of winning and secure DNC funding for Webb (who until then had been trailing in terms of both polls and fundraising). The DNC now credits Narasimhan with having helped to defeat George Allen,[7] delivering the Senate to Democrats and leading to a Democratic majority in both houses of Congress. In March 2007, Howard Dean appointed Shekar Narasimhan as national cochair of the Democratic National Committee's Indo-American Council. The "macaca incident" was important in showing how coordinated action by first- and second-generation South Asian Americans could yield big results.

In a 2009 interview, Hrishi Karthikeyan indicated that SAFO was able to get a diverse group of second-generation South Asian Americans (in terms of national origin, religion, gender, and a variety of professional backgrounds) to participate in the campaign. Most SAFO activists were in their 20s or 30s. Referring to the early days of the campaign, before Obama was declared the Democratic nominee for president, Theresa Thanjan, another activist for SAFO, similarly mentioned: "The support for Obama was very high, I'd say, with people who were thirty-five and younger. Fever pitch at college age, and then after that, probably after college to thirty-five was pretty high as well. But after thirty-five it was mostly Hillary Clinton territory." She added that she was amazed to see how many women of color were involved in Obama's campaign. "There was something about his message ... and his theme of change that really appealed to people who hadn't been involved in the process before." Thanjan said that SAFO "highlighted his background a lot. The fact that he was the son of an immigrant, the fact that he knows what it's like to have a grandmother in a Third World country." She also mentioned that there were so many South Asians involved at the higher levels in the Obama campaign, which meant that "we had pretty good representation up there, so we could send a message to them if we needed to." As the quote starting this chapter makes clear, SAFO focused on issues in the United States and not on foreign policy.

Some second-generation Indian Americans also became active in Republican groups, forming Indians for McCain in 2008, for instance. While the Indian American Republican Council was formed in 2002 by the immigrant generation, Dino Teppara, a second-generation Indian American Republican, became chair in 2009 and worked to expand it to become part of a larger center-right coalition and to include women and the second generation. Second-generation Indian American participation declined by 2012, the year that Obama ran for re-election. IALI was described as having "all but dissolved" (Haniffa 2012a, A10). Even SAFO acknowledged "a dip in enthusiasm" among members in 2012 due to the activists attending to other priorities, including raising small children (Haniffa 2012b). The *National Dance for Obama* group stepped into this breach. Led by Indian American choreographer and social justice advocate Anjali Khurana, a small group of second-generation South Asian Americans coordinated simultaneous flash mob dances (including people from all racial and ethnic backgrounds and age groups) in 19 cities around the country on October 13, 2012, and then in a smaller number of cities on November 3 and 4, 2012, in support of President

Obama's re-election campaign. The goal was to involve the millennial generation in politics and the election. While each city was encouraged to choreograph its own dance, all the flash mobs danced to the same song (composed pro bono by African American music producer Marcus Bellringer), drawing on words from Obama speeches that Anjali and her team had culled out. In a 2013 interview Anjali Khurana told me that she had "always been inspired by Obama's story." Her aim was to inspire people at a time when, according to her close friend and collaborator, "there was so much negativity, and so much vitriol in the press" and to do "something that was positive, ... to say, I support this side in a positive way." Anjali Khurana also indicated that her goal was to engage the dancers in outreach activities such as canvassing and phone banking after the dances. This took place in some localities.

Distinctive Characteristics of Second-Generation Activists

Second-generation Indian American activists contrasted with the first generation. The differences were similar to those discussed in Chapter 3 between South Asian American and Indian American activists. First, unlike the immigrant generation, which was composed almost entirely of male activists, both men and women were equally involved among second-generation activists. Second, and most importantly, unlike the immigrant generation, which turned to political activism to further business interests or consolidate community status after developing a successful career, many in the second generation developed an interest in politics early in their lives out of a desire to be part of the American political system and to be involved in policy formulation. Second-generation members often chose to go into law or public policy specifically to facilitate a career in politics or policymaking. Several Democratic activists mentioned the important role played by the *South Asian Bar Association* (SABA, with chapters in many U.S. cities) in motivating them to get involved in progressive political activism. "Navin," a second-generation Indian American Democratic activist, argued that his generation was not just publicity seeking but also interested in "making a professional career out of public policy, working in the government or running for public office which we don't see in the first generation." But he acknowledged that his generation had the advantage that the first-generation activists had "opened up doors" that he and others could use for their political development. Third, unlike the immigrant generation, which is focused primarily on foreign policy or India-centric issues, domestic issues are of greater interest to second-generation Indian Americans. As Navin explained, "I don't wake up every day fired up with a passion to do something for India, but for professional development opportunities, with an underlying respect and passion for India." He called it the 80-20 rule—the second generation were 80 percent interested in professional development and 20 percent in India. A second-generation conservative activist summarized the differences in the generational orientation toward American politics:

> I think the first generation who immigrated here, my parents' generation, focused on primarily U.S.-India relations, and they were friendly with the party of whoever was friendliest to India. The second-generation people like me, who were born and raised here, are much more focused on domestic issues. While we want positive U.S.-India relations, that's not the focus. The focus tends to be on more bread-and-butter issues like healthcare, the economy, education, things like that.

Similarly, a second-generation Democratic activist, "Diya," said, laughing: "There is a younger generation who gives money because they care about socio-economic issues and India plays no part in it. They give because they care about health care issues, trade issues. For instance, I am 38 and I give because I am interested in vesting in this country and [in] particular candidates." Finally, because of their early interest in politics, most members of the second generation also had a clearer and stronger sense of partisan ideology when compared to the immigrant generation, which they articulated eloquently.

Second-Generation Indian American Democratic Activists

Second-generation Indian Americans who were Democrats generally talked about how an interest in social justice and equality turned them into Democratic activists. Many credited their parents for this interest. "Anika" is a good example. In a 2013 interview, she declared:

> It really just comes down to equality and fairness to me, being a Democrat. And the fact that, you know, my mom's a very, very strong Gandhian... in the

sense that there's this notion of, we have enough in this world for everyone's need, but not enough for anyone's greed [laughing]. So that's this idea of sharing the wealth and I think that that's where my sense of being a part of the Democratic Party comes into play. Because it comes from this strong notion of, we need to make everyone better. You know, like, when the bottom is able to get better, then even the ones at the top will benefit.

In a 2009 interview, another second-generation Indian American woman involved in Democratic politics similarly commented:

Particular issues of concern have been issues of equality, racial discrimination, equal access to benefits, just really civil rights issues. These are all issues that I was very involved in.... I was also involved in preventing discrimination after 9/11 against our communities.... I think definitely, my experience being a minority and being the daughter of immigrants played a significant role. My parents are very vocal about their political leanings. They're Democrats and very proud of that, and they are very liberal in their views. So that also played a significant role in me becoming who I am today.

In a 2010 interview, "Vinay," an Indian American man, provided a slightly different but related motivation to get involved in work supporting the Democratic Party. He said that he had grown up during the Reagan era and that the priorities emphasized by Ronald Reagan "were kind of opposite to my values and priorities." He clarified:

Well, the Reagan era was marked by decreasing the role of government in social services and increasing the amount of money being spent on foreign, mostly fascist kind of regimes. And increasing domestic military spending, Star Wars,[8] the Cold War, we were fighting the Cold War at the time.... And so, he's bankrupting the future of the country, putting future generations in debt, cutting social services to the neediest in society, and then being bankrupted by increasing defense spending and increasing aid to regimes that were lawless.

This critique of Reagan's policies was quite different from the emphasis of several immigrant Indian American conservatives who touted their "Reagan Republican" credentials and who were nostalgic about the Reagan era. When I asked Vinay if his Indian American background played a role in his interest in Democratic politics, he indicated that it was his Christian faith, based on his upbringing in an Indian American Christian community, that was critical, particularly in the early period. "My Christian faith . . . probably has more to do with it. . . my personal life experience between my interest in politics, and the Christian faith." He specifically mentioned that his interest in social justice stemmed from his Christian values and that the Democratic Party had traditionally been rooted in Christian teachings. According to Vinay: "This has flipped only recently [where the Republican Party is now seen as embodying the Christian faith]. The role of government helping people who are least among us sounds a lot like Christian teaching. And it sounds a lot like the Democratic Party platform . . . and that's not an accident in history." Another second-generation woman said bluntly, "I'm not an issue person. So, like if you look issue-by-issue it doesn't resonate with me. I'm a partisan Democrat, so having a Democrat in the White House means the world to me."

A second-generation Democratic activist involved in SAALT mentioned in a 2007 interview that it was important for the second generation to "build coalitions with other communities of color, other disadvantaged communities" because of shared interests and concerns. Referring to the immigrant generation, he added, "I think that by saying, oh, we have money so this is why we should have a political voice, it's obviously not a very welcoming way to make political alliances with other communities." He meant that using success and wealth to distinguish Indian Americans from other groups (the model minority discourse) made it difficult for Indian Americans to forge alliances with other groups of color, even though they shared several common concerns.

Second-Generation Indian American Republicans

I talked to six second-generation Indian American Republican activists (three Hindu, two Christian, and one Muslim) about the factors that drew them to the Republican Party. The two Christians (both women) said that their parents were also Republican, but the rest said they grew up in apolitical or in Democratic households. Those who grew up in Democratic families indicated that it was the perception that the Democratic Party was more welcoming toward immigrants, or because they were living in Democratic strongholds, or in one case, because they had arrived during the Watergate scandal, that influenced their parents' Democratic partisan outlooks. Some felt that the perception that Democrats were more supportive of immigrants was somewhat accurate and that Republicans had made "irresponsible comments" about immigrants. They emphasized that Republicans needed to work harder to show support for legal immigrants and not to paint "legal" and "illegal" immigrants with the same broad brush (Republicans differentiated between these two categories, while Democrats were less likely to do so, and were also likely to use the term "undocumented" instead of "illegal"). As "Zubair" argued: "The challenge is [consequently] two-fold. One, to warn those who are making irresponsible comments, whether they're talk radio figures or other political figures, not to make those comments, and to be more careful in what they're saying. And then the challenge also is to remind Indian American friends, don't judge the entire party by the statements of a few."

Regarding their reasons for supporting the Republican Party, most mentioned fiscal policy (lower taxes, particularly on businesses and those in the higher income brackets), the free market orientation, and limited government, which would "unleash the entrepreneurial spirit." The role of faith came up in discussions with the two Christian as well as the Muslim Republicans. The Christian women talked about how their faith made them pro-life, and the Muslim man commented on how he felt that the Republican Party was more supportive of religion: "I find that ... [there is a] stronger respect for faith within the conservative movement, and that for many Indian Americans who are particularly spiritual, whether they be Hindu, Muslim, Sikh, that they would feel more comfortable ... [with the] respect that many conservatives have for the role of faith in society."

"Ruth," one of the two Christian women I talked to, focused on how she believed that the Republican Party allowed people to be productive and contributing citizens without the props that made people "satisfied with a handout." After talking about the parable of the Talents in the Bible, which she indicated was her "life motto," she elaborated:

> This hunger to take whatever little I have and make the most of it, I think is embodied in the Republican Party. And also, the idea of being stewards of the chances that we are given.... I want people to strive to be the best that they can be. You know they were created by God to do so much.

Likewise, "Kamal" argued that he felt "that the programs that Democrats support, including high taxes and very high government regulation, really stifle the ability of even the poorest of people to achieve their dreams."

Several of those I talked to also made the argument that the Republican Party should be the natural home for Indian Americans. Ravi put it this way:

> So, if a lot of Indian Americans have come to the United States seeking educational and economic opportunities as my parents did, if they want to start small businesses, if they want to be in the fields of medicine and science, those all lead me to believe that there should be less taxation, less government regulation, less command and control from the state as to what people can do. Because that's the very reason why, particularly the Indian American community has chosen life in the United States, is to seek out those freedoms that the United States affords.

Kamal also mentioned that the educational policy of the Republican Party was more in tune with what South Asian Americans want:

> South Asians put a very strong emphasis on education. Parents have a very active role when it comes to education, and, therefore, I think it's generally better to give those parents who are active in the decision making of their children more of an ability to have input and have more of a say. So, for example school choice. Republicans tend to want to give parents more of a choice as to private schools, charter schools, public schools, to have a choice which public school to attend in a given school district, to even go outside the school district, and Republicans tend to support this type of leeway, whereas, Democrats are very beholden to the teachers unions who want students to go to very specific schools in the neighborhood, whether those schools are good or bad.

Kamal, who said he had "come of age" during the Reagan period, mentioned that he was "molded by that feeling of pride in being an American, and feeling that America has a special role globally, and that the communist model was one doomed to failure," leading him to become a Republican activist (note the contrast between Kamal and Vinay, the Democratic activist mentioned earlier discussing Reaganism). "Nora," another early second-generation Republican activist, talked about how her father had made her watch a weekly television show by Milton Friedman in the 1980s that was very influential in shaping her outlook. Then she heard a speech by Reagan - and was struck and excited by the great similarities between what he said and what she had heard from Milton Friedman. This motivated her to volunteer to work for the Reagan campaign in 1984.

Second-generation Indian American Democrats and Republicans also talked about their racial identity in markedly different ways. While the former seemed to accept and embrace their racial minority status, all the second-generation Republicans, in one way or another, challenged the idea that racial background was important in the United States. Kamal argued that this emphasis on race was a Democratic obsession, not shared by Republicans: "Because they [his friends who were Democrats] only saw their role in a very race-specific position, and they could not kind of comprehend that I didn't see the world in that way. And that, more importantly, that I wasn't regarded by others in that way." And Ravi said that Republicans "don't look at it [issues] through a racial lens, which is typically what liberals do. This person is whatever, and this person is... for us, it's more of an ideological thing. You know, if you kind of agree with us on issues, that's the only thing that really matters, the ideological kinship." This articulation of an "ideological kinship" of the Republican Party is strikingly similar to Grossman and Hopkins (2016), who argue that the Republican Party "is the vehicle of an ideological movement." However, they also describe the Democratic Party as a pragmatic (and not ideological) coalition that stitches together and caters to a smorgasbord of constituencies, their group identities, and their group interests. Based on the arguments advanced by the Democratic activists mentioned here, particularly the second generation, this does not seem to be the case, since we see clearly that they perceive a strong ideological grounding for the Democratic Party (see also Edsall 2018). Again, any broader ideological basis for the Republican Party seemed to unravel with the rise of Trump, after which it more openly became a party supporting White (Christian) nationalist interests (Jones 2020; Whitehead and Perry 2020) and of those supporting it for other pragmatic reasons (e.g., as we will see later, Hindu nationalists supporting it for its anti-Muslim platform, as well as entrepreneurs benefiting from its tax policies). Since color-blindness is viewed as a trait stemming from White privilege (Bonilla-Silva 2017), and the Republican Party is White dominated, it is perhaps not surprising that color-blindness is baked into the Republican Party and is echoed by its non-White supporters as well.

Rising Hindu Nationalism and Indian American Partisan Politics

In the last chapter we saw how Hindu groups mobilized around the issue of Modi's visa denial in 2005 and became active on Capitol Hill after that (see Friedrich 2020a). That incident made U.S. Hindu nationalist supporters realize that it was not enough to get support from nonpartisan advocacy groups like the Hindu American Foundation or bipartisan political organizations like USINPAC, but that it was important to have partisan groups to work with U.S. political parties to promote support for Modi and his agenda. This outreach to U.S. partisan groups by Hindu nationalists was not just one-sided. A White American affiliated with a conservative U.S. think tank during the mid-2000s told me that he was aware of a short-lived but concerted effort among a small group of U.S. Republicans to "tag onto the [U.S.-India] nuclear deal" to gain support for India among conservatives and to link with Hindu nationalists on an anti-Islamic platform. He mentioned that part of the idea had been to sell this alliance "to the wider U.S. public with the War on Terror packaged in there and the anti-Muslim bent." He was not clear why this effort was soon abandoned.

In 2014, a few months after Modi was elected prime minister of India at the head of the BJP, Modi's Indian American fans organized a lavish reception for him at Madison Square Garden in New York City, with an estimated crowd of 19,000 people attending, including around three dozen elected American politicians (Yee 2014). Attempts to create links between Hindu nationalists and the Republican Party gained momentum after Modi's election. The most visible expression of the alliance between Hindu nationalists and the Republican Party came about with the formation of the Republican Hindu Coalition, modeled after the Republican Jewish Coalition, led by wealthy Chicago-based entrepreneur Shalabh Kumar, with Newt Gingrich serving as the honorary chairman. Kumar, who came to the United States in the late 1960s, had started out as a Democratic activist but had been persuaded to switch allegiances in 1980 by Ronald Reagan (Yokley 2015). In an article in *The Hill*, Jonathan Swan (2016) described Kumar as one of Donald Trump's "biggest financial backers" who had contributed almost $900,000 between himself and his wife, the maximum allowed, and had pledged another $1 million for Republican candidates during the 2016 election cycle.

Shalabh Kumar addressed race and religion in his interview with Swan. Regarding race, Swan quotes Kumar as saying, "A lot of people think that

Trump is somewhat of a racist. . . . His partnership with the Republican Hindu Coalition will set that aside." The article also describes how Kumar, during a meeting with Trump, "was especially won over by Trump's tough words for Pakistan, India's neighbor and nemesis; and the businessman praised Trump's views on Muslim profiling." Support for Trump because of his anti-Muslim stance also came up repeatedly in media interviews with Indian American supporters of Trump. Consequently, journalist Jeremy Peters (2016), writing about the Republican Hindu Coalition for the *New York Times*, observed: "Mr. Trump has unwittingly fashioned a niche constituency in the overlap between the Indian right and the American right, which share a lot of the same anxieties about [Islamic] terrorism, immigration and the loss of prestige that they believe their leaders have been too slow to reverse." Kumar organized a video advertisement for Trump targeting Indian Americans at the end of October 2016.[9] In the advertisement, Trump emphasized the common anti-Islamic platform, saying, "The Indian and Hindu community will have a true friend in the White House. We will defeat radical Islamic terrorism. I look forward to working with Prime Minister Modi." Trump also spoke a phrase in Hindi, "*Abki baar Trump sarkar*," which translates to, "This time a Trump government." This was instantly recognizable to a Hindu nationalist audience since it was a slogan that Modi had popularized (with his name instead of Trump's) during his 2014 election campaign in India. In another advertisement on November 1, 2016, also aimed at Hindu nationalists, the Republican Hindu Coalition attacked Hillary Clinton and linked her with Pakistan, radical Islam, and the blocking of Modi's visa:

> Hillary, sympathetic towards Pakistan, gave billions of dollars in aid and military equipment, used against India. She was instrumental in blocking PM Modi's visa. Takes contributions from countries and individuals known to support radical Islam. Her current aide Huma Abedin is of Pakistani origin[10] and will become Chief of Staff if she wins. Her husband, Bill Clinton wants to give Kashmir to Pakistan. Vote Republican. Great for you, great for US-Indian relations and great for America. This message endorsed by RHC.[11]

Kumar organized a mega, "Bollywood-themed Hindu rally" for Donald Trump in Edison, New Jersey, an area with a large Hindu Indian American settlement (S. Paul and Choksi 2016). Advertised as being a charity event to support Hindu victims of (Islamic) terror in Kashmir and West Bengal, the event consisted of a variety show by several Bollywood celebrities—many in the crowd had come to see them and not because of the political nature of the event. Next came a performance where Indian dancers were attacked by "terrorists" with guns (light sabers) and were saved by members of the U.S. Army. All the performers on stage then took the U.S. Pledge of Allegiance and sang "Born in the U.S.A." The entertainment was followed by a speech by Shalabh Kumar introducing Trump to the audience and claiming that Trump had promised a faster green card process for Indian Americans. Trump walked in; lighted a *diya* (oil lamp), a traditional Hindu ritual; and gave a short speech, starting with "I am a big fan of Hindu[12] and I am a big fan of India," ending by emphasizing that America and India would be "best friends" under his administration. Banners at the event promised green cards to Indian Americans (though Trump did not make any mention of this in his speech), and there were posters of Trump apparently sitting in a beatific yogic pose Photoshopped onto the BJP lotus symbol. Flyers depicting Hillary Clinton and Sonia Gandhi (president of the Indian Congress Party and the head of Modi's opposition party) with horns sprouting from their heads, screaming "Get Modi," were spread throughout the venue. Anti-Trump groups had organized protests outside the venue and there were some shouting matches between pro- and anti-Trumpers (S. Paul and Choksi 2016; Rizwan 2016).

Although Shalabh Kumar became one of Trump's most fervent supporters in 2016, several other Indian American Republicans criticized and distanced themselves from Trump due to his divisive campaign and said they would not vote for him. Others said they would only do so out of party loyalty (Haniffa 2016a). One immigrant Republican activist, Dr. Sampat Shivangi, also criticized Shalabh Kumar's comparison between the Republican Jewish Coalition and the Republican Hindu Coalition, arguing, "You can't compare RJC and the RHC because Israel is a Jewish state . . . but India, we are a secular country of all faiths" (Haniffa 2016b). While many Indian American Republican leaders distanced themselves from Trump in 2016, 16 percent of Indian Americans are believed to have voted for him (Ramakrishnan et al. 2017), substantially more than the 7 percent who had claimed a Republican partisan identity in 2016 (Ramakrishnan et al. 2016). An interview conducted with a Hindu American Foundation supporter in Silicon Valley in December 2016 for another project provides a clue regarding some of the possible reasons. "Rima" declared:

> I have talked with a lot of Hindus from different states and a lot of Hindus actually supported Donald Trump ... they were anti-Hillary. There is an underlying current of resentment because ... if you look at Indian community in general which happens to be mostly Hindu Indian community in United States ... we are [a] successful minority... that is why people were against Hillary. Hindu Americans or Indian Americans I should say, they felt like African Americans and Latinos would get a lot more of Hillary ... and they felt like wait, we have same issues in this case as White America [laughs]. You know we don't fall in that disadvantaged minority group and so we are discriminated against in that sense.

In other words, Rima argued that Hindu Indian Americans thought that Hillary was leaning too far toward "disadvantaged" minority groups like African Americans and Hispanics, which would hurt Hindus since they were a "successful minority" group, with similar interests as White America in this respect. It is also significant that these discussions took place *after* Trump had been elected since I learned that many Hindu American Trump supporters had not wanted others to know that they were supporting Trump during the election campaign, something Rima also hinted at in her conversation.

An Expanding Progressive South Asian American Constituency and Indian American Politics

A lot changed in the landscape of Indian American partisan activism between 2016 and 2020. The election of Donald Trump as president in 2016 and subsequent events, including the White nationalist Charlottesville march on August 12, 2017, jolted many Democrat-leaning, independent, and even relatively apolitical Indian Americans into action to reverse the xenophobia that the Republican Party unleashed, by mobilizing a South Asian American coalition. South Asian Americans are the fastest-growing demographic in the United States, and the National Asian American Survey (Ramakrishnan et al. 2017) showed that fast-growing groups like Bangladeshis and Pakistanis were even more Democrat leaning than Indian Americans. Indian American activists realized that in many swing districts and states around the country, there were enough South Asian American voters to "create a blue tsunami." Several media articles also made this case (Detsch and Gramer 2020; S. Paul 2020b; Tabernise and Geobeloff 2019).

The organization They See Blue (the name cleverly chosen to also sound like "Desi Blue" or South Asian Democrats) was formed in the San Francisco Bay Area in July 2018 by four Silicon Valley Indian American immigrant entrepreneurs to "leverage a cultural connection" with South Asian Americans (including the South Asian diaspora from other parts of the world such as the Caribbean) to flip three seats in the California Central Valley from red to blue. Through fundraising and targeted outreach to South Asian American families, They See Blue (TSB) was successful in flipping two of the three California seats and greatly reducing the margin of victory of the Republican in the third seat. Following on this success, TSB decided to focus on "flipping the three houses" (House of Representatives, Senate, and White House) in Washington, DC. They formed chapters in swing states around the country for the 2020 elections by reaching out to progressive South Asians in these states who were already active in voter outreach.

Another new progressive Indian American organization that emerged around the same time was *Indian American IMPACT* (IMPACT), an advocacy organization founded by some second-generation IALI activists, with an associated candidate training project and a fund to help Indian American candidates running for office (there was "a deluge" of Indian American candidates running for 2018 elections). Finally, South Asians for Biden was the official Biden campaign–affiliated organization. *Indian Americans for Biden* started off under the South Asians for Biden umbrella but subsequently broke away to form a separate organization. Another organization, the *AAPI Victory Fund*, was also very active in 2020. The AAPI Victory Fund was an Asian American super PAC formed before the 2016 elections to mobilize progressive Asian American voters to turn out to vote. It was founded by Shekhar Narasimhan, an Indian American who had been a long-time Democratic activist. Since the AAPI Victory Fund focused on Asian Americans more broadly, I did not include the group in my research. But they collaborated with several of the Indian American and South Asian American groups I researched that I learned about through my interviews. There were also new Indian American Republican groups that were active around the 2020 elections, including *Americans4Hindus*, a Silicon Valley–based organization supporting Republican candidates. Recognizing the importance of the South Asian American vote and how the community was divided, the Trump campaign set up several additional organizations targeting South Asian voters in August 2020—*Indian Voices for Trump*, *Hindus for Trump*, *Sikhs for Trump*, and *Muslim Voices for Trump*.[13]

In 2021, I interviewed six members of They See Blue across the United States, including some founders. I also interviewed a representative each from South Asians for Biden, Indian Americans for Biden, and Indian American IMPACT. Contact information for the Republican groups was hard to find. I was only able to interview one Indian American Republican, and he was not particularly active around the 2020 elections—he had been very active in 2016 in *Indian Americans for Trump*, which was more inclusive than the Republican Hindu Coalition. The Republican Hindu Coalition was not active in the 2020 campaign.

I talked to two founders of They See Blue and reviewed material from their webpage (theyseeblue.com) and their Facebook page (facebook.com/theyseeblue) containing interviews, articles, and blogs written by the founders (e.g., see S. Mehta 2018). One of the founders, "Harish," who described himself as having been an independent earlier, explained why the election of 2016 had ignited many Indian Americans in Silicon Valley to get involved in political activism: "There are certain fundamentals in this country, which is why many of us immigrants come here, you know, there are certain institutions, there are certain founding principles, there are certain ideals, right, that this country stands for, and all of those were being completely shattered after the election of 2016." Harish specifically meant democracy, the rule of law, a free press, respect for science and truth, and Trump shattering all of this by "treating the presidency as his own personal fiefdom." He referred me to the book *It Was All a Lie: How the Republican Party Became Donald Trump*, written by a former high-ranking Republican, Stuart Stevens (2020), who had believed in Republican ideals, "but then he realized that it was all a façade. Really speaking, what they believed in is xenophobia and divisiveness and just trying to win elections at all costs, by hook or by crook." Another co-founder, "Nikhil," who similarly described himself as being a "no party preference voter," had started his involvement in Democratic political mobilization when George W. Bush was running for re-election, since he thought the Iraq War had been "completely unnecessary." The weekend after Trump got elected, Nikhil and another Indian American started a local Silicon Valley organization, *Silicon Valley Courageous Resistance* (https://svcr.us), to resist Trump. But then, some Indian Americans felt that they needed to do something targeted specifically at South Asian Americans since this was the group they could leverage with their own backgrounds. That is how They See Blue was formed.

In contrast to the Silicon Valley founders who described themselves as "fiscally conservative, and socially liberal," several They See Blue activists in other parts of the country whom I interviewed, particularly members of the second generation, defined themselves as "progressive." Some had first become involved in left-leaning political groups such as *Swing Left* and *Indivisible* and then had broken away to form specifically South Asian American–focused groups, though many continued to be active in broader groups as well. Besides believing that they could best reach and connect with South Asian American voters due to cultural similarities, they also felt safer and more comfortable contacting South Asian Americans "because you will not be penalized for looking different or having an accent." A They See Blue activist explained that this concern was particularly due to Trump whipping up xenophobia, making South Asians nervous about contacting non–South Asian Americans.

They See Blue was an entirely volunteer organization emphasizing a "servant-leader" model (which they said they got from Abraham Lincoln) to serve voters. They focused on getting Democrats elected, rather than on one or more specific issues, and they did not fundraise for candidates. In contrast, IMPACT's primary focus was fundraising and supporting Indian American candidates and non-Indian candidates "aligned with Indian American values" (which, based on the results of the National Asian American Surveys, they defined as "pluralistic and progressive," including support for immigration reform, civil rights, and access to economic opportunities, health care, and education). But they also spent $10 million to turn out South Asian voters in Pennsylvania and Arizona, and another $2.5 million to turn out AAPI voters more broadly in Georgia ahead of the January 2021 Senate runoff elections (http://iaimpact.org). South Asians for Biden focused on the federal 2020 election and getting Biden elected. They received their messaging and their platform directly from the Biden campaign, which they then disseminated to voters. They See Blue targeted those who were Democratic or independent voters, based on past voting history. Indian Americans for Biden, on the other hand, did "not go down a party line, ... we went to all the Indian Americans in a particular district."

Each of these organizations focused on reaching out and talking to voters in a "culturally appropriate" manner, whether this included using their native languages or using cultural codes and forms of address they would recognize and be able to appreciate. Since many Indian American activists were IT workers, they developed voter lists by creating software programs to extract

South Asian American or Indian American names (in the case of Indian Americans for Biden) from the broader voter lists of the regions they were targeting. Because door-to-door canvassing was not possible in 2020 due to COVID, they used social media such as WhatsApp, Facebook, Instagram, and Twitter. They also made "multi [South Asian]-language" phone calls and "tried to really engage people who were on the fence with longer and deeper conversations." Additionally, they organized some "sign-waving rallies" and sent several post cards to voters, reminding them about voting deadlines and procedures (e.g., mail-in ballots) and the importance of their vote. Activists got involved in several events with prominent Democrats, discussed their views on podcasts, and participated in television and radio programs targeting South Asian Americans. They See Blue activists from several states around the country also supported the January 2021 mobilization in Georgia around the runoff elections.

I was curious about the issues that particularly mobilized South Asian American voter turnout around the 2020 elections and asked about this during my interviews. The number one issue that Democratic activists mentioned (also discussed on the TSB Facebook page) had to do with racism and anti-immigrant sentiments, along with the rise in hate crimes and discrimination. Harish mentioned the concern that due to the racist policies and attitudes of the Republican Party, many South Asian Americans worried that they would not be treated as "equal citizens." He added, "They themselves [i.e., the immigrants] might be able to tolerate it, but not for their children." This is a sentiment I heard several times—that South Asian Americans were most concerned that their "Brown" children had become targets of racism ("our children are being yelled at in schools and told to go back to their country") or would become such targets in the future. A TSB Facebook page post (July 3, 2020) emphasized that being financially successful may not protect South Asian Americans from xenophobia. The poster argued, "It might in fact heighten racism against us as racists perceive us as 'foreigners' who are doing better than the 'real' Americans." Other activists said that South Asian Americans had spoken about experiencing changes in the way they were treated at the border (while returning to the United States from a foreign trip) under the Trump administration, and an apparent "war" against people of color. Yet others were disturbed by alterations in voting rights laws that disenfranchised communities of color. Anti-immigrant measures that the Trump administration began to put into place were also mentioned by several activists. Entrepreneurs were indignant about the cutting back of immigration and visas (especially the H-1B and the H-4 visas) under the Trump administration, which used to "get issued and renewed in regular fashion under all previous administrations," since it directly impacted their businesses. Some also mentioned the Trump administration ending DACA and concerns about what would happen to children of H-1B immigrants (whom many Indian Americans like to call *DALCA*, emphasizing that they are children of legal immigrants) who had to leave the country when they turned 21 years of age if their parents were not able to become naturalized citizens by then.

Other motivating factors that helped turn out South Asian voters to support the Democratic Party included wanting access to affordable health care and a worry that the Affordable Care Act and the coverage for pre-existing conditions would be dismantled if Trump was elected for a second term, a fear about funding cuts for public school education "once DeVos was appointed secretary of education" (since she seemed to be focused on charter schools), the overturning of gun control policies, and the Republican distrust for science manifested by the mismanagement of COVID. Some voters were also apprehensive that women's rights to abortion would be jeopardized if Trump was re-elected. Interestingly, fears about evangelical Christian domination under a second Trump term and its impact on non-Christians were not mentioned by any of the activists as a factor motivating voters to turn to Democrats. South Asian American Democratic activists including those belonging to They See Blue and South Asians for Biden developed talking points to debunk several "myths" that on-the-fence voters might bring up, including that the economy would do less well and that their taxes would go up under Democrats, as well as the idea that Trump was good for India and that Biden was against Hindus.[14]

Of course, the selection of Kamala Harris as vice president further enthused and energized Indian Americans. In an obvious attempt to woo Indian American voters, the Biden campaign released a long and detailed statement, "Joe Biden's Agenda for Indian American Community" (http://joebiden.com/Indian-Americans/), addressing many concerns such as the bullying and xenophobic attacks that many Indian Americans had been subjected to (including attacks on houses of worship), and promising increased access to jobs and loans, to overturn some of the restrictions of immigration such the "Muslim ban," to support family unification policies, to increase temporary visas such as the H-1B and religious worker visas, to eliminate country limits for green cards, and finally, to support U.S.-India partnership. Though Trump had short ads (including a brief phrase in Hindi) targeting Indian Americans, I did not find a similar detailed agenda for Indian Americans from his campaign. The voter turnout efforts seem to have paid off since the proportion of Indian Americans who voted in the 2020 elections went up by 9 percentage points over 2016 to a stunning 71 percent (Ramakrishnan 2021).

Cleavages within the Community and Their Impact on Indian American Politics

Intergenerational cleavages continued to play a role in Indian American partisan politics around the 2020 elections. These differences reared up within They See Blue despite an attempt to forge a unified front focused on U.S.-based issues. Some immigrant members mentioned an internal division between a moderate faction (mostly comprising immigrants), who wanted to focus on electing Democrats since they believed they could take issues of concern to elected representatives once Democrats were in power, and a "Bernie" faction (supporters of Bernie Sanders, considered to be a more "radical" candidate than Joe Biden), mostly composed of the American-born generation who were much more focused on issues and, as an immigrant activist said acidly, "have this purity test they want to apply" to Democratic candidates before they decided whether or not to vote for them.

As mentioned, Indian Americans for Biden broke away from the South Asians for Biden group due to differences in orientation between the two groups. The (immigrant) representative of Indian Americans for Biden, "Girish," whom I talked to put it this way:

> Initially I was part of South Asians for Biden. Now, as part of that, I spoke to about 15 or so [Indian American] community leaders to get them involved, and the increasing sentiment I felt we got back was that they identified themselves as Indian American, not South Asian. South Asian frankly is more of a geographical identity, it is not a cultural identity. . . . So then around May-June [2020] or so, some of us within the South Asian group felt that we need to create this Indian Americans for Biden.

Girish told me that the people he approached felt that the Biden campaign needed to have a more "Indian American–focused approach" to get more traction in the community. He said that once they had formed, their numbers increased exponentially in a very short time, reaching 10,000 members by August 2020, after Kamala Harris was selected as Biden's vice presidential candidate. Generational differences between immigrants who were more likely to identify as Indian Americans and liberal second-generation members who often identified as South Asian Americans seemed to be one factor for the split since South Asians for Biden was led largely by second-generation activists and, from what I could gather, Indian Americans for Biden was a largely immigrant group.

There were also developments in India that impacted Indian American partisan activity by increasing polarization within the Indian American and South Asian American community. Recall that the BJP was re-elected in 2019 with a larger margin, emboldening them to push forward with two controversial policies: the abrogation of statehood of Jammu and Kashmir, the only Muslim-majority state in India, in August 2019 and the implementation of a new citizenship act (CAA) that discriminated against Muslims in December 2019, preceded by a clampdown on undocumented migrants (allegedly Muslims from Bangladesh) in the northeastern state of Assam. These 2019 events further galvanized the Hindu Right to mobilize in support of Modi.[15] A huge Howdy Modi event to greet Modi on his visit to the United States after his re-election was organized in Houston, Texas, on September 22, 2019, by Modi's supporters in the United States, with an estimated crowd of 50,000 people attending. Donald Trump appeared with Modi and Modi repeated the phrase Trump had used in 2016 in front of an Indian American audience: "*abki baar, Trump sarkar*"—"this time a Trump presidency"—referring to the 2020 elections and declaring his support for Trump. Outside the stadium, there were thousands of protestors demonstrating against Modi's policies. All the Democratic Indian American members of Congress except for Raja Krishnamoorthy boycotted the event (S. Paul 2019).

In candidate Joe Biden's policy paper, Agenda for Muslim American Communities (https://joebiden.com/muslimamerica/), he raised concerns about the developments in Kashmir and about the CAA (L. Jha 2020). Similarly, Kamala Harris spoke out against the CAA and condemned human rights abuses in Kashmir. These positions upset many staunch Modi supporters in the United States, and South Asian American Democratic activists reported getting questions from some voters about whether Biden and Harris were anti-India. They said they had to develop talking points to address these questions. Ro Khanna, Democratic representative from

California who had put out a tweet critical of Hindutva and of Democratic candidates who supported it,[16] came under attack from U.S. Hindutva supporters. Under the leadership of a wealthy Bay Area–based doctor, Romesh Japra, a challenger to Ro Khanna, Ritesh Tandon, also Indian American, launched his bid with the endorsement of U.S. Modi enthusiasts and ran as a Republican in the 2020 California primaries. Ro Khanna handily trounced Tandon, getting over 65 percent of the vote to Tandon's 24 percent (Haniffa 2020c). Likewise, when Muslim American congresswoman Rashida Tlaib (D-MI) criticized Modi's Kashmir policy, Modi supporters directed donations to Brenda Jones, the candidate running against her in the Michigan primaries, in an unsuccessful attempt to unseat Tlaib (Friedrich 2020b). In other words, politics in India had an important impact in shaping U.S. elections.

Family links with Hindu nationalist groups and how they should be viewed caused tensions between immigrant and second-generation Democratic activists. A small number of Indian American Democratic candidates and at least one member of the Biden campaign had such links. Sri Preston Kulkarni of Texas, who ran as a Democratic congressional candidate, was strongly supported by some U.S. members of the RSS (a key Hindu nationalist group). Kulkarni's uncle in India had been a leader of the BJP before his death in 2006. Kulkarni was a former U.S. Foreign Service official who had anticipated a posting in India, so many people were disbelieving when he claimed he did not know about the RSS. Kulkarni was also critiqued for not condemning Hindu nationalist organizations or the anti-Muslim policies of the Modi government in 2019. While many immigrant members of TSB took a pragmatic approach, arguing that Kulkarni needed the money and support of a range of groups to win, some in the second generation harshly condemned his actions. "Ekta," a second-generation TSB activist, declared, speaking to me about Kulkarni, "It's unacceptable for any Democratic candidate to accept a single penny from any member of any affiliate RSS organization" and compared it to a Democratic candidate taking money from the KKK or the Proud Boys. Amit Jani, a member of the Biden team assigned to work as his Muslim outreach coordinator, also came under attack for close family ties with Hindu nationalist groups (his parents were strong BJP and Modi supporters) and for not distancing himself from Modi's politics. Here too, many immigrant TSB leaders I talked to felt that Jani himself had no Hindu nationalist inclinations and that he should not be penalized for what his parents did (some described his being blackballed as an instance of "cancel culture"). In the end, Sri Preston Kulkarni lost his bid, apparently at least partly because some Muslim American groups withdrew their support (e.g., see I. Khan 2020), Amit Jani was "sidelined" by the Biden campaign (Rajghatta 2020), and the position of Muslim outreach coordinator was given to a Muslim American. Other Democratic candidates who came under attack for their links to Hindu nationalism included Tulsi Gabbard, a former Samoan American member of Congress from Hawaii and a practicing Hindu who ran as a presidential candidate, and Indian American congressman Raja Krishnamoorthi (D-IL).

Perhaps the biggest cleavage within the community had to do with South Asia–based religious tensions, which were undoubtedly magnified by the 2019 developments. A second-generation They See Blue activist admitted that a lot of political activism in the South Asian American community tended to happen along religious or nationalist lines, particularly among the immigrant generation. She explained that this was because "that's just their community" and because "people like to think they may have different issues and it's a chance to have your issues heard, and . . . there might be the fear of assimilating and losing who you are [within the larger India-dominated South Asian American coalition]."

South Asian American activists used two strategies to try to counter these cleavages. First, they emphasized that the U.S. elections were primarily about U.S.-based issues. "Priya" from South Asians for Biden said that she would argue:

> What happens in India doesn't affect my ability to get a job here, my ability to send my daughter to school, my health care, my environment, whether I'm being shot in a grocery store. So, while that's important and you want to of course know what's going on, that really has no impact on my vote that I cast here.

Second, and perhaps more important, they worked hard to be inclusive. Ekta, a They See Blue activist in Georgia, illustrated it this way:

> So, for example, the Georgia Muslim Voter Project—we have friends in those groups so when they have an event, we post to all of our groups. "Hey, let's come out, let's support this event, this is a Georgia Muslim Voters [event]—let's elevate what they have to say." . . . So, it's kind of through our

support and amplification that we try to give our Muslim voters options you know, if they feel too drowned out by the Indians.

Ekta also told me about a Bhutanese man who had remarked, "You know I don't really identify as South Asian," and that she had replied:

> Look, you don't have to identify as South Asian, we want to know how we can support you and your folks, so you tell us what you need. If you need resources, if you need information, we want to help you. When you have stuff going on we can amplify it for you. We are not here to replace any group.

The South Asians for Biden activist, Priya similarly described their organization as the "mother ship," which then formed several national councils "tied by identity, tied by religion" (though Girish, the Indian Americans for Biden representative, said that they had broken away to form a distinct group, not tied to South Asians for Biden) and sent out the messaging from the Biden campaign to these subgroups. In other words, the South Asian American activists tried to accommodate and include subgroups based on religion and national identity in a variety of ways.

Several South Asian American Democratic activists gave me other examples of religious polarization within the community. "Brinda" said that in many cases Hindus were voting for Trump since they approved of his attacks on Muslims.

> Indian Americans were voting for Trump because he was anti-Muslim. Yeah, mostly Hindus, yeah. So, I tried to have conversations with them about like, "Listen, do you have a mirror, can you go and look at your face?" and, "When you step out of this house, you're not among your friends, nobody knows whether you're a Hindu or a Muslim. How does his hatred for Muslims not translate to his hatred for you?"

Ekta further explained why many Hindus supported the policies of Trump. It is worth quoting at some length because it is eye-opening and elaborates on what some others had hinted at:

> Because they see Hindu supremacy as synonymous with White supremacy here. They want to be in the highest place in the pecking order

and maintain that supremacy over minorities in India and so they've used Trump as synonymous with Modi. They want a Hindu *rashtra* [country], they want Hindu supremacy, they want a Hindustan in India and so over here the candidate who is synonymous with that for them is Trump, Trump and his White Christian supremacy, Trump making the U.S. an evangelical Christian nation instead of a secular nation. Everything that Trump did is actually a mirror image of what Modi has been doing in India years before Trump came in power. And so, to them they see themselves as [similar to] the White race here.

PREMA: They do? So, this did not alienate them, this White evangelical supremacy and activism didn't alienate them as Brown Hindus?
EKTA: Of course, it did. They just wouldn't admit it, right? They saw, they are experiencing racism here but to them, they excuse it, this is what they say, "well you know, people just sometimes mistake us as Muslims who are the terrorists, but as soon as they get to know Hinduism, they'll know that we're not the terrorists, like the Muslims are the terrorists," that's exactly how they see it. So, innocent White people, if only they knew about Hinduism, they would support them and wouldn't be racist, because it's the Muslims that are terrorists and it's important for us to be seen as Hindus and not [as] the Muslim terrorists.

In other words, Ekta points out that many Hindus recognized that White Christian nationalism was a mirror image of Hindu nationalism in India. They did not feel threatened by it because they believed that White Christians understood that Hinduism and Hindus are allies, which was not the case with Muslims. So, Hindus just needed to make sure that they became visible as Hindus.

I also learned that many wealthy, high-profile religious leaders in the South Asian American community across the country (and not just Hindus) tended to be Republicans. As prominent leaders, they had much greater visibility and influence both within the community and in the wider society than most Indian American Democrats. For instance, Romesh Japra, the Republican activist in the Bay Area and founder of Americans4Hindus, is a cofounder of the Fremont Hindu temple in the Bay Area. While most Indian Americans still voted for Democrats in the 2020 elections, it is important to note that there seems to have been a substantial increase in the numbers of Indian Americans supporting Trump in 2020—studies showed that between 22 and 28 percent of Indian Americans indicated that they would vote for him (data from 2020 September Carnegie and AAPI studies) compared to the 2016 elections, where 16 percent of Indian Americans were believed to have voted for him (Ramakrishnan et al. 2017). With respect specifically to Hindu voters, it appears that there was a significant shift in their voting patterns between the 2016 and 2020 elections, from 11 percent support for Trump in 2016 to 19.8 percent support in 2020.[17]

Conclusion

Current literature on American partisan identities and voting patterns is inadequate in understanding the political formation of immigrant groups. Although several factors mold the partisan leanings of Indian Americans, we see that race and religion interacting in complicated ways in different spheres played central roles. While this interaction is central to the argument of each of the chapters of this book, it is seen most clearly in this chapter. Race does not by itself shape the partisan preferences of Indian Americans as in the case of African Americans but works in complicated but still influential ways. Early Indian American immigrants gravitated to the Democratic Party because of the support of Democrats for the immigration policies that opened the United States to new groups, their advocacy for greater social and economic equality, and the perception that Democrats were more welcoming of immigrants and racial minorities in the party. In the U.S. South, however, Republicans rather than Democrats were more likely to be open to including Indian American candidates and activists as a way of bringing some "color" into the party. The perception that Indian Americans such as Bobby Jindal were a "model minority" probably helped his rapid ascent in the Republican Party (this was discussed in several online forums). Many Indian American Republicans seem to have internalized tropes distinguishing Indians as deserving, hardworking groups different from Hispanics and Black groups since they mentioned their distaste for people "pushing through the border" and those "seeking entitlements." They also distinguished legal migrants from "illegal" groups (in contrast to Democrats, who, as mentioned, rarely mentioned this issue and used the term "undocumented" instead of "illegal").

At the same time, many Indian American Republicans activists, including highly placed members, were alienated by the White nationalism developing within the party and spoke out against it.

The "macaca" racial incident in 2006 where Republican senator George Allen targeted a second-generation Indian American led to the first unified mobilization of both Indian American generations along with other progressive groups to successfully challenge Allen's candidacy, leading to a Democratic majority in the Senate. Second-generation progressive Indian American Democrats joined coalitions with people of color and mobilized in large numbers around the candidacy of Obama (especially in 2008). As mentioned, the National Dance for Obama movement in 2012 choreographed and performed multiracial flash mob dances in cities around the country to a song composed by an African American music producer to combat the negativity in politics at the time. We have seen that even among the second generation, Democrats rather than Republicans were more likely to embrace a "person of color" identity. Second-generation Republicans preferred to embrace a color-blind ideology, arguing that racial identity was not central to their lives.

With respect to religion, Indian American Muslims felt that Democrats were more supportive of anti-discrimination policies in the workplace that would allow Muslims to thrive professionally. After the attacks of September 11, 2001, Indian American Muslims mobilized against the Patriot Act (introduced under Republican president George W. Bush), another factor turning them away from Republicans and toward Democrats. Except for these examples, there was no clear pattern regarding whether some religious groups were more likely to embrace a particular partisan identity. However, several organizers told me that LGBTQ issues and abortion seemed to be of particular concern to some Indian Christian (primarily Catholic) and Muslim groups, pushing them toward the Republican Party. The Christian nature of the Republican Party was also mentioned by several immigrant Hindu American Democratic activists. At the same time, we saw how Indian American Christian activists on both sides of the aisle argued that it was their Christian faith that motivated their activism and support for their party.

The coming to power of the Hindu nationalist BJP in 2014 in India, and of Trump in 2016, riding the wave of White Christian nationalism, brought both religion and race to the forefront of Indian American politics. Hindu nationalist supporters started reaching out to both parties to promote Modi's policies. Many U.S. politicians were receptive due to the financial clout of the group and its rising numbers. The Republican Hindu Coalition formed around an anti-Muslim platform that emphasized the linked fate and common location of Hindu and White Americans. As articulated by the woman from Silicon Valley, we see that this coalition developed based on the belief that Hillary Clinton (and the Democratic Party more generally) was more supportive of Black and Hispanic groups as opposed to "successful" minorities such as Hindus and that, consequently, Hindus and White Americans had a common interest in opposing special policies for racial minorities. Many Hindu immigrants supported Trump due to his anti-Muslim stance, which was in sync with their Hindu nationalist ideas. Hindu Republicans felt that White Americans were not against Hindus (perhaps not surprising given Newt Gingrich and Steve Bannon's strong support for the Republican Hindu Coalition) but only against Muslims. There were also several "Modi-Democrats"—supporters of Modi who tended to vote Democratic in the United States who had to be persuaded that Biden and Harris's statements against Kashmir and the CAA should not be viewed as an attack on India or Hindus. Some members of this group may have switched their allegiance to Trump (a few They See Blue activists mentioned seeing big shifts in electoral alignments among Hindus following the Howdy Modi September 2019 event in Houston, Texas, where Trump appeared on stage with Modi), and we also see this in the percentage of Hindu voters supporting Trump in 2020 versus 2016.

At the same time, rising racial xenophobia and White nationalism mobilized progressive Indian American groups to form solidarities with Muslims under a South Asian umbrella and with racial minority groups through involvement with AAPI and other coalitions—this was particularly the case in Georgia, where South Asian American Democratic groups supported the candidacies of Stacey Abrams and Raphael Warnock (African Americans fighting against White Republican domination). In short, the main takeaway is that partisan voting and identities are complex and are rarely based on single-issue politics. We see how many factors crystallizing around race and religion interacted together around U.S.-based and India-based issues to shape Indian American partisan politics.

Finally, we see fairly similar gendered generational patterns of partisan activism here as in Chapter 3, with the second generation being more interested in domestic issues and including many women leaders compared to the immigrant generation, and the second-generation seeming to be more ideologically progressive compared to more pragmatic immigrant activists.

However, generational divisions around an Indian American versus South Asian American identity seemed to have become blurred. While it was the second generation that first embraced a South Asian identity (discussed in Chapter 3), the 2016 election of Donald Trump resulted in the immigrant generation forming a South Asian American They See Blue organization to include both immigrants and the American-born from a variety of national origin backgrounds as a means to combat the bigotry emanating from the Republican Party and flip swing states blue. While IMPACT was officially described as an "Indian American" organization, the second-generation IMPACT leader I talked to told me that the organization was not "too dogmatic" about sticking to just Indian Americans, and that they were inclusive of other South Asian Americans and had supported some of them as candidates. As mentioned, they funded turnout efforts targeting South Asian voters in Pennsylvania and Arizona, as well as a larger AAPI outreach in the Georgia 2021 runoff elections. At the same time, the Indian Americans for Biden group certainly seemed to feel that they had distinctive concerns, which made them split off from the larger South Asians for Biden group.

Notes

1. Ram Rajya refers to the Kingdom of Lord Ram, or a society with peace and prosperity based on the ideals of the Hindu God Ram.
2. According to the article, Indian Americans contributed nearly $10 million toward the Democratic ticket in the 2016 elections and raised $3.3 million at a single fundraiser for Biden in September 2020 (Ghori-Ahmad and Salman 2020).
3. However, groups like Catholics do not have a clear partisan profile (Campbell 2007; Campbell, Green, and Layman 2011; J. Green 2007).
4. Many European immigrant groups in the United States were incorporated by the Democratic Party in return for votes and political patronage (K. Andersen 1979; Dahl 1961).
5. Based on the National Asian American Survey, which has been conducted since 2008, political scientist Karthick Ramakrishnan argues that the leftward swing of Asian Americans was due to the anti-immigrant rhetoric and the turn to Christian conservatism by the Republican Party (Ramakrishnan 2016).
6. Cho (2015, 53–54) argues that only Hinduism among all Asian American religions was significantly related to partisanship, increasing the likelihood of identifying as a Democrat.
7. https://www.nriInternet.com/NRIappointments/USA/Politics/A_Z/N/Shekar_Narasimhan/index.htm (accessed October 24, 2021).
8. A reference to the anti–ballistic missile program or the Strategic Defense Initiative (SDI), also known as "Star Wars," whose goal was to create a space-based shield against nuclear missiles.
9. https://www.youtube.com/watch?v=1PG2V0YnokM (accessed December 5, 2016).
10. Huma Abedin's parents were Muslims born in colonial India. Her mother's family moved to Pakistan after partition. Huma was born in Michigan.
11. https://www.youtube.com/watch?v=DFr-DlAUWkg
12. He said "Hindu" instead of Hindus, which drew a lot of mocking comments from Indian American Democrats.
13. In September 2020, the Biden campaign followed suit with two new organizations: *Sikhs for Biden* and *Hindus for Biden*—a *Muslims for Biden* organization had been created earlier in March.
14. They argued that Republican presidents have created recessions that impacted everyone and that tax increases under Democrats were not that significant, particularly considering the lack

of investment in health care, infrastructure, and education under Republicans. They challenged the idea that Trump was pro-India by pointing out that he had ended a preferential trade agreement with India, curbed legal immigration, cut H-1B and H-4B visas, and ended DACA protections. They maintained that Biden's appointment of Kamala Harris as his vice president belied the argument that he was anti-Hindu (since her mother was of Hindu background).

15. In Chapter 5, I mentioned that the 2020 Indian American Attitudes Survey showed that a majority of Indian American Hindus supported Modi and Hindutva compared to Indian Americans from other religious backgrounds (Badrinathan, Kapur, and Vaishnav 2021).
16. The specific reference was to an article on the Hindu nationalist links of Tulsi Gabbard (Friedrich 2020a).
17. Figures from the Collaborative Multiracial Post-Election Survey in 2017 and 2021 (Park and Tom 2020; Park 2023).

Conclusion

Claiming Citizenship: Race, Religion, and Political Mobilization

Claiming Citizenship shows how and why Indian Americans rally around cultural and transnational citizenship, and the importance of race and religion as central factors shaping their patterns of activism. This study of mobilization around U.S. and origin-country concerns provides a significant intervention into the literature on new immigrant groups and their patterns of incorporation into Western societies. An understanding of these topics is essential as Western societies become more racially and religiously diverse and as immigration and immigrants have taken center stage in charged debates about national identity, as well as work, education, and welfare policies.

Race and Religion as Social Location

I have argued that race and religion are not simply about skin color, culture, identity, religious beliefs, organizations, and practices but that racial and religious background also shapes the social and structural location of individuals and groups within societies, and even globally (Kurien 2022). This may be easier to understand in the case of race since we recognize that there is a racial structure and hierarchy in the United States. As a non-White group arriving in the early decades of the twentieth century, race was a significant factor impacting Indian American immigrant settlement as they faced a variety of informal and formal processes of exclusion on the West and East Coasts and Jim Crow laws in the U.S. South. Early Indian migrants recognized the link between their status as British colonial subjects and the racial hostility and denial of citizenship they experienced in the United States (since the British government did not do anything to protect them, unlike the governments of some of the other Asian migrants). Consequently, they mobilized simultaneously for Indian independence and for U.S. citizenship rights by developing an early India lobby in Washington, DC (Gould 2006). In the post–civil rights period, the ambiguous racial identity of Indian Americans emerged as a vexed issue regarding how to classify the group in the 1980 American census (whether as an Asian "discriminated minority" deserving of civil rights protections or as White), giving rise to a new round of activism. This was followed by mobilization around occupational and educational discrimination in the 1980s.

Race and skin tone continue to be important in shaping the experiences of discrimination in the everyday lives of Indian Americans in the contemporary period (Modi 2022). It also impacts the campaigns of those running for public office—a frequent tactic of opponents has been to circulate intentionally darkened pictures of Indian American candidates in a bid to make them appear threatening and have voters view them in a negative light (SAALT 2010, 21).[1] However, racial ambiguity, together with beliefs about the links between caste background and racial status based on colonial scholarship, lead Indian Americans to experience and view their racial status in a variety of ways. This affects the frames they use to mobilize. Some subgroups see themselves as similar to White ethnics (such as Jewish Americans), while others adopt the racial solidarity model of non-White groups. The particular frames adopted in turn impact mobilization strategies and the groups that organizations turn to as allies. Many other new immigrant groups in the United States have a racially ambiguous location, including Hispanics, who have a range of skin tones and who are officially classified as an ethnic, rather than a racial, group (with darker-skinned individuals in particular experiencing substantial racial discrimination); Middle Easterners and North African groups classified as White in the U.S. census who challenge this status and demand their own MENA category (Maghbouleh, Schachter, and Flores 2022); Eurasian and Central Asian groups from post-Soviet regions; and Black immigrants from the Caribbean or Africa who sometimes resist being lumped together with African Americans by emphasizing their ethnic identity (Greer 2013). Consequently, it is important to understand how an ambiguous U.S. racial location might motivate identity formation and collective action.

Religion is another important factor impacting a group's structural location, which in turn influences experiences and patterns of mobilization. The United States, unlike Canada or countries in Europe, is a highly religious country. The historical legacy of religion being the most legitimate form of ethnic expression in the United States (Warner 1993), the political success of Jewish groups, the mobilization of Christian evangelicals, and the establishment of faith-based initiatives have all reinforced the tendency for immigrant mobilization for recognition and rights to take place through religious organizations. Despite the official disestablishment of religion in the United States, there is an unofficial establishment of Protestant Christianity in the United States or what John Torpey (2010) describes as "latent" religion. A consequence is that religion is often "smuggled in" to contemporary secular discourse on major issues (Inboden 2008; S. Smith 2010). This places non-Protestant, and particularly non-Christian groups, at a structural disadvantage. As an example, the unofficial establishment of Protestant Christianity profoundly shapes the criteria that have to be met before an institution is classified as a religious organization or publicly recognized as an "American" religion at local and national levels, including by schools and school textbooks and by the administration. Many minority religions find themselves excluded or marginalized by these benchmarks (Kurien 2006a). Other research (using the cases of Buddhists, Sikhs, Muslims, and Hindus) has shown that religious minority status can serve as a motivator for civic and political activism in the face of discrimination and attacks (Chen 2002; Foley and Hoge 2007, 229) or as a means to stake a place at the table of U.S. religious pluralism (Kibria 2011; Kniss and Numrich 2007, 27; Kurien 2006b; 2007a).

While religion has been an important factor shaping the social location of groups throughout U.S. history, it gained new social significance after the attacks of September 11, 2001, and after the contemporary rise of Christian nationalism. Around two-thirds of contemporary U.S. immigrants are Christian (Jasso et al. 2006), but many introduce new types of Christianity to the United States and form their own religious institutions (Kurien 2017a). The other one-third have brought a variety of religions, transforming the United States from a Judeo-Christian country to the "world's most religiously diverse nation" (Eck 2002). Since religious institutions have been shown to impact the civic engagement of immigrants (Kniss and Numrich 2007; Kurien 2013), we need more research on the implications of this change on patterns of mobilization. Because the majority of Indian Americans belong to religions that are not well recognized or understood in the United States, a central priority has been to mobilize to obtain recognition as American traditions and the right to practice their faith, for instance, around the ability to build religious institutions and to maintain religious practices around food, clothing, and other articles of faith. Religious advocacy organizations of minority religious groups also work to reconcile their religious demands with American expectations and requirements (e.g., within the armed services, police, schools, and colleges).

The significance of religious background has grown in India as Hindutva has become the reigning ideology and consequently impacts the diaspora. Many U.S. Hindus feel the need to defend Hindu nationalist policies and view non-Hindus (in India and the diaspora) who mobilize to demand rights as a threat to the Indian nation and to Hindu Americans. Recent examples include the 2023 California bill around making caste a protected category supported by many non-Hindu groups, particularly Sikhs and Muslims, and opposed by many Hindu groups, and the 2022 talk at Google by Thenmozhi Soundararajan of Equality Labs on caste (which she had given at several other Silicon Valley companies) that was cancelled when several Google employees (presumably privileged-caste Hindus) wrote to Google managers describing Soundararajan as "Hinduphobic" and "anti-Hindu" (Tiku 2022). Hindutva supporters in the United States also activate 9/11 tropes to raise concerns about Muslim countries like Pakistan and Bangladesh. With the rise of Hindutva and attacks against religious minorities in India, non-Hindu groups in the United States on their part are strongly motivated to organize and come together to combat the rise of religious hatred and repression experienced by their coreligionists in India. This book with its study of five different religious groups (Hindus, Muslims, Christians, Sikhs, and Buddhists) makes an important contribution to understanding how religion and religious institutions motivate collective action. It shows how cleavages between Indian religious groups are reinforced in the United States as each develops separate religious organizations. Hindu American umbrella organizations tend to develop ethno-religious identity around some version of the Hindutva platform, challenged by Indian secularists, pluralists, Muslims, Sikhs, and Ambedkarites who attempt to oppose political Hinduism. We have also seen how both sides in the advocacy wars frame their grievances using religious and racial models that resonate with U.S. audiences and forge different sets of alliances to achieve their objectives.

Particularly in the post-9/11 period, religion has often been linked with race in the United States with the racialization of religion (Muslims expected to have a certain visual experience and skin color) and the religionization of race (Brown-skinned individuals who appear "foreign" believed to be Muslim). Based on her study of race and religion among second-generation Indian Americans, Khyati Joshi (2006, 89) describes many examples of the racialization of religion, where the Brown skin of her study participants was associated with a negatively viewed belief system (whether Hinduism or Islam) and the individuals were subjected to religious bigotry. South Asian Americans Leading Together (SAALT) documented the racial and religious profiling of South Asian Americans in several reports between 2001 and 2018 (https://saalt.org/resources/publications/), showing clearly how race and religion are interconnected in the United States. This includes South Asian Americans (from a range of religious backgrounds) being stopped by law enforcement without cause, having to face long interrogations about a variety of matters at ports of entry, and being questioned about faith and national origin, as well as frequent TSA searches and seizures of personal property by Customs and Border Protection agents. Many South Asian Americans encounter violent assaults, intimidatory tactics, and verbal slurs in public spaces, and schoolchildren experience religion-based bullying from classmates. SAALT also documented an escalation of xenophobic political rhetoric during election cycles, primarily motivated by anti-Muslim sentiment, but impacting all South Asian American (as well as Middle Eastern and Arab) communities.

On the other hand, for first- and second-generation U.S. immigrants belonging to Christian traditions (a large minority in the Indian case), religion might serve as a "bridge to inclusion" into the wider society (Alba, Raboteau, and DeWind et al. 2009; Foner and Alba 2008; Kurien 2017a). While most immigrant Christians worship in coethnic congregations, many of their children join nonethnic groups in school or college, and some may attend White or multiracial worship services. This was the case among Indian American Christians. Consequently, the identity frameworks of the evangelically oriented children of Indian Christian immigrants seemed to be influenced by interracial evangelical groups that de-emphasized racial differences and instead emphasized their unity as Christians. As a result, they were less likely than Indian Americans of a religious minority background to claim a racial self-identity and to label incidents of discrimination as being due to race (Kurien 2012). Since there are several well-established Christian advocacy groups in the society, Christian immigrants and their children also do not feel the need to mobilize to advance the interests of Christians in the United States, another reason that could explain the very different responses of Indian American Christians, on the one hand, and Hindu, Muslim, Sikh, and Buddhist groups on the other hand to domestic concerns.

I have also discussed an issue that is unique to South Asian Americans—the role of caste in shaping ideas of social location (including in the United States), prerogative, rights, and ability and, most importantly, in impacting social networks, consequently profoundly affecting group formation and mobilization patterns. Perhaps because of the overwhelming dominance of privileged-caste members among Indian Americans and the silence and discomfort around caste, this was not an issue that was brought up in my early interviews. Ambedkarite groups who mobilized publicly around caste were not very active in the U.S. public sphere until after 2015. Consequently, I came to recognize the significance of caste in shaping broader patterns of Indian American activism rather late in my project. Of course, the Hindu American Foundation had put out their report on caste and Hinduism in 2010 (subsequently withdrawn and updated with a revised 2011 version). They also continued to spar with the Dalit Freedom Network (DFN) and were irate about the DFN's attempts to educate the U.S. Congress about caste (one of the motivations to put out their report). But all this referred to the situation of Dalit groups in India. Anti-caste activism focused on caste discrimination taking place in the United States began primarily after the formation of Equality Labs in 2015. I have shown that groups like SAALT and Hindus for Human Rights (HfHR) supported anti-caste activism (focused on the United States and India) and allied with Ambedkarite groups. The Indian American Muslim Council (IAMC) also joined coalitions with Dalit groups around anti-caste concerns, and a variety of South Asian groups, including Ambedkarites, formed South Asian Histories for All (SAHFA) to mobilize around the California textbook issue in 2016. On the other hand, recall that USINPAC did not take up the cause of the 500 largely Dalit Indian workers at Signal in 2007 who were held as bonded laborers in Louisiana, while SAALT rallied around their case. USINPAC has not mentioned the issue of caste at all, while the Hindu American Foundation is strongly opposed to discussions of caste discrimination and any attempt to provide protections for caste status in the United States.

The issue of how caste might influence U.S. partisan activism is less evident since this is not an issue that Dalit American groups mobilize around, as far as I know. Some Dalit activists in Silicon Valley told me that questions about which politicians and parties they supported were some of the ways that other Indian Americans tried to ferret out their caste background. But this was in reference to politicians and political parties in India, specifically

Mayawati, a high-profile Dalit leader of the *Bahujan Samaj Party*, a party representing oppressed-caste groups. Caste issues did not come up in any of the interviews around U.S. partisan activism that I conducted or in the secondary analysis I undertook. This is perhaps because Dalits are a small group in the United States and because most members are recent immigrants, which may mean that many are not citizens (recall that it can take decades for Indians to obtain citizenship in the United States due to country quotas, and that groups like Immigration Voice have been mobilizing around this issue). Again, the nonprofit status of organizations such as Equality Labs and other Ambedkarite groups would prevent them from being able to get involved in political activism.

How successful is the anti-caste movement launched from the United States, targeting both India and the West, likely to be? The Indian caste system is too entrenched and too large, with too many vested interests to change easily. Fear of repercussions and lack of resources limits the ability of Indian Dalit organizations to be active on the international stage. However, transnational social movements have helped to transform oppressive social systems in countries around the world (Keck and Sikkink 1998; Tsutsui 2018). While casteism goes along with Indian immigrants, living in the West and having protections provided by the wider society where caste is not a source of stigma, in addition to support of international human rights organizations, can be a big asset for Dalit mobilization. Again, second and later generations from privileged-caste backgrounds may not be vested in the caste system to the same extent as immigrants and could become important allies in anti-caste mobilization. In fact, Ambedkarite activists probably have the best chance to successfully mobilize support to address caste discrimination in India from the diaspora. Ambedkarite activists in a variety of other countries have also been mobilizing around the anti-caste movement (Waughray 2009). A multi-institutional, multicountry strategy to educate and gain a range of allies is likely to be the most effective, long term. Dalits in the diaspora, organizing around a variety of organizations, targeting a range of audiences and institutions (governments, international human rights leaders, policymakers, academics, students, powerful international audiences, and progressive members of the Indian diaspora), with the help of international pressure and India-based organizations may be able to bring about a change in the Indian caste system and ameliorate the situation of Dalits in India and the diaspora. Though the California bill was vetoed by Governor Newsom, anti-caste activists are continuing their efforts to publicize the abominations of the caste system and to have caste discrimination recognized as a civil rights violation. While the caste system is unique, so too is the U.S. racial and ethnic system. American immigrants come from countries that have other types of stratification systems that can interact in complex ways with the American racial-ethnic pentagon (Joseph 2015; Roth 2012). Since such interaction can impact immigrant communities, origin countries, and even the wider American society, as in the Cisco case and the efforts to get caste as a protected category in the United States, we need a better appreciation of how this works.

Political Opportunity Structures and Group Characteristics

Recall that according to the literature, the political incorporation of immigrant groups is shaped by political opportunity structures (mostly those in the receiving country) as well as the characteristics and resources of groups. By emphasizing the importance of race and religion as social location instead of as just the characteristic of individual groups, I argue that the social location of a group within national (and global) structures is more important in shaping group experience than group characteristics, and that race and religion interact in shaping this structural location. This emerged clearly through my research as I saw how religious majority and minority status in the United States and India led to very similar patterns of mobilization around U.S.-based and India-based issues, with Hindus, Muslims, Sikhs, and to some extent Ambedkarite Buddhists mobilizing in very similar ways around domestic concerns about recognition and rights, and Christians, Muslims, Sikhs, and Ambedkarites getting active around the rise of Hindutva in India and attacks against minorities in almost identical ways. These similarities in patterns of activism existed even though the characteristics of these groups, their religions, and their religious institutions were very different from each other. While Hindus analogized the situation of Hindus in India and Jews in Israel (in both case the dominant group in the country), Sikhs and Muslims often drew parallels between their situation in India and those of Black and Latino groups in the United States, while Ambedkarite advocates pointed to the similarities between Black Americans under American slavery and Jim Crow and the experiences of Dalits in India (see Chapter 5).

In the early days (e.g., in 2007 when I was doing research on the Hill), the Sikh Coalition and Hindu American Foundation would sometimes collaborate on common domestic issues such as visas for religious workers in temples and gurdwaras, but I gathered that this collaboration had stopped due to tensions arising from the HAF's support for Hindu nationalism. Consequently, Sikh and Hindu groups mobilized separately around similar domestic issues. However, there was a lot of collaboration between Muslim, progressive Hindu, and Ambedkarite groups around anti-Hindutva mobilization, with Hindus for Human Rights, Equality Labs, and the Indian American Muslim Council taking leadership roles in these coalitional efforts. Sikh organizations joined in on the issue of anti-caste mobilization. Though Sikh organizations had not been part of the many congressional briefings around Hindutva and violence against minorities organized by the IAMC and HfHR, with Trudeau's September 2023 allegation about India being behind the murder of a Sikh Canadian, Sikh American organizations jumped into action asking for an inquiry and for protection for Sikh Americans painted by the Indian government as "extremists" or "terrorists." After making this argument, the Sikh Coalition went on to argue, "We believe that rising Hindutva, or hateful Hindu nationalism, in the United States is furthering such perceptions of Sikhs" (email message, September 21, 2023). Perhaps Sikh organizations will join in anti-Hindutva mobilizations in the future.

To summarize, this study makes amply clear that it is problematic to assume that individuals from the same homeland have common political interests and will mobilize under a nation-state organization to achieve those interests. Clearly, the structural location of majority or minority groups has a strong effect on patterns of mobilization in Western societies since they usually have very different histories, political interests, and social concerns. With the resurgence of religion in many parts of the world, religious cleavages have again come to the fore. As a result, majority and minority religious groups often have fundamentally different interests and agendas. This issue needs to be further studied.

Mobilization around Foreign versus Domestic Policy

Research on immigrant political mobilization usually focuses on activism either around homeland issues or around rights in their home countries. This book examines both aspects and shows the importance of understanding links as well as disjunctures between the two types of mobilizations. Turning to activism around foreign policy concerns, which I have called attempts to demonstrate "transnational citizenship," one big question is why immigrants who are naturalized U.S. citizens and who do not plan to return to their home countries are motivated to organize and mobilize around origin-country concerns. General factors such as attachment to home countries and the guilt that particularly Global South immigrants feel at making good in the West after emigrating from their home communities notwithstanding, scholars have noted specifically U.S.-centric reasons for this activism. First, some argue that the identity politics of multiculturalism "ties U.S. identity to international politics and transnational movements," since it supports the mobilization of ethnic groups around U.S. foreign affairs as a means to obtain the public American ethnic identity encouraged by multiculturalism (Shain 1999, xiv; see also B. Anderson 1998, 74; Appadurai 1996, 166). The literature on ethnic politics also notes that the central role the United States takes on the global stage has been another factor encouraging diasporic groups to mobilize in support of homeland interests and U.S. foreign policy (T. Smith 2000, 64). Again, the financial power of the U.S. diaspora is usually much greater than groups in the Global South, or even other Global North diasporas. For these reasons, politicians from Global South countries curry the support of their U.S. diasporas and try to recruit them to act as unofficial ambassadors or advocates for their country of origin. We have seen that all these factors have motivated Indian Americans to mobilize around India-centric issues. The rise of India as an economic and global power since the 1990s and its geopolitical location between Pakistan and China has also increased the significance of the country in the eyes of the U.S. administration. This is a position the diaspora is interested in harnessing. Finally, major international human rights organizations (such as the United Nations, Amnesty International, Human Rights Watch) are based in the United States. Activists mobilizing around human rights abuses in the origin country recognize the importance of having easy access to these institutions and their leaders. Recall that the activist from the International Commission on Dalit Rights pointed out to me that this was the reason he relocated the organization from London to Washington, DC.

While, as we have seen, immigrants are much more likely than the second generation to mobilize around foreign policy issues, this is not always so clear-cut. Second-generation activists on the Hill came to realize that the perception of India affected how they and the Indian American community were regarded and that they therefore needed to care about and sometimes mobilize around major India-based issues. Similarly, USINPAC's Sanjay Puri pointed out that U.S. politicians have begun to recognize that India-based concerns are not "foreign policy" issues but are concerns of their domestic constituents and, consequently, something that they had to educate themselves about and act on. We have seen that the Hindu American Foundation, although led by the second generation, has been mobilizing to support and advocate for the BJP-led government in India and its policies. Similarly, it is second-generation Sikhs who have worked to bring the lack of justice for 1984 and post-1984 Sikh victims in India to the attention of the world and human rights organizations. Second-generation Kashmiri Muslims took the lead to form organizations around the takeover of the Jammu and Kashmir state in 2019 by the Indian government. Even second-generation groups like SAALT, the Sikh Coalition, and SALDEF that focus on domestic policy have occasionally mobilized around India-based human rights issues. Although the second-generation-led political action group Indian American IMPACT focused on issues in the United States, they came out in strong support of India-born Dr. Ashish Jha, then a dean at Brown University's School of Public Health, when he spoke about the need for the United States to have a global COVID strategy and response, including helping India by sending vaccines as well as the raw materials to make vaccines.[2] Explaining this to me, an American-born leader of IMPACT argued that in many situations, such as the case of the pandemic, the global perspective of Indian Americans

> can really shed light on the best way forward.... Because I think there are other folks in the U.S. who are not of a diaspora, who don't understand what's happening in the world, are not in tune with it.... When you think about issues like climate and others, we really need people with our perspectives to understand the urgency of the United States, both for its own sake and for the world, to take on these issues. And it is a problem that other leaders who are not Indian Americans are not thinking about these global problems in a global way.

In other words, he was arguing that the immigrant-dominated nature of Indian Americans was an advantage and that even the second generation had a relatively global outlook. Consequently, we see that a transnational orientation is not something that ends with the immigrant generation, as much of the literature implies (Alba and Nee 2003; Kasinitz et al. 2008). It can continue into later generations of the diaspora. We have also seen that for many first-generation Indian Americans, mobilizing around U.S. partisan politics is a way to impact their lives in the United States *and* to be a steward for India's interests, showing that activism around domestic and foreign policy issues does not have to be an either/or matter. In fact, India-based issues were of such importance to many Indian Americans that despite the attempts of South Asian American Democratic groups formed around the 2020 elections to argue that it was U.S. issues that impacted everyday lives and that should be the focus while voting for U.S. candidates, foreign policy concerns kept turning up, often derailing the work of these Democratic organizations.

While domestic policy issues are seen as being the concern of second- and later-generation leaders of ethnic organizations, we have seen how early Indian immigrants mobilized around citizenship in the early decades of the twentieth century, and how post-1965 immigrants rallied around work and educational discrimination. More recently, it is religious advocacy organizations (mostly led by the second generation) that have been active around the right to maintain religious and cultural difference while being fully accepted and integrated in the United States: what is called "cultural citizenship." Chapter 4 demonstrated that a variety of U.S. minority religious advocacy organizations had similar patterns of mobilization around recognition and rights. But Chapter 3 also showed that sometimes organizations representing new immigrants might have opposed interests and different forms of mobilization around U.S.-based concerns. One example is the fractured activism in 2007 around the Immigration Reform Bill (which in the end was not passed). USINPAC lobbied for an increase in the H-1B quota for temporary high-skilled workers and for family-based immigration; SAALT for the maintenance of family reunification provisions and for the legalization of undocumented immigrants; Immigration Voice for the elimination of green card delays and country caps on green cards; the Asian American Hotel Owners Association (AAHOA) for increased labor immigration and against stipulations in the proposed bill that would have made employee verification provisions more cumbersome; and the Hindu American Foundation against the new restrictions on R-1 (religious workers), which would have made it more difficult for Hindu priests to enter the country.

Generational Differences in Political Activism

I have focused on generational differences in activism patterns (particularly in Chapters 3 and 6) and mentioned that the reasons the two generations got involved in activism were substantially different, as were their pathways to activism, strategies, and goals. Most of the mobilization discussed in Chapter 4 around cultural citizenship and the recognition of minority religions in the United States was led by the second generation. Conversations with a variety of second-generation activists (supporting Indian, South Asian, and religious advocacy) made clear that they wanted the American-born generation to be the face of community advocacy efforts. They argued that unlike the "uncles," they were savvy about how the U.S. system worked (as mentioned, most were U.S. trained in law or public policy). While this was not expressed directly, it was clear that they also knew they had the "right" accents and mannerisms (many mentioned wincing at the behavior and the speeches of the "uncles" on various occasions). In a December 2007 interview, "Amit," a second-generation activist in Washington, DC, gave me a brief run-through of the recent history of Indian American activism, specifically the movement from regional to national activism and the rise of second-generation activists. Speaking about his generation, he commented:

> There is more sophistication to our approach now. We are teaching a generation above us who feel that if they donate to politicians they can score for our community. But we are showing that we are more powerful if we organize. Now we are asking tough questions to candidates. We are beyond the point of just raising money. What is also important about the second generation is that we are interfacing with the leadership of larger American groups.

I asked him what he saw as the role of the first generation, and he limited it to providing funds to second-generation activists and specific advice on issues related to their expertise. He said older second-generation members immersed in the world of professional politics outside the Indian American community would furnish input on how to package a political message and how other communities were raising their profile, while the younger segment would supply the energy, time, and passion for activism. Amit added, "When the three legs of the stool come together, it is a beautiful moment." I asked him for examples when this had happened and he mentioned the macaca activism discussed in Chapter 6, as well as the Smithsonian exhibition to showcase Indian American contributions to the United States (https://smithsonianapa.org/beyondbollywood/) that he was involved with at the time (after years of work and planning, the exhibition ran from February 2014 to August 2015). There were also gendered differences in generational patterns of activism, with the activism of the immigrant generation being led almost exclusively by men, while women were much more involved as leaders among the American-born generation. In Chapter 3, I explained the reasons for these gendered differences as primarily an outcome of migration patterns, gendered cultural norms from India, and different generational pathways to activism.

While immigrants may not be aware of how their activism was critiqued by the second generation, most praised the involvement of the younger group and encouraged them to get involved. In the case of Muslim South Asian American groups, I learned that there was an intentional strategy to push forward the American-born generation as the face of Muslim American organizations after the attacks of September 11, 2001. In other cases, such as the formation of the Sikh Coalition in the aftermath of 9/11, the second generation took the initiative to organize and take over. This was also the case with the Kashmir situation in 2019 and after. One of the big differences between the generations was in the use of social media and which platforms the two generations used, with the older generation being more comfortable on Facebook, YouTube, WhatsApp, and Twitter, while the second generation used Instagram, TikTok, Snapchat, and other similar platforms.

The Role of Social Media in Activism

In an earlier project, I tracked Hindu American discussions and mobilization on Internet-based groups formed in the early 2000s and the relationship between their online and offline activism (Kurien 2007a). I also learned from an immigrant activist of the Vishwa Hindu Parishad of America (VHPA), who was mentoring and monitoring the Hindu Student Council organization that I was studying, that one of the activities of the VHPA was to develop websites, and that they had built 2,600 websites by the early 2000s (Kurien 2007a, 152). The U.S.-India Friendship Net formed in 1999 by Ram Narayan, an immigrant, was an early example of Internet-based activism around Indian American policy concerns (primarily India-centric ones). Narayanan maintained a website, which was updated regularly, and sent out email alerts to Indian Americans and their supporters (numbering over 15,000 individuals at the height of its work) regarding new developments. This was one of the platforms through which the mobilization around the U.S.-India nuclear deal took place. By the time I started research on this project in 2007, the Internet landscape had changed from websites, Internet discussion groups, and emails, with early forms of social media emerging in 2006, which the second generation used in their macaca mobilization. Subsequently, all Indian American groups and generations have used social media in their activism, though, as mentioned, the patterns of usage varied by generation. The use of social media greatly sped up communication and outreach and helped to amplify messages since messages were often forwarded by those who received them.

Udupa (2015) made the case that control over social media, in particular Twitter, had become a strategy of Hindu nationalist "tweeple" (people who tweet) in urban India (also see Shih 2023 on the role of WhatsApp as a medium for Hindutva). She showed that they did this by "putting the algorithmic rationale of the microblogging site to optimal use," exploiting "trending hashtags and trolling handles" (Udupa 2015, 445). Social media also makes it easier to fuse transnational mobilization like that around Hindutva. The U.S. diaspora has been very active on the Hindu Right Twittersphere, and quite often it is also U.S. events or the activities of individuals and groups in the United States that are the subject of the tweets emerging out of India-based BJP cells. While larger, more organized groups like the Hindu right wing have an advantage mobilizing social media around transnational concerns, even smaller groups are able to use social media to their benefit. On the international level, Ambedkarite organizations in the West have been successful in raising awareness about caste discrimination and caste violence in India and the ways in which caste discrimination works in Western societies. Ambedkarite organizations mobilized around the Cisco case and to get caste designated as a protected category in the United States. Although this was a small, largely invisible group (many members maintained their anonymity for fear of retaliation in their IT jobs), they were still successful in getting many colleges and universities, including California State University, the largest public university system in the United States, to sign on to making caste a protected category on campus. In the wake of the Cisco case, many Silicon Valley companies (with the exception of Google) organized presentations on caste so workers and managers could learn about caste discrimination and bias and how it might manifest. As mentioned, anti-caste activists were able to get the cities of Seattle and Fresno to make caste a protected category and to get the overwhelming support of the California state legislature by mobilizing wider support through their social media activism, in addition to other in-person efforts. With social media, smaller, scattered groups can coalesce into a powerful organized force that has an impact. Consequently, we may need to rethink some of the normative models of successful political organization and influence by ethnic groups.

Unified versus Diversified Ethnic Mobilization

The ethnicization model of having one major organization to represent an ethnic group homogenizes ethnic groups and their political interests. Perhaps it is also somewhat of a myth. Even though organizations like AIPAC are visible and powerful, they are supported by and linked to many others. Raj Goyle, an Indian American Democrat from Kansas and former member of the state assembly, commented on this in a 2018 media interview. Raj Goyle was one of the early second-generation Indian American politicians and one of the founders of Indian American IMPACT, discussed above and in Chapter 6. In a 2018 discussion with long-time *India Abroad* journalist Aziz Haniffa about his motivation to be a cofounder of IMPACT, Goyle mused about the Indian American obsession with the Jewish American model. Referring specifically to the variety of Indian American organizations that had mobilized around the 2020 elections, he had this to say:

> Other communities have multiple overlap organizations and many people in the Indian-American community always talk about the Jewish-American diaspora, and if you look at the Jewish-American diaspora, they have dozens of organizations that all handle some part of political engagement.... That's been a big lesson for me... a lot of people used to think that there needed to be one umbrella organization, but in reality, there needs to be multiple strong organizations that collaborate and partner. In order to build political power, our community needs *an ecosystem of organizations*, each of which can tackle a different challenge. (Haniffa 2018, 16, my italics)

In other words, Raj Goyle is arguing that having a variety of organizations, each with different strengths and catering to a different issue niche and constituency, is an asset and not a liability. However, he does indicate, as does the literature on ethnic interest groups (Brettell and Reed-Danahay 2008), that the organizations should "collaborate and partner." We see this happening in the case of the multiple Sikh American advocacy organizations, as well as many of the organizations of Indian religious minorities (particularly Muslims, Sikhs, Ambedkarites, and Hindus for Human Rights), and Indian American and Hindu American organizations such as USINPAC and the Hindu American Foundation. But we have also seen that there are points of friction and conflict between some of the organizations (e.g., between the HAF and some of the organizations of Muslims, Sikhs, and Ambedkarites; between the HAF and Hindus for Human Rights; between South Asian and Indian American organizations).

While Indian Americans might be exceptionally diverse and, in that sense, not "representative" (but see Small [2009] for a critique of that logic of case selection), other ethnic groups also have internal schisms, whether based on religion, sect, region, class, race, generation, or other differences that have not been adequately discussed or understood. The ethnicization model hides these internal cleavages and homogeneity may often be achieved at the cost of silencing minority voices. The diversity of Indian Americans contributes to theory building by helping us to understand the limits of paradigms of ethnic group mobilization, namely, that they were focusing on homogenous groups, or groups that were *made* homogenous by not recognizing internal diversity. At this juncture, the organization that claims to represent Indian Americans, modeled after AIPAC (USINPAC), is barely active, and the organization that successfully represented South Asian Americans at the national level for over 20 years (SAALT) has gone into hiatus to deal with casteism and to forge a more inclusionary leadership model. In its place, new groups such as Equality Labs, the Indian American Muslim Council, and Hindus for Human Rights have come to the fore, successfully fashioning coalitions on an anti-Hindutva and anti-caste platform. Yet, this is also a moment when Indian Americans have become extraordinarily visible on the national political stage, with two Indian Americans running, ultimately unsuccessfully, for president on the Republican side and Kamala Harris on the Democratic side who is likely to play an important role as Biden runs again for re-election. This seems to portend the need for a rethink of the classic model of political influence.

Indian Americans in the contemporary period have the advantage of having a variety of models of ethnic and racial mobilization before them, and many leaders also recognize that they do not have to settle for picking just one. "Amit," the second-generation activist mentioned above, remarked that Indian Americans had tried to telescope two different models of activism together. After telling me that the second generation had adopted elements from the "communities of color model" in addition to the dominant Jewish model embraced by the immigrant generation, he concluded by saying that as a community, "our model and identity is somewhat confused since we adopt the Jewish model and the labor movements model." But he too suggested that it was an advantage to combine different models since the Indian American community comprised different subgroups with different needs.

Does Diaspora Activism Portend an Inclusionary or Exclusionary Future?

Some scholars maintain that diaspora activism leads to the expansion of democracy and inclusion in origin as well as receiving countries. For instance, through their work on diaspora activism around authoritarian homeland regimes, Dana Moss (2022) and Alexander Betts and Will Jones (2016) argue that diasporas can contribute to the process of democratization of their homelands by taking advantage of their position outside the authoritarian home country and the resources offered by the host country to challenge repressive regimes and diffuse liberal, democratic norms. In a similar vein, scholars like Nicholls (2019) and Garbaye (2005) show how diasporic mobilization around cultural citizenship and rights deepens democracy in receiving societies through bringing a new, diverse group of citizens into the public sphere. Writing specifically about new religions, Robert Wuthnow (2021) is optimistic that the diversity of religions is a positive development for American society, and that the emergence of a variety of religious groups in the U.S. public sphere "is good for American democracy" because he believes that the advocacy and counteradvocacy of religious groups deepens civic engagement and pluralism. Likewise, Robert Jones and Eboo Patel (2022) argue that non-Protestant European immigrants extricated America from White Protestant nationalism, making it a "Judeo-Christian" country, and that contemporary non-White and non-Christian immigrants will similarly help America rise above the xenophobia of present-day White Christian nationalism to create a truly inclusive country.

However, there are others who view diasporic political activism with concern. For instance, Benedict Anderson (1998) argues that the "long-distance nationalism" of diasporic groups (focusing especially on diaspora groups in the United States) supports reactionary, anti-democratic forces and is irresponsible because it is unaccountable. Similarly, Fiona Adamson (2020) also has a negative view of diasporic activism around origin-country affairs, contending that diasporas often work as unofficial agents of home countries to promote authoritarian policies and to surveil, police, and intimidate members of the community living overseas. Mobilization around cultural citizenship is also viewed negatively by those who favor an assimilationist approach. Such scholars believe that demands by immigrant groups for the right to maintain "traditional" languages, as well as cultural and religious practices, in receiving societies can prevent immigrant integration and undermine the cultural unity of host countries. As an example, Samuel Huntington (2004) was afraid that Latino groups would adversely impact the Anglo-Protestant culture, values, and way of life of the United States. A recent survey study showed that a significant proportion of Americans, around 30 to 33 percent, felt that immigrants should not have the right to contact the media, protest, contact officials, or sign petitions, and that half or more of those surveyed felt that immigrants, particularly those who were undocumented, should be banned from engaging in any form of nonviolent protest. In other words, a large proportion of Americans want immigrants to remain socially and politically "invisible," that is, not civically or politically engaged (Langevin, Guardino, and Pugh 2022). This certainly indicates that some Americans have a negative view of new ethnic group assertion.

Based on this study of the varieties of Indian American political activism, we see that there is evidence to support both perspectives. Most political activism has been around rights and to obtain validation that they are recognized as positively contributing American groups. Part of this activism includes highlighting ways in which their values and cultures fit American society. In this sense, they are certainly integrating and even assimilating into the United States. At the same time, in some instances, Indian American activism has led to opposing mobilizations around issues and led to a barrage of scurrilous public attacks against opponents in public fora and on social media. This has resulted in American officials and policymakers feeling bewildered and unsure about what to make of the allegations and sometimes being in the position of having to adjudicate competing claims (e.g., around school textbook content and caste discrimination protection, as well as the

2019 Indian citizenship act). But this experience could also lead them to educate themselves on the issues, resulting in greater awareness and understanding of the concerns of new American groups. In short, the mobilization of immigrant groups in the Western public sphere can increase democratic participation by a more diverse group of citizens and can challenge ethnic and religious majoritarianism within Western countries, diasporic spheres, and in home countries. On the negative side, the opposing mobilizations of majority and minority diasporic groups can deepen cleavages within ethnic groups and further the fragmentation of domestic and foreign policy processes (Huntington 1997; T. Smith 2000).

The transnational identities and mobilization patterns of contemporary immigrants, particularly of religious groups, call into question conventional understandings of nationhood and citizenship and create challenges for Western societies trying to manage diversity. These challenges have led many European countries to re-evaluate, and in some cases turn away from, earlier multicultural policies as they struggle to politically integrate their new ethnic and religious groups (Vertovec and Wessendorf 2010). Contemporary U.S. immigrants confront a variety of political opportunities leading to a breadth of activism, and immigrant diasporic politics will have a decisive impact in shaping the political contours of the United States in the twenty-first century. Indian Americans are a rising political force in this country and a group where there are deep cleavages based on religious identity. This study of their mobilization patterns shows how religious status in the homeland plays a powerful role in shaping their patterns of activism around foreign policy issues in the United States. It also provides a framework to understand how globalization, multiculturalism, and new forms of technology shape the goals and methods of contemporary ethnic advocacy organizations.

Notes

1. On the other hand, in 2015, Bobby Jindal, then governor of Louisiana, was criticized for a noticeably lighter-skinned official portrait (Linshi 2015), to which he responded with a joke, "You mean I am not White?" and a critique of the obsession with skin color of the Left (Worland 2015).
2. In March 2022, Dr. Jha was appointed as the White House coronavirus response coordinator.

APPENDIX

Indian American Advocacy Organizations Studied (At Least One Person Interviewed)

Indian American Umbrella Organizations

- Association of Indians in America (AIA, formed in 1967 *around racial placement of Indians in 1980 U.S. census*)
- Federation of Indian Associations (FIA, 1976, *regional federation of Indian associations*)
- National Federation of Indian American Associations (NFIA, 1980, *national federation of regional FIA organizations*)
- Global Organization of Persons of Indian Origin (GOPIO, 1989, *to address problems faced by Indian diaspora in various countries*)

Political Education Organizations

- Indian American Forum for Political Education (IAFPE, 1982, *to promote political awareness and engagement among Indian Americans*)
- Bridging Nations (2002, *to promote dialogue between the United States, India, and China*)

Indian American Lobby Group

- United States India Political Action Committee (USINPAC, 2002, *to be the voice of Indian Americans on Capitol Hill*)

Organizations Mobilizing around U.S.-India Civilian Nuclear Deal

- U.S. India Friendship Council (2006, *a coalition of eight organizations, and later, seven, as one organization dropped out*)
- Indian American Security Leadership Council (IASLC, 2006, *to mobilize veterans' groups in support of the civilian nuclear deal*)

Trade Groups

- American Association of Physicians of Indian Origin (AAPI, 1984)
- Asian American Hotel Owners Association (AAHOA, 1985, 1989, 1994, *an organization dominated by Indian Americans, mostly from Gujarat state*)
- The Indus Entrepreneurs (TiE, 1992, *largely a software industry group of Indians and Pakistanis*)
- Immigration Voice (IV, 2006, *to mobilize around issues regarding visa backlogs and green card delays for high-skilled immigrants*)

South Asian Groups

- South Asian Americans Leading Together (SAALT, 2000, formerly South Asian Leaders of Tomorrow, *national South Asian American organization*)
- Friends of South Asia (FOSA, 2002, *based in Silicon Valley*)

Coalitional South Asian Groups Mobilizing against Hindu Nationalism

- Coalition against Genocide (2005 *to mobilize against Modi US visa and later against Hindutva attacks on Indian minorities*)
- Alliance for Justice and Accountability (2014 *formed after BJP was elected in India on an anti-Hindutva platform*)
- South Asian Histories for All (SAHFA, (2016, *around textbook changes in California*)

Hindu

- Hindu American Foundation (2003, *major national-level organization to represent Hindu interests*)
- Sadhana: Coalition of Progressive Hindus (2011, *a grassroots organization to present a progressive Hindu voice*)
- Hindus for Human Rights (HfHR, 2019, *to mobilize against Hindutva and for human rights for all groups*)

Sikh

- Sikh Council of North America (1979, *to combat discrimination against Sikhs*)
- Sikh American Legal Defense and Education Fund (SALDEF, 2004, *initially formed in 1996 as Sikh Media Watch and Resource Task Force [SMART]*)
- Sikh Coalition (2001, *after 9/11 to work for Sikh American rights and recognition*)
- United Sikhs (1999, *to help underprivileged in New York City, since 2001 focus on international issues of concern to Sikh diaspora and to help during global humanitarian crises*)

- Sikhs for Justice (2009, *for Khalistan and for Sikh rights in India*)
- Ensaaf (2004, *around justice for state-sponsored killings of Sikhs in Punjab*)
- The Surat Initiative (*educating young Sikhs on Sikh philosophy and tenets*)

Muslim

- Association of Indian Muslims of America (1985 *initially to work to uplift Muslims in India, later to oppose Hindutva and to promote secularism and communal harmony in India*)
- American Federation of Muslims from India (AFMI, 1989, *works through MPAC and CAIR to politically mobilize American Muslims*)
- Indian American Muslim Council (IAMC, 2002, *after anti-Muslim riots in Gujarat*)
- Muslim Public Affairs Council (1988 *around issues facing American Muslims*)
- Muslim Advocates (2005 *around legal action to challenge the Patriot Act as well as religious profiling*)

Christian

- Federation of Indian American Christians of North America (FIACONA, 2000, *before Prime Minister Vajpayee's visit to the United States, around attacks against Christians in India*)

Dalit

- Volunteers in the Service of India's Oppressed and Neglected (VISION, 1970s *around attacks against Dalits in India and Dalit rights*)
- Dr. Ambedkar International Mission (AIM, 2003 *to create a cultural identity for Ambedkarite Buddhists*)
- Ambedkar Association of North America (AANA, 2008, *around an Ambedkarite identity*)
- Equality Labs (2015 *an Ambedkarite organization formed by Dalit feminists to mobilize on an anti-caste platform and around other axes of oppression*)
- Dalit Freedom Network (early 2000, *became Dignity Freedom Network from 2019 focused on educating Dalit children in India*)
- Dalit Solidarity Forum (1999, *Christian-led organization that re-emerged in the public sphere in 2020 around Hindutva violence*)
- Boston Study Group
- Ambedkar-King Study Circle
- International Commission for Dalit Rights (ICDR, 2006, 2008)
- Periyar-Ambedkar organizations
- Ravidassia organizations

Kashmiri Organizations

- Kashmiri American Council (KAC, 1990, *to represent interests of Kashmiri Muslims*)
- Indo-American Kashmir Forum (IAKF, 1991, *to represent interests of Kashmiri Hindu Pandits*)
- Stand with Kashmir (2019, *to represent interests of Kashmiri Muslims*)

Organizations Mobilizing around Partisan Politics

- Indian American Republican Council (IARC, 2002)
- South Asians for Kerry (SAKI, 2004)
- Indian American Leadership Initiative (IALI, 2000, 2005)
- South Asians for Obama (SAFO, 2007)
- National Dance for Obama (2012)
- Indians for McCain (2008)
- Indian Americans for Trump (2016)
- South Asians for Biden (2020, *became South Asians for America in 2021*)
- Indian Americans for Biden (2020)
- They See Blue (TSB, 2018, 2020)
- Indian American Impact (Impact, 2018)

Organizations Studied through Secondary Research

- Indian League of America (ILA, 1973 *a pan-Indian organization based in Chicago*)

Political Education Organizations

- U.S.-India Friendship Net (1999, Ram Narayan, *this one-person organization maintained a website and sent out email alerts to Indian Americans and their supporters [over 15,000 individuals] regarding policy issues and developments*)
- Indian American Center for Political Awareness (IACPA, 1994)
- Indian American Friendship Council (IAFC, 1990 *in California, in 1996 began national activities*)

Hindu

- Vishwa Hindu Parishad of America (VHPA, 1970)
- Overseas Friends of the Bharatiya Janata Party (OFBJP)
- Hindu Swayamsevak Sangh (HSS, 1977, *overseas branch of the Rashtriya Swayamsevak Sangh*)
- Infinity Foundation (1995)
- American Hindus against Defamation (AHAD, 1997)
- Hindu International Council against Defamation (HICAD)
- Republican Hindu Coalition (2016)

Muslim

- Consultative Committee of Indian Muslims (1967)
- Indian Muslims Relief Committee (IMRC, 1980s)
- Council on Islamic Education (1990)

Sikh

- The Sikh Foundation (1967)

Kashmiri Groups

- Kashmir Study Group (KSG)
- The International Kashmir Federation (IKF)
- Americans for Kashmir (2019)

Organizations Mobilizing around Partisan Politics

- Indo-American Leadership Council of the Democratic Party (IALC, 2004)
- Republican Hindu Coalition (2016, *supporting Trump*)
- Americans4Hindus (2020, *supporting Republicans*)

References

Abramowitz, Alan, and Saunders, Kyle. 2005. "Why Can't We All Just Get Along? The Reality of a Polarized America." *The Forum* 3(2): 1–22.

Adams, Eric J. 1986. "Indian Immigrants: Educated, Affluent, and Apathetic." *India West*, July 11, p. 22.

Adamson, Fiona. 2020. "Non-state Authoritarianism and Diaspora Politics." *Global Networks* 20 (1): 150–169.

Afzal, Omar. 1991. "An Overview of Asian-Indian Muslims in the United States." Pp. 1–16 in *Indian Muslims in North America*, edited by O. Khalidi. Watertown, MA: South Asia Press.

Agarwala, Rina. 2015. "Tapping the Indian Diaspora for Indian Development." Pp. 84–110 in *The State and the Grassroots: Immigrant Transnational Organizations in Four Continents*, edited by Alejandro Portes and Patricia Fernandez-Kelly. New York: Berghahn Press.

Agarwala, Rina. 2016. "Divine Development: Transnational Religious Organizations in the US and India." *International Migration Review* 50(4): 910–950.

Agarwala, Rina. 2022. *The Migration-Development Regime: How Class Shapes Indian Emigration*. New York: Oxford University Press.

Ahrari, Mohammed E. 1991. "Indian Muslims as an American Ethnic Group: The Need for an Action Plan." Pp. 27–33 in *Indian Muslims in North America*, edited by Omar Khalidi. Watertown, MA: South Asia Press.

Ahuja, Ravi. 2008. "Networks of Subordination—Networks of the Subordinated: The Ordered Spaces of South Asian Maritime Labour in an Age of Imperialism (c. 1890–1947)." Pp. 13–48 in *Spaces of Disorder: The Limits of British Colonial Control in South Asia and the Indian Ocean Region*, edited by Ashwini Tambe and Harald Fischer-Tiné. New York: Routledge.

Alba, Richard, and Victor Nee. 2003. *Remaking the American Mainstream*. Boston: Harvard University Press.

Alba, Richard, Albert J. Raboteau, and Josh DeWind. 2009. *Immigration and Religion in America: Comparative and Historical Perspectives*. New York: New York University Press.

Alonso, Adoni, and Pedro Oiarzabal. 2010. *Diasporas in the New Media Age: Identity, Politics, and Community*. Reno: University of Nevada Press.

Alvarez, R. Michael, and Lisa García Bedolla. 2003. "The Foundations of Latino Voter Partisanship: Evidence from the 2000 Election." *Journal of Politics* 65(1): 31–49.

Ambedkar, Bhimrao Ramji. (1948) 2018. *The Untouchables, Who Were They and Why They Became Untouchables*. Chennai: Maven Books.

Ambrosio, Thomas, ed. 2002. *Ethnic Identity Groups and U.S. Foreign Policy*. Westport, CT: Praeger.

Ameri-Asia News. 1987. "Reagan Nominates Cherian to Equal Employment Opportunity Commission. First Asian Named for Sub-Cabinet Post." May–June, pp. 1–2.

Andersen, Kristi. 1979. *The Creation of a Democratic Minority, 1928–1936*. Chicago: University of Chicago Press.

Andersen, Walter. 2006. "The Indian-American Community Comes into its Political Own." *India Abroad*, September 1, pp. A12–A13.

Anderson, Benedict. 1998. "Long Distance Nationalism." Pp. 58–76 in *The Spectre of Comparisons: Nationalism, Southeast Asia and the World*. London: Verso.

Anderson, Stuart. 2011. "Waiting and More Waiting: America's Family and Employment-Based Immigration System." National Foundation for American Policy. http://www.nfap.com/pdf/WAITING_NFAP_Policy_Brief_October_2011.pdf.

Anisurrahman, Ahmad. 1991. "An American Lobby for Muslims in India: Essentials for a Required Instrument." Pp. 34–43 in *Indian Muslims in North America*, edited by Omar Khalidi. Watertown, MA: South Asia Press.

Appadurai, Arjun. 1996. *Modernity at Large: Cultural Dimensions of Globalization*. Minneapolis: University of Minnesota Press.

Aptekar, Sofya. 2008. "Highly Skilled but Unwelcome in Politics: Asian Indians and Chinese in a New Jersey Suburb." Pp. 222–243 in *Civic Hopes and Political Realities: Immigrants, Community Organizations, and Political Engagement*, edited by S. Karthick Ramakrishnan and Irene Bloemraad. New York: Russell Sage Foundation.

Arms Control Association. 2006. "The Senate and the U.S.-Indian Nuclear Deal: Issues and Alternatives." https://www.armscontrol.org/documents-reports/2006-11/senate-us-indian-nuclear-deal-issues-alternatives.

Badrinathan, Sumitra, Devesh Kapur, Jonathan Kay, and Milan Vaishnav. 2021. *Social Realities of Indian Americans: Results from the 2020 Indian American Attitudes Survey*. New York: Carnegie Endowment for International Peace.

Badrinathan, Sumitra, Devesh Kapur, and Milan Vaishnav. 2020. *How Will Indian Americas Vote? Results from the 2020 Indian American Attitudes Survey*. New York: Carnegie Endowment for International Peace.

Badrinathan, Sumitra, Devesh Kapur, and Milan Vaishnav. 2021. *How Do Indian Americans View India? Results from the 2020 Indian American Attitudes Survey*. New York: Carnegie Endowment for International Peace.

Balaji. 2014. "Resolution on Dalits Commendable but Outdated." *Huffington Post*, May 8. Retrieved August 25, 2014. http://www.huffingtonpost.com/murali-balaji/resolution-on-dalits-comm_b_5288617.html.

Bald, Vivek. 2013. *Bengali Harlem: And the Lost Histories of South Asian Americans*. Cambridge, MA: Harvard University Press.

Banerjee, Neela. 2007. "In Jews, Indian-Americans See a Role Model in Activism." *New York Times*, October 2.

Bauböck, Rainer 2003. "Towards a Political Theory of Migrant Transnationalism." *International Migration Review* 37(3): 700–723.

Baumgartner, Frank R., and Bryan D. Jones. 1993. *Agendas and Instability in American Politics*. Chicago: University of Chicago Press.

Beaty, Thalia. 2020. "Hindu Temple Ad Runs Despite Opposition." Usnews.com, August 5. https://www.usnews.com/news/us/articles/2020-08-05/times-square-advertisers-asked-not-to-run-hindu-temple-ad.

Behera, Navnita Chadha. 2006. *Demystifying Kashmir*. Washington, DC: Brookings Institution Press.

Berger, J. M. 2016. "Nazis vs. ISIS on Twitter: A Comparative Study of White Nationalist and ISIS Online Social Media Networks." Center for Cyber and Homeland Security, George Washington University. Retrieved September 1, 2020. https://research.gwu.edu/cyber.

Berwa, Laxmi N. 2000. *Asian Dalit Solidarity*. Delhi: ISPCK.

Betts, Alexander, and Will Jones. 2016. *Mobilising the Diaspora: How Refugees Challenge Authoritarianism*. Cambridge: Cambridge University Press.

Bier, David. 2018. "150-Year Wait for Indian Immigrants with Advanced Degrees." Cato Institute. https://www.cato.org/blog/150-year-wait-indian-immigrants-advanced-degrees.

Bloemraad, Irene. 2006. *Becoming a Citizen: Incorporating Immigrants and Refugees in the United States and Canada*. Berkeley: University of California Press.

Bloemraad, Irene. 2018. "Theorising the Power of Citizenship as Claims-Making." *Journal of Ethnic and Migration Studies* 44(1): 4–26.

Bob, Clifford. 2007. "Dalit Rights Are Human Rights: Caste Discrimination, International Activism, and the Construction of a New Human Rights Issue." *Human Rights Quarterly* 29(1): 167–193.

Bonilla-Silva, Eduardo. 2017. *Racism without Racists: Color-Blind Racism and the Persistence of Racial Inequality in America*. 5th ed. Lanham, MD: Rowman & Littlefield.

REFERENCES

Borge, Rosa, and Anna S. Cardenal. 2011. "Surfing the Net: A Pathway to Participation for the Politically Uninterested?" *Policy & Internet* 3(1): 1–29.

Brettell, Caroline B., and Deborah Reed-Danahay. 2008. "'Communities of Practice' for Civic and Political Engagement: A Comparison of Asian Indian and Vietnamese Immigrant Organizations in a Southwestern Metropolis." Pp. 195–221 in *Civic Hopes and Political Realities: Immigrants, Community Organizations and Political Engagement*, edited by Karthick Ramakrishnan and Irene Bloemraad. New York: Russell Sage Foundation.

Brettell, Caroline B., and Deborah Reed-Danahay. 2011. *Civic Engagements: The Citizenship Practices of Indian and Vietnamese Immigrants*. Palo Alto, CA: Stanford University Press.

Brodkin, Karen. 1998. *How Jews Became White Folks and What That Says about Race in America*. New Brunswick, NJ: Rutgers University Press.

Brown, R. Khari, and Ronald E. Brown. 2015. "Race/Ethnicity, Religion, and Partisan Leanings." *Review of Religious Research* 57: 469–505.

Browne, William P. 1990. "Organized Interests and Their Issue Niches: A Search for Pluralism in a Policy Domain." *Journal of Politics* 52(2): 477–509.

Brubaker, Rogers. 1996. *Nationalism Reframed: Nationhood and the National Question in the New Europe*. Cambridge: Cambridge University Press.

Brubaker, Rogers. 2013. "Language, Religion, and the Politics of Difference." *Nations and Nationalism* 19(1): 1–20.

Brubaker, William R., ed. 1989. *Immigration and the Politics of Citizenship in Europe and North America*. Lanham, MD: University Press of America.

Buchignani, Norman, Doreen M. Indra, and Ram Srivastava. 1985. *Continuous Journey: A Social History of South Asians in Canada*. Toronto: McClelland and Stewart in association with the Multiculturalism Directorate, Department of the Secretary of State and the Canadian Government Publishing Centre, Supply and Services Canada.

Budiman, Abby. 2021. *Indians in the U.S. Fact Sheet*. Pew Research Center. Retrieved April 29, 2020. https://www.pewresearch.org/social-trends/fact-sheet/asian-americans-indians-in-the-u-s/.

Campbell, David E., ed. 2007. *A Matter of Faith: Religion in the 2004 Presidential Election*. Washington, DC: Brookings Institution Press.

Campbell, David E., John C. Green, and Geoffrey C. Layman. 2011. "The Party Faithful: Partisan Images, Candidate Religion, and the Electoral Impact of Party Identification." *American Journal of Political Science* 55(1): 42–58.

Casanova, José. 2007. "Immigration and the New Religious Pluralism: A European Union/United States Comparison." Pp. 59–83 in *Democracy and the New Religious Pluralism*, edited by T. Banchoff. New York: Oxford University Press.

CDFEH (California Department of Fair Employment and Housing) versus Cisco Systems, Inc. et al. 2020. "Civil Rights Complaint—Employment Discrimination." Filed June 30, 2020. https://storage.courtlistener.com/recap/gov.uscourts.cand.361775/gov.uscourts.cand.361775.1.0.pdf.

Chakrapani, R. 1984. "Indian-Americans Get Assurance on Rights." *The Hindu*, February 25, p. 1.

Chakravorty, Sanjoy, Devesh Kapur, and Nirvikar Singh. 2017. *The Other One Percent: Indians in America*. New York: Oxford University Press.

Chari, Mridula. 2016. "Last Hearing Today: Should the Word 'Dalit' Be Used in California Textbooks?" *Scroll*, May 19. Retrieved August 26, 2020. https://scroll.in/article/808394/california-to-decide-today-whether-hindu-groups-can-dictate-what-dalits-call-themselves-in-textbooks.

Chatterjee, Swadesh. 2015. *Building Bridges: The Role of Indian Americans in Indo-U.S. Relations*. New Delhi: Rupa Publications.

Chen, Carolyn. 2002. "The Religious Varieties of Ethnic Presence: A Comparison between a Taiwanese Immigrant Buddhist Temple and an Evangelical Christian Church." *Sociology of Religion* 63(2): 215–238.

Cherian, Joy. 1997. *Our Relay Race: A Compilation of Selected Articles and Speeches*. Lanham, MD: University Press of America.

Cherian, Joy. 2004. "An American President Who Respected US Immigrants." *India Abroad*, June 18, p. A24.

Cherukonda, Raj. 2016. "Statement of Raj Cherukonda, Tom Lantos Human Rights Commission with the House Foreign Affairs Committee." Washington, DC. June 7, 2016. https://humanrightscommission.house.gov/sites/humanrightscommission.house.gov/files/documents/StatementofRajCherukonda_0.pdf.

Chhibber, Sumeet. 2003. "Indian Americans, Speak Now and Be Heard." March 31, 2003. https://www.sulekha.com/expressions/column.asp?cid=305794.

Chima, Jugdep S. 2010. *The Sikh Separatist Insurgency in India: Political Leadership and Ethnonationalist Movements*. New Delhi: Sage.

Cho, Richard. 2015. "Racialized Partisan Identity: The Role of Pan-Ethnic Identity in Partisan Movement among Asian Americans." Dissertation, Stony Brook University. ProQuest (10017578).

Chougule, Pratik, and Keerthika M. Subramanian. 2013. "A Community Voting against Its Interests." *India Abroad*, May 10, p. A19.

Chowdhury, Kavita. 2022. "India's Descent into a Spiral of Genocidal Hate." TheDiplomat. com, January 28. https://thediplomat.com/2022/01/indias-descent-into-a-spiral-of-genocidal-hate/.

Clough, Michael. 1994. "Grass-Roots Policymaking: Say Good-Bye to the 'Wise Men.'" *Foreign Affairs* 73(1): 2–7.

Coalition against Genocide. 2005. *How We Made U.S. Deny Visa to Modi*. http://coalitionagainstgenocide.org/news/2005/mar/21.aa.modi.php.

Coalition against Genocide. 2013a. *Affiliations of Faith, Part 1: Hindu American Foundation and the Global Sangh*. Accessed May 12, 2014. http://coalitionagainstgenocide.org/reports/2013/cag.15dec2013.haf.rss.pdf.

Coalition against Genocide. 2013b. *Affiliations of Faith, Part II: Joined at the Hip*. http://www.coalitionagainstgenocide.org/reports/2013/cag.22dec2013.haf.rss.2.pdf.

Congressional Hearing. 2014. "The Plight of Religious Minorities in India." Retrieved May 10, 2014. https://humanrightscommission.house.gov/sites/humanrightscommission.house.gov/files/documents/Hearing%20Transcript%20--20Plight%20of%20Religious%20Minorities%20in%20India.pdf.

Copland, Ian. 1991. "The Abdullah Factor: Kashmiri Muslims and the Crisis of 1947." Pp. 218–254 in *The Political Inheritance of Pakistan*, edited by D. A. Low. London: Macmillan.

Coulson, Doug. 2015. "British Imperialism, the Indian Independence Movement, and the Racial Eligibility Provisions of the Naturalization Act: *United States v. Thind* Revisited." *Georgetown Journal of Law & Modern Critical Race Perspectives* 7(1): 1–42.

Dahl, Robert A. 1961. *Who Governs: Democracy and Power in an American City*. New Haven, CT: Yale University Press.

Dalit Freedom Network (DFN). 2014. "African Americans Call for End to Oppression of Dalits in India with 'Declaration of Empathy' Signing Event at U.S. Capitol." Retrieved May 16, 2014. http://www.prweb.com/releases/Declare/Empathy/prweb11406890.htm.

Das, Rajani Kanta. 1923. *Hindustani Workers on the Pacific Coast*. Berlin and Leipzig: Walter De Gruyter & Co.

Das Gupta, Monisha. 2006. *Unruly Immigrants: Rights, Activism, and Transnational South Asian Politics in the United States*. Durham, NC: Duke University Press.

David, Rohit E. 2017. "President Trump Can Usher in True Ram Rajya: Americans Are Smarter Than So-Called Liberal Pundits." *The Times of India*, February 12. https://timesofindia.indiatimes.com/blogs/the-interviews-blog/president-trump-can-usher-in-true-ram-rajya-americans-are-smarter-than-so-called-liberal-pundits/.

De, Aparajita. 2016. "Introduction: South Asian Racialization and Belonging after 9/11: Masks of Threat." Pp. ix–xxv in *South Asian Racialization and Belonging after 9/11: Masks of Threat*, edited by Aparajita De and Hasan al Zayed. Lanham, MD: Lexington Books.

Desai, Ashwin, and Goolam Vahed. 2015. *The South African Gandhi: Stretcher-Bearer of Empire*. Stanford, CA: Stanford University Press.

Desmond, Matthew. 2012. "Disposable Ties and the Urban Poor." *American Journal of Sociology* 117(5): 1295–1335.

DeSipio, Louis. 1996. *Counting on the Latino Vote: Latinos as a New Electorate*. Charlottesville: University of Virginia Press.

Detsch, Jack, and Robbie Gramer. 2020. "Indian Americans Stir Blue Wave in Deep Red Texas." ForeignPolicy.com, October 28. https://foreignpolicy.com/2020/10/28/2020-election-indian-americans-blue-wave-texas/?utm_source=PostUp&utm_medium=email&utm_campaign=26940&utm_term=South%20Asia%20Brief%20OC&?tpcc=26940.

Dev, Atul. 2022. "A Bulldozer among the Floats at Indian Parade Divides New Jersey Town." September 22. https://www.reuters.com/world/us/bulldozer-among-floats-indian-parade-divides-new-jersey-town-2022-09-22/.

DeWind, Josh, and Renata Segura. 2014. "Diaspora-Government Relations in Forging US Foreign Policies." Pp. 3–28 in *Diaspora Lobbies and the US Government: Convergence and Divergence in Making Foreign Policy*, edited by Josh DeWind and Renata Sengupta. New York: New York University Press.

Dhingra, Pawan. 2011. "Post-9/11 Vacancies: Race, Economics, and South Asian America." *Asian American Literary Journal* 2(1.5): 130–143.

Dhingra, Pawan. 2012. *Life behind the Lobby: Indian American Motel Owners and the American Dream*. Palo Alto, CA: Stanford University Press.

Dhume, Sadanand. 2012. "What Is the Natural Political Home of Indian-Americans?" *The American*, August 29. http://www.american.com/archive/2012/august/what-is-the-natural-political-home-of-indian-americans.

DiMaggio, Paul, and Walter W. Powell. 1983. "The Iron Cage Revisited: Institutional Isomorphism and Collective Rationality in Organizational Fields." *American Sociological Review* 48(2): 147–160.

Dirks, Nicholas B. 2001. *Castes of Mind: Colonialism and the Making of Modern India*. Princeton, NJ: Princeton University Press.

Dolan, Jay P. 1992. *The American Catholic Experience: A History from Colonial Times to the Present*. Notre Dame, IN: University of Notre Dame Press.

Dollinger, Marc. 2000. *Jews and Liberalism in Modern America*. Princeton, NJ: Princeton University Press.

Dowley, Kathleen M., and Brian D. Silver. 2000. "Subnational and National Loyalty: Cross-National Comparisons." *International Journal of Public Opinion Research* 12(4): 357–371.

Dutt, Ela. 2013. "Pro and Anti Modi Activists Duke It Out in the United States." *News India Times*. http://newsindiatimes.com/pro-and-anti-modi-activists-duke-it-out-in-the-united-states/.

Dutt, Yashica. 2020. "The Specter of Caste in Silicon Valley." *New York Times*, July 14. https://www.nytimes.com/2020/07/14/opinion/caste-cisco-indian-americans-discrimination.html.

Dutta, Manoranjan. 1976. Evidence Before the U.S. House of Representatives Subcommittee on Census and Population, June 1–2, No. 94-80, pp. 33–37.

Dutta, Manoranjan. 1979. *Presentation, Civil Rights Issues of Asian and Pacific Americans: Myths and Realities*. Consultation Sponsored by the U.S. Commission on Civil Rights, Washington, DC. May 8–9, Proceedings, pp. 393–396. Original from University of Michigan.

Dutta, Manoranjan. 1982. "Asian Indian Americans: Search for an Economic Profile." Pp. 76–85 in *From India to America: A Brief History of Immigration, Problems of Discrimination, Admission and Assimilation*, edited by S. Chandrasekhar. La Jolla, CA: Population Review.

Ebaugh, Helen Rose, and Janet Saltzman Chafetz. 1999. "Agents for Cultural Reproduction and Structural Change: The Ironic Role of Women in Immigrant Religious Organizations." *Social Forces* 78(2): 585–612.

Eck, Diana. 2002. *A New Religious America: How a "Christian Country" Has Become the World's Most Religiously Diverse Nation*. San Francisco: HarperCollins.

Economic Times. 2009. "India Lobbies Hard in US to Stay Ahead." January 29. https://economictimes.indiatimes.com/news/politics-and-nation/india-lobbies-hard-in-us-to-stay-ahead/articleshow/4044733.cms.

Edsall, Thomas B. 2018. "Which Side Are You On?" *New York Times*, Opinion, May 18. https://www.nytimes.com/2018/05/10/opinion/democrats-partisanship-identity-politics.html?action=click&pgtype=Homepage&clickSource=story-heading&module=region&region=region&WT.nav=region.

Elkhanialy, Hekmat, and Ralph W. Nicholas. 1976a. "An Overview and Recommendations." Pp. 1–8 in *Immigrants from the Indian Subcontinent in the U.S.A.: Problems and Prospects*, edited by Hekmat Elkhanialy and Ralph W. Nicholas. Chicago: Indian League of America.

Elkhanialy, Hekmat, and Ralph W. Nicholas. 1976b. "Racial and Ethnic Self-Designation, Experiences of Discrimination and Desire for Legal Minority Status among Indian Immigrants in the U.S.A." Pp. 41–50 in *Immigrants from the Indian Subcontinent in the U.S.A.: Problems and Prospects*, edited by Hekmat Elkhanialy and Ralph W. Nicholas. Chicago: Indian League of America.

Emerson, Michael O. 2006. *People of the Dream: Multiracial Congregations in the United States*. Princeton, NJ: Princeton University Press.

Erikson, Robert, Michael Mackuen, and James Stimson. 2002. *The Macro Polity*. New York: Cambridge University Press.

Espino, Rodolfo, David Leal, and Kenneth J. Meier. 2008. *Latino Politics: Identity, Mobilization, and Representation*. Charlottesville: University of Virginia Press.

Espinosa, Gastón, ed. 2013. *Religion, Race, and Barack Obama's New Democratic Pluralism*. New York: Routledge.

Espiritu, Yen Le. 1992. *Asian American Pan-ethnicity: Bridging Institutions and Identities*. Philadelphia: Temple University Press.

FABRONA. 2000. "Protest by the Federation of Ambedkarites, Buddhists, and Ravidasi Organizations of North America (Fabrona)." September 8. http://www.ambedkar.org/News/hl/PROTESTBY.htm.

Fair, Christine C. 2006. "Diaspora Involvement in Insurgencies: Insights from the Khalistan and Tamil Eelam Movements." *Nationalism and Ethnic Politics* 11(1): 125–156.

Faleomavaega, Eni F. H. 2014a. "It's Official; Prime Minster Modi Is Part of U.S. Congressional History." Retrieved May 25, 2014. http://faleomavaega.house.gov/media-center/press-releases/its-official-prime-minister-modi-is-part-of-us-congressional-history.

Faleomavaega, Eni F. H. 2014b. "US Lawmakers Forge Ahead to set US-India Relations on New Course." September 24. https://www.businesstoday.in/opinion/columns/india-us-relations-on-prime-minister-narendra-modi-us-visit/story/210746.html.

Farees, Zeeshan. 2004. "USINPAC: Buying Zionist Influence, Selling Indian Interests." Ghadar, June. http://www.ghadar.insaf.net/June2004.

Federal Bureau of Investigation (FBI). 2011. "Virginia Man Pleads Guilty in Scheme to Conceal Pakistan Government Funding for His U.S. Lobbying Efforts." December 7. Retrieved May 4, 2014. http://www.fbi.gov/washingtondc/press-releases/2011/virginia-man-pleads-guilty-in-scheme-to-conceal-pakistan-government-funding-for-his-u.s.-lobbying-efforts.

Fennema, Meindert. 2004. "The Concept and Measurement of Ethnic Community." *Journal of Ethnic and Migration Studies* 30(3): 429–447.

Fennema, Meindert, and Jean Tillie. 2001. "Civic Community, Political Participation and Political Trust of Ethnic Groups." *Connections* 24(1): 26–41.

Fetzer, Joel S., and J. Christopher Soper. 2005. *Muslims and the State in Britain, France, and Germany*. New York: Cambridge University Press.

FIACONA (Federation of Indian American Christian Organizations of North America). 2000. "Forming FIACONA." January 9. http://www.fiacona.org/Press%20Releases/010920PR_discuss_forming_FIACONA.htm.

FIACONA (Federation of Indian American Christian Organizations of North America). 2011. "FIACONA Supports USCIRF Placing India on 'Watch List.'" http://persecution.in/content/fiacona-supports-uscirf-placing-india-watch-list.

Fiorina, Morris P. 1981. *Retrospective Voting in American National Elections.* New Haven, CT: Yale University Press.

Fisher, Maxine. 1980. *Indians of New York City: A Study of Immigrants from India.* New Delhi: Heritage.

Foley, Michael W., and Dean R. Hoge. 2007. *Religion and the New Immigrants: How Faith Communities Shape our Newest Citizens.* New York: Oxford University Press.

Foner, Nancy, and Richard Alba. 2008. "Immigrant Religion in the U.S. and Western Europe: Bridge or Barrier to Inclusion?" *International Migration Review* 42(2): 360–392.

Forsythe, Michael, and Veen Trehan. 2006. "India's Clout in U.S. Congress Assisted by GE, Boeing, JP Morgan." Bloomberg, July 17.

Free Press Journal. 2020. "Hindu America Foundation Boss Slams USCIRF Report: Says Group Held Multiple Hearings to Perpetuate Misinformation on India." April 29.

Friedrich, Pieter. 2020a. "The Princess of RSS and Me: The Downfall of Hindutva's Handmaiden Tulsi Gabbard." Medium.com, July 28. https://pieterjfriedrich.medium.com/the-princess-of-the-rss-and-me-d067d64a424a

Friedrich, Pieter. 2020b. "Money Trail: Diaspora Diplomacy's Financial Whitewashing of Hindutva." The Polis Project, September 27. https://www.thepolisproject.com/read/money-trail-diaspora-diplomacys-financial-whitewashing-of-hindutva/

Garbaye, Romain. 2005. *Getting into Local Power: The Politics of Ethnic Minorities in British and French Cities.* Oxford: Blackwell.

Garcia, John A. 2012. *Latino Politics in America: Community, Culture and Interests.* Lanham, MD: Rowman and Littlefield.

García, María C. 1996. *Havana USA: Cuban Exiles and Cuban Americans in South Florida 1959–1994.* Berkeley and Los Angeles: University of California Press.

Garza, Rodolpho O. de la. 2004. "Latino Politics." *Annual Review of Political Science* 7: 91–123.

Gerbaudo, Paolo, and Emiliano Treré. 2015. "In Search of the 'We' of Social Media Activism: Introduction to the Special Issue on Social Media and Protest Identities." *Information, Communication & Society* 18(8): 865–871.

Ghori-Ahmad, Safiya, and Fatima Salman. 2020. "Why Indians Matter in U.S. Politics." *Foreign Policy,* October 21. Retrieved July 20, 2021. https://foreignpolicy.com/2020/10/21/why-indian-americans-matter-in-us-politics/.

Gibson, Campbell, and Kay Jung. 2005. "Historical Census Statistics on Population Totals by Race, 1790 to 1990, and by Hispanic Origin, 1970 to 1990, for Large Cities and Other Urban Places in the United States." Working Paper No. 76, Population Division, U.S. Census Bureau, Washington, DC. Retrieved February 2005.

Gilbert, David. 2020. "Silicon Valley Has a Caste Discrimination Problem." *Vice News,* August 5. https://www.vice.com/en_us/article/3azjp5/silicon-valley-has-a-caste-discrimination-problem.

Gilmour, John. 1906. "Our First Invasion by Hindus and Mohammedans." *San Francisco Sunday Call,* November 18, p. 6. https://www.newspapers.com/image/80981496/?terms=our%2Bfirst%2Binvasion%2Bof%2Bhindus.

Glazer, Nathan. 1983. *Ethnic Dilemmas, 1964–1982.* Cambridge, MA: Harvard University Press.

Glenn, Evelyn Nakano. 2011. "Constructing Citizenship: Exclusion, Subordination, and Resistance." *American Sociological Review* 76(1): 1–24.

Glick Schiller, Nina. 2005. "Long Distance Nationalism." Pp. 570–580 in *Encyclopedia of Diasporas: Immigrant and Refugee Cultures around the World,* edited by Melvin Ember, Carol R. Ember, and Ian Skoggard. Boston, MA: Springer.

Goldberg, David Howard. 1990. *Foreign Policy and Ethnic Interest Groups: American and Canadian Jews Lobby for Israel.* Westport, CT: Greenwood.

Goldstein, Eric L. 2006. *The Price of Whiteness: Jews, Race and American Identity.* Princeton, NJ: Princeton University Press.

Gould, Harold A. 2006. *Sikhs, Swamis, Students, and Spies: The India Lobby in the United States, 1900–1946.* New Delhi: Sage Publications.

Government of India. 2001. *Report of the High-Level Committee on the Indian Diaspora.* New Delhi: Ministry of External Affairs.

Green, Donald P., Bradley Palmquist, and Eric Schickler. 2002. *Partisan Hearts and Minds: Political Parties and the Social Identities of Voters.* New Haven, CT: Yale University Press.

Green, John C. 2007. *The Faith Factor: How Religion Influences American Elections.* Westport, CT: Praeger.

Greer, Christina M. 2013. *Black Ethnics: Race, Immigration and the Pursuit of the American Dream.* New York: Oxford University Press.

Gregg, Heather S. 2002. "Divided They Conquer: The Success of Armenian Ethnic Lobbies in the U.S." Rosemary Rogers Working Paper Series, No. 13, Massachusetts Institute of Technology, Cambridge, MA.

Grossman, Matt, and David A. Hopkins. 2016. *Asymmetric Politics: Ideological Republicans and Group Interest Democrats.* New York: Oxford University Press.

Gurr, Ted R. 2000. *Peoples versus States: Minorities at Risk in the New Century.* Washington, DC: United States Institute for Peace.

HAF (Hindu American Foundation). 2005a. "Hindu American Foundation Condemns Hinduphobic Resolution in House of Representatives." March 21. Retrieved May 7, 2014. http://hafsite.org/media/news/20050321_pitts.

HAF (Hindu American Foundation). 2005b. "Hindu American Foundation Appreciates Congressional Hearing on Dalit Rights; Concerned by Biases." October 12.

HAF (Hindu American Foundation). 2009. "Briefing on Kashmir Held on Capitol Hill." http://hafsite.org/?q=media/pr/briefing-kashmir-held-capitol-hill.

HAF (Hindu American Foundation). 2010. "Hinduism: Not Cast in Caste." December 10. Retrieved December 14, 2013. http://www.hafsite.org/media/pr/hinduism-not-cast-caste-full-report.

HAF (Hindu American Foundation). 2011a. "Hinduism: Not Cast in Caste." Revised July 21. Retrieved December 14, 2013. http://hafsite.org/media/pr/hinduism-not-cast-caste-full-report.

HAF (Hindu American Foundation). 2011b. "USCIRF Hearing, March 10. Testimony and Resources." http://www.hafsite.org/media/pr/uscirf-hearing-testimony.

HAF (Hindu American Foundation). 2011c. "HAF Alleges Bias in Listing of India on Watch List." April 28. Retrieved May 16, 2014. http://hafsite.org/media/pr/haf-alleges-bias-listing-india-watch-list.

HAF (Hindu American Foundation). 2013. "Coalition against Genocide: A Nexus of Hinduphobia Unveiled." December 15. Retrieved January 10, 2014. http://hafsite.org/sites/default/files/Coalition_Against_Genocide_A_Nexus_of_HinduphobiaUnveiled.pdf.

HAF (Hindu American Foundation). 2016. "DNC Chair Candidate Keith Ellison Releases Statement after Call with Coalition of Hindu and Indian American Organizations." December 23 (via email).

Hajnal, Zoltan, and Taeku Lee. 2006a. "Immigration and Party Identification among Latinos and Asian Americans." Pp. 129–150 in *Transforming Politics, Transforming America: The Political and Civic Incorporation of Immigrants in the United States,* edited by Taeku Lee, S. Karthick Ramakrishnan, and Ricardo Ramírez. Charlottesville: University of Virginia Press.

Hamid, Aslam. 1991. "American Human Rights Activists, Legislators, Public Opinion, and the Indian Muslims." Pp. 44–47 in *Indian Muslims in North America,* edited by Omar Khalidi. Watertown, MA: South Asia Press.

Hamm, Patricia. 1996. "Mexican-American Interests in US-Mexico Relations: The Case of NAFTA." Working Paper No. 4, Center for Research on Latinos in a Global Society, University of California, Irvine.

Haney, Patrick J., and Walt Vanderbush. 1999. "The Role of Ethnic Interest Groups in U.S. Foreign Policy: The Case of the Cuban American National Foundation." *International Studies Quarterly* 43: 341–361.

Haney López, Ian. 2006. *White by Law: The Legal Construction of Race*. 10th anniversary ed. New York and London: New York University Press.

Haniffa, Aziz. 1991. "The Fight Against Professional Bias." Special Report on IAFPE Convention. August 16.

Haniffa, Aziz. 2007. "Final N-Bill by End of '07 or Early '08: Nicholas Burns." *Rediff India Abroad*. http://www.rediff.com/news/2007/feb21ndeal1.htm.

Haniffa, Aziz. 2010. "The Panun Kashmir Homeland Concept Is Something We Have to Push For." *India Abroad*, February 5, p. A17.

Haniffa, Aziz. 2011. "A Pakistani Agent in the Capital." *India Abroad*, July 29, p. A18.

Haniffa, Aziz. 2012a. "It's a Different Race: Desi Democrats Deny That the Groundswell of 2008 for Obama Has Fizzled Out This Time." *India Abroad*, September 14, p. A10.

Haniffa, Aziz. 2012b. "Dave Kumar Acknowledges Dip in Enthusiasm." *India Abroad*, September 14, p. A16.

Haniffa, Aziz. 2012c. "What's Driving Indian Americans to the Democratic Party." *India Abroad*, October 5, p. A8.

Haniffa, Aziz. 2012d. "The Republican Party Needs to Make Sincere Changes to Become a Party Inclusive of All Colors and Ethnicities." *India Abroad*, November 16, pp. A13–A14.

Haniffa, Aziz. 2012e. "Bobby Jindal Slams '47 Percent Romney, 'Dumbed-Down' Conservatism." *India Abroad*, November 23, p. A8.

Haniffa, Aziz. 2014. "New York Court Summons on Modi Has No Effect: White House." *India Abroad*, October 3, p. A42.

Haniffa, Aziz. 2015. "FIACONA Wants Modi to 'Walk the Talk' on Protecting Christians." *India Abroad*, March 27, p. A10.

Haniffa, Aziz. 2016a. "Trump Is Crazy, He's a Disgrace." *India Abroad*, November 11, pp. A8–A13.

Haniffa, Aziz. 2016b. "Fearing the GOP's Disintegration." *India Abroad*, November 11, p. A9.

Haniffa, Aziz. 2016c. "Ellison's Bid to Head DNC Disturbs Civil Rights Groups: The Hindu American Foundation and Other Groups Express Their Concerns." *India Abroad*, December 16, p. 12.

Haniffa, Aziz. 2017a. "Hearing Kashmiri's Cries: Washington Rally Presses for End of Indian Forces' Brutality." *India Abroad*, June 2, pp. 23, 25.

Haniffa, Aziz. 2017b. "Compassion for Charity?: U.S. Lawmakers Seek Reprieve in India for Compassion I'ntl." *India Abroad*, March 31, p. 21.

Haniffa, Aziz. 2017c. "Homecoming Hosted by Ranking GOP Lawmaker." *India Abroad*, September 29, p. 13.

Haniffa, Aziz. 2018. "Helping Give Candidates Their 'Can-Do': Former Kansas Lawmaker's Impact Team to Bolster Indian-American Hopefuls." *India Abroad*, February 2, pp. 13, 16.

Haniffa, Aziz. 2019a. "Indian-American Progressives and Muslims Say Modi's Action Is Illegal and Could Lead to Violence, Chaos." *India Abroad*, August 12, pp. 21, 23.

Haniffa, Aziz. 2019b. "A Bad Day for India on the Hill: India-Friendly Lawmakers Take on Trump Administration for Not Standing Up to India's Alleged Atrocities in Kashmir." *India Abroad*, November 4, pp. 10, 12, 14.

Haniffa, Aziz. 2019c. "The Way Forward in Kashmir Unveiled in Congress: Kashmiri Pandit's Prescription Is to Promote Pluralism, Reconnect and to Reintegrate the Hearts and Minds of All Kashmiris." *India Abroad*, October 28, pp. 10, 12.

Haniffa, Aziz. 2020a. "Shringla's Rationale for Hiring 2nd Lobbying Firm: Outgoing Indian Envoy and India's Next Foreign Secretary Says the Move Was Made to Engage a Changed U.S. Congress." *India Abroad*, January 20, pp. 15–16.

Haniffa, Aziz. 2020b. "Campaign against CAA Continues on Capitol Hill." *India Abroad*, February 10, pp. 8–9.

Haniffa, Aziz. 2020c. "Ro Khanna Trounces Challenger Ritesh Tandon Who Was Supported by Hindu-American Activists." *India Abroad*, March 8. https://www.indiaabroad.com/us_affa irs/ro-khanna-trounces-challenger-ritesh-tandon-who-was-supported-by-hindu-ameri can-activists/article_739f0c5c-61a0-11ea-aa58-93d503d83bde.html.

Haniffa, Aziz. 2020d. "CAA, NRC Would Render Indian Muslims Stateless." *India Abroad*, March 16, p. 23.

Haniffa, Aziz. 2020e. "'Sit-in-Satyagraha' Held in Front of Indian Embassy." *India Abroad*, February 10, p. 19.

Hardgrove, Anne. 2013. *India Federation of America and ILA Foundation Records 1970–2007.* http://chsmedia.org/media/fa/fa/M-I/ILA-inv.htm.

Harvard, Sarah A. 2017. "Muslims Who Voted for Trump Differ on His Ban but Still Agree with on One Thing: They Still Support Him." Mic.com, January 31. https://www.mic.com/artic les/167126/muslims-who-voted-for-trump-differ-on-his-ban-but-agree-on-one-thing-they-still-support-him#.ZS8V8X9yS.

Hathaway, Robert M. 2001. "Unfinished Passage: India, Indian Americans, and the U.S. Congress." *Washington Quarterly* 24(2): 21–34.

Hathaway, Robert M. 2004. "Washington's New Strategic Partnership." India-Seminar.com, June, no. 538: 68–72. https://www.india-seminar.com/2004/538/538%20robert%20 m.%20hathaway.htm.

Hauslohner, Abigail. 2019. "The Employment Green Card Backlog Tops 800,000, Most of Them Indian. A Solution Is Elusive." *Washington Post*, December 17. https://www.washing tonpost.com/immigration/the-employment-green-card-backlog-tops-800000-most-of-them-indian-a-solution-is-elusive/2019/12/17/55def1da-072f-11ea-8292-c46ee8cb3dce_st ory.html.

Heller, Deane, and David Heller. 1966. "Our New Immigration Law." *American Legion Magazine* 80(2): 6–9, 39–41. https://archive.legion.org/handle/20.500.12203/3939.

Helweg, Arthur W., and Usha M. Helweg. 1990. *An Immigrant Success Story: East Indians in America*. Philadelphia: University of Pennsylvania Press.

Hindu Immigration Hearings. 1914. "Hindu Immigration Hearings: Before the Committee on Immigration, House of Representatives." Sixty-Third Congress, Second Session. Relative to Restriction of Hindu Laborers. Friday, February 13. Washington, DC: Government Printing Office.

Hirschman, Charles. 2004. "The Role of Religion in the Origin and Adaptation of Immigrant Groups in the United States." *International Migration Review* 38(3): 1206–1233.

Ho, Elaine Lynn-Ee. 2011. "Claiming the Diaspora: Elite Mobility, Sending State Strategies and the Spatialities of Citizenship." *Progress in Human Geography* 35(6): 757–772.

Ho, Elaine Lynn-Ee, Maureen Hickey, and Brenda S. A. Yeoh. 2015. "Special Issue Introduction: New Research Directions and Critical Perspectives on Diaspora Strategies." *Geoforum* 59: 153–158.

Ho, Elaine Lynn-Ee, and Fiona McConnell. 2019. "Conceptualizing 'Diaspora Diplomacy': Territory and Populations betwixt the Domestic and Foreign." *Progress in Human Geography* 43(2): 235–255.

Hochschild, Jennifer, and John H. Mollenkopf. 2009. "Modeling Immigrant Political Incorporation." Pp. 15–30 in *Bringing Outsiders In: Transatlantic Perspectives on Immigrant Political Incorporation*, edited by Jennifer Hochschild and John H. Mollenkopf. Ithaca, NY: Cornell University Press.

Hoft, Jim. 2012. "Indian-American Coalitions Raises Millions for Mitt Romney." TheGatewayPundit.com, October 13. https://www.thegatewaypundit.com/2012/10/ind ian-american-coalitions-raises-millions-for-mitt-romney/.

Holcombe, Madeline, and Harmeet Kaur. 2021. "The Sikh Community Is in Mourning as 4 Members Were among the Victims of the Indianapolis Shooting." CNN.com, April 17. https://www.cnn.com/2021/04/17/us/indianapolis-shooting-fedex-facility-saturday/index.html.

Hong, Nicole. 2023. "How a Suspected Indian Murder-for-Hire Plot on U.S. Soil Was Foiled." *New York Times*, December 3. https://www.nytimes.com/2023/12/02/nyregion/india-sikh-assassination-attempt.html?nl=todaysheadlines&emc=edit_th_20231202.

Horowitz, Donald L. 2000. *Ethnic Groups in Conflict*. 2nd ed. Berkeley: University of California Press.

Howe, Marvine. 1984. "Sikh Parley: 'We Are United: We Are Angry.'" *New York Times*, July 29. http://www.nytimes.com/1984/07/29/world/sikh-parley-we-are-united-we-are-angry.html.

Huddy, Leonie, Lilliana Mason, and S. Nechama Horwitz. 2016. "Political Identity Convergence: On Being Latino, Becoming a Democrat, and Getting Active." *Russell Sage Foundation Journal of the Social Sciences* 2(3): 205–228.

Hudson, Lynn. 1983a "Indian Leader Urges Senate to Retain Alien Preference." *India Abroad*, March 4, pp. 1, 20.

Hudson, Lynn. 1983b. "Indians Praised for Work on Bill." *India Abroad*, May 6, p. 19.

Hunter, Shireen T. 2002. *Islam, Europe's Second Religion: The New Social, Cultural and Political Landscape*. Westport, CT: Praeger.

Huntington, Samuel P. 1997. "The Erosion of American National Interests." *Foreign Affairs* 76(5): 28–49.

Huntington, Samuel P. 2004. *Who Are We: The Challenges to America's National Identity*. New York City: Simon & Schuster.

Hutson, James H. 1998. *Religion and the Founding of the American Republic*. Washington, DC: Library of Congress.

IAMC (Indian American Muslim Council). 2011. "IAMC Responds to USCIRFS Annual Report on International Religious Freedom." May 9. Retrieved May 16, 2014. http://iamc.com/press-release/iamc-responds-to-uscirfs-annual-report-on-international-religious-freedom.

IAMC (Indian American Muslim Council). 2012. "India's Response to Its Universal Periodic Review at the United Nations Disappoints Human Rights Groups India Refuses to Agree to Adequate Steps to Protect Members of Minority Religions." http://iamc.com/press-release/indias-response-to-its-universal-periodic-review-at-the-united-nations-disappoints-human-rights-groups-india-refuses-to-agree-to-adequate-steps-to-protect-members-of-minority-religions/.

IAMC (Indian American Muslim Council). 2013. "Hindu American Foundation Reveals its Supremacist Ideology through Smear Campaign Against CAG and Indian Muslims." Retrieved May 12, 2014. http://iamc.com/press-release/hindu-american-foundation-reveals-its-supremacist-ideology-through-smear-campaign-against-cag-and-indian-muslims/.

IANS. 2020. "President Donald Trump Awards Highest Military Decoration of U.S. to Indian Prime Minister Narendra Modi." *India West*, December 22. https://www.indiawest.com/news/india/president-donald-trump-awards-highest-military-decoration-of-u-s-to-indian-prime-minister-narendra/article_6d494df2-4482-11eb-b544-5797196cbca0.html.

Ignatiev, Noel. 1995. *How the Irish Became White*. New York: Routledge.

IMC-USA (Indian Muslim Council). 2002. "Who We Are." www.imc-usa.org/cgi-bin/cfm/whoweare.cfm.

Immigration Hearing. 1965. Hearing held before Subcommittee on Immigration and Naturalization, February 10, pp. 2–3.

Inboden, William, III. 2008. *Religion and American Foreign Policy 1945–1960*. Cambridge: Cambridge University Press.

India Journal. 1999. "Separate Department to be Created for NRI's: Vajpayee." October 22, p. A3.

India Post. 2021. "HAF Seeks Legal Redress California on Caste Label." January 22, pp. 21, 23.

India West Staff Reporter. 2020. "American Sikh Caucus Co-Chair Rep. John Garamendi Supports Indian Farmers." *India West*, December 12. https://www.indiawest.com/news/global_indian/american-sikh-caucus-co-chair-rep-john-garamendi-supports-indian-farmers/article_20d646c4-3c57-11eb-8a67f45718f55bf.html.

India West Staff Reporter. 2021. "Chicago City Council Rejects Resolution Critical of Indian Government, Citizenship Amendment Act." *India West*, March 25. https://www.indiawest.com/news/global_indian/chicago-city-council-rejects-resolution-critical-of-indian-government-citizenship-amendment-act/article_2baa07ee-8d3c-11eb-b1ae-5b55f26a45e4.html.

Institute of International Education. 2016. *Top 25 Places of Origin of International Students, 2014/15-2015/16*. Open Doors Report on International Educational Exchange. https://www.chronicle.com/article/top-25-places-of-origin-of-international-students-at-u-s-colleges-2015-16/

Iyengar, Shanto. 2016. "E Pluribus Pluribus, or Divided We Stand." *Public Opinion Quarterly* 80(S1): 219–224.

Iyer, Deepa. 2015. *We Too Sing America: South Asian, Arab, Muslim, and Sikh Immigrants Shape our Multiracial Future*. New York: New Press.

Jackson, Thomas F. 2007. *From Civil Rights to Human Rights: Martin Luther King Jr., and the Struggle for Economic Justice*. Philadelphia: University of Pennsylvania Press.

Jacobson, Matthew Frye. 1999. *Whiteness of a Different Color: European Immigrants and the Alchemy of Race*. Cambridge, MA: Harvard University Press.

Jacoby, Harold S. 2007. *History of East Indians in America: The First Half-Century Experience of Sikhs, Hindus, and Muslims*. 2nd ed. Amritsar, India: B. Chattar Singh Jiwan Singh.

Jain, Sandhya. 2010. "Trans-national Hindus Seeking Vicarious Redemption." *Bharata Bharati*, December 26. http://bharatabharati.wordpress.com/2010/12/26/trans-national-hindus-seeking-vicarious-redemption-sandhya-jain/.

Janmohamed, Zahir. 2013. "U.S. Evangelicals, Indian Expats Teamed Up to Push Through Modi Visa Ban." India Blogs, *New York Times*, December 5. Retrieved May 8, 2014. http://india.blogs.nytimes.com/2013/12/05/u-s-evangelicals-indian-expats-teamed-up-to-push-through-modi-visa-ban/?_php=true&_type=blogs&_r=0.

Janmohamed, Zahir. 2014. "Their Master's Voice in Washington." *Outlook India*, February 17. Retrieved May 15, 2014. http://www.outlookindia.com/article/Their-Masters-Voice-In-Washington-/289551.

Jasso, Guillermina, Douglas S. Massey, Mark R. Rosenzweig, and James P. Smith. 2006. "The New Immigrant Survey 2003 Round 1." Accessed March 3, 2011. https://nis.princeton.edu/data.html

Jensen, Joan M. 1988. *Passage from India: Asian Indian Immigrants in North America*. New Haven, CT: Yale University Press.

Jeung, Russell, John Jimenez, and Eric Mar. 2020. "The Religious and Racial Minoritization of Asian American Voters." Pp. 201–226 in *Religion is Race: Understanding American Religion in the Twenty-First Century*, edited by Grace Yukich and Penny Edgell. New York: New York University Press.

Jha, Chandra. 1976. "Foreword." Pp v–viii in *Immigrants from the Indian Subcontinent in the U.S.A.: Problems and Prospects*, edited by Hekmat Elkhanialy and Ralph W. Nicholas. Chicago: India League of America.

Jha, Lalit K. 2009. "Indian-American Leaders to Meet Obama Team over 26/11." *Hindustan Times*. https://www.hindustantimes.com/india/indian-american-leaders-to-meet-obama-team-over-26-11/story-EnEkIHo8LX4K66aHTwFDSI.html.

Jha, Lalit K. 2020. "Joe Biden 'Disappointed' with CAA, NRC, Seeks Restoration of Rights for People in Kashmir." *The Wire*, June 26. https://thewire.in/world/us-nominee-joe-biden-caa-nrc-kashmir.

Jha, Ritu. 2012. "Exciting to See the Development of a Distinct Hindu Voice in American Politics and Public Affairs." *India Abroad*, June 1, p. A17.

Jha, Ritu. 2016. "A School for Doctors in Dharma." *India Abroad*, January 8, p. A19.
Johnston, Hugh J. M. 2014. *The Voyage of the Komagata Maru: The Sikh Challenge to Canada's Colour Bar*. Vancouver: UBC Press.
Jones, Robert P. 2016. *The End of White Christian America*. New York: Simon and Schuster.
Jones, Robert P. 2020. *White Too Long: The Legacy of White Supremacy in American Christianity*. New York: Simon & Schuster.
Jones, Robert P., and Eboo Patel. 2022. "What the Curious History of Judeo-Christian Can Teach Us about Defeating White Christian Nationalism Today." July 21. https://baptistnews.com/article/what-the-curious-history-of-judeo-christian-can-teach-us-about-defeating-white-christian-nationalism-today/#.Yuq0snbMLFA.
Jones-Correa, Michael. 1998a. *Between Two Nations: The Political Predicament of Latinos in New York City*. Ithaca, NY: Cornell University Press.
Jones-Correa, Michael. 1998b. "Different Paths: Gender, Immigration and Political Participation." *International Migration Review* 32(2): 326–349.
Jones-Correa, Michael. 2002. "Latinos and Latin America: A Unified Agenda?" Pp. 115–130 in *Ethnic Identity Groups and Foreign Policy*, edited by Thomas Ambrosio. Westport, CT: Praeger.
Jones-Correa, Michael. 2007. "Fuzzy Distinctions and Blurred Boundaries: Transnational, Ethnic, and Immigrant Politics." Pp. 44–62 in *Latino Politics: Identity, Mobilization and Representation*, edited by Rodolfo Espino, David L. Leal, and Kenneth J. Meier. Charlottesville: University of Virginia Press.
Jones-Correa, Michael, and Els de Graauw. 2013. "Looking Back to See Ahead: Unanticipated Changes in Immigration from 1986 to the Present and their Implications for American Politics Today." *Annual Review of Political Science* 16: 209–230.
Jones-Correa, Michael, and David Leal. 1996. "Becoming 'Hispanic': Secondary Panethnic Identification among Latin American Origin Groups." *Hispanic Journal of Behavioral and Social Sciences* 18(2): 214–254.
Joseph, George. 2014a. "Supreme Court Upholds Ban on Affirmative Action in Michigan: Community Divided over Decision." *India Abroad*, May 2, p. A30.
Joseph, George. 2014b. "Supreme Court's Decision Supporting Sectarian Prayers Upsets HAF." *India Abroad*, May 16, p. A10.
Joseph, Tiffany D. 2015. *Race on the Move: Brazilian Migrants and the Global Reconstruction of Race*. Palo Alto, CA: Stanford University Press.
Joshi, Khyati Y. 2006. *New Roots in America's Sacred Ground: Religion, Race and Ethnicity in Indian America*. New Brunswick, NJ: Rutgers University Press.
Jung, Moon-Kie. 2015. *Beneath the Surface of White Supremacy: Denaturalizing US Racisms Past and Present*. Palo Alto, CA: Stanford University Press.
Kalyanaraman, Srinivasan. 2011. "Hindu American Foundation Faces Desertion on Caste Report." *India Cause*. http://www.indiacause.com/blog/2011/01/04/caste-report-hindu-american-foundation-faces-desertion/.
Kamdar, Mira. 2007. "Forget the Israel Lobby. The Hill's Next Big Player Is Made in India." *Washington Post*, September 30, p. B03.
Kapur, Devesh. 2012. "The Unusual Political Leanings of Indian Americans." *Indiaspora—The Blog*, October 22. Retrieved January 23, 2013. http://indiaspora.org/blog/the-unusual-political-leanings-of-indian-americans/.
Karthikeyan, Hrishi. 2009. "The Obama Generation." *Indian American*, pp. 17–20.
Kashmeri, Zuhair, and Brian McAndrew. 2005. *Soft Target: The Real Story Behind the Air India Disaster*. 2nd ed. Toronto: James Lorimer & Company Ltd.
Kashmir Study Group. 2005. "Kashmir: A Way Forward." Retrieved May 14, 2014. http://kashmirstudygroup.com.
Kashmiri American Council. 2011. "Kashmir Resolution Key to Regional Peace: Dr. Fai." February 18.

Kasinitz, P., J. Mollenkopf, M. Waters, and J. Holdaway. 2008. *Inheriting the City: The Children of Immigrants Come of Age*. New York and Boston: Russell Sage and Harvard University Press.

Keck, Margaret E., and Kathryn Sikkink. 1998. *Activists beyond Borders: Advocacy Networks in International Politics*. Ithaca, NY: Cornell University Press.

Khalidi, Omar. 1991. *Indian Muslims in North America*. Watertown, MA: South Asia Press.

Khalidi, Usama. 1991. "Minority Experience in the United States: A Model for Indian Muslims." Pp. 60–63 in *Indian Muslims in North America*, edited by Omar Khalidi. Watertown, MA: South Asia Press.

Khan, Imad. 2020. "Sri Preston Kulkarni's Fight to Win Texas's 22nd Congressional District." TheJuggernaut.com, November 4. https://www.thejuggernaut.com/sri-preston-kulkarni-texas?mc_cid=13887cb44e&mc_eid=8ee043a486.

Khan, Muqtedar M. A. 2002. *American Muslims: Bridging Faith and Freedom*. Beltsville, MD: Amana Publications.

Kibria, Nazli. 1996. "Not Asian, Black or White? Reflections on South Asian American Racial Identity." *Amerasia Journal* 22(2): 77–86.

Kibria, Nazli. 1998. "The Racial Gap: South Asian American Racial Identity and the Asian America Movement." Pp. 69–78 in *A Part, Yet Apart: South Asians in Asian America*, edited by Lavina Dhingra Shankar and Rajini Srikanth. Philadelphia: Temple University Press.

Kibria, Nazli. 2002. *Becoming Asian American: Second-Generation Chinese and Korean American Identities*. Baltimore: Johns Hopkins University Press.

Kibria, Nazli. 2011. *Muslims in Motion: Islam and National Identity in the Bangladeshi Diaspora*. New Brunswick, NJ, and London: Rutgers University Press.

Kidd, Dustin, and Keith McIntosh. 2016. "Social Media and Social Movements." *Sociology Compass* 10(9): 785–794.

Kindy, Kimberly. 2023. "As Democrats Push to Ban Caste Discrimination, Some Indian Americans Object." *Washington Post*, November 22. https://www.washingtonpost.com/politics/2023/11/22/indian-americans-caste-discrimination-newsom-veto/?utm_campaign=wp_post_most&utm_medium=email&utm_source=newsletter&wpisrc=nl_most.

Kirk, Jason A. 2008. "Indian-Americans and the U.S.-India Nuclear Agreement: Consolidation of an Ethnic Lobby?" *Foreign Policy Analysis* 4: 275–300.

Kniss, Fred, and Paul D. Numrich. 2007. *Sacred Assemblies and Civic Engagement: How Religion Matters for America's Newest Immigrants*. New Brunswick, NJ: Rutgers University Press.

Koopmans, Ruud. 2013. "Multiculturalism and Immigration: A Contested Field in Cross-National Comparison." *Annual Review of Sociology* 39: 147–169.

Kulkarni, Bhargavi. 2020a. "Anti-CAA, NRC Protests Held Across the Country." *India Abroad*, January 27, pp. 13–14.

Kulkarni, Bhargavi. 2020b. "Republic Day of Protests." *India Abroad*, February 3, pp. 18–22.

Kulkarni, Bhargavi, and Suman Guha Mazumder. 2019. "Paradise Regained? Hindu-Americans and Kashmiri Pandits Laud Modi's Decision to End Special Status to Kashmir." *India Abroad*, August 7, p. 20.

Kumar, Rashmee. 2019. "The Network of Hindu Nationalists Behind Modi's 'Diaspora Diplomacy' in the U.S." TheIntercept.com, September 25.

Kumar, Rashmee, and Akela Lacy. 2020. "India Lobbies to Stifle Criticism, Control Messaging in U.S. Congress amid Rising Anti-Muslim Violence." TheIntercept.com, March 16. https://theintercept.com/2020/03/16/india-lobbying-us-congress/.

Kuo, Alexander, Neil Malhotra, and Cecilia Hyunjung Mo. 2017. "Social Exclusion and Political Identity: The Case of Asian American Partisanship." *Journal of Politics* 79(1): 17–32.

Kurien, Prema A. 1999. "Gendered Ethnicity: Creating a Hindu Indian Identity in the U.S." *American Behavioral Scientist* 42(4): 648–670.

Kurien, Prema A. 2001. "Religion, Ethnicity and Politics: Hindu and Muslim Indian Immigrants in the United States." *Ethnic and Racial Studies* 24(2): 263–293.

Kurien, Prema A. 2003. "To Be or Not to Be South Asian: Contemporary Indian American Politics." *Journal of Asian American Studies* 6(3): 261–288.

Kurien, Prema A. 2006a. "Multiculturalism and 'American' Religion: The Case of Hindu Indian Americans." *Social Forces* 85(2): 723–742.

Kurien, Prema A. 2006b. "Mr. President, Why Do You Exclude Us from Your Prayers?: Hindus Challenge American Pluralism." Pp. 119–138 in *A Nation of Religions: The Politics of Pluralism in Multireligious America*, edited by Stephen Prothero. University of North Carolina Press.

Kurien, Prema A. 2007a. *A Place at the Table: Multiculturalism and the Development of an American Hinduism*. New Brunswick: Rutgers University Press.

Kurien, Prema A. 2007b. "Who Speaks for Indian Americans? Religion, Ethnicity, and Political Formation." *American Quarterly* 59(3): 759–783.

Kurien, Prema A. 2012. "Decoupling Religion and Ethnicity: Second-Generation Indian American Christians." *Qualitative Sociology* 35(4): 447–468.

Kurien, Prema A. 2013. "Religion, Social Incorporation, and Civic Engagement: Second-Generation Indian American Christians." *Review of Religious Research* 55(1): 81–104.

Kurien, Prema A. 2017a. *Ethnic Church Meets Megachurch: Indian American Christianity in Motion*. New York: New York University Press.

Kurien, Prema A. 2017b. "Majority versus Minority Religious Status and Diasporic Nationalism: Indian American Advocacy Organizations." *Nations and Nationalism* 23(1): 109–128.

Kurien, Prema A. 2018. "Shifting U.S. Racial and Ethnic Identities and Sikh American Activism." *RSF: The Russell Sage Foundation Journal of the Social Sciences* 4(5): 81–98. Special issue on Immigrants and Changing Identities. https://www.rsfjournal.org/content/4/5/81.

Kurien, Prema A. 2022. "Religion as Social Location: Global and Comparative Perspectives." *Journal for the Scientific Study of Religion* 61(1): 5–20.

Kurien, Prema A. 2023. "The Racial Paradigm and Dalit Anti-Caste Mobilization in the U.S." *Social Problems* 70(3): 717–734.

Kuruvilla, Carol. 2017. "Indian-Americans Lean Left, So Why Are So Many Joining the Trump Administration?" *Huffington Post*. https://www.huffingtonpost.com/entry/indian-americans-trump-administration_us_59723f83e4b09e5f6ccf1517.

Lacroix, Thomas. 2016. "Periodizing Indian Organizational Transnationalism in the United Kingdom." Pp. 209–235 in *A Century of Transnationalism: Immigrants and Their Homeland Connections*, edited by Nancy L. Green and Roger Waldinger. Urbana: University of Illinois Press.

Lakhihal, Prashanth. 2001. "Sudarshan to Salute Hinduism's Growth." *India Post*, pp. 1, 59, 60.

Lancaster, John. 1999. "Activism Boosts' India's Fortunes." *Washington Post*. https://www.washingtonpost.com/archive/politics/1999/10/09/activism-boosts-indias-fortunes/eb725d00-aa18-4b17-963f-099f84dfa546/.

Langevin, Chris, Matt Guardino, and Jeff Pugh. 2022. *Immigrant Visibility and Political Activism Research Collaborative: Data Report and Executive Summary*. Providence College and UMass Boston. ivparc-report-final.pdf (jeffreypugh.com)

Laurence, Jonathan. 2012. *The Emancipation of Europe's Muslims: The State's Role in Minority Integration*. Princeton, NJ: Princeton University Press.

Layman, Geoffrey C., Thomas M. Carsey, and Juliana Menasce Horowitz. 2006. "Party Polarization in American Politics: Characteristics, Causes, and Consequences." *Annual Review of Political Science* 9: 83–110.

Lee, Jennifer, and Karthick Ramakrishnan. 2020. "Who Counts as Asian." *Ethnic and Racial Studies* 43(10): 1733–1756.

Lee, Joel. 2021. *Deceptive Majority: Dalits, Hinduism, and Underground Religion*. Cambridge: Cambridge University Press.

Lee, Taeku. 2008. "Race, Immigration, and the Identity-to-Politics Link." *Annual Review of Political Science* 11: 457–478.

Lee, Taeku, S. Karthick Ramakrishnan, and Ricardo Ramírez, eds. 2006. *Transforming Politics, Transforming America: The Political and Civic Incorporation of Immigrants in the United States*. Charlottesville: University of Virginia Press.

Leonard, Karen Isaksen. 1994. *Making Ethnic Choices: California's Punjabi Mexican Americans*. Philadelphia: Temple University Press.

Leonard, Karen Isaksen. 2001. "South Asian Leadership of American Muslims." Pp. 233–249 in *Muslims in the West: Sojourners to Citizens*, edited by Yvonne Haddad. New York: Oxford University Press.

Leonard, Karen Isaksen. 2003. *Muslims in the United States: The State of Research*. New York: Russell Sage Foundation.

Levitt, Peggy. 2003. "Keeping Feet in Both Worlds: Transnational Practices and Immigrant Incorporation in the United States." Pp. 177–195 in *Toward Assimilation and Citizenship: Immigrants in Liberal Nation-States*, edited by C. Joppke and E. Morawska. Basingstoke: Palgrave.

Ley, David. 2013. "Does Transnationalism Trump Immigrant Integration? Evidence from Canada's Links with East Asia." *Journal of Ethnic and Migration Studies* 39(6): 921–938.

Lien, Pei-te, Margaret Conway, and Janelle Wong. 2004. *The Politics of Asian Americans: Diversity and Community*. New York: Routledge.

Lind, Michael. 2002. "The Israeli Lobby." *Prospect*, April 1.

Lindsay, James. 2002. "Getting Uncle Sam's Ear." *Brookings Review*, Winter: 37–40.

Linshi, Jack. 2015. "Why a Bobby Jindal Portrait Sparked a Racial Controversy." Time.com, February 5. https://time.com/3695541/bobby-jindal-indian-immigration/.

Louis, Arul. 2018. "'We Are Sikhs' Campaign Wins Top Award for Public Relations Programming." *India Abroad*, March 30.

Louis, Arul. 2020. "Sikhs Can Be Counted as Separate 'Ethno-religious' Group in 2020 Census." *India West*, September 8.

Maghbouleh, Neda, Ariela Schachter, and René D. Flores. 2022. "Middle Eastern and North African Americans May Not Be Perceived, nor Perceive Themselves, to Be White." *Proceedings of the National Academy of Sciences* 119(7): e2117940119.

Mahmood, Cynthia Kepley. 2014. "'Khalistan' as Political Critique." Pp. 571–80 in *The Oxford Handbook of Sikh Studies*, edited by Pashaura Singh and Louis E. Fenech. Oxford: Oxford University Press.

Malhotra, John. 2011. "Indian Americans Support USCIRF Report on Religious Freedom." *Christian Today*, May 13. Retrieved May 16, 2014. http://www.christiantoday.co.in/articles/indian-americans-support-uscirf-report-on-religious-freedom/6260.htm.

Malhotra, Rajiv. 2003a. "Problematizing God's Interventions in History." Sulekha.com, September 6. Retrieved September 13, 2020. https://rajivmalhotra.com/library/articles/problematizing-gods-interventions-history/.

Malhotra, Rajiv. 2003b. "Does South Asian Studies Undermine India." Rediff.com, December 4.

Malhotra, Rajiv. 2003c. "Repositioning India's Brand." Rediff.com, December 9.

Malhotra, Rajiv. 2004a. "America Must Re-discover India." Rediff.com, January 20.

Malhotra, Rajiv. 2004b. "Preventing America's Nightmare." Rediff.com, January 21.

Malhotra, Rajiv. 2016. *Academic Hinduphobia: A Critique of Wendy Doniger's Erotic School of Indology*. New Delhi: Voice of India.

Marquez, Benjamin. 2003. *Constructing Identities in Mexican American Political Organizations*. Austin: University of Texas Press.

Mathias, Charles, Jr. 1981. "Ethnic Groups and Foreign Policy." *Foreign Affairs* 59(5): 975–998.

McCarthy, Niall. 2021. "Indian Talent Is in High Demand in the U.S." November 30. https://www.statista.com/chart/9008/h1b-recipients-by-country-of-birth/.

McDermott, Rachel F. 2008. "From Hinduism to Christianity, from India to New York: Bondage and Exodus Experiences in the Lives of Indian Dalit Christians in the Diaspora." Pp. 223–248 in *South Asian Christian Diaspora: Invisible Diaspora in Europe and North America*, edited by Knut A. Jacobsen and Selva J. Raj. Burlington, VT: Ashgate.

McDermott, Rachel F. 2009. "From Hinduism to Christianity, from India to New York: Bondage and Exodus Experiences in the Lives of Indian Dalit Christians in the Diaspora." Pp. 84–109 in *Pilgrims at the Crossroads: Asian Indian Christians at the North American Frontier* edited by Anand Veeraraj and Rachel Fell McDermott. Durham, NC: Lulu Publishers.

McIntire, Mike. 2006. "Indian-Americans Test Their Clout on Atom Pact." *New York Times*, June 5.

McMahon, Shawn. 2001. *Echoes of Freedom: South Asian Pioneers in California, 1899–1965*. Berkeley: Center for South Asian Studies, University of California, Berkeley.

McMahon, Shawn. 2005. *Fight for Equality: International Medical Graduates in the United States*. Riverdale, MD: Potomac Publishing.

McNickle, Chris. 1993. *To Be Mayor of New York: Ethnic Politics in the City*. New York: Columbia University Press.

Medina, Jennifer. 2016. "Debate Erupts in California over Curriculum on India's History." *New York Times*, May 6. Retrieved August 26, 2020. https://www.nytimes.com/2016/05/06/us/debate-erupts-over-californias-india-history-curriculum.html.

Mehra, Beloo. 2003. "Political Coming-of-Age for Indian-Americans." June 17. https://www.sulekha.com/column.asp?cid=305830.

Mehta, Purvi. 2013. "Recasting Caste: Histories of Dalit Transnationalism and the Internationalization of Caste Discrimination." PhD dissertation, University of Michigan.

Mehta, Sunil. 2018. "A Call to Arms (from a Reluctant Warrior)." Medium.com.

Melwani, Lavina. 2009. "Meet the Young Hindu American Foundation." *Hinduism Today Magazine*, April/May/June. https://www.hinduismtoday.com/magazine/april-may-june-2009/2009-04-meet-the-young-hindu-american-foundation/.

Metcalf, Barbara D., and Thomas R. Metcalf. 2002. *A Concise History of India*. Cambridge: Cambridge University Press.

Mishra, Sangay K. 2016. *Desis Divided: The Political Lives of South Asian Americans*. Minneapolis: University of Minnesota Press.

Misir, Deborah N. 1996. "The Murder of Narvoz Mody: Race, Violence and the Search for Order." *Amerasia Journal* 22(2): 55–76.

Mistry, Dinshaw. 2013. "The India Lobby and the Nuclear Agreement with India." *Political Science Quarterly* 128(4): 717–746.

Modi, Radha. 2022. "Shifting Legibility: Racial Ambiguity in the U.S. Racial Hierarchy." *Ethnic and Racial Studies*. Published online April 20, 2022.

Modood, Tariq. 2005. *Multicultural Politics: Racism, Ethnicity and Muslims in Britain*. Minneapolis: University of Minnesota Press.

Modood, Tariq 2010. "Multicultural Citizenship and Muslim Identity Politics." *Interventions* 12(2): 157–170.

Moore, Deborah Dash. 1981. *At Home in America: Second Generation New York Jews*. New York: Columbia University Press.

Mora, Cristina G. 2014. *Making Hispanics: How Activists, Bureaucrats & Media Constructed a New America*. Chicago: University of Chicago Press.

Morning, Ann. 2001. "The Racial Self-Identification of South Asians in the United States." *Journal of Ethnic and Migration Studies* 27(1): 61–79.

Moss, Diana M. 2022. *The Arab Spring Abroad: Diasporic Activism against Authoritarian Regimes*. Cambridge: Cambridge University Press.

Mozumdar, Suman Guha. 2019a. "Indian-Americans Cheer Green Card Bill." *India Abroad*, July 17. https://www.indiaabroad.com.

Mozumdar, Suman Guha. 2019b. "OJBJP Launches Phone Campaign Ahead of Elections." *India Abroad*, January 3, p. 14.

Mozumdar, Suman Guha. 2020a. "Identity Politics and Census 2020: The Sikhs' Bid for Separate Ethnic Identity in the U.S. Raises Questions and Concerns." *India Abroad*, February 10, pp. 22–25.

Mozumdar, Suman Guha. 2020b. "The Pushback: Campaigns in Support of India's Citizenship Laws Gather Momentum in the U.S." *India Abroad*, January 6, pp. 8–9.

Nadal, Kevin L. 2019. "The Brown Asian American Movement: Advocating for South Asian, Southeast Asian, and Filipino American Communities." *Asian American Policy Review* 29: 2–11.

Nagel, Caroline R., and Lynn A. Staeheli. 2008. "Integration and the Negotiation of 'Here' and 'There': The Case of British Arab Activists." *Social & Cultural Geography* 9(4): 415–430.

Nanjappa, Vicky. 2020. "Pro Khalistan SJF Instigating Sikhs in the Army, Youth to Rise in Mutiny against India." OneIndia.com, December 9. https://www.oneindia.com/india/pro-khalistan-sjf-instigating-sikhs-in-army-youth-to-rise-in-mutiny-against-india-nia-3187209.html.

Naujoks, Daniel. 2013. *Migration, Citizenship, and Development: Diasporic Membership Policies and Overseas Indians in the United States.* New Delhi: Oxford University Press.

Newfield, Christopher, and Avery F. Gordon. 1996. "Multiculturalism's Unfinished Business." Pp. 76–115 in *Mapping Multiculturalism*, edited by A. Gordon and C. Newfield. Minneapolis: University of Minnesota Press.

News India Staff Writer. 1980. "Chief Testifies before Immigration Policy Body." *News India*, May 16.

Nibber, Gurpreet Singh. 2015. "Referendum 2020? Khalistan Divides, Unites, Sikhs Abroad." *Hindustan Times*, August 4. Accessed January 5, 2017. http://www.hindustantimes.com/punjab/referendum-2020-khalistan-divides-unites-sikhs-abroad/story-QBIfntRdW0zF7kVpw9XgmN.html.

Nicholls, Walter J. 2019. *The Immigrant Rights Movement: The Battle over National Citizenship.* Stanford, CA: Stanford University Press.

Nimbark, Ashkant. 1980. "Some Observations on Asian Indians in an American Educational Setting." Pp. 247–271 in *The New Ethnics: Asian Indians in the United States*, edited by P. Saran and E. Eames. New York: Praeger.

Nimer, Mohammed. 2002. *The North American Muslim Resource Guide: Muslim Community Life in the United States and Canada.* New York: Routledge.

Nomani, Azra. 2006. *Standing Alone: An American Woman's Struggle for the Soul of Islam.* Reprint ed. San Francisco: HarperOne.

Noorani, A. G. 2011. "Article 370: A Constitutional History of Jammu and Kashmir." Oxford Scholarship Online, September. https://academic.oup.com/book/26414.

Ochoa, Enrique C., and Gilda Ochoa, eds. 2005. *Latino Los Angeles: Transformations, Communities, Activism.* Tucson: University of Arizona Press.

Okamoto, Dina. 2014. *Redefining Race: Asian American Panethnicity and Shifting Ethnic Boundaries.* New York: Russell Sage Foundation.

Okamoto, Dina, and G. Cristina Mora. 2014. "Panethnicity." *Annual Review of Sociology* 40: 219–239.

Omi, Michael, and Howard Winant. 2015. *Racial Formation in the United States.* 3rd ed. New York: Routledge.

Omvedt, Gail. 2004. "The UN, Racism, and Caste." Pp. 187–193 in *Caste, Race and Discrimination: Discourses in International Context*, edited by Sukhadeo Thorat and Umakant. New Delhi: Rawat Publications.

Ong, Aihwa. 1996. "Cultural Citizenship as Subject-Making: Immigrants Negotiate Racial and Cultural Boundaries in the United States." *Current Anthropology* 37(5): 737–762.

Overseas Tribune Staff Writer. 1986. "No Cut in Medicare Funding for FMGs." *Overseas Tribune*.

Pais, Arthur. 2013. "We Should Be in the Army Not as Exceptions but as Freely as Other Minorities." *India Abroad*, July 26, p. A18.

Park, Jerry. 2023. "Asian Americans, Religion, and the 2020 Elections." Unpublished manuscript.

Park, Jerry, and Joshua C. Tom. 2020. "Political Trajectories of Asian Americans: Bringing Religion In." *AAPI Nexus* 17(1&2).

Paul, David M., and Rachel Anderson Paul. 2009. *Ethnic Lobbies and US Foreign Policy*. Boulder, CO: Lynne Rienner.

Paul, Sonia. 2019. "'Howdy Modi' Was a Display of Indian American's Political Power." TheAtlantic.com, September 23. https://www.theatlantic.com/politics/archive/2019/09/howdy-modi-rally-trump-divides-indian-diaspora/598600/.

Paul, Sonia. 2020a. "How Hindu Nationalism Could Shape the Election." Politico, October 30. Retrieved July 20, 2021. https://www.politico.com/news/magazine/2020/10/30/hindu-nationalism-election-indian-american-voters-433608.

Paul, Sonia. 2020b. "'A Political Awakening': South Asians Play Growing Role in U.S. Elections." TheJuggernaut.com, September 3. https://www.thejuggernaut.com/a-political-awakening-south-asians-2020-elections?mc_cid=aeb1764649&mc_eid=8ee043a486.

Paul, Sonia, and Mansi Choksi. 2016. "How Donald Trump Ended Up at a Bollywood-Themed Hindu Rally in New Jersey." October 20. https://theworld.org/stories/2016-10-19/how-donald-trump-ended-bollywood-themed-hindu-rally-new-jersey.

Però, Davide, and David Solomos. 2010. "Introduction: Migrant Politics and Mobilization: Exclusion, Engagements, Incorporation." *Ethnic and Racial Studies* 33: 1–8.

Peters, Jeremy W. 2016. "Among Donald Trump's Biggest U.S. Fans: Hindu Nationalists." October 14. http://www.nytimes.com/2016/10/15/us/politics/indian-americans-trump.html?_r=0.

Pew Research Center. 2011. *Lobbying for the Faithful. Online Directory of Religious Advocates: Kashmiri American Foundation*. https://www.pewresearch.org/religion/2011/11/21/lobbying-for-the-faithful-exec/.

Pew Research Center. 2012. *Asian Americans: A Mosaic of Faiths*. https://www.pewresearch.org/religion/2012/07/19/asian-americans-a-mosaic-of-faiths-overview/.

Pew Research Center. 2015. *America's Changing Religious Landscape*. http://www.pewforum.org/2015/05/12/americas-changing-religious-landscape.

Pew Research Center. 2017. *U.S. Indian Population Living in Poverty, 2015*. https://www.pewresearch.org/social-trends/chart/u-s-indian-population-living-in-poverty/.

Pew Research Center. 2019. *First and Second Generation Share of the Population 1900–2017*. https://www.pewresearch.org/hispanic/chart/first-and-second-generation-share-of-the-population/.

Pew Research Center. 2023. *Religion among Asian Americans*. October 11. https://www.pewresearch.org/religion/2023/10/11/religion-among-asian-americans/

Philpott, Daniel. 2009. "Has the Study of Global Politics Found Religion?" *Annual Review of Politics* 12: 183–202.

Portes, Alejandro, and Rubén Rumbaut. 2014. *Immigrant America: A Portrait*. 4th ed. Berkeley: University of California Press.

Potts, Michel. 1994. "Indian, Asian Hotel Owners Groups Join Forces at Meet." *India West* 20(5): C53.

Prashad, Vijay. 1998. "Crafting Solidarities." Pp. 105–126 in *A Part, yet Apart: South Asians in Asian America*, edited by Lavina Dhingra Shankar and Rajini Srikanth. Philadelphia: Temple University Press.

Puri, Harish K. 2011. *Ghadar Movement: A Short History*. New Delhi: National Book Trust, India.

Putnam, Robert. 2000. *Bowling Alone: The Collapse and Revival of American Community*. New York: Simon & Schuster.

Rai, Mridu. 2004. *Hindu Rulers, Muslim Subjects: Islam, Rights, and the History of Kashmir*. Princeton, NJ: Princeton University Press.

Rai, Mridu. 2019. "History of Betrayals in Kashmir." Frontline.com. https://frontline.thehindu.com/cover-story/kashmir-history-of-betrayals/article29053014.ece

Raj, Yashwant. 2017. "Barack Obama, the First 'Indian American' President." *Hindustan Times*, January 22. https://www.hindustantimes.com/world-news/barack-obama-the-first-indian-american-president/story-FzmviWUyMnmbnFf6xygOjM.html.

Rajagopal, Arvind. 1995. "Better Hindu Than Black? Narratives of Asian Indian Identity." Presented at the annual meetings of the SSSR and the RRA, St. Louis, MO.

Rajagopal, Arvind. 2001. *Politics after Television: Hindu Nationalism and the Reshaping of the Public in India*. Cambridge: Cambridge University Press.

Rajan, Radha. 2011. "Hindu American Foundation's Motivated 'Report': Cast in Hubris and Deception." Bharatabharati. http://bharatabharati.wordpress.com/2011/01/07/hindu-american-foundations-motivated-%E2%80%98report%E2%80%99-cast-in-hubris-and-deception-radha-rajan/.

Rajghatta, Chidanand. 2011. "As Pak Lobbying Falls on ISI Sword, 'Hai-Fai' among Kashmiri Pandits." *The Times of India*, July 21. http://timesofindia.indiatimes.com/world/us/As-Pak-lobbyist-falls-on-ISI-sword-Hai-Fai-among-Kashmiri-Pandits/articleshow/9314477.cms.

Rajghatta, Chidanand. 2020. "Biden Sidelines pro-Modi Indian American as Muslim Outreach Coordinator after Liberal Firestorm." *The Times of India*, March 11. https://timesofindia.indiatimes.com/world/us/biden-sidelines-pro-modi-indian-american-as-muslim-outreach-coordinator-after-liberal-firestorm/articleshow/74582191.cms.

Ramakrishnan, Karthick S. 2016. "How Asian Americans Became Democrats." *American Prospect*, July 16. Retrieved July 20, 2021. https://prospect.org/civil-rights/asian-americans-became-democrats/.

Ramakrishnan, Karthick S. 2021. "In 2020, AAPIs Saw the Highest Increases in Voter Turnout." Data Bits, May 20. https://aapidata.com/blog/2020-record-turnout/.

Ramakrishnan, Karthick S. 2023. "Face the Facts: South Asian Americans Need Representation in Asian America." Blog, February 24. https://aapidata.com/blog/facts-south-asians-2023/

Ramakrishnan, Karthick S., Janelle Wong, Jennifer Lee, and Taeku Lee. 2016. "Report on Registered Voters in the Fall 2016 National Asian American Survey (NAAS)." October 5. http://naasurvey.com/wp-content/uploads/2016/10/NAAS2016-Oct5-report.pdf.

Ramakrishnan, Karthick S., Janelle Wong, Jennifer Lee, and Taeku Lee. 2017. "2016 Post-Election National Asian American Survey (NAAS)." May 16. https://naasurvey.com/wp-content/uploads/2017/05/NAAS16-post-election-report.pdf

Rana, Junaid. 2017. "Policing Kashmiri Brooklyn." Pp. 256–268 in *FBI and Religion: Faith and National Security before and after 9/11*, edited by Sylvester A. Johnson and Steven Weitzman. Berkeley: University of California Press.

Rangarajan, Raj S. 2002. "Four Community Groups Join Forces for Unity." *India West*, October 11, p. A28.

Rao, Ramesh. 2003. "It's India Not South Asia." *The Subcontinental: A Journal of South Asian American Political Identity* 1(1): 27–40.

Rashid, Iffat. 2020. "Theatrics of a 'Violent State' or 'State of Violence': Mapping Histories and Memories of Partition in Jammu and Kashmir." *South Asia: Journal of South Asian Studies* 43(2): 215–231.

Ravishankar, Ra, and Shefali Chandra. 2004. "Brahminizing the Diaspora." Editorial, *Ghadar*, June. https://www.ghadar.insaf.net/June2004.

Redden, Elizabeth. 2016. "Return to Sender." Inside Higher Education, February 22. https://www.insidehighered.com/news/2016/02/22/uc-irvine-moves-reject-endowed-chair-gifts-donor-strong-opinions-about-study.

Reed-Danahay, Deborah, and Caroline B. Brettell. 2008. *Citizenship, Political Engagement, and Belonging: Immigrants in Europe and the United States*. New Brunswick, NJ: Rutgers University Press.

Reedy, George E. 1991. *From the Ward to the White House: The Irish in America*. New York: Maxwell Macmillan.

Rekhi, Shefali. 1998. "Vajpayee Government Woos NRIs with Resurgent India Bonds, Makes Impressive Gains." *India Today*, June 24. https://www.indiatoday.in/magazine/economy/story/19980831-vajpayee-government-woos-nris-with-resurgent-india-bonds-makes-impressive-gains-826991-1998-06-23

Retis, Jessica, and Roza Tsagarousianou, eds. 2019. *The Handbook of Diasporas, Media, and Culture*. Medford, OR: Wiley-Blackwell.

Rice, Condoleeza. 2000. "Campaign 2000: Promoting the National Interest." *Foreign Affairs*, 79(1): 45–62.

Rizwan, Sahil. 2016. "The 12 Most Incredible and Absurd Things That Happened at the 'Hindus for Trump' Bollywood Event." Buzzfeed.com, October 16. https://www.buzzfeed.com/sahilrizwan/big-fan-of-hindu?utm_term=.ccG3qymRP&ref=mobile_share#.rnqBJlERj.

Rogers, Reuel R. 2006. *Afro-Caribbean Immigrants and the Politics of Incorporation: Ethnicity, Exception, or Exit*. New York: Cambridge University Press.

Rohatgi, Anubha. 2020. "Govt Blocks 40 Websites of Banned Pro-Khalistan Group Sikhs for Justice." HindustanTimes.com, July 5. https://www.hindustantimes.com/india-news/govt-blocks-40-websites-of-banned-pro-khalistan-group-sikhs-for-justice/story-XGpEigOtBauJegATFLmLpK.html.

Rosaldo, Renato. 1994. "Cultural Citizenship in San Jose, California." *Polar* 17: 57–63.

Roth, Wendy D. 2012. *Race Migrations: Latinos and the Cultural Transformation of Race*. Stanford, CA: Stanford University Press.

Rubinoff, Arthur G. 2001. "Changing Perceptions of India in the U.S. Congress." *Asian Affairs: An American Review* 28(1): 37–60.

Ruiz, Neil G. 2017. *Key Facts about the U.S. H1-B Visa Program*. April 27. Pew Research Center.

SAALT. 2001. "Terrorists Bring War Home in More Ways Than One." https://saalt.org/wp-content/uploads/2012/09/American-Backlash-report.pdf?eType=EmailBlastContent&eId=e8844d1f-311e-486e-ba95-c1bfdb8c0b17.

SAALT. 2010. "From Macacas to Turban Toppers: The Rise in Xenophobic and Racist Rhetoric in American Political Discourse." October. http://saalt.org/wp-content/uploads/2012/09/From-Macacas-to-Turban-Toppers-Report-October-20101.pdf.

SAALT. 2018. "Communities on Fire: Confronting Hate Violence and Xenophobic Political Rhetoric." http://saalt.org/wp-content/uploads/2018/01/Communities-on-Fire.pdf.

SACW.net. 2014. "Hindu Nationalism in the United States: A Report on Nonprofit Groups." http://www.sacw.net/IMG/pdf/US_HinduNationalism_Nonprofits.pdf.

Sahni, Manmeet. 2021. "Biden-Harris Is Diminishing India's Hindutva Lobby in the White House." Religion Unplugged, February 1. Retrieved February 14, 2021. https://religionunplugged.com/news/2021/2/1/biden-harris-is-diminishing-indias-hindutva-lobby-in-the-white-house.

Salim, Mariya. 2019. "A Historic Congressional Hearing on Caste in the US." Thewire.in. Retrieved August 2, 2019. https://thewire.in/caste/a-historic-congressional-hearing-on-caste-in-the-us.

Samson, Frank L. 2015. "Asian American Attitudes towards a US Citizenship Path for Illegal Immigrants: Immigration Reform as Racialized Politics." *Journal of Ethnic and Migration Studies* 41(1): 117–137.

Sanchez, Bob. 2004. "Pledge of Allegiance – To India." *The Social Contract* 14: 4 (Summer). (https://www.thesocialcontract.com/artman2/publish/tsc1404/article_1241.shtml).

Saperstein, Aliya, and Andrew M. Penner. 2012. "Racial Fluidity and Inequality in the United States." *American Journal of Sociology* 118(3): 676–727.

Saujani, Reshma. 2004. "A Campaign in First Persons." *Indian Life and Style—Politics (India West)*. Retrieved July 18, 2007. www.indianlifeandstyle.com/Politics.htm.

Saund, Dalip Singh. 1960. *Congressman from India*. New York: E. P. Dutton and Company.

Savarkar, Vinayak D. (1923) 1969. *Hindutva: Who Is a Hindu*. Bombay: S. S. Savarkar.

Sazawal, Vijay. 2013. "Resolving the Kashmir Conundrum: A Way Forward." September 11. https://www.kashmirforum.org/resolving-the-kashmir-conundrum-a-way-forward/

Schaffer, Howard. 2009. *The Limits of Influence: America's Role in Kashmir*. Washington, DC: Brookings University Press.

Schaffer, Teresita. 2005. *Kashmir: The Economics of Peace Building*. A Report of the CSIS South Asia Group with the Kashmir Study Group. Washington, DC: CSIS Press.

Segura, Gary M., and Helena Alvez Rodrigues. 2006. "Comparative Ethnic Politics in the United States: Beyond Black and White." *Annual Review of Political Science* 9: 375–395.

Selod, Saher. 2018. *Forever Suspect: Racialized Surveillance of Muslim Americans in the War of Terror*. New Brunswick, NJ: Rutgers University Press.

Shain, Yossi. 1999. *Marketing the American Creed Abroad: Diasporas in the U.S. and Their Homelands*. Cambridge: Cambridge University Press.

Shani, Giorgio. 2008. *Sikh Nationalism and Identity in a Global Age*. New York: Routledge.

Sharma, Ashok. 2017. *Indian Lobbying and its Influence in US Decision Making*. New Delhi: Sage Publications.

Sharma, Nitasha T. 2016. "Hip Hop Music-Anti/Racism-Empire: Post-9/11 Brown and a Critique of U.S. Empire." In *Audible Empires: Music/Transnationalism/Postcoloniality*, edited by Ronald Radano and Tejumola Olaniyan. Durham, NC: Duke University Press.

Shih, Gerry. 2021. "India's Farmers Call Off Protests for Now, after Government Agrees to Additional Demands." *Washington Post*, December 9. https://www.washingtonpost.com/world/2021/12/09/india-farmers-end-protests/.

Shih, Gerry. 2023. "Inside the Vast Digital Campaign by Hindu Nationalists to Inflame India." *Washington Post*, September 26. https://www.washingtonpost.com/world/2023/09/26/hindu-nationalist-social-media-hate-campaign/?utm_source=Pew+Research+Center&utm_campaign=8d9e32f4fa-EMAIL_CAMPAIGN_2023_09_27_05_08&utm_medium=email.

Shukla, Aseem. 2010a. "Exclusivists versus Pluralists: Very Different Paths to the One Truth." *Washington Post/Newsweek*, On Faith Panel. http://newsweek.washingtonpost.com/onfaith/panelists/aseem_shukla/2010/07/the_question_posed_here_on.html

Shukla, Aseem. 2010b. "Haley and America's Religious Litmus Test." *Washington Post/Newsweek*, On Faith Panel, June 23. http://newsweek.washingtonpost.com/onfaith/panelists/aseem_shukla/2010/06/what_nikki_haleys_victory_does_not_mean.html.

Shukla, Aseem. 2010c. "Tell and Don't Ask." *Washington Post/Newsweek*, On Faith Panel. http://newsweek.washingtonpost.com/onfaith/panelists/aseem_shukla/2010/02/tell_and_dont_ask.html.

Shukla, Suhag. 2008. "Hindu American Political Advocacy." *Swadharma* 3. www.swadharma.org/public/Swadhamav3.pdf.

Shukla, Suhag. 2010. "Caste, Hinduism, and Human Rights." HuffPost, December 10, 2010, updated May 25, 2011. https://www.huffpost.com/entry/hinduisms-white-elephant-_b_794813.

Shukla, Suhag. 2020. "Trumpian Tactics Against India's Citizenship Law" *India Abroad*, February 10, pp. 7, 10.

Sikhs for Justice. 2011. "India Placed on Human Rights 'Watch List.'" May 9. http://panthic.org/articles/5349.

Singh, Gurharpal, and Darshan Singh Tatla. 2006. *Sikhs in Britain: The Making of a Community*. London and New York: Zed Books.

Singh, Harpreet. 2011. "Continuing Violence against Religious Minorities." Sikh Siyasat, May 5. Retrieved May 16, 2014. http://www.sikhsiyasat.net/2011/05/05/continuing-violence-against-religious-minorities-india-on-us-watch-list/.

Singh, Khushwant. 2005. *A History of the Sikhs, Vol 2: 1839–2004*. Delhi: Oxford University Press.

Singh, Pritam. 2005. "Hindu Bias in India's 'Secular' Constitution: Probing Flaws in the Instruments of Governance." *Third World Quarterly* 26(6): 909–926.

Singh, Prithvi Raj. 1996. "The 'Fighting Machine' and Hindus, Letter to the editor." *India Post* October 11, p. A26.

Singh, Prithvi Raj. 1997. "A Time of Agony and a Time for Joy." *India Post* August 15, pp. A9, A26.

Singh, Sardar Hukam. 1949. Speech in Constitutional Assembly Debates (CAD): The Official Report 12 Vols. Delhi 1946–1950. Vol XI, 21 November 1949 Speech (East Punjab: Sikh representative). https://eparlib.nic.in/bitstream/123456789/763258/1/cad_29-08-1949.pdf

Sirohi, Seema. 2018. "World Hindu Congress Courts Controversy Besides Hindus." Thewire. in, September 6. https://thewire.in/world/world-hindu-congress-courts-controversy-besides-hindus.

Skrentny, John. 2002. *The Minority Rights Revolution*. Cambridge, MA: Harvard University Press.

Small, Mario Luis. 2009. "'How Many Cases Do I Need?': On Science and the Logic of Case Selection in Field-Based Research." *Ethnography* 10(1): 5–38.

Smith, Anthony D. 1986. *The Ethnic Origins of Nations*. Oxford: Wiley-Blackwell.

Smith, Steven D. 2010. *Disenchantment of Secular Discourse*. Cambridge, MA: Harvard University Press.

Smith, Tony. 2000. *Foreign Attachments: The Power of Ethnic Groups in the Making of American Foreign Policy*. Cambridge, MA: Harvard University Press.

Snedden, Christopher. 2001. "What Happened to Muslims in Jammu? Local Identity, 'the Massacre of 1947' and the Roots of the 'Kashmir Problem.'" *South Asia: Journal of South Asian Studies* 24(2): 111–134.

Sohi, Seema. 2014. *Echoes of Mutiny: Race, Surveillance and Indian Anticolonialism in North America*. New York: Oxford University Press.

Soulsman, Gary. 2006. "Soft Voice, Strong Message." *News Journal*, April 2. Retrieved April 16, 2020. http://www.ijtihad.org/soft-voice-strong-message.htm.

Soundararajan, Thenmozhi. 2016. "Erasing Caste: The Battle over California Textbook and Caste Apartheid." HuffPost, May 3, updated December 6, 2017. https://www.huffpost.com/entry/erasing-caste-the-battle_b_9817862.

Soundararajan, Thenmozhi. 2017. "Why It Is Time to Dump Gandhi." Medium.com. Retrieved May 24, 2017. https://medium.com/@dalitdiva/why-it-is-time-to-dump-gandhi-b59c7399fe66.

Soundararajan, Thenmozhi. 2020. "A New Lawsuit Shines a Light on Caste Discrimination in the U.S. and around the World." *Washington Post*, July 13. https://www.washingtonpost.com/opinions/2020/07/13/new-lawsuit-shines-light-caste-discrimination-us-around-world/.

Soundararajan, Thenmozhi, and Sinthujan Varatharajah, 2015. "Caste Privilege 101: A Primer for the Privileged." TheAerogram.com, February 10. http://theaerogram.com/caste-privilege-101-primer-privileged/.

Sridaran, Lakshmi. 2019. "High-Skilled Immigrants Bill Is Dangerous." *India Abroad*, pp. 8, 22.

Srinivasan, Rajeev. 2000. "Why I Am Not a South Asian." Rediff.com, March 19. https://www.rediff.com/news/2000/mar/19rajeev.htm.

Staerklé, Christian, Jim Sidanius, Eva G. T. Green, and Ludwin E. Molina. 2010. "Ethnic Minority-Majority Asymmetry in National Attitudes around the World: A Multilevel Analysis." *Political Psychology* 31(4): 491–519.

Stepick, Alex, Guillermo Grenier, Max Castro, and Marvin Dunn. 2003. *This Land Is Our Land: Immigrants and Power in Miami*. Berkeley: University of California Press.

Stevens, Stuart. 2020. *It Was All a Lie: How the Republican Party Became Donald Trump*. New York. Alfred A. Knopf.

Swami, Praveen. 2006. "PMO in Secret Talks with Secessionists." *The Hindu*, January 25.

Swan, Jonathan. 2016. "Hindu-American Emerges as Trump Mega-Donor." *The Hill*, July 19. Retrieved July 20, 2021. https://thehill.com/homenews/campaign/288377-hindu-american-emerges-as-trump-mega-donor.

Tabernise, Sabrina, and Robert Geobeloff. 2019. "How Voters Turned Virginia from Deep Red to Solid Blue." *New York Times*, November 9. https://www.nytimes.com/2019/11/09/us/virginia-elections-democrats-republicans.html?auth=login-email&login=email.

Takaki, Ronald. 1989. *Strangers from a Different Shore: A History of Asian Americans*. Boston: Little, Brown and Company.

Talbott, Strobe. 2006. *Engaging India: Diplomacy, Democracy, and the Bomb*. Washington, DC: Brookings Institution Press.

Tellis, Ashley. 2008. "The Merits of Dehyphenation: Explaining US Success in Engaging India and Pakistan." *Washington Quarterly* 31(4): 21–42.

Teltumbde, Anand. 2017. *Dalits: Past, Present, and Future*. New York: Routledge.

Thapar, Romila, Michael Witzel, Jaya Menon, Kai Friese, and Razib Khan. 2019. *Which of Us Are Aryans? Rethinking the Concept of Our Origins*. New Delhi: Aleph Book Company.

Therwath, Ingrid. 2007. "Working for India or against Islam? Islamophobia in Indian American Lobbies." *South Asia Multidisciplinary Academic Journal*, October. Retrieved May 12, 2013. https://journals.openedition.org/samaj/262

Tiku, Nitasha. 2022. "Google's Plan to Talk about Caste Bias Led to 'Division and Rancor.'" *Washington Post*, June 2. https://www.washingtonpost.com/technology/2022/06/02/google-caste-equality-labs-tanuja-gupta/.

Torpey, John. 2010. "A (Post-) Secular Age? Religion and the Two Exceptionalisms." *Social Research* 77(1): 269–296.

Trautman, Thomas. 1997. *Aryans and British India*. Berkeley: University of California Press.

Trotter, Virginia Y., and Bernard Michael. 1975. *Report of the Ad Hoc Committee on Racial and Ethnic Definitions of the Federal Interagency Committee on Education*. Washington, DC: Federal Interagency Committee on Education.

Tsutsui, Kiyoteru. 2018. *Rights Make Might: Global Human Rights and Minority Social Movements in Japan*. New York: Oxford University Press.

Udupa, Sahana. 2015. "Internet Hindus: Right-Wingers as New India's Ideological Warriors." Pp. 432–449 in *Handbook of Religion and the Asian City: Aspiration and Urbanization in the Twenty-First Century*, edited by Peter Van der Veer. Berkeley: University of California Press.

USCIRF Annual Report. 2018. *India, Tier 2*. https://www.uscirf.gov/sites/default/files/Tier2_INDIA.pdf.

USINPAC. 2009. "US National Security and US-India Strategic Relations." November.

USINPAC. 2014. "American Flag Flown Over US Capitol in Honor of BJP President Rajnath Singh." Retrieved May 18, 2014. http://www.usinpac.com/index.php/latest-press-release/2473-american-flag-flown-over-u-s-capitol-in-honor-of-bjp-president-rajnath-singh.

Uslaner, Eric M. 2002. "Cracks in the Armor? Interest Groups and Foreign Policy." Pp. 355–277 in *Interest Group Politics*, edited by Allan J. Cigler and Burdett A. Loomis. Washington DC: CQ Press.

Varadarajan, Latha. 2010. *The Domestic Abroad: Diasporas in International Relations*. New York: Oxford University Press.

Varshney, Ashutosh. 2021. "India's Democratic Exceptionalism Is Now Withering Away. The Impact Is Also External." Indianexpress.com, February 23. https://indianexpress.com/article/opinion/columns/elected-government-death-of-democracy-india-7200030/.

Venkataramakrishnan, Rohan 2019. "Who Is Linking Citizenship Act to NRC? Here Are Five Times That Amit Shah Did So." December 20. https://scroll.in/article/947436/who-is-linking-citizenship-act-to-nrc-here-are-five-times-amit-shah-did-so.

Vertovec, Steven, and Susanne Wessendorf. 2010. *The Multicultural Backlash: European Discourses, Policies and Practices*. London and New York: Routledge.

Villarreal, Roberto E., and Norma G. Hernandez. 1991. "Old and New Agendas: An Introduction." Pp. xv–xxvi in *Latinos and Political Coalitions: Political Empowerment for the 1990s*, edited by Roberto E. Villareal and Norma G. Hernandez. Santa Barbara, CA: Greenwood Press.

Visvanathan, Shiv. 2001. "The Race for Caste: Prolegomena to the Durban Conference." *Economic and Political Weekly*, July 7, pp. 2512–2516.

Viswanath, Sunita, and Raju Rajagopal. 2021. "The Case Against Cisco: The Imperative of Outlawing Caste Discrimination in the United States." Americankahani.com, February 28. https://americankahani.com/perspectives/the-case-against-cisco-the-imperative-of-outlawing-caste-discrimination-in-the-united-states/.

Waldman, Amy. 2002. "A Secular India or Not? At Strife Scene, Vote Is Test." *New York Times*, December 12, p. A18.

Warner, R. Stephen. 1993. "Work in Progress toward a New Paradigm for the Sociological Study of Religion in the United States." *American Journal of Sociology* 98(5): 1044–1093.

Warner, R. Stephen. 2006. "The De-Europeanization of American Christianity." Pp. 233–255 in *A Nation of Religions: The Politics of Pluralism in Multireligious America*, edited by Stephen Prothero. Chapel Hill: University of North Carolina Press.

Waters, Mary C. 1999. *Black Identities: West Indian Immigrant Dreams and American Realities*. New York and Cambridge: Russell Sage Foundation and Harvard University Press.

Waughray, Annapurna. 2009. "Caste Discrimination: A Twenty-First Century Challenge for UK Discrimination Law?" *Modern Law Review* 72(2): 182–219.

Wayland, Sarah. 2004. "Ethnonationalist Networks and Transnational Opportunities." *Review of International Studies* 30: 405–426.

Whitehead, Andrew L., and Samuel L. Perry. 2020. *Taking America Back for God: Christian Nationalism in the United States*. New York: Oxford University Press.

Whittle, Thomas. G. 2006. "Ambassador for Freedom Dr. Sayyid Muhammad Syeed." *Freedom Magazine*. Retrieved April 16, 2020. https://www.freedommag.org/english/vol36i1/page22.htm.

Wildman, Sarah. 2001. "All for One." *New Republic*, December 24. https://www.thenewrepublic.com122401/diarist122401.html.

Williams, Raymond B. 1988. *Religions of Immigrants from India and Pakistan: New Threads in the American Tapestry*. Cambridge: Cambridge University Press.

Williams, Raymond B. 1996. *Christian Pluralism in the United States: The Indian Immigrant Experience*. Cambridge: Cambridge University Press.

Wimmer, Andreas. 1997. "Who Owns the State: Understanding Ethnic Conflict in Post-Colonial Societies." *Nations and Nationalism* 3(4): 631–665.

Wimmer, Andreas, and Nina Glick Schiller. 2002. "Methodological Nationalism and Beyond: Nation-State Building, Migration, and the Social Sciences." *Global Networks* 2(4): 301–334

Wittkopf, Eugene R., and James M. McCormick, eds. 1998. *The Domestic Sources of American Foreign Policy: Insights and Evidence*. 3rd ed. Lanham, MD: Rowman and Littlefield.

Wong, Janelle. 2018. "The Evangelical Vote and Race in the 2016 Election." *Journal of Race, Ethnicity, and Politics* 3(1): 81–106.

Wong, Janelle, S. Karthick Ramakrishnan, Taeku Lee, and Jane Junn. 2011. *Asian American Political Participation: Emerging Constituents and Their Political Identities*. New York: Russell Sage Foundation.

Wong, Janelle, Kathy Rim, and Haven Perez. 2008. "Protestant Churches and Conservative Politics: Latinos and Asians in the United States." Pp. 271–299 in *Civic Hopes and Political Realities: Immigrant, Community Organizations, and Political Engagement*, edited by S. Karthick Ramakrishnan and Irene Bloemraad. New York: Russell Sage Foundation.

Worland, Justin. 2015. "Here's Bobby Jindal's Response to a Racial Controversy over His Portrait." Time.com, February 9. https://time.com/3701081/bobby-jindal-portrait-2016-presidential-election/.

Wright, Matthew, and Irene Bloemraad. 2012. "Is There a Trade-Off between Multiculturalism and Socio-Political Integration? Policy Regimes and Immigrant Incorporation in Comparative Perspective." *Perspectives on Politics* 10(1): 77–95.

Wright, Theodore P., Jr. 1991. "Limitations on the Human Rights Approach to Problems of the Muslim Minority in India." Pp. 48–57 in *Indian Muslims in North America*, edited by Omar Khalidi. Watertown, MA: South Asia Press.

Wuthnow, Robert. 2021. *Why Religion Is Good for American Democracy*. Princeton, NJ: Princeton University Press.

Yang, Fenggang, and Helen Rose Ebaugh. 2001. "Transformations in New Immigrant Religions and Their Global Implications." *American Sociological Review* 66(2): 269–288.

Yee, Vivian. 2014. "At Madison Square Garden, Chants, Cheers, and Roars for Modi." *New York Times*, September 28. https://www.nytimes.com/2014/09/29/nyregion/at-madison-square-garden-chants-cheers-and-roars-for-modi.html.

Yokley, Eli. 2015. "GOP Hindu-American Political Arm Emerges for 2016 Elections." Rollcall.com, November 20. http://www.rollcall.com/news/home/new-hindu-political-arm-emerge-2016-elections.

Zong, Jie, and Jeanne Batalova. 2015. "Indian Immigrants in the United States." Migration Policy Institute, May 6. https://www.migrationpolicy.org/article/indian-immigrants-united-states-2013.

Zutshi, Chitralekha. 2019. *Oxford India Short Introductions: Kashmir*. New Delhi: Oxford University Press.

Index

For the benefit of digital users, indexed terms that span two pages (e.g., 52–53) may, on occasion, appear on only one of those pages.

1984 Living History Project, 217–18
2014 Remembrance Project, 217–18
80-20 Initiative, 60
9/11, 5–6, 8–9, 270, 276–77
    activism before and after, 151–59, 218, 277–78, 287
    and Afghanistan, 113
    and hate crimes, 28, 177–78
    and Hinduism, 78–79
    and Kashmiri Muslims, 95–96, 225
    responses to, 118–20, 130–31
    and South Asian American organizations, 16–17, 106–7, 118, 244–45

AAPI Victory Fund, 258, 260, 271–72
abortion, 237, 251, 262, 270
Abraham, Thomas, 56–57, 59–60
Abrams, Stacey, 271
academia, U.S., 167–70, 189–90
academic Hinduism, 78–79
Academic Hinduphobia, 168–69
Ackerman, Gary L., 78
Adamson, Fiona, 292
Adityanath, Yogi, 227
Adivasi, 166
Adrian College, 153–54
Advocates for Human Rights, 202
affirmative action, 21–23, 26–27, 70–71, 144–45, 212, 233
Afghanistan, 108–9, 113
Africa, 50, 57, 157–58
African American mobilization, 16
Agarwala, Rina, 57, 90–92
Agenda for Muslim American Communities, 264–65
Ahluwalia, Waris Singh, 160–61
Ahmed, Akbar S., 153–54
Ahmed, Parvez, 153–54, 183–84
Ahrari, Mohammed E., 86–87
airports, 159–60, 277–78
Akali Dal, 76
Akins, Harrison, 205–6

Al Qaeda, 95–96
Albany, New York, 205–6
Alien Contract Labor Law, 38–39
Alien Tort Claims Act, 198–99, 218–20
All-India Christian Council (AICC), 84
Allen, George, 144, 245
Alliance for Justice and Accountability (AJA), 198–200, 203
Alphabet Workers Union, 178–79
Alwaleed, Prince, 170
Amazon, 179–80
Ambedkar Association of North America (AANA), 82–84, 215–16
Ambedkar Bhavan, New Delhi, 84
Ambedkar International Center, 82–83, 175–76
Ambedkar International Mission, Dr. (AIM), 81–83
Ambedkar King Study Circle, 179–80
Ambedkar, Bhimrao Ramji, 8–9, 17, 21–23, 70, 169–70, 175–76, 190–91
Ambedkarite Buddhism, 81–82
Ambedkarite studies, 169–70
Ambedkarites, 22–23, 25–26, 81, 145, 159, 164, 175–76, 190, 213–14, 279–80
    and caste, 279, 280–81, 288–89
    and civil rights, 176–77, 178–81
    and education, 170, 172, 173–74
    and mobilization, 195–96, 198–99, 277, 281
    post-9/11, 151–52, 159
    and religious freedom, 208–9
Ambegaonkar, Prakash, 132
American Association of Physicians of Indian Origin (AAPI), 61–62, 124–25, 141
American Civil Liberties Union (ACLU), 182
American Federation of Muslims from India (AFMI), 86, 90–91
American Hellenic Institute Public Affairs Committee (AHIPAC), 17
American Hindus against Defamation (AHAD), 152
American identity, 89–90, 99, 118

328 INDEX

American India Public Affairs Committee, 208–9
American Israel Public Affairs Committee (AIPAC), 2, 130–31, 133–34, 286, 289
  as model, 17, 23–24, 86–87, 120–24, 150, 290–91
American Jewish Committee (AJC), 68, 125–26, 133–34, 157–58
American Jewish Congress, 68
American Justice Center, 198–99
American Medical Association (AMA), 62
American Muslim Council (IAMC), 201–2, 204–7, 208–9, 282
American Muslim Institution, 184–85
American values, 151–52, 185, 275–76
Americans for Hindus, 231
Americans for Kashmir, 224–25
Americans4Hindus, 258, 268–69
Amnesty International, 201–2
Amritsar, India, 76–77
anarchism, 42
Anderson, Benedict, 194–95, 292
anti-Christian actions, 193
anti-colonialism, 35, 39–44, 47–48
anti-conversion laws, 201–2, 213
Anti-Defamation League, 68
anti-Hindu nationalism, 8–9, 81
anti-immigration stances, 237, 241, 261–62
anti-Muslim actions, 194, 197, 198, 202, 206, 253, 254–55, 265–66, 267, 270–71
Anti-Racial Harassment Bill, 59–60
anti-Semitism, 68
anti-Sikh actions, 202–3, 216, 217–20
apartheid, 39, 166, 212, 213–14, 226
Arab American communities, 144
Arab American groups, 118–19
Arab spring, 12
Arizona, 260, 271–72
Armed Forces Special Powers Act, 74–75
Armenian Assembly of America, 17
art museums, 167–68
Arya Samaj, 46–47, 69–70
Aryan identity, 6, 23, 45–46, 53–54, 65, 107
Asian American Hotel Owners Association (AAHOA), 62–63, 124–25, 142, 198–99, 285
Asian American Legal Defense and Education Fund (AALDEF), 16, 144, 151
Asian American organizations, 13, 26–27
Asian American Voters Coalition, 58–59
Asian Americans, 147, 232, 233
Asian Americans against Affirmative Action (4A), 60

Asian Indians, category of, 26–27, 53–55, 65, 187–88
Asian Pacific American caucus, 136–37
Asian Pacific American organizations, 28, 146–47
Asiatic Barred Zone Act, 44, 51, 54–55
Asiatic Exclusion League, 38, 51
assimilation, 9–10, 13, 16–17, 38
Association of Indian Muslims of America (AIM), 86, 87, 88, 90–91, 197, 198, 205–6, 208–9
Association of Indians in America (AIA), 52–53, 54–55, 56–57, 58–59, 107
atheism, 22–23, 70, 83–84
Atlanta, Georgia, 62–63
aunties, 116–17
Australia, 43–44, 129–30
AWACS planes, 108, 114
Ayodhya mosque, 79–80
Ayodhya, India, 72
Azadi movement, 74–75

Babri mosque, 72, 77–78, 198, 208–9
Bahujan Samaj Party, 279–80
Bangladesh, 12, 143, 157–58, 200–1, 264, 277
Bangladesh caucus, 136–37
Bangladeshi identity, 116–17, 118–19, 257
Bannon, Steve, 237, 270–71
Barkatullah, Abdul Hafiz Mohamed (Maulavi), 41–42
Barry, John, 41
Barve, Kumar, 121
Basilica of the National Shrine of the Immaculate Conception (Washington, DC), 101
Basu, Amrita, 59, 63
beards, 97
Bell Labs, 60, 81
Bell, W. Kamau, 167
Bellingham, Washington, 38, 39–40
Bellringer, Marcus, 246–47
Bengal, India, 42, 47–48, 255–56
Bengali communities, North America, 33–34, 35, 38–39, 40–41, 116–17
Bera, Ami, 1, 236–37
Berlin Indian Committee, 42
Berwa, Laxmi, 175, 210
Betts, Alexander, 291
Bharatiya Janata Party (BJP), 27, 71–73, 77–78, 79–80, 81, 101, 172, 264, 283–84
  and anti-Dalit attacks, 84, 209
  and Hindu nationalism, 111, 203–4, 208–9, 213–14, 254, 270–71
  and Indian farmers' protest, 220–21

leadership, 197, 203, 265–66
  and nuclearization, 111, 134–35
  and Trump, 255–56
  and USINPAC, 139
Bhargava, Anju, 185–86
Bhopal, India, 41
Biden, Joe, 1, 208–9, 218–20, 235–36, 258, 260–61, 262–66, 267, 270–72, 290
Bin Laden, Osama, 155–56
bindis, 59–60
bipartisanship, 132, 218–20, 244
BIPOC models of activism, 8–9
Black communities, 80, 167, 175, 212–13, 216, 226, 232, 239, 257, 270–71, 275, 281
  and early Indian immigrants, 33–34, 39, 42
Black feminism, 213–14
Black identities, 13, 53–54
Black Lives Matter (BLM), 167, 224–25, 226
Blasio, Bill de, 208–9
Bloemraad, Irene, 9–10
Boggs, Patton, 135–36
Bollywood, 255–56
Boston, 164
Boston Study Group (BSG), 169–70
Brahmanical Hinduism, 22–23
Brahmins, 6, 21–22, 74, 173–74, 178–79
Brandeis University, 178
Brettell, Caroline, 18
Bridging Nations, 132
British Army, 35
British Columbia, 32, 33
British Defense of India Act (1915), 42–43
British East India Company, 73
British House of Lords, 187–88
British Merchant Shipping Act (1894), 38–39
British Race Relations Act (1976), 187–88
British-U.S. relations, 39–41, 45–46, 48, 64–65, 94, 129–30
Brown University, 283–84
Brownback, Sam, 113
Buck, Ken, 142–43
Buddhism, 8–9, 22–23, 70–71, 81, 175, 190–91
Buddhist Indian American organizations, 4–5, 28–29
Buddhists, 166, 186–87
Buffalo, New York, 224–25
bullying, 189–90, 262–63
Burns, Nicholas, 2–3
Burton, Dan, 97–98, 109–11
Bush, George, 62, 100, 114–15, 157, 242–43, 244
Bush, George W., 2–3, 131, 133–35, 259, 270
business sector, 27–28, 79–80, 110, 111–12, 125–27, 130–31, 147–48, 237, 247–48, 254–55

California, 19–20, 26, 32, 40–41, 64–65, 83–84, 142–43, 167–68, 182, 277, 288–89
  and Asian exclusionism, 45–46
  and early Indian immigration, 33, 35, 37–38, 43–44
  and education, 171–75, 185
  race riots in, 38
  and Sikhs, 99, 218–21
California Alien Land Law (1913), 45–46
California Department of Fair Employment and Housing (CDFEH), 178–79
California State University, 167–68, 288–89
Cambridge, Massachusetts, 205–6
Caminetti, Anthony, 43–44
campaigns
  educational, 170
  political, 125–26, 128, 252–53, 260
  public relations, 132–33, 160–61, 163, 223
Canada, 81, 97–98, 142–43, 218–20, 221
  early immigration to, 33, 36–37, 39–42, 43–44, 64–65
Capitol Hill Hearing on Protecting the Civil Rights of Muslims, 177
Carter, Jimmy, 26–27
caste, 11, 23, 25–26, 116–17, 196, 207–8, 279
  activism against, 8–9, 28, 70, 82–84, 138–39, 159, 164, 165–66, 177–81, 190–91, 279, 280–81, 288–89
  activism against, India, 209–16
  background of, 21–23
  and civil rights, U.S., 151–52, 178–81
  and conversion, 69–73
  education about, 163–67, 169–70, 172–75
  and Indian independence movement, 42
  and migration, 6–7, 80–81
  and religious freedom, 205–6, 208–9
  and SAALT, 145–47
  and U.S. citizenship, 45–46
Caste Freedom Index (CFI), 215
Catholic University of America, 101
Catholicism, 68, 101, 236–37, 270
CBS, 161–62
Cellar, Emmanuel, 48
Center for Dharma Studies, 168–69
Center for Islamic and Arabic Studies, San Diego State University, 170
Center for Pluralism, 184–85
Center for Sikh Studies, Claremont Lincoln University, 167–68
Chandigarh, Punjab, 76
Charleston, South Carolina, 177–78
Charlottesville march, 257
Chatterjee, Swadesh, 132–33, 134–35, 240

Chaudhary, Ved, 59–60
Cherian, Joy, 57, 58–60, 63
Cherukonda, Raj, 215–16
Chicago, 50–51, 53–54, 55–57, 86, 199–200, 227
Chima, Jugdep, 76–77
China, 78–79, 110, 135, 205–6, 213
Chinese Americans, 114–15
Chinese immigrants, 43–44
Chopra, Deepak, 163
Choudry, Ibrahim, 47–48
Chowdhury, Ishani, 96
Christian Indian organizations, U.S., 4–5, 28–29, 100–3, 159, 191, 194, 198–99
Christian South Asians, 166
Christianity, 21, 22–23, 27, 69–70, 83–84, 88–89, 116–17, 121, 176–77, 185–86, 190, 193, 213, 231–32
    conservative, 183, 231–32
    and conversion, 70, 130–31, 202–3, 211
    and DFN, 84–85
    and Hindu nationalism, 70–71, 72, 81, 91–92
    and politics, 195–96, 236–37, 249–51, 262, 275–76, 278, 281
    and religious freedom, 194, 209
Church, Denver S., 43–44
Circular-i-Azadi (Circular of Freedom), 40–41
Cisco Systems, 178–81, 280–81, 288–89
citizenship, 9–10, 26, 113–14
    cultural, 10–12, 150–52, 189–91, 274, 285–86, 291–92
    transnational, 11, 32–33, 64–65, 103–4, 194–95, 274, 282–83, 293
    multicultural, 9–11, 15–17, 23–24, 150–51
    Indian, 203–4, 205–6
    U.S., 23, 26, 32–33, 45–49, 65, 89, 142, 274–75
Citizenship Act Amendment (CAA), 203–6, 209, 227, 264–65, 270–71
civic advocacy, 115–16, 136–37, 154, 275–77
Civil Rights Act (1964), 51, 58–59
Civil Rights Commission, 58–59
civil rights movement, 16, 28, 42, 49, 151
civil rights, immigrant, 50, 52, 105, 117, 118, 138–39, 230, 280–81
    post-9/11, 118–19, 150, 152, 156–57, 176–82
Claremont University, 170
Clinton, Bill, 112–13, 130, 133–34
Clinton, Hillary, 246, 254–56, 257, 270–71
CNN, 160–61, 163
Coalition Against Genocide (CAG), 198, 201–2
Coalition for Partnership, 132–33
Coalition to Stop Genocide, 205–6, 208–9
Cold War, 49, 108–9, 249

colonialism, 6–7, 19–20, 26, 34, 67–68, 88, 165–66, 274–75
    and caste, 23, 69–71, 180–81
    and Hindu–Muslim conflict, 70–71
    and suppression of Indian independence, 39–41, 42–43, 49
    and U.S. racialization, 36–37, 64–65
Colorado, 142–43
Columbia University, 21–22, 56–57, 169–70
Comcast, 160–61
Communism, 49, 108–9, 201–2, 209
Compassion International, 200
conferences and conventions
    advocacy, 59–60, 67, 86–87, 211, 212–13, 227–28
    Kashmir, 93
    Sikh, 97–98
Congress Party, 193, 217–18, 255–56
Congressional Asian Pacific American Caucus, 136–37
Congressional Caucus on India and Indian Americans, 78, 110, 222–23
Congressional Human Rights Caucus, 210
Connecticut, 48, 56–57
Consultative Committee of Indian Muslims, 86
Continuous Journey Regulation (Canada), 33
conversion, 84, 140–41, 200, 202–3, 211, 212–13, 236–37
Conyers, John, 200–1
Cordoba House mosque, 184–85
Cornerstone, 223
Coulson, Doug, 45–46
Council of Khalistan, 97–98, 109–10
Council on American-Islamic Relations (CAIR), 87, 93, 152, 154, 157–58, 159–60, 181, 188–89, 227
Council on Islamic Education, 170
Countering Violent Extremism (CVE) program, 177
COVID-19, 25, 145, 162, 165–66, 177–78, 227, 260–61, 262, 283–84
Cuban American mobilization, 17
Cuban American National Foundation (CANF), 17
cultural citizenship, 10–12, 150–52, 189–91, 274, 285–86, 291–92
Curtis, Lisa, 221–22

D'Souza, Joseph, 84–85, 213
DACA, 142, 261–62
Daily Show, the, 161–62
Dalit Coalition, 198–99
Dalit Diva, 82–83

Dalit Freedom Network (DFN), 84–85, 211, 212–13, 279
Dalit/Ambedkarite organizations, U.S., 80–84, 167
Dalits, 6–7, 25–26, 27, 28–29, 70, 116–17, 158, 166, 186–87, 199–200, 207
and caste, 21–23, 70, 80, 178–81, 190–91, 196, 209–12, 226, 279–80
and education, 175
against Gandhi, 169–70
and Hindu nationalism, 91–92
and mobilization, 8–9, 107, 159, 280–81
and religious conflict, 72–73
Das, Taraknath, 40–42, 47–48
Day, Richard, 58
Dayal, Har, 41–42
Dayal, John, 202
Dean, Howard, 245
Delhi, India, 206, 220–21
democracy, 49, 67, 153, 212, 291
Democratic National Committee (DNC), 245
Democratic National Convention, 183–84, 200, 242–43, 244
Democrats, 133–34, 142–43, 180–81, 186–87, 200, 208–9, 222–23, 230
Indian American, 4–5, 11–12, 29–30, 108, 123–73, 231–32, 238–39, 242–43, 244–46, 247–50, 269–70
Latinx, 233
Muslim, 243
and South Asian American, 257–63
voting for, 235–37
demographics, Indian Americans
background of, 19–24
and political incorporation, 12
and SAALT, 138–39
and Sikhs, 37–38
in U.S., 2
denaturalization, 165
Desai, Moraji, 81
Desai, Nirav, 118
descent-based discrimination, 212–13, 214–16
Desi identities, 105, 117
deterritorialized imagined communities, 216
Dev, Atul, 227
devadasi system, 210–11
Dhaliwal, Sandeep Singh, 186–87
Dharm, Pratima, 183
Dharma Civilization Foundation (DCF), 168–69
Dhingra, Pawan, 62–63
Diamond Jubilee (1897), 35

diaspora activism, 30, 91–92, 220–21, 280–81, 291–93
diaspora diplomacy, 194–95
diaspora politics, 9–10, 113–14, 194–98, 224–26, 227
and India-Pakistan conflict, 111–14
diaspora strategies, 11, 194–95
Diwali, 182–83, 185–86
doctors, Indian, 60–62
doctors' organizations, Indian American, 4–5, 16–17, 65
Dogras, 73–74
domestic issues, U.S., 23–24, 30, 151, 159, 186–87, 278, 282–85
and Hindu American Foundation, 157–58, 282
and mobilization, 12, 189–91
and multicultural citizenship, 16–17
and racial discrimination, 52–63
and SAALT, 136–37
and second-generation, 7–9, 28, 107, 128, 146–47, 148, 246–48, 266, 283–84, 285
see also hate crimes
domestic violence organizations, 138–39
dotbusters, 59–60
Dravidian identity, 23, 53–54
DREAM Act, 142, 188–89
Dukakis campaign, 108
Durbin, Richard, 142–43
Dutt, Yashica, 164
Dutta, Manoranjan, 52–55, 63, 107

Eck, Diana, 181
economic factors, 108–9, 233, 236–37, 248, 251, 282–83
economic liberalism, 108–9, 110, 111–12
Edison, New Jersey, 255–56
education, 50–51, 97, 146, 189–90, 274
and Dalits, 85, 214, 280–81
and Indian Americans, 19–20, 56–57
and Kashmiri Muslims, 73, 224–25
and partisan politics, 241, 252
and post-9/11 stereotypes, 159–76
Educators' Society for Heritage of India, 144
elections, India, 11–12, 17, 93, 113–14, 133–34, 138–41, 203
elections, U.S., 25, 231, 240
and Indian American candidates, 258, 260, 264–66, 290
and South Asian American votes, 258
voting patterns, 231–32, 235–37, 260–62, 268–69, 271–72
Elkhanialy, Hekmat, 53–54
Ellison, Keith, 140–41, 200, 201–2

Engel, Eliot, 223
English language, 19–20, 56–57, 88–89, 136–37
Ensaaf, 217–18
Equal Employment Opportunity Commission, 58–59
equal opportunity, 59–60
Equality Labs, 82–83, 138–39, 146–47, 159, 164, 165–66, 174–75, 179–81, 290
　and caste, 188, 213–14, 277, 279–80, 282
　and religious freedom, 198–99, 205–6
Ethan Allen, 93–94
ethnic cleansing, 73–74, 94–95, 143
ethnic formation, 68–69
ethnic identity, 195–96
ethnic models, 146, 148, 289–91
ethnic unity, 4–5, 13–14, 106
　and U.S.-India nuclear deal, 3
ethnicization model, 289–90
ethnology, 23
European Economic Community, 95–96
European Union, 212

Fa-Hsien, 165–66
Facebook, 179–80, 214, 259, 260–62, 287
Fai, Ghulam Nabi, 93, 221–22
Fairness for High- Skilled Immigrants Act (2019), 142–43
Faith Based and Neighborhood Partnership, 185–86
Faleomavaega, Eni, 139–41, 202
family reunification, 44, 50, 57, 58, 59, 62–63, 97, 126–27, 142, 285
family values, 237
FBI, 144, 154–55, 177–78, 221–22, 227
Federation of Ambedkarites, Buddhists, and Ravidasi Organizations of North America (FABRONA), 81
Federation of Indian American Christian Organizations of North America (FIACONA), 100, 101–2, 191, 193, 199–201, 204–5
Federation of Indian Associations (FIA), 56–57
Fennema, Miendert, 18
FICE, 52
Fidelis, 201–2
Fiji, 59–60, 157–58
first-generation Indian Americans, 27–28, 36–37, 116–17, 123–24, 136, 144–45, 146, 147–48, 197, 244, 286–87
　and AIPAC, 120–24
　and gender, 147–48, 271–72
　and identity, 119–20, 263–64
　and Kashmiri Muslims, 224–25
　and mobilization, 7–8, 12
　and partisan politics, U.S., 238–39, 243, 245, 269–70
Fisher, Maxine, 50–51, 53–54
flash mob dances, 246–47
Floyd, George, 165, 167
Foreign Contribution Regulation Act (FCRA), 213
Foreign Medical Graduate Examination in Medical Sciences, 61–62
foreign medical graduates (FMGs), 26–27
foreign policy
　see homeland issues
Fox News, 160–61
Free Hindusthan, 40–41
Freedom House, 204–5
Fremont Hindu temple, 268–69
Fresno, California, 160–61, 180–81
Fresno, California, 288–89
Friedman, Milton, 252–53
Friends of Freedom for India (FFI), 47–48

Gabbard, Tulsi, 140–41, 199–200, 202, 236–37, 265–66
Gandhi, 46–47, 48, 70, 75, 169–70, 175–76, 190–91
Gandhi day of service, 118
Gandhi, Indira, 76–77, 210
Gandhi, Mahatma, 205–6, 248–49
Gandhi, Rajiv, 108
Gandhi, Sonia, 255–56
gender, 7–8, 25–26
　and generational status, 247–48, 271–72, 286–87
　and leadership, 147–48
generational status, 4–5, 25–26, 30, 64, 147–48, 231–32, 286–87
　and AIPAC model, 120–24
　and caste, 7
　and ethnic politics, 23–24
　and Indian American politics, 263–69
　and mobilization, 27–28, 105
　and South Asian American organizations, 114–18
genocide, 72–73, 218–20, 222–23, 224–25
Georgetown University, 170
Georgia, 260–61, 266–67, 271–72
Georgia Muslim Voter Project, 266–67
Gephardt, Dick, 118
Germany, 37–38, 44, 46–47
Ghadar movement, 26, 36–37, 41–44, 45–48, 65, 75, 98–99
Ghadar-di-gunj (Echoes of Mutiny), 42, 47–48

Ghouse, Mike, 184–85
Gingrich, Newt, 254, 270–71
Glazer, Nathan, 50
Global Organization of People of Indian Origin (GOPIO), 59–60, 144
globalization, 9–10, 15–16, 23–24
Golden Temple, 76–77, 97–99
Google, 179–80, 277
Gore, Al, 244
Gould, Harold, 48
government regulation, 251–52
Goyle, Raj, 289
Gray's Inn, 21–22
green cards, 90, 126–27, 135–36, 142–43, 255–56
Grossman, Matt, 253
Gujarat, India, 62–63, 72, 91–92, 101, 130–31, 139–41, 194, 197–99, 200–2
gun violence, 188–89
Gurmukhi, 41–42
Guyana, 59–60

H-1B visas, 19–20, 22–23, 27–28, 90, 126–27, 130–31, 142–43, 159, 261–62, 285
H-2B visas, 142
H-4 visas, 142–43, 261–62
Haley, Nikki, 1, 236–37
Hall, George E., 54–55
Haniffa, Aziz, 222–23, 241–42, 289
Harris, Kamala, 1, 142–43, 262–64, 270–71, 290
Harvard Kennedy School, 82–83
Harvard University, 60, 170
Haryana, India, 76, 220–21
hate crimes, 59–60, 105, 118–19, 137, 144, 151, 164–65, 177–78, 189–90, 230, 238–39
 and Hindus, 185–86
 and Muslims, 153–54, 159
 and Sikhs, 155–56, 162, 186–88, 190
 and voting, 261–62
Hathaway, Robert, 110–11, 121, 125–26
Hawaii, 236–37
health care issues, 127, 188–89, 248, 262
hearings, 54–55, 177, 188–89
Helms, Jesse, 97–98, 240
Henry Hyde United States– India Peaceful Cooperation Act, 2–3, 131
Heritage Foundation, 221–22
High-level Committee on the Indian Diaspora, 113–14
hijabs, 159–60, 182
Hindu American Awareness and Education Month, 185

Hindu American Foundation (HAF), 79, 96, 140–41, 151–52, 157–58, 163–66, 171–72, 182–83, 200, 282, 285
 and caste, 211–13, 216, 226, 279, 282–83
 and civil rights, 176–77, 180–81
 and education, 165–66, 172–75
 and Kashmir, 221–23, 227–28
 and partisan politics, 254, 256
 and political voice, 185–86
 and religious freedom, 193–94, 199–200, 201–3, 204–5, 206, 208–9
Hindu American organizations, 4–5, 25–26, 27–29, 77–80, 130–31, 168–69, 194, 231–32
 and civil rights, 176–78, 181
 and education, 159–60, 163–67, 170, 171–72, 190
 and inclusion, 182–85
 post-9/11, 157–58
Hindu American Seva Charities (HASC), 185–86
Hindu American Summit, 186–87
Hindu caucus, 186–87
Hindu Coalition, 230
Hindu Education Foundation (HEF), 172
Hindu Immigration Hearings (1914), 43–44
Hindu International Council against Defamation (HICAD), 152, 157
Hindu Kashmiris (Hindu Brahmins/Pandits), 92–97, 203–4
Hindu nationalism, 5–6, 27, 28–29, 65–66, 69–73, 77–78, 165–66, 227–28, 231–32, 253, 281
 activism against, 206–7, 264–65, 290
 and bipartisanship, 29–30
 and BPJ, 111, 203–4
 and caste, 6–7, 69–73, 163–64, 190–91, 214
 and Dalits, 8–9, 83
 and diaspora politics, 111–12, 196–97, 277
 and education, 172
 and generational divides, 265–66
 and Indian American partisanship, 254–57
 and Kashmir, 224–25, 227
 and Muslims, 90–92
 and religious conflict, 67–68, 86
 and religious minorities, 103–4, 199–200, 201–2, 203–9
 and social media, 288–89
 and Trump, 264, 267–68, 270–71
 and USINPAC, 140–41
Hindu studies, 168–69
Hindu Swayamsevak Sangh (HSS), 168–69
Hindu temples, 185–86, 208–9
Hinduphobia, 174, 176–77, 200–1, 277

Hindus, 16–17, 21–23, 62–63, 83–84, 88–89, 118–19, 120, 151–52, 236–37
and early U.S. immigration, 32–34, 35, 41, 51
and JINSA, 125–26
and mobilization, 27–28, 40–41, 107, 146, 235–36, 257, 281–82
and religious conflict, 67–68, 72–73, 130–31, 188
and religious freedom, 150–51, 209, 257
and second-generation, 115, 146–47
and White nationalism, 265–68
Hindus for Human Rights (HfHR), 180–81, 186–87, 190–91, 204–9, 214, 279, 282, 290
Hindus for Trump, 258
Hindustan Association of America, 43–44
Hindustan Association of the Pacific Coast, 41–42
Hindustan Ghadar Party, 41–42
see also Ghadar movement
Hindustan Information Service, 46–47
Hindustani Association, 40–41
Hindustani Association of America, 46
Hindutva
see Hindu nationalism
Hofstra University, 167–68
homeland issues, 30, 49, 131, 136–37, 156–57, 282–85
and Christian Indians, 28, 191
and diaspora politics, 194–97
and ethnic mobilization, 13–14, 15–16
and first-generation Indians, 7–9, 27–28, 147, 148, 238–39, 247–48, 283–84
and identity, 11, 12, 107
and partisan politics, U.S., 239–40
and religious status, 28–29, 194–95
homosexuality, 163
Hong Kong, 32
Hopkins, David, A., 253
Hopkinson, William C., 41
hotel industry, 62–63
hoteliers organizations, Indian American, 4–5, 16–17, 65
see also AAHOA
House Resolution (HR 417), 201–2
housing, 50–51
Howard University, 175
HSS (Hindu Swayamsevak Sangh), 77–78
HuffPost, 163, 212–13
human rights, 67, 74–75, 86–87, 103–4, 282–83
and Dalits, 81, 210–11, 213–16
in India, 109–10, 138–39, 140–41, 199–200, 201–2, 206–7, 283–84
and Kashmir, 92, 93, 94–95

and Muslims, 90–91
and Sikhs, 97–98, 218–20
Human Rights Commission, 202–3
Human Rights Watch, 201–2, 210–11
Huntington, Samuel, 292
Hurricane Katrina, 142
Hyderabad India, 85

ICE, 177
identities, 26
Muslim American, 88–90
ideological kinship, 253
illegal immigration, 44
Illinois, 19–20, 161–62
immigrants, European, 13, 14–15, 63, 68
immigrants, Indian
see first-generation Indian Americans
Immigration and Naturalization Act (1965), 56
immigration policy, 26–27, 80, 233, 250–51
early history of, 19–20, 38–40
and racial exclusion, 36–37, 42–46, 48, 49, 65
immigration reform, 142–43, 242–43
immigration studies, 36
Immigration Voice, 135–36, 142–43, 279–80, 285
Imperial Valley, California, 37–38, 46, 48–49
inclusion, 182–85, 291–93
income levels, 19–20, 55, 146, 147–48, 231, 238–39, 242–43, 250, 268–69
India Association for American Citizenship, 47–48
India caucus, 203
India Day Parade, 56–57, 227
India Home Rule League, 46–47
India League of America, 47–48, 56–57
India Welfare League, 47–48
Indian American advocacy organizations, 2–3, 4–5, 7–8, 11–12, 24–25, 141–46
diversity of, 5–6, 18
and generational differences, 124, 146, 147
history of, 26–28
and professionalism, 130–31, 136–37
recent, 139–41
religious, 28, 77–104
see also names of organizations
Indian American Catholic Association (IACA), 101
Indian American Forum for Political Education (IAFPE), 57, 58–62, 63, 124–25, 240
Indian American identity, 107, 146–47
Indian American IMPACT (IMPACT), 145, 258–59, 260, 271–72, 283–84, 289
Indian American Leadership Center, 117
Indian American Leadership Initiative (IALI), 227–28, 244, 246–47

Indian American Muslim Council (IAMC), 91–92, 193, 198–200, 201–2, 227, 279, 282, 290
Indian American Security Leadership Council (IASLC), 3, 132
Indian American Task Force on Terrorism, 128–29
Indian Americans, 3–4
  background to, 19–24, 26
  post-1965, history of, 49–64
  pre-1965, history of, 37–49
Indian Americans for Biden, 258, 260–61, 263, 271–72
Indian Americans for Trump, 259
Indian Army, 85, 97–98
India caucus, 67, 107, 108–14, 130–31, 136–37, 142, 222–23
Indian census, 73–74
Indian constitution, 21–22, 74, 75, 95–96, 190–91, 201–2, 205–6, 209
Indian consulates, 97–98
Indian Day Parade, 100
Indian embassy, 107, 129, 132–33, 205–6, 223
Indian External Affairs Ministry, 111–12
Indian farmers' protest, 218–21, 227
Indian government, 93–94, 97–98, 105, 106, 108, 111–12, 193, 200, 213–14, 221
  and anti-Sikh actions, 97–99
  and caste, 212
  and Kargil Conflict, 112
  and Kashmir, 222–25
  Ministry of External Affairs, 113–14
  and religious minorities, 210, 282
Indian identity, 89, 99, 117, 118–19, 231–32, 236–37, 263–64, 271–72
Indian independence, 36–37, 274–75
  and early Indian immigrants, 26, 40–46, 64
  and racial status, 46–49, 64–65
Indian languages, 23
Indian League of America (ILA), 54–56
Indian Muslims Relief Committee (IMRC), 86–87
Indian National Congress Association of India, 46–47, 48
Indian Voices for Trump, 231, 258
Indiana, 133–34
Indians for McCain, 246–47
Indiaspora, 145
Indivisible, 260
Indo American Hospitality Association, 62–63
Indo-American Kashmir Forum (IAKF), 94–95, 221–22
Indo-Caribbean identity, 116–17, 258
Indo-Chinese relations, 132

Indo-Pakistan tensions, 111–14
Indo-Pakistan war (1965), 76
Industrial Workers of the World, 42
Infinity Foundation, 78–79, 168–69
information technology (IT) sector, 6, 19–20, 22–23, 159
information technology associations, Indian American, 4–5
Instagram, 214, 260–61, 287
institutional isomorphism, 8–9, 150–51
interfaith work, 153–54, 157, 158, 165–66, 177–78, 182, 183–86, 188–89, 190
Interfaith Youth Core, 184–85
International Association of American Physicians (IAAP), 61–62
International Atomic Energy Agency, 134–35
International Commission for Dalit Rights (ICDR), 215, 282–83
International Justice Program of the Advocates for Human Rights, 199–200
International Kashmir Federation (IKF), 94, 96–97
international medical graduates (IMGs), 61–62
International Monetary Fund (IMF), 108–9, 141
International Society for Krishna Consciousness (ISKCON), 157–58
Internet tools, 119–20, 135–36, 153–54, 164–67, 169–70, 218–20
Invading the Sacred, 168–69
Iran, 206
Iranian hostage crisis (1979– 1980), 97
Iraq war, 242–43, 259
Irish American mobilization, 16, 17
Irish nationalists, 40–41
IRS, 52–53
ISIS, 12
Islam, Frank, 184–85
Islamic Resource, 184–85
Islamic Society of North America (ISNA), 87, 93, 153–54, 188–89
Islamic Society of Orange County, 184–85
Islamophobia, 160–62, 165, 166, 188–89, 190
Israel, 2–3, 120–22, 125–26, 133–34, 194–95, 201–2, 226, 256, 281
Iyer, Deepa, 117, 136–38, 144–45

Jacobson, Mathew Frye, 13
Jains, 186–87
Jammu, India, 29–30, 73–74, 92–93
Jammu and Kashmir state, 29–30, 73–74, 92, 94, 95–96, 141, 203–4, 221–22, 225, 264, 283–84
  see also Kashmir

Jani, Amit, 265–66
Janmohamed, Zahir, 200, 201–2
Japan, 48, 49, 65, 129–30
Japanese American Citizens League (JACL), 151
Japanese American mobilization, 16
Japanese and Korean Exclusion Leagues, 38
Japanese Burakumin leaders, 214–15
Japanese immigrants, 43–44, 45–46
Japra, Romesh, 264–65, 268–69
Jayapal, Pramila, 1, 188, 223–25
Jersey City, New Jersey, 59–60
Jewish American mobilization, 16, 17, 27–28, 59–60, 86–87, 107, 146, 275–76, 289
and USINPAC, 124–31
Jewish Americans, 55–56, 68
Jewish Anti-Defamation League, 152
Jewish Institute for National Security Affairs (JINSA), 125–26
Jews, 183, 206, 209, 226, 275, 281
Jha, Ashish, 283–84
Jha, Chandra, 55–56
Jim Crow laws, 32–33, 39, 212–13, 281
Jindal, Bobby, 130–31, 236–37, 241–42, 244, 269–70
John Hopkins University, 81
Johnson, Lyndon B., 242–43
Joint Committee, 56–57
Jones, Brenda, 264–65
Jones, Robert, 291
Jones, Will, 291
Joshi, Khyati, 277–78

Kabir Panth, 69
Kabir panthis, 83–84
Kalra, Ash, 184–85
Kalsi, Kamaljeet Singh, 181–82
Kamble, Raju, 81, 169–70
Kamdar, Mira, 2–3
Kapany, Narinder Singh, 167–68
Kapoor, Aman, 135–36, 143
Kapur, Ramesh, 108, 132
Kargil Conflict, 105, 112–13
Karthikeyan, Hrishi, 244–47
Kashmir, 28–29, 67, 85, 87, 92, 114, 141, 196, 203–4, 205–6, 208–9, 221–25, 255, 264
and U.S., 264–65, 270–71
Kashmir Imbroglio, 73–75
Kashmir Study Group (KSG), 92, 93–94
Kashmir Valley, 74–75, 94, 96–97
Kashmiri American Council (KAC), 92, 93, 221–22, 224–25

Kashmiri Hindus (Kashmiri Pandits), 141, 222–23, 224–25, 255–56
Kashmiri Muslims of North America, 93, 103–4, 221–23, 224–25, 226–28
Kashmiri organizations, U.S., 92–97
Kashmiri separatism, 222
Kathwari, Farooq, 93–94
Kaul, P.K., 108
Kawaja, Kaleem, 90–91, 205–6
Kennedy, Edward, 49–50
Kennedy, John F., 242–43
Kenya, 57
Kerala, 100
Kerry, John, 242–43, 244–45
Keshavan, Narayan D., 78
Khalidi, Omar, 86–87
Khalidi, Usama, 86–87
Khalistan Affairs Center, 97–98
Khalistan movement, 76–77, 97–99, 103–4, 216–21
Khalistanis, 186–87, 227
Khalsa Diwan Society, 40–41, 43–44
Khan, Dada Amir Haider, 47–48
Khan, Daisy, 184–85
Khan, Mubarek Ali, 48
Khan, Muqtedar, 153–54, 183–84
Khandelwal, Madhulika, 118–19
Khanna, Ro, 1, 188, 227–28, 236–37, 264–65
Khateeb, Shaheen, 91–92
Khomeini, Ayatollah, 97
Khurana, Anjali, 246–47
King, Martin Luther, Jr., 175–76, 190–91, 212–13
Kirk, Jason, 131
kirpan, 37–38, 159–60, 181–82
Know-Nothing Party, 68
Kolluri, Kris, 118
Komagata Maru, 42
Korean Americans, 52–53
Koul, Lalit, 221–22
Krishnamoorthi, Raja, 1, 142–43, 236–37, 264, 265–66
Ku Klux Klan, 68
Kulkarni, Sri Preston, 265–66
Kumar, K. V., 56, 223
Kumar, Shalabh, 230, 254–56

Lacroix, Thomas, 98–99
Lacy, Akela, 223
Lakhihal, Prashanth, 78
langar, 162, 182–83, 190, 220–21
language states, 76
Latinx communities, 226, 233, 241–42, 257, 270–71, 275, 281, 292
Latinx identities, 13, 106–7
Lautenberg Amendment, U.S., 206, 209

leadership, 107, 145–46, 189, 282, 286
    Kashmiri, 203–4
    Muslim American, 153–54, 197
League of United Latin American Citizens
    (LULAC), 151
Lee, Jennifer, 147
Lee, Joel, 69–70
Left Front, 134–35
LGBTQ rights, 237, 242–43, 270
Lindsay, James M., 2
Livingston Proposal, 93–94
lobbying, Indian American, 107, 108–14
    AIPAC as inspiration, 2–3, 23–24
    and Dalits, 83, 84–85
    and early Indian immigrants, 26, 46–48
    and ethnic mobilization, 13–14, 15–16, 17
    generational, 123, 274–75
    and green cards, 135–36
    Hindu, 78, 201–2, 225
    and IMGs, 61–62
    and Indian farmers' protest, 220–21
    and Kargil Conflict, 112–13
    and Kashmir, 96–97, 221–22
    and Muslims, 86–87, 90–91
    and nuclear deal, 131–35
    and Sikhs, 97–98
    and WWII, 36–37
Lofgren, Zoe, 142–43
London School of Economics, 21–22
London, England, 35
Los Angeles, California, 67, 97–98, 159–62
Louisiana, 279
Luce-Celler Act (1946), 48–49
Luce, Clare Booth, 48

macaca incident, 245, 270, 287–88
Madison Square Garden, 198–99
Maharashtra, India, 22–23, 70, 81–82
Malhotra, J., 193
Malhotra, Rajiv, 78–79, 168–69, 185
Mandalaparthy, Nikhil, 207–8
Mansuri, Shabbir, 170
marches, 97–98
marginalized groups, 158, 190, 244–45, 275–76
marriage, 21, 32–34, 37–38, 39
Mason, George, 170
mass shootings, 138–39
Massachusetts, 133–34
massacres, 73–74
Mayawati, Kumari, 279–80
McDermott, John, 108–9
McDermott, Rachel, 83
media coverage, 59, 128–29, 147

    and AIPAC, 121
    and Ambedkar, 169–70
    of anti-colonialism, 41–42
    and anti-Sikh actions, India, 97–99
    and caste, 163–64, 179–81, 203–4, 211, 212–13
    and early Indian immigrants, 32, 33–34
    and hate crimes, 177–78
    and Hindus, 77–78, 183, 185–86
    and Indian Christians, 101
    and Indian detainees, U.S., 138–39
    and Indian farmer's protest, 220–21
    and Indian Republicans, 254–55
    and interfaith work, 184–85
    and Kargil Conflict, 112–13
    and Kashmir, 222–23, 227
    and post-9/11 education, 160–63, 164–65
    and religious minorities, India, 199–200
    and SAALT, 144–45
    and SAFO, 245
    and SAKI, 244–45
    and Sikhs, 162, 190, 218–20
    and U.S. Indian politics, 230–31
    and voting, U.S., 236–37, 241–42, 260–61
Medicare, 61–62
Meghani, Mihir, 79–80
Memorial Day, 162
methodology of book, 5–17, 24–30
Mexican American Legal Defense and
    Education Fund (MALDEF), 16, 151
Mexican American mobilization, 16
Mexican communities, 37–38
Mexico, 44
Microsoft, 179–80
Midsouth Indemnity Association, 62–63
migrant justice, 176–77
millennials, 246–47
Minaj, Hasan, 161–62
minorities, ethnic, 14, 187–88
    Indian Americans as, 23–24, 26–27, 52–53,
        55–56, 63, 257, 270–71
minorities, racial, 189–90, 235–37
    and Indian Americans, 32–33, 51, 65–66, 146
    and South Asian Americans, 106–7, 167
    and voting, U.S., 235–37
minorities, religious, 28, 88–89, 188, 194–95,
        206, 225–26, 231–32, 275–76, 289
    and advocacy, U.S., 67–68, 103, 140–41, 150–
        52, 189–90, 282, 285
    and anti-Hindu nationalism, 197–98, 208–9
    and cultural citizenship, U.S., 189–91
    and diaspora politics, 196
    in India, 197–209
    Jews as, 120–21

minority mobilization, 16
minority nationalism, 11
Mishra, Debashish, 105, 117, 118–19
Mishra, Sangay, *Desis Divided*, 5
Mississippi, 133–34
Mnuchin, Steve, 141
mobilization patterns, 4–5, 6–7, 23–24, 26, 195–96, 281
   and generational status, 7–8, 146–48, 290–91
   and national origins, 13–14, 18, 27–28
   and racial discrimination, history of, 56–60
   and religious freedom, 150–51, 194, 217, 275–76, 285
   and South Asian American voters, 261–62
Modi, Narendra, 29–30, 139, 141, 196, 197, 198–99, 200–1, 203, 206–7, 208, 217–18
   and Hindu nationalism, 231, 237, 254, 264–65, 267–68, 270–71
   and Kashmir, 220–21, 223
   and Republicans, 254–55
Mora, Cristina, 106–7
mosques, 71–72, 77–78, 79–80, 165, 177, 184–85, 230
   attacks on, 198, 206, 208–9
Moss, Dana, 291
motel industry, 62–63
Mughal period India, 69, 165–66
multicultural citizenship, 9–11, 150–51
   and ethnic lobbies, 15–17, 23–24
multiculturalism, 90–91, 157, 196, 282–83
Multifaith Voices for Peace and Justice, 199–200
multireligiosity, 8–9, 146–47, 182–83, 190, 196, 203
Mumbai, India, 128–29
Muslim Advocates, 154–55, 165, 177–78, 188–89
Muslim American organizations, 28–29, 85–92, 146–47, 194
   and diaspora politics, 196–97
   and education, 159–63, 164–67, 170
   and inclusion, 182–83, 190
   post-9/11, 153–55
   and religious freedom, 181–82, 194
Muslim Kashmiris, 73–75, 92–97
Muslim nationalism, 65, 71
Muslim Public Affairs Council (MPAC), 87, 159–61, 164–65, 188–89
Muslim reform, 184–85
Muslim Voices for Trump, 258
Muslims, 16–17, 21, 27–28, 32, 83–84, 118–19, 144, 158, 166, 183, 185, 207
   and civil rights, 150–51, 176–77, 180–81
   conversion to, 70

Dalit, 83
   and Democratic Party, 242–43, 270
   early Indian immigrants as, 33, 35, 38–39
   and Hindu nationalism, 69–70, 72–73, 78–79, 277
   and identity, 154–55
   and mobilization, 107, 152–55, 167, 195–96, 281–82
   and religious freedom, 194, 209, 226
   and religious conflict, 67–68, 70–71, 72–73, 130–31
   South Asian American, 154–55
   and U.S. immigration, 85
   voting patterns, 235–36
Myanmar, 205–6

Nanak, Guru, 69, 75, 182–83
Narasaki, Karen, 156
Narasimhan, Shekar, 245, 258
Narayanan, Ram, 132–33, 287–88
Nashville, Tennessee, 62–63
National Asian American Survey, 147
National Association for the Advancement of Colored People (NAACP), 16, 59–60, 63, 151
National Association of Americans of Asian Indian Descent (NAAAID), 56, 58–59
National Association of Muslim Lawyers (NAML), 154–55
National Coalition of South Asian Organizations (NCSO), 137–38
National Committee for Indian Independence, 47–48
National Dance for Obama, 246–47, 270
National Federation of Indian American Associations, 56–57, 58–59 (NFIA), 108, 114, 124–25, 144
National Iranian American Council, 143
National Organization of Indian Associations, 132
National Register of Citizenship (NRC), 204, 205–6
national security, 144
National Sikh Campaign (NSC), 160–61
nationalism, 5, 75, 107
   and home rule, 46–47
   long-distance, 23–24, 194–95, 292
   and mobilization, 27–28, 42
   and racial formation, 36, 64–65
Navayana Buddhism, 70
Nehru, Jawaharlal, 67–68, 75, 97–98, 108–9
Nepal, 143
Nevada, 133–34

New Delhi, 84, 125
New England, 68
New Jersey, 19–20, 33–34, 52–53, 56–57, 61, 77–78, 110, 152, 227
New Orleans, Louisiana, 39
New York (state), 19–20, 38–39, 48, 52–53, 56–57
New York, New York, 53–54, 81, 82–83, 155–57, 158, 162, 182, 198–200
   and Dalits, 83, 175–76
   early mobilization in, 39, 41, 46–48
   and Patriot Act, 244–45
   and SAALT, 116
   and Sikhs, 97–98, 218–20
Newsom, Gavin, 180–81, 231, 280–81
Nicholas, Ralph, W., 53–54
Nijjar, Hardeep Singh, 218–20
Nikore, Varun, 244
Noah, Trevor, 161–62
Nomani, Azra, 184–85
Non-Alignment Movement (NAM), 108–9
nonresident Indians (NRIs), 111–12
nonviolence, 48, 157, 205–6
North Carolina, 133–34
Norton, Eleanor Holmes, 212–13
nuclear deal, U.S.-India, 2–4, 131–35, 194–95, 240, 254, 287–88
nuclear Non-Proliferation Treaty, 111, 131
nuclear testing, 112, 113
nuclearization, 2–4, 107, 111–14

Oak Creek, Wisconsin, 177–78
Obama, Barack, 1, 96, 183, 185–86, 236–37, 241–42, 245–47
Occupy movement, 12
Office of Strategic Services (OSS), 48
Okamoto, Dina, 106–7
Omi, Michael, 36
Omvedt, Gail, 210
Ong, Aihwa, 10–11
opportunity structures, 12–13, 14–15, 30, 189–90, 281–82
Oregon, 37–38, 40–42
Organization of Islamic Cooperation, 88
Orientalism, 33–34
Overseas Citizen of India (OCI), 113–14
Oxford University, 41

Pai, Ajit, 1
Pakistan, 27–28, 73–74, 107, 137–38, 143, 157–58, 200, 277
   and citizenship, 113–14
   and Cold War, 108–10
   and Kargil Conflict, 112–14
   and Kashmir, 92, 93–97, 221–22, 224–25, 227, 255
   and religious freedom, 200–1
   and U.S. politics, 130
   and USINPAC, 140–41
Pakistan caucus, 136–37
Pakistan League of America, 48
Pakistani identity, 89, 90–91, 115–17, 118–19, 257
Palestine Solidarity Movement, 224–25, 226
Palestinian activists, 87
Pallone, Frank, 110
Pan-Aryan Association, 41
pan-ethnic model, 9, 28, 106–7, 147, 148, 244–45
pan-Indian American organizations, 52–53
Pannun, Gurpatwant Singh, 218–20
parades, 162
Parivar, Sangh, 201–2
Parker, Karen, 218–20
partisan politics, U.S., 3–4, 7–8, 227–28, 231–34, 279–80
   Asian American, 234–35
   first-generation Indian Americans, 238–43, 284–85
   Indian American, 235–37
   second-generation Indian Americans, 244–47
   and South Asian American organizations, 115–16
partition, India–Pakistan, 27–28, 67–68, 71, 74, 75, 92, 95–96, 114, 244–45
Pasadena, California, 162
Patel subcaste, 62–63
Patel, Dinesh, 60
Patel, Eboo, 184–85, 291
PBS, 160–61
Pearl Harbor attack, 65
Pelosi, Nancy, 133–34
Penn State University, 153–54
Pennsylvania, 260, 271–72
Periyar, 23
Person of Indian Origin (PIO) cards, 111
Peters, Jeremy, 254–55
Peterson, Lisa, 220–21
Phillips, Robin, 202
Philpott, Daniel, 67–68
Phule, Jyotirao, 23
Pillai, Jan, 56
Pitts, Joseph, 140–41, 200–2

pluralism, 67, 88, 91–92, 146–47, 150–51, 184–85, 194–95, 260
  and Hinduism, 163
  Indian, 197, 206–7, 226, 277
  institutional, 5
  and Islam, 153
  and Kashmir, 93
  and minorities, 197–99
  and multiculturalism, 10–11
  U.S., 157
podcasts, 165–66, 260–61
policing, 159–60, 165, 220–21
political incorporation, 12–13, 14–15
political voice, 185–89
Pope Francis, 182
poverty, 188–89, 200, 252
Powell, Colin, 113
Prabhudoss, John, 100, 101, 200–1
Prestholdt, Jennifer, 199–200
Princeton University, 52–53
Progressive Caucus, 223
progressives, 247–48, 260, 270
  AJA, 198–99
  Hindu, 158, 165–66, 173–74, 180–81, 190–91, 196, 206–7, 214, 282
  and Kashmir, 222–23
  Muslim, 154–55, 184–85
  and religious freedom, 208–9
  Sikh, 160–61
  and TSB, 260
  and U.S. Congress, 199–200
protests, 97–98, 205–6, 216, 218, 255–56
public service announcements, 160–61
Punjab communities, North America early, 33, 34, 35, 41, 42
Punjab, India, 37–38, 42–43, 76, 99, 103–4, 196, 202–3, 217–21
Punjabi Hindus, 74, 203–4
Puri, Ram Nath, 40–41
Puri, Sanjay, 125–28, 130–31, 135–37, 139, 227–28, 282–83
Putnam, Robert, 18

Queens, New York, 155–57
queer South Asians, 167
Quraishi, Asifa, 154–55
Quran, the, 167

race riots, 38, 40–41
racial classification, 49–56, 275
racial discrimination, 105, 136–37, 254–55
  and early Indian immigrants, 26, 32–33, 36–46, 48, 49, 50–51, 64–65
  and Gandhi, 169–70
  and Indian Christians, 159
  and mobilization, history of, 52–64
  against Muslims, U.S., 103
  post-9/11, 153–59, 162, 164–65
  and profiling, 138–39, 144, 184–85, 230
  and SAALT, 144
  and Trump administration, 29–30, 254–55, 261–62
  and voting, 261–62
racial formation, 36, 49, 64–65
racial solidarity model, 28, 107, 146–47, 190, 277, 290–91
racial status, 45–49
racialization, 274
  and caste, 6, 23, 146, 209–15, 216, 226, 275, 280–81
  and generational status, 7, 28, 107, 147
  and mobilization, 11, 13, 167
  and pan-ethnicity, 106–7
  and partisan politics, 231–33, 253, 269–70
  and religion, 5–6, 8–9, 15, 226, 277–78
  and South Asian, U.S., 115
Rai, Lala Lajpat, 46–47
Raj, Udit, 84
Ram, Hindu God 73
Ram temple movement, 71–72
Ramadan, 182–83
Ramakrishnan, Karthick, 1, 147
Ramaswamy, E.V. (Periyar), 22–23, 70
Ramaswamy, Vivek, 1
rape, 213–14
Rashtriya Swayamsevak Sangh (RSS), 71–72, 77–78, 203, 208, 209, 265–66
Rathod, Jayesh, 115–16
Ravidas, 69, 83–84
Ravidassia sabhas, 82–83
Ravidassia temple, 175–76
Reagan, Ronald, 26–27, 29–30, 58–59, 60, 100, 114–15, 249, 252–53, 254
recognition, 182–85
Reed-Danahay, Deborah, 18
refugees, 203–4
religion, 42, 168–69, 182–83, 274
  Abrahamic, 157, 163, 168–69, 185, 190–91
  accommodation of, 181–82
  and caste, 6–7, 22–23, 146
  and civil rights, 181–82
  and diaspora, 11, 16, 21, 68–69
  and politics, 14–15, 231–32, 275–76
  and racialization, 5–6, 8–9, 15
  and Republicans, 251, 270

religious advocacy organizations, U.S., 77–103, 276–77
religious conflict
    background, India, 69–73, 197
    Kashmir Imbroglio, 73–75
    and partisan politics, 267
    Sikh Khalistan Movement, 75–77
religious discrimination, 28, 138–39, 160–61, 165, 166, 176–77, 275–76
    in India, 193–94, 203–4
religious freedom, 194, 199–206, 208–9, 213, 276–77
Religious Freedom and Restoration Act, 176–77
religious nationalism, 27–28
Republic Day, India, 205–6
Republican debates, 1
Republican Hindu Coalition, 4–5, 254–55, 256, 259, 270–71
Republican Jewish Coalition, 254, 256
Republican National Convention, 183–84
Republican values, 259
Republicans, 142–43, 186–87, 200–1, 203, 223, 235–36
    and Hindu nationalism, 254
    Indian American, 4–5, 11–12, 29–30, 231–32, 238–39, 241–43, 246–47, 250–53, 270
    voting for, 235–37
Resolving Extended Limbo for Immigrant Employees and Families Act (RELIEF), 142–43
Resurgent India Bond, 111–12
Rihanna, 221
Romney, Mitt, 241–42
Roosevelt, Franklin D., 26, 48
Rosaldo, Renato, 10–11
Rose Bowl Parade, 162
Rubinoff, Arthur, 112–13
rural outmigration, Indian, 34
Rusk, Dean, 49
Rutgers University, 52–53

Sacramento, California, 220–21
Sadhana, 151–52, 164–65, 173–74, 176–77, 180–81, 190–91, 206–7, 208, 214
Sadhana: Coalition of Progressive Hindus, 158
Sagar, D.B., 215
Sahi, Ajit, 199–200
Saint Thomas, 100
same-sex marriage, 165–66
San Diego, California, 176–77
San Francisco Bay Area, California, 32, 38, 40–41, 62–63, 82–83, 168–69, 174, 179–80, 205–6, 258, 264–65
    early immigrant mobilization in, 41–42
    and Muslims post-9/11, 154–55
    and Sikhs, 97–98, 217–18
San Francisco Bulletin, 41
San Jose, California, 185–86, 199–200
Sanders, Bernie, 263
Sangh Parivar, 71–72, 77–78, 79–80
Sanskritic Hinduism, 70
satyagraha, 48, 205–6
Saudi Arabia, 87–88, 169–70, 213
Saujani, Reshma, 244–45
Saund, Dalip Singh, 46, 48–49, 64–65
Savarkar, Vinayak Damodar, 69–70
Syeed, Sayyid M. 153–54, 184–85
Sazawal, Vijay, 94
Schiller, Glick, 194–95
Scottish independence, 218–20
seamen, 33–34, 38–39, 47–48
Seattle, Washington, 38, 180–81, 205–6, 288–89
second-generation Indian Americans, 1, 159, 184–85, 271–72, 284–85
    as activists, 247–53
    and AIPAC, 121–24
    and Asian American organizing, 115, 146–47, 263–64, 266
    and domestic issues, 247–48, 266
    and gender, 147–48, 271–72
    and homeland policy, 227–28
    and IMPACT, 258
    and India caucus, 110
    and Kashmiri Muslims, 224–25
    and mobilization, 7–8, 12, 28, 106–7, 286
    and partisan politics, 244–47, 248–53, 269–70
    post-9/11, 151, 154–56
    and SAALT, 144–45, 146
    Sikh, 181–82, 217–20
    and U.S. national politics, 11–12
secularism, 5, 68, 86, 90–92, 150–51, 185–86, 195–96
    Indian, 197, 205–6, 277
    and minorities, 198–99
secularist groups, 140–41
Senate Foreign Relations Committee, 240
Shah, Navin, 61, 62
Shah, Raj, 1
Shah, Salim, 170
Shani, Giorgio, 218
Sharma, Kapil, 110–11
Sherman, Brad, 202–3
Sherman, Rita, 168–69
Shia studies, 170
Shingal, Mira and Ajay, 168–69

shuddi rituals, 69–70
Shukla, Aseem, 163, 185, 236–37
Shukla, Suhag, 79–80, 185–86, 200, 203, 221–22
Siddiqui, Muzammil, 184–85
Siddiqui, Zafar, 184–85
Signal International, 142
Sikh American Legal Defense and Education Fund (SALDEF), 156–57, 159–61, 164–66, 186–88, 220–21, 227–28, 284
Sikh American organizations, 4–5, 28–29, 97–100, 138–39, 146–47, 218–20, 221, 289
  and caste, 282
  and civil rights, 176–77, 180–82
  and diaspora politics, 196–97
  and education, 159–67, 170–71, 174, 190
  and inclusion, 182–85, 187–88
  and India issues, 194
  and Khalistan, 217–18
  post-9/11, 155–57, 177–78
Sikh caucus, 186–87, 220–21
Sikh Coalition, 155–56, 159–60, 161–62, 163, 164–65, 167, 170–71, 186–87, 202–3, 217–18, 220–21, 282, 283–84
  and civil rights, 174, 177–78, 181–82
  and Kashmir, 227–28
Sikh Council of North America, 97
Sikh Day Parade, 100, 162, 218
Sikh Empire, 35, 73
Sikh Foundation, 97–98, 167–68
Sikh Khalistan Movement, 75–77
Sikh Media Watch and Resource Task Force (SMART), 152, 156–57
Sikh nationalism, 65, 218–20
Sikh parade, 187
Sikh studies, 167–68
Sikh temple, 177–78
Sikhism, 37–38, 185
Sikhs, 16–17, 21, 22–23, 27, 88–89, 116–17, 118–19, 144, 152, 166–67
  as early immigrants, U.S., 33, 35, 37–38, 39–41, 42, 44–48, 64–65
  and Hindu nationalism, 81, 91–92, 277
  and human rights, 109–10
  and identity, 99
  and Khalistan, 216–21, 227
  as minorities, 202–3
  and mobilization, 107, 167–68, 195–96, 281
  and partition, 76–115
  and religious conflict, 70–71, 72
  and religious freedom, 194, 209, 226
  as religious minority, U.S., 150–51
  and second-generation, U.S., 115
  and U.S. advocacy, 67

U.S. immigration of, 97
  voting patterns, 235–36
Sikhs for Justice, 193, 218–20
Sikhs for Trump, 258
Silicon Valley Courageous Resistance, 259
Silicon Valley, California, 142–43, 164, 179–80, 188, 256, 258, 259–60, 270–71, 279–80, 288–89
Simon, Larry, 178
Simpson-Mazzoli Immigration Bill, 57
Simpson, Alan, 58
Singh, Gulab, 73
Singh, Hari, 74
Singh, J. J., 47–48, 64–65
Singh, Jaideep, 167
Singh, Jaswant, 112, 240
Singh, Manmohan, 2–3, 131
Singh, Rajnath, 139–40
Singh, Ranjit, 35
Singh, Shoba, 81
Singh, Simran Jeet, 163
singing, 205–6
skilled foreign workers, 19–20, 50, 142–43, 285
  doctors, 60–62
Skrentny, John, 16
slavery, 173, 174, 226, 281
Snapchat, 287
social justice, 115, 117, 146–47, 158, 167, 206–7, 246–47, 248
social media, 30, 165, 169–70, 224–25, 259, 287–89
  and macaca incident, 245, 287–88
  and mobilization, 9, 12, 165, 214, 260–61
socialism, 42, 108–9
Sodhi, Balbir Singh, 155–56
Solarz, Stephen, 109–11
Soundararajan, Thenmozhi, 82–83, 164, 174–75, 179–80, 188, 205–6, 213–14, 277
South Africa, 169–70, 212, 216
South Asia Institute, 169–70
South Asia Solidarity Initiative, 199–200, 205–6
South Asian American organizations, 4–5, 27–28, 114–18, 136–39, 141–46, 147, 172, 238–39, 246
  and elections, U.S., 244–45
  and second-generation progressives, 28, 29–30
South Asian Americans, 45–46, 105–7, 115–20, 142, 144, 145–46, 147, 230, 277–78
  and caste, 164
  post-9/11, 151
  and progressive politics, 257–63
South Asian Americans Leading Together (SAALT), 115–16, 117–18, 136–39,

142–46, 147–48, 151, 188, 208–9, 250, 277–78, 279, 283–84, 285
South Asian Bar Association (SABA), 247–48
South Asian Histories for All (SAHFA), 172, 173–74, 279
South Asian identity, 231–32, 271–72
South Asians for Biden, 258–59, 262, 263, 267
South Asians for Kerry (SAKI), 244–45
South Asians for Obama, 244–47
Soviet Union, 108–9, 206, 209
Sri Lanka, 143, 205–6
Sri Lankan identity, 115–16
Sridaran, Lakshmi, 143
Srinivasan, Rajeev, 106, 119–20
St. Paul, Minnesota, 205–6
Stand with Kashmir, 224–25
Stanford University, 86–87, 160–61
State Bank of India, 111–12
stereotypes, 152, 159–76
Stevens, Stuart, 259
students, 142
   and 9/11, 153–54
   and anti-colonialism, 35, 46
   and caste, 166, 178
   and discrimination, 26–27, 60–62, 175, 274–75
   and immigration, 44, 56–57
   as international, 19–20
   and racialized college groups, 114–15
   and second-generation, 147–48
Students Against Hindutva Ideology, 206–7, 208–9
Subcontinental Institute, 118
Subcontinental, The, 118
Surat Initiative, 217–18
Surrey, British Columbia, 218–20
surveillance
   and American Muslims, 154–55, 165, 188–89
   of early Indian immigrant mobilization, 40–41, 42–43
racial, 138–39
   and Sikh separatism, 98–99
surveys
   of Americans, 19, 292
   of Asian Americans, 20f, 147, 233, 235–36, 257, 260
   by Equality Labs, 166, 174–75, 180–81, 188
   of Indian Americans, 50–51, 53–54, 55–56, 165–66, 187, 196
Swan, Jonathan, 254–55
Swing Left, 260
swing states, 30, 230, 231, 258, 271–72
Syeed, Sayyid, 87, 88

Syrian Christians, 100

Take Back Yoga campaign, 163
Talbott, Strobe, 112
Taliban, the, 95–96, 120
Tandon, Ritesh, 264–65
Tanzania, 57
Tellis, Ashley, 130
Temple University, 56
temples, 103
Teppara, Dino, 246–47
terrorism, 95–99, 113, 120–21, 127–29, 141, 157, 201–2, 221–22, 254–56, 268, 282
Texas, 19–20, 82–83, 118–19, 133–34, 161–62, 186–87, 208, 265–66
   and civil rights, 176–77
   and textbooks, 170–71
Texas India Forum, 203
textbooks, 170–75, 185–86, 189–90, 279
textile peddlers, 33–34, 38–39
Thanedar, Shri, 1, 186–87, 236–37
Thanjan, Theresa, 246
That's So Hindu (podcast), 165–66
The United Shades of America with W. Kamau Bell, 161–62
They See Blue (TSB), 258, 259–62, 265–67, 271–72
Thind, Bhagat Singh, 45–46, 64–65
Thomas, George, 62
Thunberg, Greta, 221
TikTok, 287
Tillie, Jean, 18
Times Square, New York, 208–9
Tlaib, Rashida, 224–25, 264–65
Toronto, Ontario, 218–20
Torpey, John, 275–76
Torture Victim Protection Act, 198–99
trade organizations, 4–5, 16–17, 146
   and discrimination, history of, 32–66
transnational citizenship, 11, 32–33, 64–65, 103–4, 194–95, 274, 282–83
transnational organization, 9–10, 45–46, 67–68, 71–72, 221, 227, 280–81
Transnational Repression Policy Act, 218–20
transnational turn, 36
Transportation Security Administration (TSA), 159–60
trials, 42–43, 44, 52–53
tribal Indians, 72–73, 81, 215–16
Trinidad, 59–60
Tripathi, Rohit, 205–6
Trudeau, Justin, 282

Trump, Donald, 29–30, 103, 164–65
  administration of, 1, 142–43, 144, 165, 176–77, 203, 222–23, 230, 261–62
  anti-, 259–60, 262
  election of, 237, 253, 254, 257, 262–63, 264, 271–72
  and India, 206
  and Republican Hindu Coalition, 4–5
  supporters of, 103, 241, 255–57, 258, 267, 268–69, 270–71
turbans, 45–46, 97, 155–56, 159–62, 177–78, 181–82, 190, 220–21
Twitter, 82–83, 214, 260–61, 287

U.S. Affordable Care Act, 188–89, 262
U.S. Air Force, 181–82
U.S. Army, 45–46, 181–82, 255–56
  Hindus in, 183
U.S. Atomic Energy Act, 131
U.S. Bill of Rights, 185
U.S. Capitol, 212–13
U.S. census, 26–27, 32–33, 36, 51, 138–39, 164–65, 187–88, 274–75
  and racial status, 52–53, 54–55, 65
  and Sikhs, 190
U.S. Center for Medicare and Medicaid Services, 1
U.S. Chamber of Commerce, 132–33, 142–43
U.S. Civil Rights Act, 50, 178–79, 208–9
U.S. Commission on Civil Rights, 55
U.S. Commission on International Religious Freedom (USCIRF), 96, 193, 194, 202, 204–6
U.S. Congress, 65, 67, 105, 122, 123–24, 142–43, 182–83, 220–21
  and caste, 212, 215, 279
  and Dalits, 83, 84–85, 211
  and Hindu nationalism, 78, 140–41, 198–200, 209
  and Hindus, 46–47, 183, 185–87, 188, 236–37
  Indian Americans in, 1, 46, 48–49
  and Indian Christians, 101, 109–10
  and Indian immigrant exclusion, 38, 43–44, 48
  and Kashmir, 93, 94, 222–23
  and Muslims, 140–41, 165
  and nuclear deal, 131, 132–35
  and religious minorities, India, 200–3
  and Sikhs, 97–98, 177–78, 186–87, 217–20
  and support for India, 109–11, 112–13, 240
  and U.S.-India nuclear deal, 2–3
  and USINPAC, 125–83
U.S. Council on Foreign Relations, 2

U.S. Customs and Border Protection, 138–39, 277–78
U.S. Department of Health and Human Services, 56
U.S. Department of Transportation, 56
U.S. Environmental Protection Agency, 56
U.S. Federal Communications Commission, 1
U.S. Homeland Security, 136–37
U.S. House Foreign Affairs Committee, 109–10, 223
U.S. House Foreign Affairs Subcommittee on Asia and Pacific, 139–40
U.S. House of Representatives, 54–55, 108–9, 110, 139–41, 142–43, 165, 186–87, 200–1
U.S. House of Representatives Foreign Affairs Subcommittee on
  Asia, the Pacific, and Nonproliferation, 141, 142
U.S. House Resolution 417, 140–41
U.S. Immigration Act (1924), 44
U.S. Immigration Act (1965), 11–12, 19–20, 49–56, 59, 63, 97
U.S. Immigration Reform Bill, 285
U.S. Immigration Service, 50–51
U.S. Indian Business Council, 132–33
U.S. Indian Political Action Committee (USINPAC), 96, 139, 142, 144, 145, 201–3, 279, 285
  and Kashmir, 222–23, 227–28
  and nuclear deal, 2, 3
U.S. Justice Department, 136–37, 177–78
U.S. Muslim ban, 165, 184–85, 188–89, 190, 262–63
U.S. National Park Service, 160
U.S. National Security Committee, 129
U.S. Patriot Act, 118–19, 130–31, 154–55, 165, 190, 242–43, 244–45, 270
U.S. Pledge of Allegiance, 255–56
U.S. Seaman's Act (1915), 38–39
U.S. Select Committee on Immigration and Refugee Policy, 57, 58
U.S. Senate, 132–33, 143, 177–78, 183
U.S. Small Business Administration, 56
U.S. State Department, 119–20
U.S. Supreme Court, 45–46, 65, 144, 244
U.S.-India Friendship Council, 3, 132–35, 227
U.S.-India Strategic Dialogue, 140–41, 201–2, 215–16
Udupa, Sahana, 288–89
Uganda, 57
UN Committee on the Elimination of Racial Discrimination (CERD), 210–11

UN Sub-Commission on the Prevention of Discrimination and Protection of Minorities, 214–15
UN Sustainable Development Goals, 215–16
uncles, 116–17, 122–23, 124, 136, 243, 244–45, 286
undocumented immigrants, 142, 144–45, 164–65, 285, 292
Unfinished Legacy of Dr. B. R. Ambedkar Conference, 169–70
United Chinese Americans, 143
United Nations, 1, 74, 81, 95–96, 97–98, 212, 215, 218–20
   and Dalits, 83
United Nations Commission on Human Rights, 210
United Nations Human Rights Council, 93
United Nations Human Rights Council (UNHCR), 94
United Sikhs, 156–57, 164–65, 182, 220–21
United States Commission on Religious Freedom (USCIRF), 193
United States India Political Action Committee (USINPAC), 125–31, 145–46, 201–2, 283–84
United States v. Bhagat Singh Thind, 45, 47–48, 51, 65
United States-India Business Alliance (USIBA), 125
United We Dream, 143
United Sikhs, 187–88
University of California, Berkeley, 35, 45–46
   Graduate Theological Union, 167–69
University of California, Irvine, 168–69
University of California, Riverside, 167–68
University of California, Santa Barbara, 167–68
University of California, Santa Cruz, 167–68
University of Michigan, 167–68
University of Southern California, 168–69
unskilled labor
   and early immigrant Indians, 43–44, 46–47
untouchable groups, 21–22, 23, 69–70, 81, 165–66, 180–81, 190–91, 211, 212–14
Urdu, India, 41–42
USAID, 215–16
Uttar Pradesh, India, 227

Vaisakhi, 182–83
Vajpayee, Atal Bihari, 81, 101, 112–13, 183, 197
Vancouver, BC, 38, 40–41
   immigration to, 42
Vedic age, 70–71
Vedic Foundation (VF), 172

Vedic texts, 23
Verma, Seema, 1
Virginia, 144, 171–72
Virginia Military Institute, 131
Vishwa Hindu Parishad, 208
Vishwa Hindu Parishad (VHP), 71–72
Vishwa Hindu Parishad of America (VHPA, 152
Vishwa Hindu Parishad of America (VHPA), 77–78, 79–80, 287–88
Viswanath, Sunita, 214
Volunteers in the Service of India's Oppressed and Neglected (VISION), 81, 175, 210–11

Walt Disney World, 182
Warnock, Raphael, 271
Washington (state), 33, 37–38, 40–41
Washington, DC, 47–48, 57, 61, 79, 82–83, 200–1
   and advocacy, 189
   and Dalits, 84–85, 175–76, 210, 211, 282–83
   and Hindus, 46–47, 186–87, 207–8
   and IALI, 244
   and Immigration Voice, 135–36
   and India caucus, 110
   Indian Christians in, 101
   and Indian Muslims, 86, 87
   and post-9/11 advocacy, 154–55, 156
   and religious freedom, 205–6
   and second-generation, 123
   second-generation in, 286
   and Sikhs, 97–98
   and South Asian American organizations, 117, 118
   and USINPAC, 128–29, 145
Watergate scandal, 250–51
Webb, James, 245
welfare, 274
WhatsApp, 261–62, 287
White Americans, 233, 257, 270–71
White Christians, 101, 159, 235–36
   and Dalits, 84–85
White ethnics, 275
White House, 112–13, 123, 182–83, 254–55
White models of activism, 8–9
White nationalism, 12, 153–54, 165, 166, 177–78, 257, 265–66, 267–68, 269–70, 271
   Christian, 241–42, 253, 267–68, 291
   post-9/11, 155–56, 177
White privilege, 164, 253
whiteness
   and Asian immigrants, 26–27, 45–46, 274–75
   and European immigration, 13, 16, 36
   and Indian immigrants, 52–56, 63, 65

Wikipedia, 214
Wildman, Sarah, 118–19
Wilson, William, 43–44
Wilson, Woodrow, 43–44
Winant, Howard, 36
women, 241–42, 246
   Dalit, 213–14
   Indian, 70–71, 172
   Indian American, 60, 184–85, 246–47, 271–72
   South Asian, 138–39
Women in the World Summit, 213–14
Women's Islamic Initiative for Spirituality and Equality, 184–85
Woodrow Wilson International Center, 110–11
workplace equity, 177, 178–80, 189–90, 238–39, 243, 270, 274–75
Workplace Religious Freedom Act, 182
World Bank, 215
World Hindu Congress, 199–200
World Kashmir Awareness Forum, 221–22
World Sikh Organization, 97–98

World Trade Center, 184–85
World War I, 36–37, 38–39, 44, 45–46
World War II, 26, 36–37, 48, 49, 65
Wulf, Norman A., 133–34
Wuthnow, Robert, 291

xenophobia, 29–30, 68, 144, 237, 257, 259–60, 261–63, 271, 277–78, 291

Yemen, 213
Yengde, Suraj, 82–83
yoga, 163
Young India, 46–47
Young India Association (YIA), 205–6
YouTube, 25, 78–79, 207–8, 218–20, 245, 287
Yuba City, California, 162, 187

Zachariah, George K., 57
Zachariah, Zachariah P., 241–42
Zulu Africans, 169–70
Zutshi, Jeevan, 94, 96–97